The IMA Volumes
in Mathematics
and Its Applications

Volume 20

Series Editors
Avner Friedman   Willard Miller, Jr.

Institute for Mathematics and
its Applications
IMA

The **Institute for Mathematics and its Applications** was established by a grant from the National Science Foundation to the University of Minnesota in 1982. The IMA seeks to encourage the development and study of fresh mathematical concepts and questions of concern to the other sciences by bringing together mathematicians and scientists from diverse fields in an atmosphere that will stimulate discussion and collaboration.

The IMA Volumes are intended to involve the broader scientific community in this process.

Avner Friedman, Director
Willard Miller, Jr., Associate Director

* * * * * * * * * *

IMA PROGRAMS

1982-1983	**Statistical and Continuum Approaches to Phase Transition**
1983-1984	**Mathematical Models for the Economics of Decentralized Resource Allocation**
1984-1985	**Continuum Physics and Partial Differential Equations**
1985-1986	**Stochastic Differential Equations and Their Applications**
1986-1987	**Scientific Computation**
1987-1988	**Applied Combinatorics**
1988-1989	**Nonlinear Waves**
1989-1990	**Dynamical Systems and Their Applications**
1990-1991	**Phase Transitions and Free Boundaries**

* * * * * * * * * *

SPRINGER LECTURE NOTES FROM THE IMA:

The Mathematics and Physics of Disordered Media
> Editors: Barry Hughes and Barry Ninham
> (Lecture Notes in Math., Volume 1035, 1983)

Orienting Polymers
> Editor: J.L. Ericksen
> (Lecture Notes in Math., Volume 1063, 1984)

New Perspectives in Thermodynamics
> Editor: James Serrin
> (Springer-Verlag, 1986)

Models of Economic Dynamics
> Editor: Hugo Sonnenschein
> (Lecture Notes in Econ., Volume 264, 1986)

Dijen Ray-Chaudhuri

Coding Theory and Design Theory

Part I
Coding Theory

With 13 Illustrations

Springer-Verlag
New York Berlin Heidelberg
London Paris Tokyo Hong Kong

Dijen Ray-Chaudhuri
Department of Mathematics
Ohio State University
Columbus, Ohio 43210
USA

Series Editors

Avner Friedman
Willard Miller, Jr.
Institute for Mathematics and Its Applications
University of Minnesota
Minneapolis, MN 55455 USA

Mathematical Subject Classification Codes:11T71, 94Bxx.

Library of Congress Cataloging-in-Publication Data

Coding theory and design theory / Dijen Ray-Chaudhuri, editor.
    p. cm. — (The IMA volumes in mathematics and its
 applications ; v. 20–21)
    "Based on the proceedings of a workshop which was an integral part
of the 1987–88 IMA program on applied combinatorics"—Foreword.
  Includes bibliographical references.
    Contents: v. 1. Coding theory — v. 2. Design theory.
    ISBN 0-387-97228-5 (v. 1 : alk. paper). — ISBN 0-387-97231-5 (v.
2 : alk. paper)
    1. Coding theory. 2. Experimental design. I. Ray-Chaudhuri,
Dijen, 1933– II. Series.
 QA268.C68   1990
 003'.54—dc20   89-26336

Printed on acid-free paper.

Camera-ready copy prepared by the IMA.
Printed and bound by Edwards Brothers, Inc., Ann Arbor, Michigan.
Printed in the United States of America.

9 8 7 6 5 4 3 2 1

ISBN 0-387-97228-5 Springer-Verlag New York Berlin Heidelberg
ISBN 3-540-97228-5 Springer-Verlag Berlin Heidelberg New York

The IMA Volumes
in Mathematics and its Applications

Current Volumes:

Volume 1: Homogenization and Effective Moduli of Materials and Media
Editors: Jerry Ericksen, David Kinderlehrer, Robert Kohn, J.-L. Lions

Volume 2: Oscillation Theory, Computation, and Methods of Compensated Compactness
Editors: Constantine Dafermos, Jerry Ericksen,
David Kinderlehrer, Marshall Slemrod

Volume 3: Metastability and Incompletely Posed Problems
Editors: Stuart Antman, Jerry Ericksen, David Kinderlehrer, Ingo Muller

Volume 4: Dynamical Problems in Continuum Physics
Editors: Jerry Bona, Constantine Dafermos, Jerry Ericksen, David Kinderlehrer

Volume 5: Theory and Applications of Liquid Crystals
Editors: Jerry Ericksen and David Kinderlehrer

Volume 6: Amorphous Polymers and Non-Newtonian Fluids
Editors: Constantine Dafermos, Jerry Ericksen, David Kinderlehrer

Volume 7: Random Media
Editor: George Papanicolaou

Volume 8: Percolation Theory and Ergodic Theory of Infinite Particle Systems
Editor: Harry Kesten

Volume 9: Hydrodynamic Behavior and Interacting Particle Systems
Editor: George Papanicolaou

Volume 10: Stochastic Differential Systems, Stochastic Control Theory and Applications
Editors: Wendell Fleming and Pierre-Louis Lions

Volume 11: Numerical Simulation in Oil Recovery
Editor: Mary Fanett Wheeler

Volume 12: Computational Fluid Dynamics and Reacting Gas Flows
Editors: Bjorn Engquist, M. Luskin, Andrew Majda

FOREWORD

This IMA Volume in Mathematics and its Applications

Coding Theory and Design Theory Part I: Coding Theory

is based on the proceedings of a workshop which was an integral part of the 1987-88 IMA program on APPLIED COMBINATORICS. We are grateful to the Scientific Committee: Victor Klee (Chairman), Daniel Kleitman, Dijen Ray-Chaudhuri and Dennis Stanton for planning and implementing an exciting and stimulating year-long program. We especially thank the Workshop Organizer, Dijen Ray-Chaudhuri, for organizing a workshop which brought together many of the major figures in a variety of research fields in which coding theory and design theory are used.

Avner Friedman

Willard Miller, Jr.

PREFACE

Coding Theory and Design Theory are areas of Combinatorics which found rich applications of algebraic structures. Combinatorial designs are generalizations of finite geometries. Probably, the history of Design Theory begins with the 1847 paper of Reverand T.P. Kirkman "On a problem of Combinatorics", Cambridge and Dublin Math. Journal. The great Statistician R.A. Fisher reinvented the concept of combinatorial 2-design in the twentieth century. Extensive application of algebraic structures for construction of 2-designs (balanced incomplete block designs) can be found in R.C. Bose's 1939 Annals of Eugenics paper, "On the construction of balanced incomplete block designs". Coding Theory and Design Theory are closely interconnected. Hamming codes can be found (in disguise) in R.C. Bose's 1947 Sankhyā paper "Mathematical theory of the symmetrical factorial designs". The same paper also introduced the packing problem in projective spaces - the central problem in the construction of optimum linear codes. Coding theory has developed into a rich and beautiful example of abstract sophisticated mathematics being applied successfully to solve real-life problems of communication. Applications of deep theorems of Algebraic Geometry for construction of linear codes by V.D. Goppa and others created much excitement. Much work remains to be done to make the algebraic geometric codes practical and implementable. Theory of t-designs for $t > 2$ is in a state of rapid development. The 1987-88 Applied Combinatorics Program of IMA decided to devote the period from May 1, 1988 to June 25, 1988 to concentration on Design Theory and Coding Theory. It was particularly appropriate as many of the specialists that were invited worked in both of these areas.

The purpose of this section of the Applied Combinatorics Year was to bring together Coding Theorists, Design Theorists and Statisticians in the area of experimental designs, to exchange informations and ideas on the latest developments, to encourage interactions and to create an inspiring and stimulating research environment. This purpose was well served. Before the beginning of the workshops from May 1 to June 10, 1988 the pace was relaxed with plenty of time for research exchanges. During this period lectures of J.H. van Lint on Algebraic Geometric Codes was a particularly popular event. In this period there were also lectures by E. Assmus, R.A. Bailey, C-S. Cheng, M. Deza, A.S. Hedayat, S.L. Ma, V. Pless, D.K. Ray-Chaudhuri, N. Singhi, R.M. Wilson and L. Teirlinck. The periods of workshops, Coding Theory, June 13–17, 1988 and Design Theory, June 20–25, 1988 were much more intense with forty (40) lectures altogether. Symposium on Statistical theory of Experimental Designs attracted many statisticians with lively lectures by eight prominent statisticians. Most of the participants submitted their papers for publication in this volume on Coding Theory and Design Theory. Unfortunately a few fine lectures are not submitted for inclusion in these Proceedings.

Thanks are due to IMA director Professor A. Friedman, Associate director W. Miller, Jr. and IMA staff for their extremely helpful attitude and generous assistance. I take this opportunity to offer special thanks to Mrs. P. Brick, Mr. S. Skogerboe, and Mrs. K. Smith for their preparation of the manuscripts.

CONTENTS — PART I

CONTENTS — PART II

BAER SUBPLANES, OVALS AND UNITALS

E.F. ASSMUS, Jr.† AND J.D. KEY†*

1. Introduction. In this paper we examine some of the types of codewords that can occur in codes associated with finite projective and affine planes, exploring further the notions that were introduced in [1]. There we defined the hull, $H_p(\mathcal{D})$, of a design $\mathcal{D}$ over a finite field F_p, where p is a prime that divides the order n of the design: if $C_p(\mathcal{D})$ denotes the code of $\mathcal{D}$ over F_p, defined to be the space spanned by the characteristic functions of the blocks of $\mathcal{D}$, then $H_p(\mathcal{D}) = C_p(\mathcal{D}) \cap C_p(\mathcal{D})^\perp$, where $X^\perp$ denotes the subspace orthogonal to X with respect to the standard inner product. In the case where $\mathcal{D}$ is a finite projective plane Π, and π any affine part of Π, we showed that affine planes obtained by "derivation" from π (see [1]) could be obtained from minimal-weight vectors of $H_p(\pi)^\perp$. Since $H_p(\pi)^\perp$ is the image of the natural projection of $H_p(\Pi)^\perp$, we were led to examine the nature of codewords of the code $H_p(\Pi)^\perp$, and, in particular, those codewords that could give rise to minimal-weight (i.e. weight-n) vectors in $H_p(\pi)^\perp$ and $C_p(\pi)$. The support of such a vector must form either a line or a blocking set for Π; examples of these, other than lines, are Baer subplanes meeting the line at infinity for π in a line segment, or, in the even-order case, ovals meeting that line in two points.

Here we examine the codewords arising from some standard configurations of points in a projective plane Π, for example, Baer subplanes, unitals and ovals, and we look at the designs formed by taking as blocks the set of all the configurations of a given type, and the relationship of their codes to the codes $H_p(\Pi)$, $C_p(\Pi)$, $C_p(\Pi)^\perp$, and $H_p(\Pi)^\perp$ of the plane. Thus in particular we obtain the following for desarguesian planes:

PROPOSITION. *Let $\Pi = PG(2, q^2)$, $q = p^r$, and let $\mathcal{S}$, $\mathcal{U}$ and $\mathcal{H}$ be the designs consisting of the points of Π and the Baer subplanes, unitals and hermitian unitals, respectively, as blocks. Then $C_p(\mathcal{S})$, $C_p(\mathcal{U})$ and $C_p(\mathcal{H})$ all contain $C_p(\Pi)$, and are in $H_p(\Pi)^\perp$. When $p = 2$, $C_2(\Pi) = C_2(\mathcal{H})$.*

If $\Pi = PG(2, q)$, $q = p^r$, and $\mathcal{O}$ is the design with blocks the ovals of Π, then if p is odd, $C_p(\mathcal{O}) = F_p^N$ where $N = q^2 + q + 1$; if $p = 2$, $C_2(\mathcal{O}) \subseteq C_2(\Pi)^\perp$.

We can show that $C_2(\mathcal{O}) = C_2(\Pi)^\perp$ for $q = 2, 4, 8$, and 16. In fact, for $q = 16$, taking the orbit of any oval under a Singer cycle will give a generating set for $C_2(\Pi)^\perp$. For $q = 8$ and 16 these computations were carried out using the Cayley language on the Birmingham University VAX.

We conjecture that $C_p(\Pi) = C_p(\mathcal{H})$ for $\Pi = PG(2, q^2)$ for q any power of p, although the assertion is only proven in the case $p = 2$. It may even be true, for

---

†Department of Mathematics, Lehigh University, Bethlehem, PA 18015

†Department of Mathematical Sciences, Martin Hall, Clemson University, Clemson, SC 29634

*Permanent address: Department of Mathematics, University of Birmingham, Birmingham B15 2TT, U.K.

any unital U of $\Pi = PG(2, q^2)$, that U is hermitian if and only if the characteristic function of U is in $C_p(\Pi)$; these questions are closely related to intersection properties of unitals with unitals, and unitals with Baer subplanes, and they perhaps should be investigated more thoroughly.

The Proposition follows from Lemmas and Corollaries in Section 3. In Section 4 we obtain, for any affine translation plane π, some classes of vectors that will always be in $C(\pi)^\perp$, and hence obtain a class of vectors in $C(\Pi)^\perp$ for a projective translation plane.

2. Notation and Background. For any finite incidence structure $\mathcal{D}$ with point set $\mathcal{P}$ and block set $\mathcal{B}$, where $|\mathcal{P}| = N$, $C_p(\mathcal{D})$ will denote the code of $\mathcal{D}$ over the field F_p, i.e. $C_p(\mathcal{D})$ is the subspace of F_p^N spanned by the rows of an incidence matrix for $\mathcal{D}$ with the blocks indexing the rows and the points the columns. For $\mathcal{D}$ a design of order n, only primes p that divide n can possibly give non-trivial codes $C_p(\mathcal{D})$. We denote the dual code of $C_p(\mathcal{D})$ by $C_p(\mathcal{D})^\perp$, i.e. $C_p(\mathcal{D})^\perp = \{v | v \in F_p^N, (u, v) = 0$ for all $u \in C_p(\mathcal{D})\}$, where (u, v) denotes the standard inner product of vectors u and v. The hull of $\mathcal{D}$ at p, $\mathrm{Hull}_p(\mathcal{D}) = H_p(\mathcal{D})$, is defined to be $C_p(\mathcal{D}) \cap C_p(\mathcal{D})^\perp$, and usually we will omit the subscript p when it is clear from the context.

For $\mathcal{D}$ a projective plane Π, with point set $\mathcal{P}$ and line set $\mathcal{L}$, we have $|\mathcal{P}| = N = n^2 + n + 1$, where n is the order of Π. For $L \in \mathcal{L}$, $|L| = n + 1$, and we take $p | n$. Then it is well known that $3n - 2 \leq \dim(C_p(\Pi)) \leq \frac{N+1}{2}$, and that $C_p(\Pi)$ has minimum weight $n + 1$ with minimal-weight vectors the scalar multiples of the rows of the incidence matrix (see, for example, [10]). Bruen and Ott [4] have recently improved the lower bound to $n\sqrt{n} + 1$.

We use the following notation for codes and codewords in F_p^N. If $v \in F_p^N$ then for $Q \in \mathcal{P}$, v_Q denotes the coordinate of v at Q; $\mathrm{Supp}(v) = \{Q | Q \in \mathcal{P}, v_Q \neq 0\}$ is the support of v. For any subset X of $\mathcal{P}$, we define the vector v^X by $v_Q^X = 1$ if $Q \in X$, $v_Q^X = 0$ if $Q \notin X$. We denote $v^{\mathcal{P}}$ by J, the all-one vector. A vector will be called a constant vector if all the non-zero entries v_Q are equal.

A Baer subplane Σ of Π when $n = m^2$ is a subset of $m^2 + m + 1$ points and $m^2 + m + 1$ lines of π with the property that Σ is a projective plane of order m. Then every element of Π meets Σ in 1 or $m + 1$ elements of Σ.

A unital $\mathcal{U}$ of Π when $n = m^2$ is a subset of $m^3 + 1$ points X with the property that every line of Π meets X in 1 or $m + 1$ points. Then the structure with point set X and block set the set of all line segments of Π that contain $m + 1$ points of X forms a unitary design, i.e. a design with parameters $2 - (m^3 + 1, m + 1, 1)$. If $\pi = PG(2, q^2)$, the desarguesian plane of order q^2, where $q = p^r$, then the absolute points and non-absolute lines of a unitary polarity form a hermitian unital in Π. For $q > 2$ there are non-hermitian unitals in $PG(2, q^2)$: see [11].

An oval in Π is an $(n + 1)$-arc for n odd, and an $(n + 2)$-arc for n even. For $\Pi = PG(2, q)$, when q is odd, the ovals are just the conics, i.e. the absolute points of an orthogonal polarity [6]. For q even, a conic together with its nucleus is an oval, but for $q > 8$ other ovals also exist.

On the point set $\mathcal{P}$ of Π we define the structures $\mathcal{S}$, $\mathcal{U}$, $\mathcal{H}$ and $\mathcal{O}$ where the blocks are given as follows:

$\mathcal{S}$: the Baer subplanes of Π, when $n = m^2$;

$\mathcal{U}$: the unitals in Π, when $n = m^2$;

$\mathcal{H}$: the hermitian unitals in Π, when $\Pi = PG(2, q^2)$;

$\mathcal{O}$: the ovals in Π, of size $n + 1$ for n odd, $n + 2$ for n even.

In [1, Prop. 1] we reproved the following well-known facts (see [13], for example) concerning the hull of Π when p divides n:

$$H(\Pi) = \langle v^L - v^M | L, M \in \mathcal{L} \rangle = \{v | v \in C(\Pi) \text{ and } \sum_Q v_Q = 0\},$$

$$H(\Pi)^\perp = \langle J \rangle \oplus C(\Pi)^\perp.$$

Terminology for projective planes may be found in [7]. In particular, a (P,L)-elation of Π is a collineation of Π that fixes every line through the point $P \in L$, and every point on the line L. If every possible (P, L)-elation exists, then Π is (P, L)-transitive. If, for a line L, Π is (P, L)-transitive for all $P \in L$, then L is called a translation line for Π, the group of all elations with axis L is the translation group of L, and Π is a translation plane. A Singer cycle for Π is a collineation of order N that acts regularly on the points and on the lines of Π. For $\Pi = PG(2, q)$, Singer cycles always exist, but no other projective plane is known with a regular cyclic collineation group.

3. Codewords in Hull $(\Pi)^\perp$. In all the following, Π will denote a projective plane of order n, with point set $\mathcal{P}$, line set $\mathcal{L}$, where $N = |\mathcal{P}| = |\mathcal{L}| = n^2 + n + 1$. The codes $C(\Pi)$, $C(\Pi)^\perp$, $H(\Pi)$, $H(\Pi)^\perp$ all have length N and are defined over the field F_p, where $p|n$. We write $B(\Pi) = H(\Pi)^\perp$.

LEMMA 1. *A constant vector $v \in F_p^N$ is in $B(\Pi)$ if and only if $|Supp(v) \cap L|$ taken modulo p is independent of L.*

Proof. Let $X = \text{Supp}(v)$, so that $v = \beta v^X$, where $\beta \in F_p$. Suppose $v \in B(\Pi)$. Then, since $H(\Pi) = \langle v^L - v^M | L, M \in \mathcal{L} \rangle$ (see section 2), $(v, v^L - v^M) = 0$, so that (v, v^L) is independent of $L \in \mathcal{L}$. Thus $(v, v^L) = (\beta v^X, v^L) = \beta |X \cap L|$, and hence $|X \cap L|$ is also independent of L (mod p).

Conversely, if $|X \cap L| = \alpha$ is constant modulo p, then $(v^X, v^L) = \alpha$ for all L, so that $(v^X, v^L - v^M) = 0$ for all $L, M \in \mathcal{L}$, and $v^X \in B(\Pi)$. Thus, since v is a constant vector, $v = \beta v^X \in B(\Pi)$.

COROLLARIES.

1. *If X is the set of points of a Baer subplane of Π, where $n = m^2$, then $v^X \in B(\Pi)$.*

2. *If X is the set of points of a unital in Π, where $n = m^2$, then $v^X \in B(\Pi)$.*

3. *If X is an oval in Π where n is odd, then $|X| = n + 1$ and $v^X \notin B(\Pi)$.*

4. *If X is an oval in Π when n is even, then $|X| = n + 2$, and for $p = 2$, $v^X \in C_2(\Pi)^\perp \subset B_2(\Pi)$.*

5. If $\Pi = PG(2, q)$, where $q = p^s$, and $s = ht$, then if X is the set of points of $\Sigma = PG(2, p^t)$ in its natural embedding in Π, $v^X \in B(\Pi)$ if and only if $h \in \{1, 2\}$.

Proof. If $h = 2$ then Σ is a Baer subplane, and Corollary 1 applies. Let $h \geq 3$. Then $K = F_{p^s}$ is a vector space of dimension h over $F = F_{p^t}$; let x_1, x_2, x_3 be three elements of K that are linearly independent over F. Using homogeneous coordinates for Π, the line $\langle (x_1, x_2, x_3)' \rangle$ will not meet the set $X = \{\langle (y_1, y_2, y_3) \rangle | y_i \in F\}$, which forms the points of a subspace $\Sigma = PG(2, p^t)$. However, some lines of Π will clearly meet Σ in $p^t + 1$ points. Lemma 1 shows that $v^X \notin B(\Pi)$.

LEMMA 2. *Let $X \subseteq \mathcal{P}$ with $v^X \in C(\Pi)$. If $Y \subseteq \mathcal{P}$ with $v^Y \in B(\Pi)$ and $|Y \cap L| \equiv |X \cap L| \pmod{p}$ for all L, then $|X \cap Y| \equiv |X| \pmod{p}$.*

Proof. By Lemma 1, $v^X \in C(\Pi)$ implies that $|X \cap L|$ is independent of L, modulo p. Now $(v^X - v^Y, v^L) = (v^X, v^L) - (v^Y, v^L) \equiv |X \cap L| - |Y \cap L| \equiv 0 \pmod{p}$, for all $L \in \mathcal{L}$, so $v^X - v^Y \in H(\Pi)$. Hence $(v^X - v^Y, v^X) \equiv |X| - |X \cap Y| \equiv 0 \pmod{p}$, since $v^X \in C(\Pi)$. Hence $|X \cap Y| \equiv |X| \pmod{p}$.

COROLLARIES.

1. *If X is the set of points of a Baer subplane of $\Pi = PG(2, q^2)$, then $v^X \notin C(\Pi)$.*

Proof. $|X| = q^2 + q + 1 \equiv 1 \pmod{p}$, where $q = p^r$. In Π there is a Baer subplane Y that meets X in a line segment of size $q + 1$, and in one other point off the line. Then $|X \cap L| \equiv 1 \equiv |Y \cap L| \pmod{p}$ and $|X \cap Y| = q + 2 \equiv 2 \pmod{p}$. But $v^Y \in B(\Pi)$ from Lemma 1, so $v^X \notin C(\Pi)$.

2. *If X is a unital in Π and $v^X \in C(\Pi)$ then the intersection of every unital and Baer subplane of Π with X must be of cardinality $\equiv 1 \pmod{p}$.*

In connection with Corollary 2 above, we note that intersection properties of hermitian unitals, and of hermitian unitals with Baer subplanes, have been examined by Kestenband [9] and Bruen & Hirschfeld [3] respectively.

LEMMA 3. *Let $X \subseteq \mathcal{P}$, $|X| \equiv \alpha \pmod{p}$. Suppose there exists a flag (P, L) with $P \notin X$ such that*

(i) *for every $M \in \mathcal{L}$ with $M \neq L$ and $P \in M$ we have $|X \cap M| \equiv \beta \pmod{p}$ with $\beta \not\equiv 0 \pmod{p}$;*

(ii) *Π is (P, L) transitive.*

Let $E = \{g \mid g$ is a (P, L)-elation of $\Pi\}$, $\mathcal{B} = \{X^g | g \in E\}$, and $\mathcal{D}$ the structure $(\mathcal{P}, \mathcal{B})$.

Then $J - v^L \in C_p(\mathcal{D})$.

Proof. Let $u = \sum_{g \in E} v^{X^g}$. The subgroup E, which has order n, acts regularly on the points of each of the lines $M \neq L$ through P. Thus $u_Q = n \equiv 0 \pmod{p}$ for $Q \in L \cap X$; $u_Q = 0$ for $Q \in L$, $Q \notin X$; $u_Q = |M \cap X| \equiv \beta \pmod{p}$ for $Q \notin L$. Thus $u = \beta(J - v^L) \in C_p(\mathcal{D})$, whence $J - v^L \in C_p(\mathcal{D})$ since $\beta \neq 0$.

CoROLLARIES.

1. If $J \in C_p(\mathcal{D})$, then $v^L \in C_p(\mathcal{D})$.

2. If $|X| \equiv \alpha \not\equiv 0 \pmod{p}$, and if Π has a Singer cycle s, then with $\mathcal{B}_1 = \{X^g | g \in \langle E, s \rangle\}$ and $\mathcal{D}_1 = (\mathcal{P}, \mathcal{B}_1)$, $J \in C_p(\mathcal{D}_1)$, and $v^L \in C_p(\mathcal{D}_1)$ for any line L satisfying the given conditions.

Proof. Let $w = \sum_{h \in \langle s \rangle} v^{X^h}$. Then $w_Q = \alpha \not\equiv 0 \pmod{p}$ for all $Q \in \mathcal{P}$, so $w = \alpha J \in C_p(\mathcal{D}_1)$.

3. If $\Pi = PG(2, q^2)$ then $C(\mathcal{S}) \supset C(\Pi)$.

Proof. By Lemma 2, Corollary 1, $C(\mathcal{S}) \neq C(\Pi)$. Let X be a Baer subplane and let L be any line of $\mathcal{L}$, $P \notin L$, $P \notin X$. Then $\alpha = 1 = \beta$ and all the conditions are satisfied. Since Π has a Singer cycle, Corollary 2 above gives $C(\mathcal{S}) \supset C(\Pi)$. (See also Note 1 below.)

4. If $\Pi = PG(2, q^2)$ and X is any unital embedded in Π, then, with $\mathcal{D}_1$ the structure defined in Corollary 2, $C(\mathcal{D}_1) \supseteq C(\Pi)$. In particular, $C(\mathcal{H}) \supseteq C(\Pi)$.

Proof. As in 3 above, if X is a unital, $\alpha = 1 = \beta$ and again all the conditions are satisfied. See also Note 2 below.

5. If $\Pi = PG(2, q)$ with q even then $C(\mathcal{O}) \supseteq H(\Pi)$; in fact, the containment is strict when $q > 2$.

Proof. Since the cardinality of an oval is $q + 2$ and all vectors in $H(\Pi)$ have weight congruent to zero mod 4, the second assertion is obvious once we prove the first. But if Y is an oval and L is a line meeting Y twice, we apply Lemma 2 with $X = Y - L$ and P one of the two points of $X \cap L$. Then $J + v^L$ is in $C(\mathcal{O})$ for every L and hence $v^L + v^M$ for every L and M. We remark that $\mathcal{O}$ could have been taken to be the orbit of any oval under $PGL_3(q)$ and, in particular, we could have taken $\mathcal{O}$ to be simply all ovals obtained as a conic together with its nucleus.

Notes.

1. For $\Pi = PG(2, q^2)$, $C(\mathcal{S}) \supset C(\Pi)$, and we conjecture that, for q prime, $C(\mathcal{S}) = H(\Pi)^{\perp}$. This is true, by computation, for $q^2 = 4$, 9 and 25.

2. It has been shown by Bagchi and Sastry [2] that if $\mathcal{D}$ is a symmetric incidence structure of even order with a polarity, and if X is the set of absolute points of the polarity, then $v^X \in C_2(\mathcal{D})$. Thus for $\Pi = PG(2, q^2)$ where $q = 2^r$ and X a hermitian unital, $v^X \in C_2(\Pi)$, and hence $C_2(\Pi) = C_2(\mathcal{H})$. (The inclusion $C_2(\mathcal{H}) \subseteq C_2(\Pi)$ can also be proved from the results of Fisher, Hirschfeld and Thas [5].)

That the result of Bagchi and Sastry also holds for odd order is not true, i.e. if X is the set of absolute points of a polarity σ of a symmetric structure $\mathcal{D}$ of odd order, then v^X need not be in $C(\mathcal{D})$. For example, if $\mathcal{D} = PG(2, q)$ with q odd, and if σ is an orthogonal polarity, then X is an oval, and $v^X \notin B(\Pi) \supset C(\Pi)$, by Lemma 1. However, we have found, by computation, that for $q = 9$ or 25,

$C(\mathcal{H}) = C(\Pi)$. Also, for $q = 9$, $C_3(\Pi) \subset C_3(\mathcal{U})$. This last inequality was shown by using the construction of Metz [11] to find a non-hermitian unital in $PG(2,9)$. Moreover, we believe that a unital X has $v^X \in C(\Pi)$, where $\Pi = PG(2,q^2)$, if and only if X is hermitian.

LEMMA 5. *Let $X \subseteq \mathcal{P}$ with $|X| \equiv \alpha \not\equiv 0 \pmod{p}$. Suppose that $L \in \mathcal{L}$ satisfies $X \cap L = \emptyset$, where L is a translation line for Π, and H its translation group. If $\mathcal{B} = \{X^g | g \in H\}$ and $\mathcal{D} = (\mathcal{P}, \mathcal{B})$, then $J - v^L \in C(\mathcal{D})$.*

Proof. Let $w = \sum_{g \in H} v^{X^g}$. Then $w_Q = 0$ for $Q \in L$, and $w_Q = \alpha$ for $Q \notin L$, since H acts regularly on $\mathcal{P} \backslash L$. Thus $w = \alpha(J - v^L) \in C(\mathcal{D})$, so $J - v^L \in C(\mathcal{D})$.

COROLLARY. *For $\Pi = PG(2,q), q$ odd, $C(\mathcal{O}) = F_p^N$.*

Proof. We first show that $C(\mathcal{O}) \supset C(\Pi)$. An oval has $q + 1$ points, so $\alpha = 1$ in the Lemma. Each line L of $\mathcal{L}$ is exterior to some oval, and is a translation line for Π. So $J - v^L \in C(\mathcal{O})$ for all $L \in \mathcal{L}$. We need only show that $J \in C(\mathcal{O})$, and this follows, as usual, by taking a Singer cycle s for Π, and then setting $w = \sum_{g \in \langle s \rangle} v^{X^g} = (q+1)J = J \in C(\mathcal{O})$. That $C(\mathcal{O}) \neq C(\Pi)$ follows from Lemma 1, and the observations above. Thus $C(\mathcal{O}) \supset C(\Pi)$.

For q odd, the ovals are precisely the conics, and through any five points, no three collinear, there passes a unique oval: see [6]. Let $\mathcal{T}$ be a triangle of points $\{A, B, C\}$, with edges the lines K, L and M. A simple count yields that $\mathcal{T}$ is on $(q-1)^2$ ovals. Call this set of ovals $\mathcal{B}$. Every point of Π not on K, L or M is on x members of $\mathcal{B}$, where $x(q^2 + q + 1 - 3q) = x(q-1)^2 = (q-1)^2(q-2)$, i.e. $x = (q-2)$. Let $v = \sum_{X \in \mathcal{B}} v^X$. Then $v_Q = 0$ for $Q \in K, L, M$, and $Q \notin \{A, B, C\}$; $v_Q = 1$ for $Q \in \{A, B, C\}$; $v_Q = -2$ for $Q \notin K, L, M$. Let $w = 2(v^K + v^L + v^M) - (v + 2J)$. Then $w = v^{\mathcal{T}}$ and $w \in C(\mathcal{O})$, since $C(\mathcal{O}) \supset C(\Pi)$. This holds for any triangle, so we clearly have that $\langle J \rangle^{\perp} \subseteq C(\mathcal{O})$, since any generator of $\langle J \rangle^{\perp}$ can be obtained from the vector $v^{\mathcal{T}_1} - v^{\mathcal{T}_2}$, where $\mathcal{T}_1$ and $\mathcal{T}_2$ are suitably chosen distinct triangles with an edge in common. Since $J \in C(\mathcal{O})$, $J \notin \langle J \rangle^{\perp}$, it follows that $C(\mathcal{O}) = F_p^N$.

The proposition stated in the Introduction now follows from the Lemmas and Corollaries.

4. Translation Planes. Let $V = V_{2s}(p)$, and $q = p^s$. Then a spread in V is a set of $q + 1$ subspaces S_i, $i = 0, \ldots, q$, each of dimension s over F_p, such that $S_i \cap S_j = \{0\}$ for all $i \neq j$. An affine translation plane is formed by taking the vectors of V as points, and the spread elements and all their translates (or cosets) as lines: see [12].

For any $r \neq 2s$, let $\mathcal{L}(r)$ denote the set of r-flats (i.e. supspaces and translates) of V over F_p. Let $\mathcal{D}(r)$ denote the 2-design formed by taking the vectors of V as points, and the members of $\mathcal{L}(r)$ as blocks. Then $\mathcal{D}(r)$ is the design defined by the affine geometry $AG(2s, p)$ of points and r-flats, and usually denoted by $AG(2s, p) : r$ or $A_{2s,r}(p)$ (see [8]). Let $B(r) = C(\mathcal{D}(r))$ over F_p. In [1] we showed that if π is a translation plane of order q, then

$$C(\pi) \subseteq B(s) \subseteq \mathrm{Hull}(\pi)^{\perp}.$$

LEMMA 6. *If π is a translation plane of order $q = p^s$, then $B(r) \subseteq \text{Hull}(\pi)^\perp$ if and only if $r \geq s$. If $r > s$, then $B(r) \subseteq C(\pi)^\perp$.*

Proof. Notice first that if $2s \geq r_1 \geq r_2$ then $B(r_1) \subseteq B(r_2)$, since if $X \in \mathcal{L}(r_1)$, then v^X can be written as a sum of vectors v^Y where the Y are translates of the same space in $\mathcal{L}(r_2)$.

Let $X \in \mathcal{L}(r)$ and, without loss of generality, suppose that X is a subspace of V. Let S_i, $i = 0, 1, \ldots, q$ be a spread for π. We show first that $|X \cap S_i| > 1$ for all i if and only if $r > s$. For suppose $|X \cap S_i| > 1$ for all i. Then $X - \{0\} = \cup_{i=0}^s (X \cap S_i - \{0\})$ which is a disjoint union, so $p^r - 1 \geq (p^s + 1)(p - 1)$, i.e. $p^r \geq p^{s+1} - p^s + p$, so that $p^r > p^{s+1} - p^s = p^s(p - 1)$, and hence $r > s$. Conversely, if $r > s$ and $X \cap S_i = \{0\}$ for some i, then $\dim(X + S_i) = r + s > 2s$, which is impossible. Thus $X \cap S_i \neq \{0\}$ for all i if and only if $r > s$, which is equivalent to the statement $B(r) \subseteq C(\pi)^\perp$ if and only if $2s \geq r > s$, since $(v^X, v^{S_i}) \equiv 0 \pmod{p}$ for all S_i and all their translates.

If $r \leq s$ then there is a value of i for which $X \cap S_i = \{0\}$. Then $|X \cap (a + S_i)| = 1$ for all translates $a + S_i$ of S_i if and only if $r = s$. Thus $v^X \in \text{Hull}(\pi)^\perp$ if and only if $r \geq s$.

COROLLARY. *If Π is a finite projective translation plane of order $q = p^s$, L a translation line and $\pi = \Pi^L$, then if $X \in \mathcal{L}(r)$, where $r > s$, the vector v of length $q^2 + q + 1$ with $v_Q = 1$ for $Q \in X$, $v_Q = 0$ for $Q \in L$ or $Q \notin X$, is in $C(\Pi)^\perp$.*

Proof. This follows from [1, Proposition 2] since $C(\pi)^\perp$ is the image of the projection of the space $\{u | u \in C(\Pi)^\perp \text{ and } u_Q = 0 \text{ for } Q \in L\}$, into $F_p^{q^2}$.

Acknowledgement.

The second author, Jennifer Key, would like to thank Bryn Mawr College and the Association of Women in Mathematics for the award of the Emmy Noether lectureship at Bryn Mawr College for the spring semester 1988. The lectureship was established to commemorate the name of Emmy Noether, who taught at Bryn Mawr from 1933 to 1935.

REFERENCES

[1] E.F. ASSMUS, JR. AND J.D. KEY, *Affine and projective planes*, Discrete Math., Special Coding Theory Issue (to appear).

[2] BHASKAR BAGCHI AND N.S. NARASIMHA SASTRY, *Even order inversive planes, generalized quadrangles and codes*, Geometriae Dedicata, 22 (1987), pp. 137-147.

[3] A.A. BRUEN AND J.W.P. HIRSCHFELD, *Intersections in projective space I*, Combinatorics, Math. Z., 193 (1986), pp. 215–225.

[4] A.A. BRUEN AND U. OTT, *On the p-rank of incidence matrices and a question of E.S. Lander*, (preprint).

[5] J.C. FISHER, J.W.P. HIRSCHFELD AND J.A. THAS, *Complete arcs in planes of square order*, Annals of Discrete Math., 30 (1986), pp. 243–250.

[6] J.W.P. HIRSCHFELD, *Projective Geometries over Finite Fields*, Oxford, 1979.

[7] D.R. HUGHES AND F.C. PIPER, *Projective Planes*, Springer Graduate Texts in Mathematics (1973).

[8] D.R. HUGHES AND F.C. PIPER, *Design Theory*, Cambridge University Press, 1985.

[9]   BARBU C. KESTENBAND, *Unital intersections in finite projective planes*, Geometriae Dedicata, 11 (1981), pp. 107–117.

[10] E.S. LANDER, *Symmetric Designs: an Algebraic Approach*, London Mathematical Society Lecture Notes #74, Cambridge University Press, 1983.

[11] RUDOLF METZ, *On a class of unitals*, Geometriae Dedicata, 8 (1979), pp. 125–126.

[12] T.G. OSTROM, *Finite Translation Planes, Lecture Notes in Mathematics, 158*, Springer, 1970.

[13] H. SACHAR, *The F_p span of the incidence matrix of a finite projective plane*, Geometriae Dedicata, 8 (1979), pp. 407–415.

ON THE LENGTH OF CODES
WITH A GIVEN COVERING RADIUS

RICHARD A. BRUALDI†* AND VERA S. PLESS‡**

Abstract. We further develop techniques for showing the non-existence of short codes with a given covering radius. In particular we show that there does not exist a code of codimension 11 and covering radius 2 which has length 64. We conclude with a table which gives the best available information for the length of a code with codimension m and covering radius r for $2 \leq m \leq 24$ and $2 \leq r \leq 24$.

1. Introduction. We consider binary linear codes C of length n and dimension k, called $[n, k]$-codes. The **covering radius** of C is the smallest integer r such that each binary n-tuple has (Hamming) distance at most r to some codeword in C. Let $m = n - k$ be the **codimension** of C, and let H be an m by n **parity check matrix** for C and hence a generator matrix for the **dual code** $C^{\perp}$. By a **syndrome** we mean a binary column vector of length m. The covering radius of C is also the smallest integer r such that every syndrome is the sum of r or fewer columns of H. Determining the covering radius of a code is in general a difficult problem [4].

In [2] the following **length function** was defined to facilitate investigations on the covering radius. Let r and m be positive integers with $r \leq m$. Then $\ell(m, r)$ equals the smallest length of a code of codimension m and covering radius r; equivalently, $\ell(m, r)$ equals the smallest integer n for which there exists an m by n matrix H such that each syndrome is the sum of at most r columns of H. The following properties of the length function are given in [2]:

$$\text{(1.1)} \qquad \ell(m, 1) = 2^m - 1 \text{ and } \ell(m, m) = m.$$

$$\text{(1.2)} \qquad \ell(m, r) \geq \ell(m, r + 1).$$

$$\text{(1.3)} \qquad \ell(m + 1, r) \geq \ell(m, r) + 1.$$

$$\text{(1.4)} \qquad \ell(m + 1, r + 1) \leq \ell(m, r) + 1.$$

$$\text{(1.5)} \qquad \ell(m, r) \geq \min\{n : \sum_{i=0}^{r} \binom{n}{i} \geq 2^m\}.$$

The lower bound in (1.5) is the **first feasible length** [2] for a code of codimension m and covering radius r, but this bound seems to be rarely attained except in trivial circumstances.

$$\text{(1.6)} \qquad \ell(m, r) = m + 1 \text{ for } m > r \geq \lceil \frac{m}{2} \rceil.$$

$$\text{(1.7)} \qquad \ell(2s + 1, s) = 2s + 5 \text{ for } s \geq 1.$$

$$\text{(1.8)} \qquad \ell(2s, s - 1) = 2s + 6 \text{ for } s \geq 4.$$

†Department of Mathematics, University of Wisconsin, Madison, WI 53706
*Research partially supported by National Science Foundation Grant No. DMS-8421521
‡Department of Mathematics, University of Illinois at Chicago, Chicago, IL 60680
**Research partially supported by National Security Agency Grant No. MDA 904-85-H-0016

In addition we have

(1.9)
$$\ell(2s + 1, s - 1) = 2s + 7 \text{ for } s \geq 6.$$

Proof. By (1.3) and (1.8)

$$\ell(2s + 1, s - 1) \geq \ell(2s, s - 1) + 1 = 2s + 7 \quad (s \geq 4).$$

By [5, Theorem 23] it follows that for $s \geq 6$ there exists a $[2s + 7, 6]$-code with covering radius $s - 1$, and hence $\ell(2s + 1, s - 1) \leq 2s + 7$. $\square$

In the next section we develop further the techniques of [2] and [3] for showing the nonexistence of codes of covering radius 2 with a prescribed codimension and length. In particular we show that there does not exist a code of covering radius 2 with codimension 11 and length 64 (64 is the first feasible length). This settles a question in [2] and implies that $\ell(11, 2) \geq 65$.

In the last section we extend and update the table of values for the length function given in [2].

2. Further results on the covering radius. Let $A_0, A_1, \ldots, A_n$ and $B_0, B_1, \ldots, B_n$ denote respectively the weight distributions of the $[n, k]$-code C and the $[n, m]$-code $C^\perp$. Let $u_1, u_2, \ldots, u_n$ denote the columns of a parity check matrix H for C, and let r denote the covering radius of C. Because each syndrome is a sum of r or fewer columns of H, the number

(2.1)
$$g(n, m, r) = \sum_{j=0}^{r} \binom{n}{j} - 2^m$$

is a nonnegative integer.

Calderbank and Sloane [3] define the **syndrome graph** $\mathcal{G}(C)$ as follows. The vertices of $\mathcal{G}(C)$ are the subsets of $\{1, 2, \ldots, n\}$ of cardinality at most r. Two such subsets X and Y are joined by an edge if and only if

(2.2)
$$\sum_{i \in X} u_i = \sum_{j \in Y} u_j.$$

The graph $\mathcal{G}(C)$ is the graph of an equivalence relation and because C has covering radius r, $\mathcal{G}(C)$ has 2^m connected components each of which is a complete graph. We remark that the graph $\mathcal{G}(C)$ is independent of the choice of the parity check matrix H for C. However the following **induced subgraph** $\mathcal{G}_0(C)$ depends on the choice of first row of H. The vertices of $\mathcal{G}_0(C)$ are those subsets X of $\{1, 2, \ldots, n\}$ of cardinality at most r for which $\sum_{i \in X} u_i$ has first coordinate equal to 0. Because the graph is induced, the edges are defined by (2.2). It follows that $\mathcal{G}_0(C)$ has 2^{m-1} connected components, each of which is a connected component of $\mathcal{G}(C)$.

We now assume that $r = 2$ and make the following observations.

(2.3) [3] A vector of weight 3 or 4 in C gives three edges of $\mathcal{G}(C)$ no two of which have a vertex in common.

(2.4) If $A_1 = A_2 = 0$, then two vertices of $\mathcal{G}(C)$ which are joined by an edge are disjoint (as subsets of $\{1, 2, \ldots, n\}$) and at most one of the vertices is a singleton set.

(2.5) If $A_1 = A_2 = 0$, then the number of edges of $\mathcal{G}(C)$ equals $3(A_3 + A_4)$.

This follows from the fact that when $A_1 = A_2 = 0$, each edge of $\mathcal{G}(C)$ comes from a vector of weight 3 or 4.

(2.6) [3] The number of edges of $\mathcal{G}_0(C)$ is at least $A_3 + A_4$.

PROPOSITION 2.1. *Suppose that C has covering radius 2 and $A_1 = A_2 = 0$. Then*

$$\frac{1}{3}\binom{g(n,m,2)+1}{2} \geq A_3 + A_4 \geq \frac{g(n,m,2)}{3}.$$

Proof. The number of vertices of $\mathcal{G}(C)$ is $2^m + g(n,m,2)$. Let the sizes of the connected components be $k_i(1 \leq i \leq 2^m)$. Then the number of edges of $\mathcal{G}(C)$ is

$$\sum_{i=1}^{2^m}\binom{k_i}{2}.$$

We have

$$\binom{g(n,m,2)+1}{2} \geq \sum_{i=1}^{2^m}\binom{k_i}{2} \geq \sum_{i=1}^{2^m}(k_i - 1) = g(n,m,2).$$

The conclusion now follows from (2.5). $\square$

Given an $[n,k]$-code of even covering radius we now show how to construct another $[n,k]$-code with a no larger covering radius. If u is a binary vector, $\overline{u}$ denotes the vector for which $u + \overline{u}$ is an all 1's vector.

PROPOSITION 2.2. *Let*

$$H = \left[\begin{array}{c|c} 1 & u \\ \hline 0 & \\ \vdots & H_1 \\ 0 & \end{array}\right]$$

be a parity check matrix for an $[n,k]$-code with even covering radius r. Then

$$H' = \left[\begin{array}{c|c} 1 & \overline{u} \\ \hline 0 & \\ \vdots & H_1 \\ 0 & \end{array}\right]$$

is a parity check matrix for an $[n,k]$-code C' with covering radius at most r.

Proof. Let s be any syndrome and suppose that s is the sum of $j \leq r$ columns of H. If j is even and column 1 is not used, then s is the sum of the j columns of H' with the same index; if j is even and column 1 is used, then s is the sum of $j-1$ columns of H. If j is odd and column 1 is not used, then $j \leq r-1$ (because r is even) and s is the sum of the columns of H' with the same index and also column 1; if j is odd and column 1 is used, then s is the sum of j columns of H'. $\square$

COROLLARY 2.3. *Suppose that the covering radius of the $[n,k]$-code C is 2.*

(i)   If n is even, then there exists an $[n,k]$-code with covering radius 2 in which the all 1's vector is either in the code or in a coset of weight 2.

(ii)   If n is odd, then there exists an $[n,k]$-code with covering radius 2 in which the all 1's vector is either in the code or in a coset of weight 1.

Proof. Because C has covering radius 2, the all 1's vector is in a coset of weight at most 2. First suppose that n is even and that the all 1's vector is in a coset of weight 1. Without loss of generality we may assume

$$H = \begin{bmatrix} 1 & & x_1 \\ 0 & & x_2 \\ \vdots & & \vdots \\ 0 & & x_m \end{bmatrix}$$

where x_i has even weight ($i = 1, 2, \ldots, m$). The code C' of Proposition 2.2 has parity check matrix H' all of whose rows have even weight. Hence the all 1's vector is in C'. Hence (i) holds. In a similar way one proves (ii). □

LEMMA 2.4. *Suppose that C has covering radius 2 and that $A_1 = A_2 = 0$. If the graph $\mathcal{G}_0(C)$ contains a complete graph K_t, then $\mathcal{G}_0(C)$ contains at least $2\binom{\lceil \frac{t}{2} \rceil}{2} + 2\binom{\lfloor \frac{t}{2} \rfloor}{2}$ pairwise vertex disjoint edges, none of which meets K_t.*

Proof. By (2.4) at most one of the vertices of K_t is a singleton set. If the set $\{i, j\}$ of cardinality 2 is a vertex of K_t, then the columns u_i and u_j of the parity check matrix H have the same first coordinate. Suppose that ℓ of the vertices of K_t arise from columns with first coordinate 0 and $t - \ell$ arise from columns with first coordinate 1. Then it follows from (2.4) and (2.5) that $\mathcal{G}_0(C)$ has a collection of

$$2\binom{\ell}{2} + 2\binom{t-\ell}{2}$$

pairwise vertex disjoint edges none of which meets a vertex of K_t. □

THEOREM 2.5.

$$\ell(11, 2) \geq 65.$$

Proof. Suppose to the contrary that there exists a code C of length 64 and codimension 11 having covering radius 2. Let H be a parity check matrix for C. Because 64 is the first feasible length for codimension 11, $A_1 = A_2 = 0$. It follows from [2, Lemma 4.6] that a nonzero vector in $C^\perp$ has weight w where $27 \leq w \leq 38$. It was shown in [2] that the vectors in $C^\perp$ of weights $0, 27$, and 38 form a subcode as do the vectors of weights 0 and 38; in addition $B_{38} = 0, 1$, or 3. We now show that $B_{27} \leq 2$.

Suppose $B_{27} \geq 3$ so that $B_{38} > 0$. Let v and u be vectors in $C^\perp$ of weights 27 and 38, respectively. Then $u + v$ has weight 27. Let w be a vector in $C^\perp$ of weight

27 with $w \neq v, u + v$. Then $v + w$ has weight 38 and $v + w \neq u$. We now have the contradiction: $(v + w) \cdot u \equiv v \cdot u \equiv w \cdot u \equiv 1 \pmod 2$. Hence $B_{27} \leq 2$.

Suppose $B_{27} \geq 1$. Then $B_{27} = 1$ and $B_{38} = 0$, or $B_{27} = 2$ and $B_{38} = 1$. We may choose H to be of the form

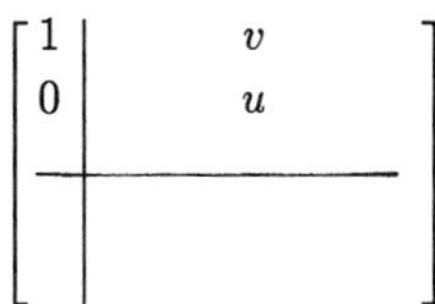

where the first row has weight 27 and the second row, if $B_{38} = 1$, has weight 38. We now apply Proposition 2.2 and obtain a code with covering radius 2 and no vectors of weight 27. Hence we may assume that $B_{27} = 0$.

We now show that $B_w = 0$ for $30 \leq w \leq 35$. If not, we may suppose that the first row of H has one of these weights w. The number of components of the graph $\mathcal{G}_0(C)$ is 2^{10} and the number of vertices is

$$2^{10} + \begin{cases} 1 & \text{if} \quad w = 32 \quad \text{or} \quad 33, \\ 3 & \text{if} \quad w = 31 \quad \text{or} \quad 34, \\ 7 & \text{if} \quad w = 30 \quad \text{or} \quad 35. \end{cases}$$

We have $g(64, 11, 2) = 33$. Hence by (2.6) and Proposition 2.1 $\mathcal{G}_0(C)$ has at least 11 edges. This gives a contradiction if $31 \leq w \leq 34$. Now suppose that $w = 30$ or 35. Then it follows that $\mathcal{G}_0(C)$ contains a complete graph K_4 as a subgraph. By Lemma 2.4 $\mathcal{G}_0(C)$ has a set of 4 pairwise vertex disjoint edges none of which meets the K_4. We now conclude that the connected components of $\mathcal{G}_0(C)$ with more than 1 vertex are one K_4 and four K_2's. Since this gives only 10 edges, we have a contradiction. Hence $B_w = 0$ for $30 \leq w \leq 35$, and the only possible nonzero weights of vectors in $C^\perp$ are $28, 29, 36, 37$ and 38.

Using the fact that $A_{38} \leq 3$, one may now show that there is no nonnegative integral solution to the MacWilliams identities. $\square$

3. A table for the length function. We now extend and update the table for the length function. This table uses the properties (1.1) through (1.9) of the length function and incorporates improvements resulting from work of Ashlock [1], Calderbank and Sloane [3], Kibler [6], Simonis [7], and van Wee [8]. We give the best available information for $\ell(m, r)$ with $2 \leq m \leq 24$. By (1.1) and (1.6) we may confine our attention to $2 \leq r \leq \lceil \frac{m}{2} \rceil = 12$.

m/r	2	3	4	5	6	7	8	9	10	11	12
2	2										
3	4	3									
4	5	5	4								
5	9	6	6	5							
6	13	7	7	7	6						
7	18-19	11	8	8	8	7					
8	24-26	14	9	9	9	9	8				
9	33-41	16-18	13	10	10	10	10	9			
10	46-58	19-22	16	11	11	11	11	11	10		
11	65-90	23	17-20	15	12	12	12	12	12	11	
12	91-119	30-38	19-24	18	13	13	13	13	13	13	12
13	128-182	37-55	23-25	19	17	14	14	14	14	14	14
14	181-246	47-71	27-29	20-26	20	15	15	15	15	15	15
15	256-374	59-88	31-37	23-27	21	19	16	16	16	16	16
16	362-495	74-120	36-51	26-30	22-25	22	17	17	17	17	17
17	512-750	93-149	43-66	30-35	24-29	23	21	18	18	18	18
18	724-1006	117-181	51-81	34-41	27-33	24-29	24	19	19	19	19
19	1024-1518	147-244	61-98	38-48	29-36	25-31	25	23	20	20	20
20	1448-2015	185-308	72-115	43-63	33-40	27-31	26-31	26	21	21	21
21	2048-2976	233-372	85-147	49-80	36-44	30-38	27-32	27	25	22	22
22	2896-4062	294-500	101-179	56-112	40-45	33-42	29-33	28-31	28	23	23
23	4096-6048	370-621	120-208	65-127	45-60	35-45	30-37	29-34	29	27	24
24	5793-8127	466-749	143-237	74-156	50-75	39-47	34-41	30-35	30-35	30	25

Table: $\ell(m,r)$ for $2 \leq m \leq 24$ and $2 \leq r \leq 12$.

The lower bounds in the table are obtained from the sphere covering bound (1.5) with the exception of the following improvements:

$$\ell(6,2) = 13, [5]$$
$$\ell(9,2) \geq 33, \ell(10,2) \geq 46, \ell(12,2) \geq 91 [2]$$
$$\ell(9,3) \geq 16, [7]$$
$$\ell(14,4) \geq 27, \ell(16,5) \geq 26, \ell(17,6) \geq 24, \ell(21,7) \geq 30,$$
$$\ell(22,7) \geq 33, \ell(22,8) \geq 29, [8]$$
$$\ell(7,2) \geq 18, \ell(8,2) \geq 24 [3]$$
$$\ell(13,4) \geq 23, \ell(15,5) \geq 23, \ell(17,5) \geq 30, \ell(18,5) \geq 34,$$
$$\ell(18,6) \geq 27, \ell(20,6) \geq 33, \ell(24,8) \geq 34, [9]$$

In some instances (1.3) gives a better result than the sphere covering bound when $\ell(m,r)$ is known. The fact that $\ell(11,2) = 23$ follows from the binary Golay code. All the other exact values in the table are consequences of one of (1.6) to (1.9).

The upper bounds in the table are obtained as follows. Some of these were given in the table in [2]. The upper bound for $\ell(m,2)$ with $m \geq 10$ follows from Theorems 3.2 and 3.3 of [2]. Kibler [6] showed by construction that $\ell(8,2) \leq 26$, $\ell(9,2) \leq 41$, and $\ell(9,3) \leq 18$. Ashlock [1] showed by construction that $\ell(8,2) \leq 26$, $\ell(9,2) \leq 41$, and $\ell(12,3) \leq 38$. The remainder of the upper bounds follow by taking the amalgamated direct sum (ADS) [5] of codes with a known covering radius. The codes used were the codes constructed in the proofs of Theorems 3.2 and 3.3 of [2], some of the codes given in Graham and Sloane [5], the Golay and Hamming codes, and the codes constructed by Kibler and Ashlock. Some of the codes used in the ADS constructions were known to be normal because the code had a weight 3 vector. For those codes which were not known to be normal, we verified that the covering radius of the code obtained by an ADS construction had the required value.

Acknowledgement.

We are greatly indebted to Vanessa Job for the computations that gave many of the upper bounds for the length function in the table. We also thank A.R. Calderbank and N.J.A. Sloane for sending us a copy of [3].

REFERENCES

[1]   D. Ashlock. private communication.
[2]   R.A. Brualdi, V.S. Pless and R.M. Wilson, *Short codes with a given covering radius*, IEEE Trans. Inform. Theory (to appear).
[3]   A.R. Calderbank and N.J.A. Sloane, *Inequalities for covering codes*, preprint.
[4]   G.D. Cohen, M.G. Karpovsky, H.F. Mattson, Jr., and J.R. Schatz, *Covering radius – survey and recent results*, IEEE Trans. Inform. Theory, IT-31 (1985), pp. 328–343.
[5]   R.L. Graham and N.J.A. Sloane, *On the covering radius of codes*, IEEE Trans. Inform. Theory, IT-31 (1985), pp. 385–401.
[6]   R. Kibler. private communication
[7]   J. Simonis, *The minimal covering radius t[15, 6] of a 6-dimensional binary linear code of length 15 is equal to 4*, preprint.
[8]   G.J.M. van Wee, *Improved sphere bounds on the covering radius of codes*, preprint.
[9]   I.S. Honkala, *Modified bounds for covering codes*, preprint.

THE DIFFERENTIAL ENCODING OF COSET CODES BY ALGEBRAIC METHODS

A.R. CALDERBANK*

Abstract. A trellis code is a method of encoding a binary data stream as a sequence of real vectors that are transmitted over a noisy channel. Trellis codes are used in modems designed to achieve data rates of up to 19.2 kb/s on dial-up voice telephone lines. Coset codes are trellis codes based on lattices and cosets. The signal constellation is finite, and signal points are taken from $2N$-dimensional lattice L, with an equal number of points taken from each coset of a sublattice M. One part of the input data stream selects cosets of M in L and the other part selects points from those cosets. An important practical problem is that of channel phase shifts which cause a rotation of every 2-dimensional constituent of a $2N$-dimensional signal through the same multiple of $90°$. We describe the structure of coset codes and an algebraic method of resolving this phase ambiguity.

1. Introduction. A *trellis code* is a method of encoding a binary data stream as a sequence of real vectors that are transmitted over a noisy channel. The vectors are selected from a finite set called the *signal constellation*. Trellis codes based on lattices and cosets are called *coset codes*. Coset codes were proposed by Calderbank and Sloane in [5], but the name was coined by Forney who investigated their structure in a sequence of papers [6,7,8]. Here the signal points are taken from a $2N$-dimensional lattice L and the signal constellation contains an equal number of points from each coset of a sublattice M. The $2N$ components of a signal point are transmitted as N consecutive 2-dimensional symbols. One part of the input data stream selects cosets of M in L and the other part selects points from these cosets.

The performance of a trellis code is determined by the minimum squared distance d^2 between output sequences corresponding to distinct input sequences. For coset codes this minimum squared distance is determined by the minimum norm in M and by the method of selecting cosets. The *norm* $N[C]$ of a coset C is the minimum norm of a point in C, and the *multiplicity* $\text{Mult}[C]$ is the number of points in C with the minimum norm. Let u, u' be distinct input sequences, let $T = (T_k), T' = (T'_k)$ be the corresponding coset sequences, and let $x = (x_k), x' = (x'_k)$ be the corresponding output sequences. If $T = T'$ then $\|x_k - x'_k\|^2 \geq N[M]$ for some k. If $T_i = T'_i$ for $i < k_1$ and $i > k_2$ then

$$\|x - x'\|^2 \geq \sum_{i=k_1}^{k_2} N[T_i - T'_i] = d^2(T, T')$$

and the number of sequences $x' = (x'_k)$, $x'_k \in T'_k$ at distance $d^2(T, T')$ from x is $\prod_{i=k_1}^{k_2} \text{Mult}[T_i - T'_i]$, provided the signal points x_k fall in the interior of the signal constellation (if there are boundary points then there are fewer sequences x'). If

---

*AT&T Bell Laboratories, Murray Hill, New Jersey 07974

$d_1^2 = N[M]$, and $d_2^2 = \min\limits_{T \neq T'} d^2(T, T')$, then the minimum squared distance $d^2 = \min(d_1^2, d_2^2)$.

We shall say that two trellis codes are *equivalent* if the two methods of selecting signal points have the same distance properties. For coset codes we require that for every pair of inputs u, u', the corresponding coset sequences $(A_k), (A'_k)$ and $(T_k), (T'_k)$ satisfy $N[A_k - A'_k] = N[T_k - T'_k]$ for all k.

We suppose that the trellis encoder slides a window of size $\nu + k$ along k parallel binary data sequences. The state of the encoder is the ν-tuple of prior input bits and the shape of the window (the choice of ν particular prior input bits) determines the possible transitions between states. The problem of determining the minimum squared distance d^2 is at worst the problem of finding a minimum cost path in a directed graph with $2^{2\nu}$ vertices labeled by pairs of states. However for very symmetric trellis codes the complexity of the problem can be greatly reduced.

Binary convolutional codes are *regular*: this means that for any pair of inputs u, u' the Hamming distance between the corresponding outputs x, x' depends only on the modulo 2 sum $u \oplus u'$. Figure 1A is the trellis diagram of the binary convolutional code $[1 + D^2, 1 + D + D^2]$. Regularity makes calculation of the minimum squared distance much easier since it allows us to assume that one of the inputs u, u' is the zero sequence.

Next consider the trellis encoder $f. \; \mathbf{F}_2^3 \to \mathbf{R}$ given by

$$(1) \qquad\qquad f(a_1 a_2 a_3) = (-1)^{a_2} - 2\big((-1)^{a_1 + a_2 + a_3}\big)$$

that was considered by Calderbank and Mazo in [1]. The rate of this code is 1 bit/1-dimensional signal and the trellis diagram is shown in Figure 1B. The *figure of merit* for a trellis code is the minimum squared distance d^2 normalized by the average transmitted signal power P where

$$P = \frac{1}{2^{\nu + k}} \sum_{a \in \mathbf{F}_2^{\nu + k}} \|f(a)\|^2.$$

For the code given by (1), the minimum squared distance $d^2 = 36$ and the average power $P = 5$. The performance of a trellis code is measured against uncoded transmission at the same rate. Uncoded transmission at rate 1 bit/dimension uses the signal constellation $\{\pm 1\}$. For uncoded transmission the minimum squared distance $d^2 = 4$ and the average power $P = 1$.

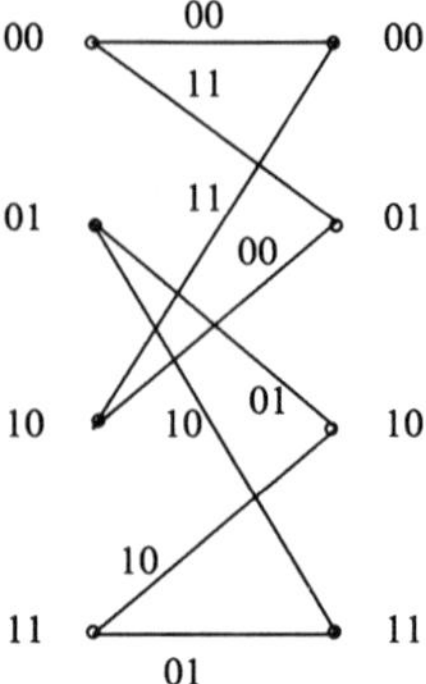

Fig. 1A. Trellis diagram for the binary convolutional code $[1 + D^2, 1 + D + D^2]$.

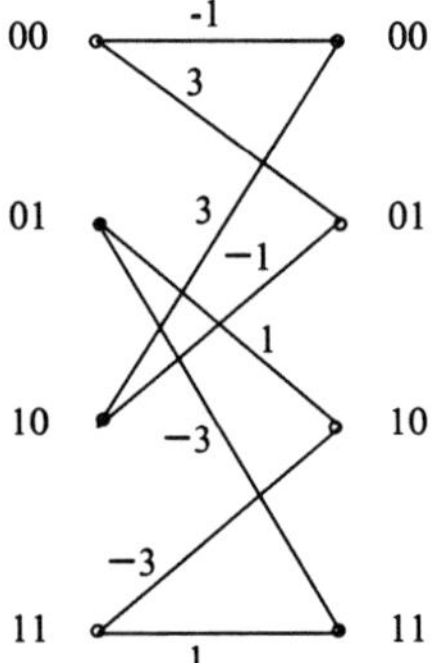

Fig. 1B. Trellis diagram for the code $f(a_1 a_2 a_3) = (-1)^{a_2} - 2(-1)^{a_1 + a_2 + a_3}$.

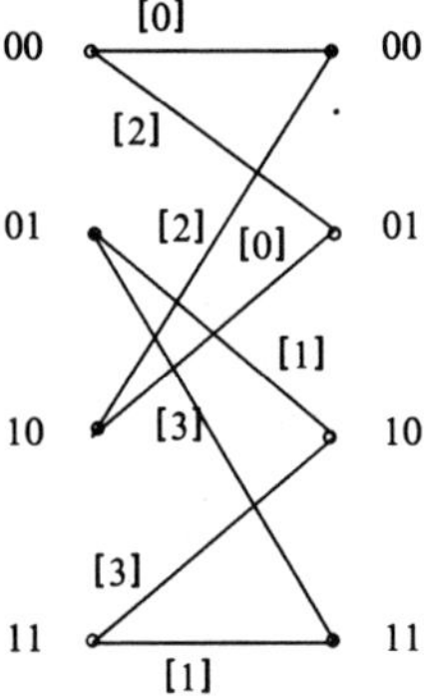

Fig. 1C. Trellis diagram for the code $[2 \ 1 \ 2]$.

The *coding gain* is

$$10 \log_{10} \frac{(d^2/P)\,\text{coded}}{(d^2/P)\,\text{uncoded}} = 10 \ \log_{10} \frac{36}{20} = 2.5 \ dB.$$

Calderbank, Mazo and Wei [3] (see also [2]) obtained an upper bound on the normalized minimum squared distance d^2/P of a trellis code with rate k bits/n-dimensional signal that is given by

$$\frac{d^2}{P} \le \min_{i \ge 1} \left[2 \left(\frac{2^{tk}}{2^{tk} - 1} \right) \ \left(\frac{\nu}{k} + t \right) \right].$$

They also derive stronger asymptotic results for large memory ν using the sphere packing bounds of Kabatiansky and Levenshtein [11]. It is possible to obtain lower bounds by probabilistic methods (see [1]) and for $k = 1$ we have

$$\frac{9}{50}(\nu + 1) \le \frac{d^2}{P} \le \frac{8}{3}(\nu + 2)$$

which is not very strong. For $n = 1, k = 1$, and $\nu = 2$, we do not even know the best 4-state code.

We return to the trellis encoder $f : \mathsf{F}_2^3 \to \mathsf{R}$ given by (1). Given $a = (a_1, a_2, a_3)$, $a' = (a_1', a_2', a_3')$ in F_2^3, let $a \oplus a' = (b_1, b_2, b_3)$. Then

$$(2) \qquad |f(a) - f(a')| \ge \min_{\epsilon_1, \epsilon_2 = \pm 1} [2(\epsilon_1 b_2 + 2\epsilon_2(b_1 \oplus b_2 \oplus b_3))]^2$$

provides a lower bound on $|f(a) - f(a')|^2$ that depends only on the modulo 2 sum $a \oplus a'$. This allows us to find a lower bound on the minimum squared distance d^2 by finding a minimum cost path in a graph with just 4 vertices. The 4 vertices are labeled by binary 2-tuples and the vertex labeled z represents the set of pairs of states $\{y, y \oplus z\}$ where $y \in \mathsf{F}_2^2$. The edge joining $e_1 e_2$ to $e_2 e_3$ corresponds to the 3-tuple $e = (e_1, e_2, e_3)$ and is labeled by the lower bound on $|f(a) - f(a \oplus e)|^2$ provided by (2). This graph is called the *state transition diagram* and is shown in Fig. 2.

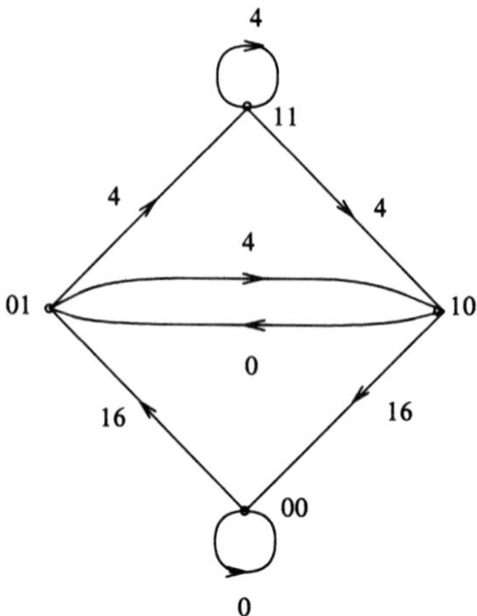

Fig. 2. The state transition diagram for the code $f(a_1a_2a_3) = (-1)^{a_2} - 2(-1)^{a_1+a_2+a_3}$.

Figure 2 reveals $d^2 \geq 36$ and that $d^2 = 36$ is only possible for inputs u, u' that differ in a single coordinate position. Now

$$|f(a) - f(a \oplus (010))|2 = \begin{cases} 36, & \text{if } (a, (101)) = 1 \\ 4, & \text{if } (a, (101)) = 0 \end{cases}$$

where $(\ ,\ )$ denotes the usual dot product. Given an input u, there exists an input u' at distance 36 from μ if and only if there exists a 3-subsequence of u that is orthogonal to (101). For $u = \dots 0011001100 \dots$ there is no input u' at distance 36. The code given by (1) is not regular but it is still possible to determine the minimum squared distance by solving a minimum cost path problem in a graph with $2^{\nu} = 4$ vertices.

Trellis coded modulation schemes have adopted in international standards for both 14.4 Kb/s private-line modems and 9.6 Kb/s switched network modems. These applications require data rates of 6 bits/2-dim signal and 4bits/2-dim signal respectively. Coset codes allow the theorist to work with the larger signal constellations required by the modem applications.

A 4-state, 1-dimensional coset code based on the integer lattice $L = Z$ and on the sublattice $M = 4Z^2$ is shown in Fig. 1c. The code is described by the generator matrix $G = [2\ 1\ 2]$; if the input at time k is a_k, then the coset output at time k is $T_k = 4Z + 2a_{k-2} + a_{k-1} + 2a_k = [2a_{k-2} + a_{k-1} + 2a_k]$. This code is regular; for all $a, b \in Z_2^3$ we have

$$N(f(a) - f(b)) = N(f(a \oplus b)).$$

The state transition diagram is shown in Fig. 3 where the edge corresponding to the 3-tuple e is labeled by $N(f(e))$. The distance $d^2 = \min(d_1^2, d_2^2) = 9$, since $d_1^2 - 16$ and $d_2^2 = 9$. This coset code can be used to transmit data at $k = k_2 + 1$ bits/1-dim signal; we form a signal constellation of size 2^{k_2+2} with 2^{k_2} points in each coset of $4\mathbf{Z}$ in $\mathbf{Z}$. One bit selects the coset and the other k_2 bits select the signal point within the coset. Since coded transmission requires twice as many signal points as uncoded transmission the average signal power P increases by a factor of 4, and the coding gain approaches $10 \log_{10} \left(\dfrac{9}{1} \times \dfrac{1}{4} \right) = 3.3 \ dB$ as $k_2 \to \infty$.

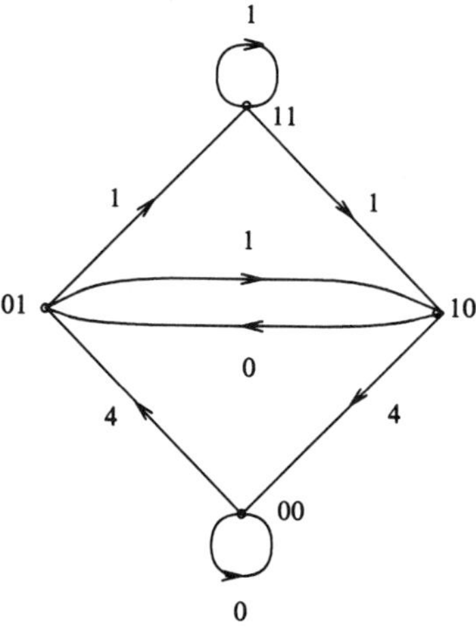

Fig. 3. The state transition diagram for the code [2 1 2].

Calderbank and Sloane [5] have used results of Fricker and others (see [10]) to analyze the asymptotic coding gain provided by coset codes. For an s-dimensional lattice L with density Δ the coding gain approaches

$$(3) \qquad 10 \log_{10} \left\{ \frac{s+2}{3} \frac{d^2}{d_1^2} \Delta^{2/s} 2^{2k_1/s} \right\} \ dB$$

as $k_2 \to \infty$.

The subject of trellis coded modulation began with the work of Ungerboeck [12] who showed that coding gains of the order of 3 dB could be obtained with simple 4-state codes and that coding gains of the order of 6 dB could be obtained with 128 state codes. Ungerboeck designed trellis encoders by matching the output of a binary convolutional code with the signal point using a technique called "mapping by set-partitioning." These original codes were based on 1- and 2-dimensional signal constellations. Work on trellis coded modulation schemes using higher dimensional signal constellations began with the examples presented by Forney et al. [9] and by Calderbank and Sloane [4]. The theory has been developed in recent papers by Calderbank and Sloane [5], Wei [15], and by Forney [6,7,8].

In many modulation schemes the collection of 2-dimensional constituents of the $2N$-dimensional signal points is closed under rotation through 90°. After a channel phase shift, every 2-dimensional constituent may have been rotated through $90°, 180°$, or $270°$, and it is important to overcome this phase ambiguity. One method of resolving the phase ambiguity is differential encoding of the input data prior to trellis encoding, provided that the trellis code is properly chosen. The first example is due to Calderbank and Mazo [1], but this example works by coupling two 1-dimensional trellis encoders. The first true 2-dimensional example is due to Wei [14], who also found a way of introducing feedback was discovered independently by Ungerboeck. The methods described by Calderbank and Mazo and by Wei are based on finding a transformation of inputs that corresponds to $90°$ rotation of outputs. We shall combine this idea with the lattice/coset approach to design a large class of trellis codes that are transparent to $90°$ phase shifts. We shall focus on the case where the lattice $L = \mathbf{Z}^2$, spanned by (0,1), (1,0), and $M = \phi^3(L)$ where $\phi = \begin{bmatrix} 1 & 1 \\ 1 & -1 \end{bmatrix}$ is a linear transformation that multiplies norms by 2. However, we begin with a short discussion of canonical forms for highly symmetric trellis encoders.

2. Canonical Forms for Trellis Encoders. We consider a trellis encoder that slides a window of size $\nu + k$ along k parallel binary data sequences. We ignore the shape of the window and regard the encoding function f as a map from $\mathbf{F}_2^{\nu+k}$ to $\mathbf{R}^n$. We suppose (following Ungerboeck [12]) that the size of the signal constellation is 2^{k+1}. Now let S_j denote the set of $2^k(\nu+k)$-tuples corresponding to edges leaving state j. The uniformity condition introduced Zehavi and Wolf in [16] is that the collection of distances $\|f(y) - f(y \oplus e)\|^2 \mid y \in S_j\}$ is independent of the state j, and depends only on the *error vector* e. We define a *uniform trellis code* to be a code satisfying the Zehavi-Wolf uniformity condition. The uniformity condition makes possible a consistent labeling of edges in the state transition diagram with sets of pairwise distances; the edge corresponding to the $(\nu + k)$-tuple e is labeled $\{\|f(y) - f(y \oplus e)\|^2 \mid y \in S_j\}$. It is then possible to bound the performance of the code by modifying the generating function method described by Viterbi and Omura in [13].

Example. The trellis encoder $f : \mathbf{F}_2^3 \to \mathbf{R}$ given by $f(a_1 a_2 a_3) = (-1)^{a_2} - 2(-1)^{a_1+a_2+a_3}$ is uniform. The edge labeling of the state transition diagram is shown in Fig. 4.

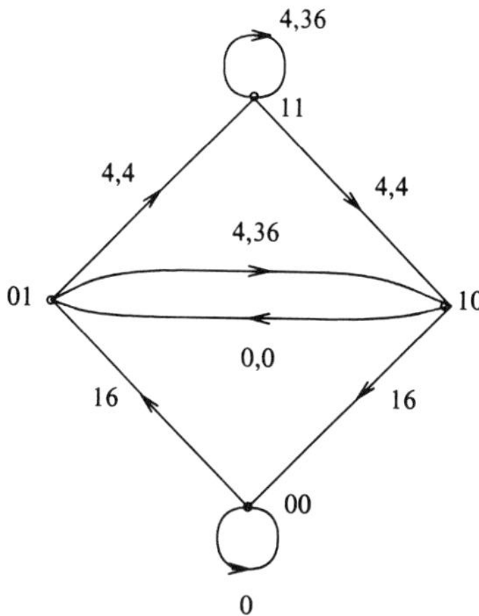

Fig. 4. The edge labeling for the uniform code $f(a_1a_2a_3) = (-1)^{a_2} - 2(-1)^{a_1+a_2+a_3}$.

Zehavi and Wolf make the additional assumption that the encoding function f operates on the outputs of a rate $k/(k+1)$ binary convolutional code. This means that there exist $y_j \in \mathsf{F}_2^{\nu+k}$, $j = 1, \ldots, k+1$ such that $f(a)$ is determined by the $k+1$ dot products (a, y_j). For $k = n = 1$ the uniformity condition is very restrictive and there is only one example.

PROPOSITION 2.1. *Let $f : \mathsf{F}_2^{\nu+1} \to \mathbf{R}$ be a uniform trellis code with a signal constellation of size 4. Then the signal constellation is $\{\pm w_1, \pm w_2\}$ and the signal points are used equally often. There exist $y_1, y_2 \in \mathsf{F}_2^{\nu+1}$ such that for all $a \in \mathsf{F}_2^{\nu+1}$, the label $f(a)$ depends only on $f(0)$ and on the dot products $(a, y_1), (a, y_2)$.*

Proof. The signal constellation is $\{x_1, x_2, x_2, x_4\}$, where $x_1 < x_2 < x_3 < x_4$, and there is only one way to realize $|x_4 - x_1|$ as a difference of edge labels; if $f(\nu) - f(\nu \oplus e) = x_4 - x_1$, then $f(\nu) = x_4$ and $f(\nu \oplus e) = x_1$. The edges leaving state j are labeled $f(j0)$ and $f(j1)$. If $\{f(j0), f(j1)\} = \{x_1, x_4\}$ for some state j, then uniformity implies every edge is labeled x_1 or x_4, and this contradicts the assumption that there are 4 signal points.

Suppose that $f(j\epsilon_1) = x_1, f(l\epsilon_2) = x_4$, and let $e_1 = (j\epsilon_1) \oplus (l\epsilon_2)$. Then uniformity with respect to e_1 implies $|\{f(j0), f(j1)\} \cap \{x_1, x_4\}| = 1$ for every state j. Now uniformity with respect to $e_2 = (0 \ldots 01)$ implies $\{f(j0), f(j1)\} = \{x_1, x_2 + a\}$ or $\{x_4, x_4 - a\}$. Note that $x_1 + a \neq x_4 - a$ for otherwise there are only 3 signal points. Since x_1, x_4 are used equally often, it follows that every signal point is selected $2^{\nu-1}$ times. Since we obtain an equivalent code by subtracting the average of the transmitted signals from each label, we may assume that this average is zero, and that $x_4 = -x_1$.

The sums $e + e'$ of error vectors e, e' that interchange labels x_1 and x_4 form a subgroup G of $\mathsf{F}_2^{\nu+1}$ of order $2^{\nu-1}$. This subgroup preserves the edge labeling. Now

$F_2^{\nu+1} = \langle G, e_1, e_2 \rangle$ and every error vector has a well defined action on edge labels. There exist $y_1, y_2 \in F_2^{\nu+1}$ such that $y_1^{\perp} = \langle G, e_2 \rangle$ and $\langle y_1, y_2 \rangle^{\perp} = G$. For $a \in F_2^{\nu+1}$, the label $f(a)$ depends only on $f(0)$ and the inner products $(a, y_1), (a, y_2)$.

One method of constructing uniform trellis encoders $f : F_2^{\nu+1} \to \mathbf{R}^n$ is to begin with a rate $k/(k+1)$ binary convolutional code determined by vectors $y_1, \ldots, y_{k+1} \in F_2^{\nu+1}$. For $a \in F_2^{\nu+1}$ let $\overline{a}$ denote the restriction of a to the last k coordinates. We assume that $\overline{y}_1 = 0$ and that $\langle \overline{y}_2 \ldots, \overline{y}_{k+1} \rangle = F_2^k$. The condition $\overline{y}_1 = 0$ splits the states into two classes, and the condition $\langle \overline{y}_2, \ldots, \overline{y}_{k+1} \rangle = F_2^k$ ensures that the 2^k edges leaving a given state receive different labels. The label $f(a)$ is determined by the inner products $(a, y_j), j = 1, \ldots, k+1$. The 2^{k+1} labels split into two sets s, s' according to the inner product with y_1. It is easy to see that if s' is obtained from s by applying an isometry then the encoder f is uniform. Is this the only way to construct uniform trellis encoders?

Finally we consider symmetric trellis encoders based on the lattice $L = \mathbf{Z}^2$ and the sublattice $M = \phi^N(L)$ where $\phi = \begin{bmatrix} 1 & 1 \\ 1 & -1 \end{bmatrix}$ is a norm-doubling map. For any integer x, let $(x)_2$ be the exact power of 2 dividing x. Let $L_0 = L = \mathbf{Z}^2$, and let $L_j = \phi^j(L_0)$. Then the sublattice L_j has index 2 in L_{j-1} and we may choose vectors $x_j \in L_{j-1} \backslash L_j, j = 1, 2, \ldots, N$. Every coset $L_N + y$ in L_0/L_N has a unique representation as a linear combination

$$(4) \qquad L_N + y = \sum_{j=1}^{N} c_j(L_n + x_j),$$

where $c_j = 0$ or $1, j = 1, 2, \ldots, N$ (For $L = \mathbf{Z}$ and $M = 2^N \mathbf{Z}$ the corresponding representation is just the binary representation of a positive integer.) We ignore the memory structure and regard the trellis encoder f as a function $F_2^{\nu+1}$ onto L_0/L_N. Uniqueness of the representation (4) allows us to write

$$(5) \qquad f(a) = \sum_{j=1}^{N} f_j(a)(L_N + x_j),$$

and to express f as a linear combination of functions $f_j : F_2^{\nu+k} \to F_2, j = 1, \ldots, N$.

PROPOSITION 2.2. *Let* $f : F_2^{\nu+1} \to L_0/L_N$ *be a trellis encoder such that*

$$(N[f(a) - f(b)])_2 = (N[f(a \oplus b)])_2$$

for all $a, b \in F_2^{\nu+k}$. *Then there exist* $y_1, \ldots, y_N \in F_2^{\nu+k}$ *such that* $(N[f(a)])_2 = i$ *if and only if* $(a, y_i) = 1$ *and* $(a, y_j) = 0$ *for* $j < i$.

Proof. Let $H_0 = F_2^{\nu+k}$ and let

$$H_j = \{a \in F_2^{\nu+k} | f_1(a) = f_2(a) = \cdots = f_j(a) =\}$$

for $j = 1, 2, \ldots, N$. We claim that H_j is a subspace of H_0 and that f_j is linear on H_{j-1}. The proof is by induction on j.

If H_j is a subspace then for all $a, b \in H_j$

$$\begin{aligned}
f_{j+1}(a) \neq f_{j+1}(b) &\iff f(a) - f(b) \in L_j/L_N \backslash L_{j+1}/L_N \\
&\iff (N[F(a) - f(b)])_2 = j \\
&\iff (N[F(a \oplus b)]_2 = j \\
&\iff f(a \oplus b) \in L_j/L_N \backslash L_{j+1}/L_N \\
&\iff f_{j+1}(a \oplus b) = 1.
\end{aligned}$$

Thus for all $a, b \in H_j$

$$f_{j+1}(a) + f_{j+1}(b) = f_{j+1}(a \oplus b),$$

and in particular H_{j+1} is a subspace. This proves the claim.

The function f is constant on cosets of H_N, since if $a \oplus b \in H_N$ then $N[f(a) - f(b)] = N[f(a \oplus b)] = 0$ and so $f(a) = f(b)$. There exist $y_1, \ldots, y_N$ such that $\langle y_1, \ldots, y_j \rangle^{\perp} = H_j$. Then $(N[f(a)])_2 = i$ if and only if $a \in L_i/L_N \backslash L_{i+1}/L_N$ and the result follows.

Example. Here $N = 3$. The 8 cosets of L_3 in L_0 are listed in Table 1 together with norms and multiplicities. The coset norms are all powers of 2. Proposition 2.2 implies that every regular trellis code based on L_0/L_3 is equivalent to a trellis code obtained from a rate 2/3 binary convolutional code determined by vectors $y_1, y_2, y_3 \in \mathbf{F}_2^{\nu+2}$, according to the rule

(6)
$$f(a) = \sum_{j=1}^{3} (a, y_j)(L_3 + x_j).$$

We illustrate this with an example

coset	name	norm	multiplicity
(0,0)	A	0	1
(2,0)	B	4	4
(1,1)	C	2	2
(1,3)	D	2	2
(0,3)	E	1	1
(0,1)	F	1	1
(3,0)	G	1	1
(1,0)	H	1	1

Table 1. Coset representatives, names, norms, and multiplicities for the 8 cosets of $\phi^3(\mathbf{Z}^2)$ in $\mathbf{Z}^2$.

Calderbank and Sloane [5] specify the method of selecting cosets by a generator matrix. The matrix

$$G_1 = \left[\begin{array}{c|cc|cc} 1 & 2 & 1 & 1 & 2 \\ 1 & 0 & 0 & 1 & 0 \end{array}\right]$$

determines an 8-state trellis code. The columns of G_1 are to be read as cosets of L_3 in L_0. If the inputs at time k are b_k, a_k then the coset output at time k is

$$T_k = L_3 + a_k(2,0) + b_k(1,1) + a_{k-1}(2,0) + a_{k-2}(1,1).$$

Calderbank and Sloane proved that a trellis code specified by a generator matrix is regular if exactly one column of the generator matrix is chosen from outside the sublattice $L_1 = \phi(L_0)$. Following Proposition 2.2 we write the trellis encoder f in the form

$$f(a) = f_1(a)(L_3 + (3,0)) + f_2(a)(L_3 + (1,3)) + f_3(a)(L_3 + (2,0)).$$

Let $e_j, j = 1, 2, \ldots, 5$ be the standard basis of $\mathbf{F}_2^5$. Then $H_0 = \mathbf{F}_2^5$, $H_1 = (\langle e_1, e_2, e_4, e_5 \rangle, H_2 = \langle e_2, e_5, e_1 + e_4 \rangle$, and $H_3 = \langle e_1 + e_4, e_2 + e_5 \rangle$. We choose $y_1 = (0,0,1,0,0), y_2 = (1,0,0,1,0)$ and $y_3 = (0,1,0,0,1)$. The function $f^* : \mathbf{F}_2^5 \to L_0/L_3$ given by

$$f^*(a) = (a, y_1)(L_3 + (3,0)) + (a, y_2)(L_3 + (1,3)) + (a, y_3)(L_3 + (2,0))$$

determines an equivalent trellis code.

The same analysis applies to codes based on the lattice $L = \mathbf{Z}$ and on the sublattice $M = 2^N \mathbf{Z}$.

3. The Design of Two-Dimensional Trellis Codes that are Transparent to 90° Phase Shifts. We shall explain the method by means of an example; a 32-state code suitable for coded transmission at rate 4 bits/2-dimensional symbol. The 32 point signal constellation is shown in Fig. 5. Signal points are labeled by pairs uT where u is a binary pair and $T \in L_0/L_3$ is a coset. This labeling satisfies

P1) if $x = u_1 T_1, y = u_2 T_2$ are signal points and if $x = R(y)$ then $u_1 = u_2$,

where R denotes anticlockwise rotation through 90°. To label larger signal constellations simply add extra digits to the binary part of the label while following rule P1. Figure 5 demonstrates that rotation through 90° permutes the 8 cosets. This permutation can be realized by adding the coset $R(y) - y$ to the coset y, but of course the difference $R(y) - y$ depends on x.

The input data stream is divided into 4 bit blocks; two bits select the coset and the other two bits select the signal point from within the coset. The generator matrix

(7)
$$G_2 = \left[\begin{array}{c|cc|cc|cc} 0 & 1 & & 0 & 1 & 0 & 1 \\ 2 & 1 & x & 2 & 1 & 2 & 1 \end{array}\right]$$

defines a 32-state regular trellis code (here $x \in L_0 \backslash L_1$). If the inputs at time k are b_k, a_k then the coset output at time k is $T_k = L_3 + G u_k$ where $u_k = (a_{k-3}, b_{k-2}, b_{k-1}, a_{k-1}, b_k, a_k)^T$. The minimum squared distance $d^2 = 6$ ($d_1^2 = 8$, $d_2^2 = 6$) and the *path multiplicity* (the number of inputs u' at minimum distance 6 from a given input u) is 16. The coset T_k is a linear combination of columns of G_2. The design of a 32-state code transparent to $90°$ channel phase shifts requires 2 ingredients:

(1) a permutation P of the set $\{00, 01, 10, 11\}$ of order 4.

(2) a rule G^* for selecting cosets such that the following diagram commutes:

(8)

$$
\begin{array}{ccc}
(b_k, a_k) & \xrightarrow{\;\;G^*\;\;} & (T_k) \\[2mm]
\downarrow & & \downarrow \\[2mm]
(P(b_k, a_k)) & \xrightarrow{\;\;G^*\;\;} & (R(T_k))
\end{array}
$$

In other words, P applied to inputs induces $90°$ rotation outputs.

We choose the permutation $P : (b, a) \to (a + b, \bar{a})$ so that $P : (0,0) \to (0,1) \to (1,0) \to (1,1)$. The generator matrix

(9)
$$
G^* = \left[\; \begin{matrix} 0 \\ 2 \end{matrix} \;\middle|\; \begin{pmatrix} 1 \\ 1 \end{pmatrix} + a_{k-2} \begin{pmatrix} 0 \\ 2 \end{pmatrix} x \;\middle|\; \begin{matrix} 0 \\ 2 \end{matrix} \;\; \begin{matrix} 1 \\ 1 \end{matrix} \;\middle|\; \begin{matrix} 0 \\ 2 \end{matrix} \;\; \begin{matrix} 1 \\ 1 \end{matrix} \;\right]
$$

is obtained from G_2 by changing a single column. The coset T_k output at time k is given by

$$
\begin{aligned}
T_k = {}& a_k(1,1) + b_k(2,0) + a_{k-1}(1,1) + b_{k-1}(0,2) + a_{k-2}x + \\
& b_{k-2}[(1,1) + a_{k-2}(2,0)] + a_{k-3}(0,2).
\end{aligned}
$$

The difference between G_2 and G^* is the introduction of the non-linear term $b_{k-2} a_{k-2}(2,0)$

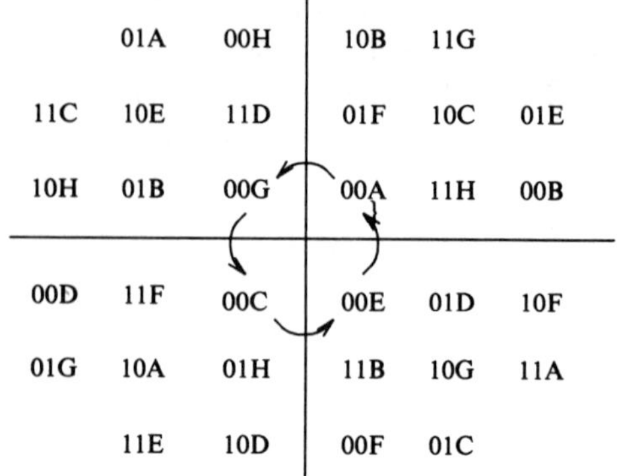

Rotation through 90°

$A = (0,0)$ $\xleftrightarrow{+(2,0)}$ $B = (2,0)$

$\downarrow +(3,0)$ $\downarrow +(3,0)$

$G = (3,0)$ $\xleftrightarrow{+(2,0)}$ $H = (1,0)$

$\downarrow +(0,3)$ $\downarrow +(0,3)$

$C = (1,1)$ $\xleftrightarrow{+(2,0)}$ $D = (1,3)$

$\downarrow +(1,0)$ $\downarrow +(1,0)$

$E = (0,3)$ $\xleftrightarrow{+(2,0)}$ $F = (0,1)$

$\downarrow +(0,1)$ $\downarrow +(0,1)$

Rotation Through 180°

$$\left.\begin{array}{l} A = (0,0) \\ C = (1,1) \\ B = (2,0) \\ D = (1,3) \end{array}\right\} +(1,1)$$

$$\left.\begin{array}{l} G = (3,0) \\ E = (0,3) \\ H = (1,0) \\ F = (0,1) \end{array}\right\} +(1,3)$$

Fig. 5. The effect of 90° rotation on the 8 cosets of L_0/L_3.

(cf. Wei [14]). We shall describe how to choose $x \in L_0 \backslash L_1$ so that (8) commutes. First we check that $p^2 : (b_k, a_k) \to (\overline{b}_k, a_k)$ corresponds to $180°$ rotation of outputs:

$$G^*[a_{k-3}, \overline{b}_{k-2}, a_{k-2}, \overline{b}_{k-1}, a_{k-1}, \overline{b}_k, a_k] - G^*[a_{k-3}, b_{k-2}, a_{k-2}, b_{k-1}, a_{k-1}, b_k, a_k]$$

$$= (1,1) + a_{k-2}(2,0)$$

$$= \begin{cases} (1,1), & \text{if } T_k \in L_1 \\ (1,3), & \text{if } T_k \notin L_1 \end{cases}.$$

Figure 5 shows that this difference is just $R^2(T_k) - T_k$. Next we check that $P(b_k, a_k) \to (a_k + \beta_k, \overline{a}_k)$ corresponds to $90°$ rotation of outputs:

$$G^*[\overline{a}_{k-3} a_{k-2} + b_{k-2}, \overline{a}_{k-2}, a_{k-1} + b_{k-1}, \overline{a}_{k-1}, a_k + b_k, \overline{a}_k]$$

$$\qquad - G^*[a_{k-3}, b_{k-2}, a_{k-2}, b_{k-1}, a_{k-1}, b_k, a_k]$$

$$= (2,0) + (a_{k-2} + b_{k-2})[(1,1) + \overline{a}_{k-2}(2,0)] + b_{k-2}[(1,1) + a_{k-2}(2,0)]$$

$$\quad + (\overline{a}_{k-2} - a_{k-2})x + a_{k-1}(2,0) + (1,1) + a_k(2,0) + (1,1)$$

$$= (\overline{a}_{k-2} - a_{k-2})x + a_{k-2}(1,1) + (a_k + a_{k-1} + b_{k-2} + 1)(2,0)$$

$$= \begin{cases} x + (2,0), & \text{if } a_{k-2} = 0, \ a_k + a_{k-1} + b_{k-2} = 0 \\ x, & \text{if } a_{k-2} = 0, \ a_k + a_{k-1} + b_{k-2} = 1 \\ -x + (1,3), & \text{if } a_{k-2} = 1, \ a_k + a_{k-1} + b_{k-2} = 0 \\ -x + (1,1), & \text{if } a_{k-2} = 1, \ a_k + a_{k-1} + b_{k-2} = 1 \end{cases}$$

$$= \begin{cases} x + (2,0), & \text{if } T_k = (0,0) \text{ or } (2,0) \\ x, & \text{if } T_k = (1,1) \text{ or } (2,0) \\ -x + (1,3), & \text{if } T_k = x \text{ or } x + (2,0) \\ -x + (1,1), & \text{if } T_k = x + (1,1) \text{ or } x + (1,3) \end{cases}$$

If we choose $x = (1,0)$ then Fig. 5 shows that this difference is just $R(T_k) - T_k$.

States in the trellis diagram are labeled by 5 prior input bits and edges between states come in gangs of four. Let s, s' be state labels and let E_0 be the edge from s to s' that is labeled by the coset T and triggered by the input (b, a). For $i = 1, 2, 3$ there is an edge E_i from $P^i(s)$ to $P^i(s')$ that is labeled by $R^i(T)$ and triggered by the input $P^i(b, a)$. We transform this trellis code into a single finite state machine with built in transparency to $90°$ phase shifts by introducing feedback. The idea is to trigger the edges E_0, E_1, E_2, E_3 with the same input (b', a') and it requires that the encoder be decoupled from the input data stream.

The binary vector $c = (c_7, c_6, c_5, c_4, c_3, c_2, c_1)$ corresponds to the edge from state $c_7, c_6, c_5, c_4, c_3)$ to state $(c_5, c_4, c_3, c_2, c_1)$. We require two functions $c_1' = f_1(c), c_2' = f_2(c)$ such that

(1) $f_1(c) = f_i(p^j(c))$, for $i = 1, 2$ and $j = 0, 1, 2, 3$,

(2) if $f_i(c_7, c_6, c_5, c_4, c_3, c_2, c_1) = f_i(c_7, c_6, c_5, c_4, c_3, d_2, d_1)$ for $i = 1, 2$, then $c_1 = d_1$ and $c_2 = d_2$.

The second condition ensures that the 4 edges leaving a given state are triggered by different outputs. It is straightforward to verify that the functions

$$(10) \qquad c_1' = f_1(c_7, c_6, c_5, c_4, c_3, c_2, c_1) = c_1 + c_3$$
$$c_2' = f_2(c_7, c_6, c_5, c_4, c_3, c_2, c_1) = c_2 + \overline{c}_4 + c_1 c_3$$

satisfy (1) and (2). Next we require functions g_1, g_2 such that

$$(11) \qquad c_1 = g_1(c_7, c_6, c_5, c_4, c_3, c_2', c_1'),$$
$$c_2 = g_2(c_7, c_6, c_5, c_4, c_3, c_2', c_1').$$

We choose

$$g_1(c_7, c_6, c_5, c_4, c_3, c_2', c_1') = c_3 + c_1'$$
$$(12) \qquad g_2(c_7, c_6, c_5, c_4, c_3, c_2', c_1') = c_2' + \overline{c}_4 + c_3 \overline{c}_1'$$

The new finite state encoder is shown in Fig. 6. Note that the same functions $f_i, g_i, i = 1, 2$ can be used to transform any trellis code with the property that the transformation $P : (b, a) \to (a + b, \overline{a})$ applied to inputs corresponds to 90° rotation applied to outputs. Theorem 3.1 shows that this 32-state trellis code is not an isolated example.

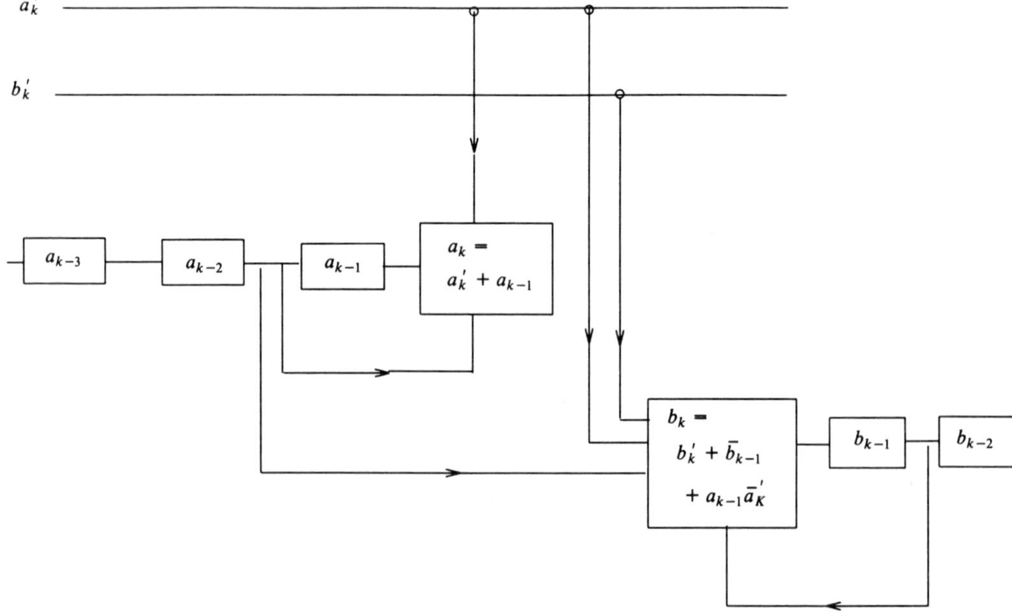

Fig. 6.   A finite state encoder with built in transparency to 90° phase shifts (matched to the transformation $P: (b, a) \to (a + b, \overline{a})$).

THEOREM 3.1. *Let $z_0, z_1, \ldots, z_l = (1,1)$ or $(1, 3)$, let $j \in \{1, 2, \ldots, l-1\}$ and let*

$$G = [G_l | G_{l-1} | G_{l-2} | \ldots | G_0]$$

where

$$(1) \quad G_i = \begin{bmatrix} 0 & z_i^T \\ 2 & \end{bmatrix} \quad \text{for } i \neq j, \text{ and}$$

$$(2) \quad G_j = \begin{cases} \left[z_j^T + a_{k-j}\binom{0}{2}, x^T \right], & \text{if } z_j + l(2,0) = (1,1) \\[2ex] \left[z_j^T + \overline{a}_{k-j}\binom{0}{2}, x^T \right], & \text{if } z_j + l(2,0) = (1,3) \end{cases}$$

Then it is possible to choose $x \notin L_1$ so that the transformation $P : (b, a) \to (a + b, \overline{a})$ applied to inputs induces $90°$ rotation of output cosets.

Proof. We give details only for the case $z_j + l(2,0) = (1,1)$, since the other case is very similar. We have

$$G[a_{k-l} + b_{k-l}, \overline{a}_{k-l}, \ldots, a_k + b_k, \overline{a}_k]^T - G[b_{k-l}, a_{k-l}, \ldots, b_k, a_k]^T$$

$$= \left(\sum_{i \neq j} a_{k-i} \right)(2,0) + \left(\sum_{i \neq j} z_i \right) + (\overline{a}_{k-j} - a_{k-j})x$$

$$+ (a_{k-j} + b_{k-j})(z_j + \overline{a}_{k-j}(2,0)) + b_{k-j}(z_j + a_{k-j}(2,0))$$

$$= a_{k-j}z_j + \left(\sum_{i \neq j} z_i \right) + \left(b_{k-j} + \sum_{i \neq j} a_{k-i} \right)(2,0)$$

$$(13) \qquad + (\overline{a}_{k-j} - a_{k-j})x$$

$$= \begin{cases} x + \left(\sum_{i \neq j} z_i \right), & \text{if } a_{k-j} = 0, \ b_{k-j} + \sum_{i \neq j} a_{k-i} = 0 \\[1ex] x + \left(\sum_{i \neq j} z_i \right) + (2,0), & \text{if } a_{k-j} = 0, \ b_{k-j} + \sum_{i \neq j} a_{k-i} = 1 \\[1ex] -x + \left(\sum_i z_i \right), & \text{if } a_{k-j} = 1, \ b_{k-j} + \sum_{i \neq j} a_{k-i} = 0 \\[1ex] -x + \left(\sum_i z_i \right) + (2,0), & \text{if } a_{k-j} = 1, \ b_{k-j} + \sum_{i \neq j} a_{k-i} = 1 \end{cases}$$

Now $T_k = (0,0)$ or $(2,0)$ if and only if $a_{k-j} = 0$, $b_{k-j} + \sum_{i \neq j} a_{k-i} = 0$. It follows from Fig. 5 that

$$x + \left(\sum_{i \neq j} z_i \right) = (3,0).$$

Hence $x = (3,0) + l(1,1)$ or $x = (1,0) + l(1,1)$,

$$-x + \left(\sum_i z_i \right) = z_j + (1,0) = (0,3) + l(2,0),$$

and (13) becomes

$$
\begin{aligned}
&G[a_{k-l} + b_{k-l}, \bar{a}_{k-l}, \ldots, a_k + b_k, \bar{a}_k] - G[b_{k-l}, a_{k-l}, \ldots, b_k, a_k] \\
&= \begin{cases}
(3,0), & \text{if } T_k = (0,0) \text{ or } (2,0) \\
(1,0), & \text{if } T_k = (1,1) \text{ or } (1,3) \\
(0,3) + l(2,0), & \text{if } T_k = (1,0) + l(1,1) \text{ or } (3,0) + l(1,1) \\
(0,1) + l(2,0), & \text{if } T_k = (1,0) + (l+1)(1,1) \text{ or } (3,0) + (l+1)(1,1)
\end{cases}
\end{aligned}
$$

Figure 5 shows that this difference is just $R(T_k) - T_k$ so the proof is complete.

REMARK. The conclusions of Theorem 3.1 hold for a more general class of matrices G. It is possible to replace a block $G_i, i \neq j$, with $\begin{bmatrix} 0 & 0 \\ 0 & 0 \end{bmatrix}$, $\begin{bmatrix} 0 & 0 \\ 0 & 2 \end{bmatrix}$ or $\begin{bmatrix} 0 & 0 \\ 2 & 0 \end{bmatrix}$, but then the rule for selecting the nonlinear block G_j may also change. For example, the 8-state code

$$
\begin{bmatrix} 0 \\ 2 \end{bmatrix} \begin{pmatrix} 1 \\ 3 \end{pmatrix} + a_{k-1} \begin{pmatrix} 0 \\ 2 \end{pmatrix}, \begin{pmatrix} 0 \\ 3 \end{pmatrix} \begin{vmatrix} 0 & 1 \\ 2 & 1 \end{vmatrix}
$$

satisfies the conclusions of the theorem.

Trellis codes specified by a non-linear generator matrix G are not regular, there exist inputs u_k, u'_k corresponding to outputs T_k, T'_k such that $N[Gu_k - Gu'_k] \neq N[G(u_k \oplus u'_k)]$ (and $\text{Mult}[Gu_k - Gu'_k] \neq \text{Mult}[G(u_k \oplus u'_k)]$). For the 32-state code given by (7) take $u_k = (0|00|00|00)^T$, $u'_k = (0|10|01|00)^T$, $w_k = (0|01|00|00)^T$, $w'_k = (0|11|01|00)^T$. then $u_k \oplus u'_k = w_k \oplus w'_k = (0|10|01|00)$ but

$$
G^* u_k - G^* u'_k = (0,0) \quad \text{and} \quad G^* w_k - G^* w'_k = (2,0).
$$

In fact trellis codes specified by a non-linear generator matrix G do not satisfy the uniformity condition introduced by Zehavi and Wolf. For the 32-state example, the uniformity condition is violated for all error vectors e satisfying $G^* = (0,0)$ or $(2,0)$. However the class of trellis codes considered in Theorem 3.1 are still very symmetric.

THEOREM 3.2. *Let G be a generator matrix satisfying the hypothesis of Theorem 3.1. Let $u_k = (b_{k-l}, a_{k-l}, \ldots, b_k, a_k)^T$, $u'_k = (b'_{k-l}, a'_{k-l}, \ldots, b'_k, a'_k)^T$ be the inputs corresponding to outputs $T_k = Gu_k, T'_k = Gu'_k$. Then either*

$$(1) \quad N[Gu_k - Gu'_k] = N[G(u_k \oplus u'_k)], \quad \text{or}$$

$$(2) \quad G(u_k \oplus u'_k) = (0,0) \quad \text{or} \ (2,0), \ b_{k-j} \neq b'_{k-j}, \text{and}$$

$$
a_{k-j} = a'_{k-j} = \begin{cases}
1, & \text{if } z_j + l(2,0) = (1,1) \\
0, & \text{if } z_j + l(1,0) = (1,3)
\end{cases}
$$

Proof. Again we give details only for the case $z_j + l(2, 0) = (1, 1)$. If $a_{k-j} \neq a'_{k-j}$ then exactly one of T_k, T'_k is in $L_1 = \phi(L)$ and $N[Gu_k - Gu'_k] = N[G(u_k \oplus u'_k)] = 1$. If $a_{k-j} = a'_{k-j} = 0$ then $2Gu'_k = (0, 0)$ and

$$Gu_k - Gu'_k = G(u_k \oplus u'_k - 2Gu'_k = G(u_k \oplus u'_k).$$

If $a_{k-j} = a'_{k-j} = 1$ then

$$Gu_k - Gu'_k = G(u_k \oplus u'_k) + (2, 0),$$

and Table 1 shows that adding $(2,0)$ to a coset T preserves the norm $N(T)$ except when $T = (0, 0)$ or $(2, 0)$.

REMARKS. The conclusions of Theorem 3.2 hold for a more general class of generator matrices G. We require only that 2 columns of G (not necessarily adjacent) form a non-linear block and that the remaining columns all represent cosets from the sublattice $\phi(L)$. For a coset T define

$$N^*(T) = \begin{cases} N(T), & \text{if} \quad T \neq (0, 0) \text{ or } 2, 0) \\ 0, & \text{if} \quad T = (0, 0) \text{ or } 2, 0). \end{cases}$$

Then Theorem 3.2 implies

$$N^*(Gu_k - Gu'_k) = N^*(G(u_k \oplus u'_k))$$

Regularity of N^* makes possible a consistent labeling of the edges in the state diagram, and we can obtain a lower bound on the minimum squared distance by solving a minimum cost problem. This lower bound gives the true minimum squared distance; there is only one non-linear term and given the sequence $u_k \oplus u'_k$) it is possible to find u_k, u'_k such that for all $kN(Gu_k - Gu'_k) = N^*(G(u_k \oplus u'_k))$. However, the path multiplicity (and indeed the minimum distance) may change from one input sequence to another (cf. Section 1).

REFERENCES

[1] A.R. CALDERBANK AND J.E. MAZO, *A new description of trellis codes*, IEEE Trans. Inform. Theory, IT-30 (1984) pp. 784-791,.

[2] A.R. CALDERBANK, J.E. MAZO, AND H.M. SHAPIRO, *Upper bounds on the minimum distance of trellis codes*, Bell Syst. Tech. J. 62 (1983) pp. 2617-2646.

[3] A.R. CALDERBANK, J. E. MAZO, AND V.K. WEI, *Asymptotic upper bounds on the minimum distance of trellis codes*, IEEE Trans. Commun., COM-33 No. 4 (1985), pp. 305-309.

[4] A.R. CALDERBANK AND N.J.A. SLOANE, *Four-dimensional modulation with an eight-state trellis code*, Bell Syst. Tech. J. 64 (1985), pp. 1005-1018.

[5] A.R. CALDERBANK AND N.J.A. SLOANE, *New trellis codes based on lattices and cosets*, IEEE Trans. Inform. Theory, vol. IT-33 (1987), 177-195.

[6] G.D. FORNEY J., *Coset codes I: geometrical classification*, to appear in IEEE Trans. Inform. Theory.

[7] G.D. FORNEY JR., *Coset codes II: Binary lattices and related codes*, submitted to IEEE Trans. Inform. Theory.

[8] G.D. FORNEY JR., *Coset codes III: Ternary codes, lattices and trellis codes*, submitted to IEEE Trans. Inform. Theory.

[9] G.D. FORNEY JR., R.G. GALLAGER, G.R. LANG, F.M. LONGSTAFF AND S.U. QUERESCHI, *Efficient modulation for band-limited channels*, IEEE J. Select. Areas Commun., SAC-2 (1984), 632-647.

[10] F. FRICKER, *Einführung in Die Gitterpunktlehre*, Boston, MA: Birkhäuser (1982).

[11] G.A. KABATIANSKY AND V.I. LEVENSHTEIN, *Bounds for packing on a sphere and in space* (in Russian), Probl. Peredachi Inform., 14, no. 1 (1978), pp. 3–25; transl. in Probl. Inform. Transmiss., 14, no. 1 (1978), pp. 1–17.

[12] G. UNGERBOECK, *Channel coding with multilevel/phase signals*, IEEE Trans. Inform. Theory, IT-28 (1982), pp. 55–67.

[13] A. J. VIBERBI AND J.K. OMURA, *Principles of digital communication and coding*, New York: McGraw-Hill (1979).

[14] L.F. WEI, *Rotationally invariant convolutional channel coding with expanded signal space – II: Nonlinear codes*, IEEE J. Select. Areas Commun., SAC-2 (1984) pp. 672–686.

[15] L.F. WEI, *Trellis coded modulation with multidimensional constellations*, to appear in IEEE Trans. Inform. Theory.

[16] E. ZEHAVI AND J.K. WOLF, *On the performance evaluation of trellis codes*, IEEE Trans. Inform. Theory, IT-33 (1987), pp. 196–202.

FAMILIES OF CODES WITH FEW DISTINCT WEIGHTS FROM SINGULAR AND NON-SINGULAR HERMITIAN VARIETIES AND QUADRICS IN PROJECTIVE GEOMETRIES AND HADAMARD DIFFERENCE SETS AND DESIGNS ASSOCIATED WITH TWO-WEIGHT CODES

I.M. CHAKRAVARTI*

Summary. In this paper, we present several doubly infinite families of linear projective codes with two-, three- and five distinct non-zero Hamming weights together with the frequency distributions of their weights.

The codes have been defined as linear spaces of coordinate vectors of points on certain projective sets described in terms of Hermitian and quadratic forms - non-degenerate and singular - in projective spaces. The weight-distributions have been derived by considering the geometry of intersections of projective sets by hyperplanes in relevant projective spaces. Results from Bose and Chakravarti (1966) and Chakravarti (1971) on the Hermitian geometry and Bose (1964), Primrose (1951) and Ray-Chaudhuri (1959, 1962) have been used in the enumeration of weights and their frequencies.

The paper has been organized as follows. Preliminary definitions, concepts and results on Hermitian geometry [from Bose and Chakravarti (1966) and Chakravarti (1971)] are given in Section 1.

Two families of two-weight codes $\mathcal{C}(V_{N-1})$ and $\mathcal{C}(\bar{V}_{N-1})$ over $GF(s^2)$ and associated families $\mathcal{C}'(V_{N-1})$ and $\mathcal{C}'(\bar{V}_{N-1})$ over $GF(s)$ together with their weight-distributions are given in Section 2. Here V_{N-1} denotes a non-degenerate Hermitian variety in $PG(N, s^2)$ and $\bar{V}_{N-1}$ is its complement and a code $\mathcal{C}(S)$ is defined as the linear space of the coordinate vectors of the points in the projective set S. These codes have been otherwise obtained by Wolfmann (1975, 1977) from quadrics and by Calderbank and Kantor (1986) from the rank three representation of unitary groups. However, this latter paper was not available to the author while he presented his results at Marseille (1986).

The eigenvalues of the adjacency matrix $A = B_2 - B_1$ (B_i is the incidence matrix of the ith associates $i = 1, 2$) of the strongly regular graph (two-class association scheme) on $s^{2(N+1)}$ vertices defined by the two-weight code $\mathcal{C}'(V_{N-1})$ over $GF(s)$ and the (p^i_{jk}) parameters of the two-class association scheme are given in Section 3.

In section 4, we show that for $s = 2$, B_2 (the association matrix of the second associates) of the two-class association scheme of Section 3, is the incidence matrix a symmetric BIB design with parameters $v = 2^{2(N+1)}$, $k = 2^{2N+1} + (-2)^N$, $\lambda = 2^{2N} + (-2)^N$ and $2B_2 - J$ is a Hadamard matrix of order $2^{2(N+1)}$. Similarly, $I + B_1$ is the incidence matrix of a symmetric BIB design with parameters $v = 2^{2(N+1)}$, $k = 2^{2N+1} - (-2)^N$. Further, it is shown that the $2^{2N+1} + (-2)^N$ codewords

---

*Department of Statistics, University of North Carolina, Chapel Hill, NC 27599-3260

each of weight $(2^{2N} - (-2)^N)$, which are non-adjacent to the null codeword form a Hadamard difference set (Menon 1960, Mann 1965) with parameters $v = 2^{2N+2}$, $k = 2^{2N+1} + (-2)^N$, $\lambda = 2^{2N} + (-2)^N$ and the $(2^{2N+1} - (-2)^N - 1)$ codewords each of weight 2^{2N} together with the null codeword form a Hadamard difference set with parameters $v = 2^{2N+2}$, $k = 2^{2N+1} - (-2)^N$, $\lambda = 2^{2N} - (-2)^N$, for integer N. These difference sets also appear in Wolfmann (1977) and Calderbank and Kantor (1986). But our presentation in terms association matrices is of special interest to statisticians.

In Section 5, a family of five-weight linear codes and the associated weight-distributions are derived. A code here is defined as the linear span of a projective set which is the intersection of a non-degenerate Hermitian variety and the complement of one of the secant hyperplanes. These codes are believed to be new.

In Sections 6 and 7, we consider codes which are linear spans of projective sets defined in terms of degenerate Hermitian and quadratic forms in projective spaces. The motivation here is to explore how the code parameters behave when the basic projective set is not purely a subspace nor a non-degenerate Hermitian or quadric variety but an amalgam of the two, which still admits a geometric description (and algebraic equations).

In section 6, the basic projective set is a degenerate Hermitian variety V_{N-2}^o which is the intersection of a non-degenerate Hermitian variety V_{N-1} in $PG(N, s^2)$ with one of its tangent hyperplanes. The code $\mathcal{C}(V_{N-2}^o)$ which is the linear space generated by the coordinate vectors of the points of V_{N-2}^o, is shown to be a tri-weight code. Its weight-distribution as a code over $GF(s^2)$ as well as that of its sister code over $GF(s)$ are given. This family seems to be new.

In section 7, a degenerate quadric Q_{N-1}^o which is the intersection of a non-degenerate quadric Q_N in $PG(N, s)$ with one of its tangent hyperplanes, is taken as the basic projective set. The code $\mathcal{C}(Q_{N-1}^o)$ which is the linear space of the coordinate vectors of the points of Q_{N-1}^o is shown to be a tri-weight code both for odd and even N. The frequency distributions of the weights are given for both odd and even N. For odd N, both the cases elliptic and hyperbolic have been considered. These families supplement whose obtained by Wolfmann (1975) from non-degenerate quadrics, and these codes for odd N, are believed to be new. For even N and $s = 2$, this code was given by Dowling (1969). This is not a cyclic code, but he showed that this can be made cyclic by adding all permutations of the codewords and $2(2^{2t} - 1)$ other codewords. The weight-distribution of the code given in our Table 7.1, corresponds to Games's (1986) table for $N = 2t - 1$, $r = 1$, $q = s$. Games (1986) calculated the sizes and their respective multiplicities of intersections by hyperplanes of a degenerate quadric (cone) of order r in $PG(N, q)$, for $N - r$ even.

1. Introduction. The geometry of Hermitian varieties in finite dimensional projective spaces have been studied by Jordan (1870), Dickson (1901), Dieudonné (1971), and recently, among others by Bose (1963, 1971), Segre (1965, 1967), Bose and Chakravarti (1966) and Chakravarti (1971). In this paper, however, we have used results given in the last two articles.

In h is any element of a Galois field $GF(s^2)$, where s is a prime or a power of a prime, then $\bar{h} = h$ is defined to be conjugate to h. Since $h^2 = h$, h is conjugate to $\bar{h}$. A square matrix $H = (h_{ij})$, $i, j = 0, 1, \ldots, N$, with elements from $GF(s^2)$ is called Hermitian if $h_{ij} = \bar{h}_{ji}$ for all i, j. The set of all points in $PG(N, s^2)$ whose row-vectors $\underline{x}^T = (x_0, x_1, \ldots, x_N)$ satisfy the equations $\underline{x}^T H \underline{x}^{(s)} = 0$ are said to form a Hermitian variety V_{N-1}, if H is Hermitian and $\underline{x}^{(s)}$ is the column vector whose transpose is $(x_0^s, x_1^s, \ldots, x_N^s)$. The variety V_{N-1} is said to be non-degenerate if H has rank $N+1$. The Hermitian form $\underline{x}^T H \underline{x}^{(s)}$ where H is of order $N+1$ and rank r can be reduced to the canonical form $y_0 \bar{y}_0 + \cdots + y_r \bar{y}_r$ by a suitable non-singular linear transformation $\underline{x} = A\underline{y}$. The equation of a non-degenerate Hermitian variety V_{N-1} in $PG(N, s^2)$ can then be taken in the canonical form $x_0^{s+1} + x_1^{s+1} + \cdots + x_N^{s+1} = 0$.

Consider a Hermitian variety V_{N-1} in $PG(N, s^2)$ with equation $\underline{x}^T H\, \underline{x}^{(s)} = 0$. A point C in $PG(N, s^2)$ with row-vector $\underline{c}^T = (c_0, c_1, \ldots, c_N)$ is called a **singular** point of V_{N-1} if $\underline{c}^T H = \underline{0}^T$ or equivalently, $H\underline{c}^{(s)} = \underline{0}$. A point of V_{N-1} which is not singular is called a **regular** point of V_{N-1}. Thus a non-singular point is either a regular point of V_{N-1} or a point not on V_{N-1}, in which case it is called an **external** point of $PG(N, s^2)$, with respect to V_{N-1}. It is clear that a non-degenerate V_{N-1} cannot possess a singular point. On the other hand, if V_{N-1} is degenerate and rank $H = r < N + 1$, the singular points of V_{N-1} constitute a $(N - r)$-flat called the **singular space** of V_{N-1}.

Let C be a point with row vector $\underline{c}^T$. Then the **polar space** of C with respect to the Hermitian variety V_{N-1} with equation $\underline{x}^T H \underline{x}^{(s)} = 0$, is defined to be the set of points of $PG(N, s^2)$ which satisfy $\underline{x}^T H \underline{c}^{(s)} = 0$.

When C is a singular point of V_{N-1}, the polar space of C is the whole space $PG(N, s^2)$. When, however, C is either a regular point of V_{N-1} or an external point, $\underline{x}^T H \underline{c}^{(s)} = 0$ is the equation of hyperplane which is called the **polar hyperplane** of C with respect to V_{N-1}. Let C and D be two points of $PG(N, s^2)$. If the polar hyperplane of C passes through D, then the polar hyperplane of D passes through C. Two such points C and D are said to be **conjugates** to each other with respect to V_{N-1}. Thus the points lying in the polar hyperplane of C are all the points which are conjugates to C. If C is a **regular** point of V_{N-1}, the polar hyperplane of C passes through C; C is thus self-conjugate. In this case, the polar hyperplane is called the **tangent hyperplane** to V_{N-1} at C.

When V_{N-1} is non-degenerate, there is no singular point. To every point, there corresponds a unique polar hyperplane, and at every point of V_{N-1}, there is a unique tangent hyperplane. If C is an external point, its polar hyperplane will be called a **secant hyperplane.**

The number of points in a non-degenerate Hermitian variety V_{N-1} in $PG(N, s^2)$ is $\phi(N, s^2) = (s^{N+1} - (-1)^{N+1})(s^N - (-1)^N)/(s^2 - 1)$.

A polar hyperplane $\mathcal{S}_{N-1}$ of an external point $\mathcal{D}$ (also called a secant hyperplane) in $PG(N, s^2)$ intersects a non-degenerate Hermitian variety V_{N-1}, in a non-degenerate Hermitian variety V_{N-2} of rank N. It has $(S^N - (-1)^N)(s^{N-1} - (-1)^{N-1})/(s^2 - 1)$ points.

A tangent hyperplane $\mathcal{T}_{N-1}$ to a non-degenerate V_{N-1} at a point C, intersects

V_{N-1} in a degenerate V_{N-2} of rank $N-1$. The singular space of V_{N-2} consists of the single point C.

The number of points in a degenerate Hermitian variety V_{N-1} of rank $r < N+1$ in $PG(N, s^2)$ is $(s^2-1)f(N-r, s^2)\phi(r-1, s^2) + f(N-r, s^2) + \phi(r-1, s^2)$, where $f(k, s^2) = (s^{2(k+1)} - 1/(s^2-1)$. Thus the number of points in a degenerate V_{N-2} of rank $N-1$, is

$$(1.1) \quad \begin{aligned} &(s^2-1)f(0, s^2)\phi(N-2, s^2) + f(0, s^2) + \phi(N-2, s^2) \\ &= 1 + (s^{N-1} - (-1)^{N-1})(s^{N-2} - (-1)^{N-2})s^2/(s^2-1). \end{aligned}$$

2. Two-weight codes from non-degenerate Hermitian varieties in projective spaces. Consider the code $\mathcal{C}(V_{N-1})$ over $GF(s^2)$, which is the linear space generated by the coordinate vectors of the points on a non-degenerate Hermitian variety V_{N-1} in $PG(N, s^2)$. This variety has $(s^{N+1} - (-1)^{N+1})(s^N - (-1)^N)/(s^2-1) = n$ (say) points. Thus a matrix $G = (g_{ij})\, i = 0, 1, \ldots, N, j = 1, \ldots, n$, whose columns are the coordinate vectors of the n points on V_{N-1}, is a generator matrix of the code $\mathcal{C}(V_{N-1})$ which is a projective linear code $(n, k = N+1)$. Now, a tangent hyperplane meets V_{N-1} at $1 + (s^{N-1} - (-1)^{N-1})(s^{N-2} - (-1)^{N-2})s^2/(s^2-1))$ points and a secant hyperplane meets V_{N-1} at $(s^N - (-1^N)(s^{N-1} - (-1)^{N-1}/(s^2-1)$ points; hence this code $\mathcal{C}(V_{N-1})$ has only two distinct non-zero weights w_1 and w_2 (say), where

$$(2.1) \quad \begin{aligned} w_1 &= (s^{N+1} - (-1)^{N+1})(s^N - (-1)^N)/s^2 - 1) \\ &\quad - (s^{N-1} - (-1)^{N-1})(s^{N-2} - (-1)^{N-2})s^2/(s^2-1) - 1 = s^{2N-1} \\ w_2 &= (s^{N+1} - (-1)^{N+1})(s^N - (-1)^N)/(s^2-1) \\ &\quad - (s^N - (-1)^N)(s^{N-1} - (-1)^{N-1})/s^2 - 1 = s^{2N-1} + (-s)^{N-1}. \end{aligned}$$

The frequency f_{w_1} of the code-words with weight w_1 is equal to the number of tangent hyperplanes (same as the number of points on V_{N-1}) multiplied by (s^2-1). The frequency f_{w_2} of codewords of weight w_2 is the number of secant hyperplanes (same as the number of external points in $PG(N, s^2)$) multiplied by (s^2-1). Thus

$$(2.2) \quad \begin{aligned} f_{w_1} &= (s^{N+1} - (-1)^{N+1})(s^N - (-1)^N), \\ f_{w_2} &= (s^{2(N+1)} - 1) - (s^{N+1} - (-1)^{N+1})(s^N - (-1)^N) \\ &= (s-1)(s^{2N+1} + (-s)^N). \end{aligned}$$

Let $\bar{V}_{N-1}$ denote the set of external points of $PG(N, s^2)$ with respect to V_{N-1}. Thus $\bar{V}_{N-1}$ is the complement of V_{N-1}. Considering the intersections of $\bar{V}_{N-1}$ by tangent and secant hyperplanes, we get another sequence $\mathcal{C}(\bar{V}_{N-1})$ of two-weight linear projective codes in s^2 symbols, with parameters $\bar{n} = (s^{2N+1} + (-s)^N)/(s+1)$, $\bar{k} = N+1$, $\bar{w}_1 = s^{2N} - s^{2N-1}$, $\bar{w}_2 = s^{2N} - s^{2N-1} - (-s)^{N-1}$, $f_{\bar{w}_1} = (s^{N+1} - (-1)^{N+1})(s^N - (-1)^N)$, $f_{\bar{w}_2} = (s-1)(s^{2N+1} + (-s)^N)$.

Now a projective linear (n, k) code over $GF(s^r)$ with weights $w_i, i = 1, \ldots, t$, determines a projective linear (n', k') code over $GF(s)$ with weights $w_i', i = 1, \ldots, t$,

$n' = n(s^r - 1)/(s - 1)$, $k' = kr$, $w'_i = s^{r-1}w_i$, $i = 1,\ldots,t$, (Delsarte, 1972). Hence the code $\mathcal{C}(V_{N-1})$ over $GF(s^2)$ determines a sister code $\mathcal{C}'(V_{N-1})$ over $GF(s)$ with parameters $n' = (s^{N+1} - (-1)^{N+1})(s^N - (-1)^N)/(s - 1)$, $k = 2(N + 1)$, $w'_1 = s^{2N}$; $w'_2 = s^{2N} - (-s)^N$, $f_{w'_1} = (s^{N+1} - (-1)^{N+1})(s^N - (-1)^N)$, $f_{w'_2} = (s - 1)(s^{2N+1} + (-s)^N)$.

Similarly, the code $\mathcal{C}(\bar{V}_{N-1})$ over $GF(s^2)$ determines a code $\mathcal{C}'(\bar{V}_{N-1})$ over $GF(s)$ with parameters $\bar{n}' = s^{2N+1} + (-s)^N$, $\bar{k}' = 2(N + 1)$, $\bar{w}'_1 = s^{2N+1} - s^{2N}$, $\bar{w}'_2 = s^{2N+1} - s^{2N} + (-s)^N$, $f_{w'_1} = (s^{N+1} - (-1)^{N+1}(s^N - (-1)^N)$, $f_{w'_2} = (s - 1)(s^{2N+1} + (-s)^N)$.

The family $\mathcal{C}'(V_{N-1})$ of two-weight codes over $GF(s)$ is a subfamily of the one derived by Wolfmann (1978) from non-degenerate quadrics. This is because a non-degenerate Hermitian form over $PG(N, s^2)$ becomes a non-degenerate quadric over $PG(2N + 1, s)$ (Dickson, 1958, p. 144). It is elliptic if N is even and hyperbolic if N is odd (see, for instance, Heft, 1971).

3. Strongly regular graphs of Latin square and negative Latin square types, from two-weight codes. Delsarte (1972) has shown that a two-weight projective (n, k) code over $GF(s)$ determines a strongly regular graph on $v = s^k$ vertices (a two-class association scheme) and that the eigenvalues ρ_i of the adjacency matrix $A = B_2 - B_1$ of the graph (B_i is the association matrix of the ith associates, $i = 1, 2,$: see, for instance, Bose and Mesner 1959) are given by

$$(3.1) \qquad (w_2 - w_1)\rho_0 = 2mv/s - (w_1 + w_2)(v - 1),$$
$$(w_2 - w_1)\rho_1 = w_1 + w_2 - (1 + (-1)^i)v/s, \quad i = 1, 2,$$

with $v = s^k$, $m = n(s - 1)$, w_1 and w_2 are the two distinct non-zero weights of codewords. One can calculate the parameters p^i_{jk}, $i, j, k = 1, 2$, of the two-class association scheme from ρ_1, ρ_2, n_1 and n_2, where n_i is the number of codewords of weight $w_i, i = 1, 2$.

Writing $(\rho_1 + \rho_2)/2 = -\gamma$, $(\rho_1 - \rho)/2 = \sqrt{\Delta}$ and $\Delta^2 = \gamma^2 + 2\beta + 1$, one can show that $(\beta + \gamma)/2 = p^2_{12}$ and $(\beta - \gamma)/2 = p^1_{12}$. Then $p^1_{11} = n_1 - 1 - p^1_{12}$, $p^1_{22} = n_2 - p^1_{12}$, $p^2_{11} = n_1 - p^2_{12}$, $p^2_{22} = n_2 - 1 - p^2_{12}$ (see, for instance, Bose and Mesner 1959).

Thus the graph on $s^{2(N+1)}$ vertices corresponding to the code $\mathcal{C}'(V_{N-1})$ over $GF(s)$ is strongly regular and the eigenvalues of its adjacency matrix $A = B_2 - B_1$, are $\rho_0 = (s^{2N+1} + (-s)^N)(s - 1) - (s^{N+1} - (-1)^{N+1})(s^N - (-1)^N) = n_2 - n_1$, $\rho_1 = 1 - 2(-s)^N$ and $\rho_2 = 1 + 2(s - 1)(-s)^N$. As a two-class association scheme its parameters are $n_1 = (s^{N+1} - (-1)^{N+1})(s^N - (-1)^N)$,

$n_2 = (s - 1)(s^{2N+1} + (-s)^N), p^1_{12} = (s - 1)s^{2N}$,

$p^2_{12} = (s - 1)s^{2N} - (s - 2)(-s)^N - 1, p^1_{11} = s^{2N} - (s - 1)(-s)^N - 2, p^2_{11} =$

$s^{2N} - (-s)^N, p^1_{22} = s^{2N}(s - 1)^2 + (-s)^N(s - 1), p^2_{22} = s^{2N}(s - 1)^2 + (-s)^N(2s - 3)$.

For $N = 2$, this family gives the two-class negative Latin square association scheme $NL_g(s^3)$ with $g = s^2 - 1$, given by Mesner (1967, pp. 579-580). Mesner considered two points on an $EG(3, s^2)$ to be first associates if the line joining the two points, shared a point with a non-degenerate Hermitian curve in the ideal plane of the $PG(3, s^2)$ in which $EG(3, s^2)$ is embedded. Thus at first sight our construction generalizes Mesner's family based on the Hermitian curve. However, it is to be noted that for every odd N, our family is the same as the hyperbolic family which is called pseudo-Latin square $L_g(s^{N+1})$, $g = s^N + 1$ and for every even N, our family is the same as the elliptic family which Mesner called the negative Latin square $NL_g(s^{N+1})$, $g = s^N - 1$, (Mesner 1966, p. 578). See also Hubaut (1975, pp. 374-379, C. $12^{\pm}$).

Similarly, one can verify that the eigenvalues of the adjacency matrix $\bar{A} = \bar{B}_2 - \bar{B}_1$ of the strongly regular graph on $v = s^{2(N+1)}$ vertices corresponding to the two-weight projective code $\mathcal{C}'(\bar{V}_{N-1})$ over $GF(s)$ are $\bar{\rho}_0 = f_{w_2'} - f_{w_1'}$, $\bar{\rho}_1 = 1 + 2(s-1)(-s)^N$ and $\bar{\rho}_2 = 1 - 2(-s)^N$. Thus it is clear that the sequence of two-weights codes $\bar{\mathcal{C}}'(\bar{B}_N)$ over $GF(s)$ gives rise to essentially the same two sequences of (Latin square type $L_g(n)$ and negative Latin square type $NL_g(n)$) two-class association schemes, as derived from the sequence of codes $\mathcal{C}'(V_{N-1})$.

4. Hadamard difference sets, Hadamard matrices and symmetric BIB designs from the association schemes. For $s = 2$, the parameters of the two-class association scheme corresponding to the two-weight binary projective code $\mathcal{C}'(V_{N-1})$ are $n_1 = (2^{N+1} - (-1)^{N+1})(2^N - (-1)^N)$, $n_2 = 2^{2N+1} + (-2)^N$, $p_{12}^1 = 2^{2N}$, $p_{12}^2 = 2^{2N} - 1$, $p_{11}^1 = 2^{2N} - (-2)^N - 2$, $p_{11}^2 = 2^{2N} - (-2)^N$, $p_{22}^1 = 2^{2N} + (-2)^N$, $p_{22}^2 = 2^{2N} + (-2)^N$.

The equality $p_{22}^1 = p_{22}^2 = 2^{2N} + (-2)^N$ implies that the matrix $B_2 -$ the association matrix of the second associates (non-adjacent vertices) is the incidence matrix of a symmetric BIB design with parameters $v = 2^{2(N+1)}$, $k = 2^{2N+1} + (-2)^N$, $\lambda = 2^{2N} + (-2)^N$ and $2B_2 - J$ is a Hadamard matrix of order $2^{2(N+1)}$ which corresponds to the Hadamard difference set $v = 2^{2N+2}$, $k = 2^{2N+1} + (-2)^N$, $\lambda = 2^{2N} + (-2)^N$.

Consider the $(2^{2N+1} + (-2)^N)$ codewords each of weight $(2^{2N} - (-2)^N)$ which are non-adjacent to (second associates of) the null codeword. The null codeword and codeword of weight 2^{2N} are adjacent to (first associates of) each other and among the non-adjacent vertices of the null codeword, there are $p_{22}^1 = 2^{2N} + (-2)^N$ codewords which are also non-adjacent to the given codeword of weight 2^{2N}. This implies that the given code vector can be expressed as the differences of $2^{2N} + (-2)^N$ pairs of code vectors each of weight $(2^{2N} - (-2)^N)$. Similarly, since $p_{22}^2 = 2^{2N} + (-2)^N$ it follows that every codeword of weight $2^{2N} - (-2)^N$ can be expressed as the differences of $2^{2N} + (-2)^N$ pairs of codevectors each of weight $(2^{2N} - (-2)^N)$.

Thus the codewords of weight $2^{2N} - (-2)^N$ form a difference set with $v = 2^{2N+2}$, $k = 2^{2N+1} + (-2)^N$, $\lambda = 2^{2N} + (-2)^N$.

Again, $p_{11}^1 + 2 = p_{11}^2 = 2^{2N} - (-2)^N$. Thus the $(2^{2N+1} - (-2)^N - 1)$ codewords each of weight 2^{2N} together with the null codeword form a difference set with $v = 2^{2N+2}$, $k = 2^{2N+1} - (-2)^N$, $\lambda = 2^{2N} - (-2)^N$.

5. A family of five weight codes. Code defined as a linear span of a projective set which is the intersection of a non-degenerate Hermitian variety and the complement of one of the secant hyperplanes. Let $\mathcal{S}^0_{N-1}$ be a hyperplane in $PG(N, s^2)$ which is not one of the tangent hyperplanes of the non-degenerate Hermitian variety V_{N-1}. Then $\mathcal{C}^0_{N-1}$ intersects V_{N-1} in a non-degenerate Hermitian variety V^0_{N-2}. Let X denote the set of points on V_{N-1} which are not on V^0_{N-2}, that is, $X = V_{N-1}\backslash V^0_{N-2}$. Then the number points in X is

(5.1)
$$|X| = [(s^{N+2} - (-1)^{N+1})(s^N - (-1)^N) - (s^N - (-1)^N)(s^{N-1} - (-1)^{N-1})]/(s^2 - 1)$$
$$= s^{2N-1} + (-s)^{N-1}.$$

Let $\mathcal{C}(X)$ be the code over $GF(s^2)$, which is the linear space generated by the coordinate vectors of the points in X. Then $\mathcal{C}(X)$ has $n = s^{2N-1} + (-s)^{N-1}$, $k = N + 1$.

Let $\mathcal{S}_{N-1}$ be another hyperplane, distinct from $\mathcal{S}^0_{N-1}$, which is a secant to V_{N-1}. Then $\mathcal{S}_{N-1}$ intersects V_{N-1} in a non-degenerate V_{N-2} and meets $\mathcal{S}^0_{N-1}$ in a $(N-2)$-flat $\mathcal{S}^0_{N-2}$. Now, $\mathcal{S}^0_{N-2}$ intersects V^0_{N-2} in a non-degenerate V^0_{N-3} if it is a secant to V^0_{N-2} and in a *degenerate* V^0_{N-3}, if it is a tangent. Thus, every secant $\mathcal{S}_{N-1}$ distinct from $\mathcal{S}^0_{N-1}$, meets X either in $s^{2N-3} + (-s)^{N-2}$ points or in s^{2N-3} points. Thus

(5.2)
$$|X| - |X \cap \mathcal{S}_{N-1}| = (s+1)[s^{2N-2} - s^{2N-3} - (-s)^{N-2}] = w_1 \text{ (say), or}$$
$$= s^{2N-1} - s^{2N-3} + (-s)^{N-1} = w_2 \text{ (say).}$$

Further, each $(N-2)$-flat $\mathcal{S}^0_{N-2}$ of $\mathcal{S}^0_{N-1}$, which is a tangent to V^0_{N-2} at the point P (say), is contained in exactly one hyperplane which is tangent to V_{N-1} at P and in $(s^2 - 1)$ secant hyperplanes (excluding $\mathcal{S}^0_{N-1}$). Thus the number of secant hyperplanes which meet X in s^{2N-3} points is

(5.3)
$$\{(s^N - (-1)^N)(s^{N-1} - (-1)^{N-1})/(s^2 - 1)\}(s^2 - 1)$$
$$= (s^N - (-1)^N)(s^{N-1} - (-1)^{N-1}).$$

Again, an $(N-2)$-flat $\mathcal{S}^0_{N-2}$ of $\mathcal{S}^0_{N-1}$, which is a secant to V^0_{N-2}, is contained in $(s+1)$ hyperplanes which are tangents to V_{N-1} and in $(s^2 - s - 1)$ secant hyperplanes (excluding $\mathcal{S}^0_{N-1}$). Thus the number of such secant hyperplanes is
(5.4)
$$(s^2 - s - 1)[((s^2)^N - 1)/(s^2 - 1) - (s^N - (-1)^N)(s^{N-1} - (-1)^{N-1})/(s^2 - 1)]$$
$$= (s^2 - s - 1)(s^{2N-1} + (-s)^{N-1})/(s + 1).$$

Thus it follows that in $\mathcal{C}(X)$, there are

$$f_{w_1} = (s - 1)(s^2 - s - 1)(s^{2N-1} + (-s)^{N-1}) \text{ codewords each of weight } w_1,$$
$$f_{w_2} = (s^N - (-1)^N)(s^{N-1} - (-1)^{N-1})(s^2 - 1) \text{ codewords each of weight } w_2, \text{ and}$$
$$f_{w_3} = (s^2 - 1)\text{codewords each of weight } w_3 = s^{2N-1} + (-s)^{N-1}.$$

Let C be a point of V_{N-2}^0 and let $\mathcal{T}_{N-1}(C)$ be the hyperplane tangent to V_{N-1} at C. Then the intersection of $\mathcal{T}_{N-1}(C)$ and V_{N-1} is a degenerate Hermitian variety V_{N-2} with $1+s^2(s^{N-1}-(-1)^{N-1})(s^{N-2}-(-1)^{N-2})/(s^2-1)$ points. But $\mathcal{T}_{N-1}(C)$ meets $\mathcal{S}_{N-1}^0$ in an $(N-2)$-flat $\mathcal{T}_{N-2}^0(C)$ which is tangent to V_{N-2}^0 at C. Thus $\mathcal{T}_{N-2}^0$ meets V_{N-2}^0 in a degenerate V_{N-3}^0 consisting of $1+(s^{N-2}-(-1)^{N-2})(s^{N-3}-(-1)^{N-3})s^2/(s^2-1)$ points. Thus

$$(5.5) \qquad |X \cap \mathcal{T}_{N-1}(C)| = |V_{N-1} \cap \mathcal{T}_{N-1}(C)| - |V_{N-2}^0 \cap \mathcal{T}_{N-2}^0(C)|$$
$$= s^{2N-3} + (-s)^{N-1}.$$

Let

$$w_4 = |X| - |X \cap \mathcal{T}_{N-1}(C)| = s^{2N-1} - s^{2N-3} = s^{2N-3}(s^2-1)$$

and let $f_{w_4} = (s^2-1)$. (no. of points on V_{N-2}^o)

$$(5.6) \qquad = (s^N - (-1)^N)(s^{N-1} - (-1)^{N-1}).$$

Then in $\mathcal{C}(X)$ there are f_{w_4} codewords each of weight w_4.

Let $\mathcal{T}_{N-1}(P)$ be the tangent hyperplane to V_{N-1} at a point P which is not on V_{N-2}^0. Then $\mathcal{T}_{N-1}(P)$ meets V_{N-1} in a degenerate V_{N-2} consisting of

$$1 + (s^{N-1} - (-1)^{N-1})(s^{N-2} - (-1)^{N-2})s^2/(s^2-1)$$

points. But $\mathcal{T}_{N-1}(P)$ intersects $\mathcal{S}_{N-1}^o$ in an $(N-2)$-flat $\mathcal{S}_{N-2}^o$ which is not a tangent to V_{N-2}^o. Thus $\mathcal{S}_{N-2}^o$ meets V_{N-2}^o in a non-degenerate V_{N-3}^o consisting of $(s^{N-1} - (-1)^{N-1})(s^{N-2} - (-1)^{N-2})/(s^2-1)$ points. Hence

$$|X \cap \mathcal{T}_{N-1}(P)| = |V_{N-1} \cap \mathcal{T}_{N-1}(P)| - |V_{N-2}^o \cap \mathcal{S}_{N-2}^o|$$
$$(5.7) \qquad = s^{2N-3} + (-s)^{N-1} + (-s)^{N-2}.$$

Let $w_5 = |X| - |X \cap \mathcal{T}_{N-1}(P)| = s^{2N-1} - s^{2N-3} - (-s)^{N-2}$, and $f_{w_5} = (s^2-1)$. (No. of points in X) $= (s^2-1)(s^{2N-1}) + (-s)^{N-1})$. Thus in $\mathcal{C}(X)$ there are f_{w_5} codewords each of weight w_5. Thus the linear projective code $\mathcal{C}(X)$ over $GF(s^2)$ has five distinct non-zero weights w_i with corresponding frequencies $f_{w_i}, i = 1,2,3,4,5$. It follows that $\mathcal{C}(X)$ determines a linear projective code $\mathcal{C}'(X)$ over $GF(s)$ with parameters $n' = n(s+1) = (s+1)(s^{2N-1} + (-s)^{N-1})$, $k' = 2k = 2(N+1)$, $w_i' = sw_i, i = 1,2,3,4,5$, and the associated frequencies $f_{w_i}, i = 1,\ldots,5$ remain unchanged.

6. A family of three-weight codes from degenerate Hermitian varieties in projective spaces. Consider the section of a non-degenerate Hermitian variety V_{N-1} in $PG(N, s^2)$ with the tangent space $\mathcal{T}_{N-1}(C)$ at a point C on V_{N-1}. This section is a degenerate $V_{N-2}^o(C)$ of rank $N-1$ and its singular space consists of the single point C.

A $(N-2)$-space $\mathcal{S}_{N-2}$ contained in $\mathcal{T}_{N-2}(C)$ but not containing C, intersects $V_{N-2}^o(C)$ in a non-degenerate Hermitian variety V_{N-3} of rank $N-1$. Every point of $V_{N-2}^o(C)$ lies on some line joining C to a point of V_{N-3}. Thus the number of points on $V_{N-2}^o(C) = 1 + (s^{N-1} - (-1)^{N-1})(s^{N-2} - (-1)^{N-2})s^2/(s^2 - 1)$.

Let $\mathcal{C}(V_{N-2}^o)$ be the code over $GF(s^2)$ which is the linear space of the coordinates of the points on $V_{N-2}(C)$. This is a linear projective code with $n = 1 + (s^{N-1} - (-1)^{N-1})(s^{N-2} - (-1)^{N-2})s^2/(s^2 - 1)$ and $k = N$.

There are $\{[(s^2)^N - 1] - [(s^2)^{N-1} - 1]\}/(s^2 - 1) = (s^2)^{N-1}$ $(N-2)$-spaces $\mathcal{S}_{N-2}$ in $\mathcal{S}_{N-1}(C)$ which do not pass through C. Each such $\mathcal{S}_{N-2}$ meets $V_{N-2}^o(C)$ in a non-degenerate V_{N-3} with $(s^{N-1} - (-1)^{N-1})(s^{N-2} - (-1)^{N-2})/(s^2 - 1)$ points. Thus in $\mathcal{C}(V_{N-2}^o)$ there are

$$f_{w_1} = (s^2 - 1)(s^2)^{N-1} = s^{2N} - s^{2N-2}$$

codewords each of weight

$$
\begin{aligned}
w_1 &= 1 + s^2(s^{N-1} - (-1)^{N-1})(s^{N-2} - (-1)^{N-2})/(s^2 - 1) \\
&\quad - (s^{N-1} - (-1)^{N-1})(s^{N-2} - (-1)^{N-2})/(s^2 - 1) \\
&= s^{2N-3} + (-s)^{N-1} + (-s)^{N-2}.
\end{aligned}
$$

Let $\mathcal{S}_{N-2}^*$ be a fixed $(N-2)$-flat contained in $\mathcal{T}_{N-2}(C)$, not passing through C and let V_{N-3}^* a non-degenerate variety of rank $N-1$, denote the intersection of $\mathcal{S}_{N-2}^*$ and $V_{N-2}^o(C)$. Let $\mathcal{T}_{N-3}(D)$ be the tangent space to V_{N-3}^* at D which is a regular point of $V_{N-2}^o(C)$. Then the $(N-2)$-space $\mathcal{T}_{N-2}(C, D)$ which is the join of the point C and $\mathcal{T}_{N-3}(D)$, is the tangent space to $V_{N-2}^o(C)$ at D and to every point on the line joining D to C. The tangent space $\mathcal{T}_{N-2}(C, D)$ intersects $V_{N-2}^o(C)$ in a degenerate variety $V_{N-3}^o(C, D)$ of rank $N-3$ and its singular space is the line joining C and D.

Number of points on such $V_{N-3}^o(C, D)$ (degenerate of order 2) is

$$
\begin{aligned}
&(s^2 - 1)(s^2 + 1)(s^{N-3} - (-1)^{N-3})(s^{N-4} - (-1)^{N-4})/(s^2 - 1) \\
&\quad + s^2 + 1 + (s^{N-3} - (-1)^{N-3})(s^{N-4} - (-1)^{N-4})/(s^2 - 1) \\
&= 1 + s^2 + s^4(s^{2N-7} + (-s)^{N-3} + (-s)^{N-4} - 1)/(s^2 - 1)
\end{aligned}
$$

Thus

$$
\begin{aligned}
w_2 &= 1 + s^2(s^{N-1} - (-1)^{N-1})(s^{N-2} - (-1)^{N-2})/(s^2 - 1) \\
&\quad - 1 - s^2 - s^2(s^{2N-5} + (-s)^{N-1} + (-s)^{N-2} - s^2)/(s^2 - 1) = s^{2N-3}
\end{aligned}
$$

is the weight of a codeword which corresponds to the tangent space $\mathcal{T}_{N-2}(C, D)$ in $\mathcal{T}_{N-1}(C)$. The number of such $\mathcal{T}_{N-2}(C, D)$ is equal to the number of regular points D on $V_{N-3}^o(C)$, that is the number of points on V_{N-3}^* a non-degenerate Hermitian variety. Thus the frequency f_{w_2} of the codewords in $\mathcal{C}(V_{N-2}^o)$ of weight w_2 is

$$f_{w_2} = (s^{N-1} - (-1)^{N-1})(s^{N-2} - (-1)^{N-2}).$$

Let S_{N-3}^* be a $(N-3)$-flat in S_{N-2}^*, which is not a tangent to V_{N-3}^*. Let S_{N-2} be the join of C and S_{N-3}^*. Since S_{N-3}^* meets V_{N-3}^* in a non-degenerate Hermitian variety V_{N-4}, the section of $V_{N-2}^o(C)$ with S_{N-2} is a degenerate V_{N-3}^* which consists of all the points on the lines joining C to the points of V_{N-4}. Let

$$
\begin{aligned}
w_3 &= |V_{N-2}^o(C)| - |V_{N-3}^*| \\
&= 1 + s^2(s^{N-1} - (-1)^{N-1})(s^{N-2} - (-1)^{N-2})/(s^2 - 1) \\
&\quad - 1 - s^2(s^{N-2} - (-1)^{N-2})(s^{N-3} - (-1)^{N-3})/(s^2 - 1) \\
&= s^{2N-3} + (-s)^{N-1}.
\end{aligned}
$$

Thus w_3 is the weight of a codeword which corresponds to an $(N-2)$-flat S_{N-2} which passes through C, but is not a tangent to $V_{N-2}^o(C)$. Number of such $(N-2)$-flats S_{N-2} = Number of S_{N-3} in S_{N-2}^* − Number S_{N-3} in S_{N-2}^*, which are tangents to V_{N-3}^*, is

$$
\begin{aligned}
((s^2))^{N-1} - 1)/(s^2 - 1) &- (s^{N-1} - (-1)^{N-1})(s^{N-2} - (-1)^{N-2})/(s^2 - 1) \\
&= (s^{2N-3} + (-s)^{N-2})/(s+1)
\end{aligned}
$$

Thus the frequency f_{w_3} of codewords of weight w_3 is

$$
\begin{aligned}
(s^2 - 1)(s^{2N-3} &+ (-s)^{N-2})/(s+1) \\
&= (s-1)(s^{2N-3} + (-s)^{N-2}).
\end{aligned}
$$

It follows that $\mathcal{C}(V_{N-2}^o)$ determines a linear projective code $\mathcal{C}'(V_{N-2}^o)$ over $GF(s)$ with parameters

$$
\begin{aligned}
n' &= n(s+1) = (s+1) + \{s^2(s^{N-1} - (-1)^{N-1})(s^{N-2} - (-1)^{N-2})\}/(s-1), \; k' = 2k, \\
(6.1) \quad w_1' &= sw_1 = s^{2N-2} - (-s)^N - (-s)^{N-1}, w_2' = sw_2 = s^{2N-2}, \\
w_3' &= sw_3 = s^{2N-2} - (-s)^N
\end{aligned}
$$

and the frequencies f_{w_i} $\;$ $i = 1, 2, 3$ remain unchanged.

7. Families of three-weight codes from degenerate quadrics (cones) in projective spaces. Let Q_N be a non-degenerate quadric in $PG(N, s)$ and let $\mathcal{T}_{N-1}(P)$ be the hyperplane, tangent to Q_N at P. Then the intersection of $\mathcal{T}_{N-1}(P)$ and Q_N is a cone $Q_{N-1}^o(P)$ of rank N and order 1 and its vertex consists of the single point P.

A $(N-2)$-flat S_{N-2} contained in $\mathcal{T}_{N-1}(P)$ but not passing through P, intersects Q_N in a non-degenerate quadric Q_{N-2}. The points of $Q_{N-1}^o(P) = \mathcal{T}_{N-1}(P) \cap Q_N$, are then all the points on the lines joining P to the points of Q_{N-2}. $Q_{N-1}^o(P)$ has then $1 + s\psi(N-2, 0)$ points where $\psi(N-2, 0)$ is the number of points on Q_{N-2}.

Let S_{N-3}^* be a $(N-3)$-flat contained in an S_{N-2}^* which is one of the $(N-2)$-flats of $\mathcal{T}_{N-1}(P)$, not passing through P. Suppose that S_{N-3}^* is not a tangent of $Q_{N-2}^* = S_{N-2}^* \cap Q_{N-1}^o(P)$. Then S_{N-3}^* intersects Q_{N-2}^* (a non-degenerate quadric)

44

in a non-degenerate Q_{N-3}^*. Then the join of P and $\mathcal{S}_{N-3}^*$ which is a $(N-2)$-flat $\mathcal{S}_{N-2}(P) = P\dot{\cup}\mathcal{S}_{N-3}^*$ passing through P, intersects $Q_{N-1}^o(P)$, in a cone Q_{N-2}^o of order 1 with its vertex a single point P.

Now suppose that $\mathcal{T}_{N-3}^*(R)$ and $(N-3)$-flat contained in $\mathcal{S}_{N-2}$, is a tangent to Q_{N-2}^* at R. Then $\mathcal{T}_{N-3}^*(R)$ intersects Q_{N-2}^* in a cone Q_{N-3}^o of order 1 with R as its vertex. Hence the join of P and $\mathcal{T}_{N-3}^*(R)$ which is an $(N-2)$-flat $\mathcal{T}_{N-2}^*(P,R)$ (say) intersects $Q_{N-1}^o(P)$ in a cone $Q_{N-2}^o(P,R)$ of order 2 and the line joining P and R is its vertex.

Let $\mathcal{C}(Q_{N-1}^o(P))$ be the code over $GF(s)$, which is the linear space generated by the coordinate vectors of the points on the cone $Q_{N-1}^o(P)$. The weight-distributions of the linear projective codes are next derived treating the two cases (i) $N = 2t$ and (ii) $N = 2t - 1$ separately.

(i) $\underline{N = 2t}$. In this case, Q_{2t} is a non-degenerate quadric in $PG(2t, s)$ and $Q_{2t-1}^o(P)$ is the intersection of Q_{2t} with its tangent hyperplane $\mathcal{T}_{2t-1}(P)$ at a point P of Q_{2t}. Thus $Q_{2t-1}^o(P)$ is a cone of order 1 with P as its vertex. Thus

$$
\begin{aligned}
|Q_{2t-1}^o(P)| &= \text{number of points on } Q_{2t-1}^o(P) \\
&= 1 + s\psi(2t - 2, 0) = 1 + s(s^{2t-2} - 1)/(s - 1) \\
&= (s^{2t-1} - 1)/(s - 1).
\end{aligned}
$$

The code $\mathcal{C}(Q_{2t-1}^o(P))$ which is the linear space generated by the coordinate vectors of $Q_{2t-1}^o(P)$ has then the parameters $n = (s^{2t-1} - 1)/(s - 1)$, $k = 2t$.

A $(2t-2)$ flat $\mathcal{S}_{2t-2}$ contained in $\mathcal{T}_{2t-1}(P)$ but not passing through P intersects $Q_{2t-1}^o(P)$ in a non-degenerate quadric Q_{2t-2}. Thus

$$
w_1 = (s^{2t-1} - 1)/(s - 1) - (s^{2t-2} - 1)/(s - 1) = s^{2t-2}
$$

is the number of points of $Q_{2t-1}^o(P)$ which are not on such a $(2t-2)$-flat. The number f_{w_1} of such $(2t-2)$-flats in $\mathcal{T}_{2t-1}(P)$ is given by

$$
f_{w_1} = (s^{2t} - 1)/(s - 1) - (s^{2t-1} - 1)/(s - 1) = s^{2t-1}.
$$

Let $\mathcal{S}_{2t-3}^*$ be a $(2t-3)$-flat contained in $\mathcal{S}_{2t-2}^*$ which is one of the $(2t-2)$-flats of $\mathcal{T}_{2t-1}(P)$, not passing through P and assume further that $\mathcal{S}_{2t-3}^*$ is not a tangent to $Q_{2t-2}^* = \mathcal{S}_{2t-2}^* \cap Q_{2t-1}^o(P)$. Then the join of P and $\mathcal{S}_{2t-3}^*$ is a $(2t-2)$-flat $\mathcal{S}_{2t-2}(P)$ of $\mathcal{T}_{2t-1}(P)$, passing through P. $\mathcal{S}_{2t-2}(P)$ meets $Q_{2t-1}^o(P)$ in a cone $Q_{2t-2}^o(P)$ of order 1 with P as its vertex and $Q_{2t-2}^o(P)$ consists of all the points on the lines joining P to the points of a non-degenerate Q_{2t-3}^* which is the intersection of $\mathcal{S}_{2t-3}^*$ and Q_{2t-2}^*.

Number of points on $Q_{2t-2}^o(P) = |Q_{2t-2}^o(P)| = 1 + s\psi(2t - 3, 0)$, where $\psi(2t - 3, 0)$ is the number of points on Q_{2t-3}^*. Thus $|Q_{2t-2}^o(P)| = 1 + s(s^{t-1} + 1)(s^{t-2} - 1)/(s-1)$, if Q_{2t-3}^* is elliptic, $= 1 + s(s^{t-1} - 1)(s^{t-2} + 1)/(s - 1)$ if Q_{2t-3}^* is hyperbolic. Then $w_2 = (s^{2t-1} - 1)/(s - 1) - 1 - s(s^{t-1} + 1)(s^{t-2} - 1)/(s - 1) = s^{2t-2} + s^{t-1}$ is the number of points of $Q_{2t-1}^o(P)$ which are not on $\mathcal{S}_{2t-2}^*(P)$, if Q_{2t-3}^* is elliptic. Let f_{w_2} denote the number of such $\mathcal{S}_{2t-2}^*(P)$ flats.

If Q^*_{2t-3} is hyperbolic, then

$$w_3 = (s^{2t-1} - 1)/(s - 1) - 1 - s(s^{t-1} - 1)(s^{t-2} + 1)/(s - 1)$$
$$= s^{2t-2} - s^{t-1},$$

is the number of points on $Q^o_{2t-1}(P)$ which are not an $S^*_{2t-2}(P)$. Let f_{w_3} denote the number of such $(2t - 2)$-flats $S^*_{2t-2}(P)$.

Let $\mathfrak{T}_{2t-3}(R)$ be a $(2t - 3)$-flat in S^*_{2t-2} which is a tangent to Q^*_{2t-2} at a point R in Q^*_{2t-2}. Hence $\mathfrak{T}_{2t-3}(R)$ meets Q^*_{2t-2} in a cone $Q^o_{2t-2}(R)$ of order 1 and its vertex is the point R. The join of P and $\mathfrak{T}_{2t-3}(R)$ which is a $(2t-2)$-flat $\mathfrak{T}_{2t-2}(P, R)$ intersects $Q^o_{2t-1}(P)$ in a cone $Q^o_{2t-2}(P, R)$ of order 2 and its vertex is the line joining P and R. Then

$$|Q_{2t-2}(P, R)| = (s^2 - 1)/(s - 1) + s^2\psi(2t - 4, 0) = (s + 1) + s^2(s^{2t-4} - 1)/(s - 1)$$
$$= (s^{2t-2} - 1)/(s - 1).$$

Thus

$$w_4 = (s^{2t-1} - 1)/(s - 1) - (s^{2t-2} - 1)/(s - 1) = s^{2t-2}$$

is the number of points of $Q^o_{2t-1}(P)$ which are not on $\mathfrak{T}_{2t-2}(P, R)$. Then the number f_{w_4} of such flats, which is equal to the number of points on Q^*_{2t-2}, is given by $f_{w_4} = (s^{2t-2} - 1)/(s - 1)$. Now, $f_{w_2} + f_{w_3} =$ (number of $(2t - 2)$-flats in $\mathfrak{T}_{2t-1}(P)$, passing through P) - (number of $(2t - 3)$-flats in a $(2t - 2)$-flat S^*_{2t-2} of $\mathfrak{T}_{2t-1}(P)$, not passing through P and tangents to $Q^*_{2t-2}) = (s^{2t-1} - 1)/(s - 1) - (s^{2t-2} - 1)/(s - 1) = s^{2t-2}$.

Now $Q^o_{2t-1}(P)$ has $(s^{2t-1} - 1)/(s - 1)$ points and each point is on $(s^{2t-1} - 1)/(s - 1)$ $(2t - 2)$-flats contained in $\mathfrak{T}_{2t-1}(P)$. Hence counting (point, $(2t - 2)$-flat) pairs in two ways, one gets

$$f_{w_1} = (s^{2t-2} - 1)/(s - 1) + f_{w_2}(s^{2t-2} - 1)/(s - 1) + f_{w_2}(s^{2t-2} - s^t + s^{t-1} - 1)/(s - 1)$$
$$+ f_{w_3}(s^{2t-2} + s^t - s^{t-1} - 1)/(s - 1)$$
$$= (s^{2t-2} - 1)/(s - 1) \times (s^{2t-1} - 1)/(s - 1), f_{w_2} + f_{w_3} = s^{2t-2}, f_{w_1} = s^{2t-1},$$
$$f_{w_4} = (s^{2t-2} - 1)/(s - 1).$$

Solving these equations, one gets

$$f_{w_2} = (s^{2t-2} - s^{t-1})/2, \quad f_{w_3} = (s^{2t-2} + s^{t-1})/2.$$

Thus the weight-distribution of the $\mathcal{C}(Q^o_{2t-1}(P))$ is
(7.1)

weight	frequency
0	1
s^{2t-2}	$(s - 1)\{s^{2t-1} + (s^{2t-2} - 1)/s - 1\} = s^{2t} - s^{2t-1} + s^{2t-2} - 1$
$s^{2t-2} + s^{t-1}$	$(s - 1)(s^{2t-2} - s^{t-1})/2 = (s^{2t-1} - s^{2t-2} - s^t + s^{t-1})/2$
$s^{2t-2} - s^{t-1}$	$(s - 1)(s^{2t-2} + s^{t-1})/2 = (s^{2t-1} - s^{2t-2} + s^t - s^{t-1})/2$
	s^{2t}

Thus this is a tri-weight linear projective code over $GF(s)$ with $n = (s^{2t-1} - 1)/(s - 1)$ and $k = 2t$.

(ii) $\underline{N = 2t-1}$ In this the case Q_{2t-1} is a non-degenerate quadric in $PG(2t - 1, s)$ and $Q^o_{2t-2}(P)$ is the intersection of Q_{2t-1} and its tangent hyperplane $\mathcal{T}_{2t-2}(P)$ at a point P. Thus $Q^o_{2t-2}(P)$ is a cone of order 1 and P is its vertex. Then the number of points on $Q^o_{2t-2}(P)$ is

$$
\begin{aligned}
|Q^o_{2t-2}(P)| &= 1 + s\psi(2t - 3, 0) \\
&= 1 + s(s^{t-1} + 1)(s^{t-2} - 1)/(s - 1) = (s^{2t-2} - s^t + s^{t-1} - 1)/(s - 1), \\
&\quad \text{if } Q_{2t-1} \text{ is elliptic;} \\
&= 1 + s(s^{t-1} - 1)(s^{t-2} + 1)/(s - 1) = (s^{2t-2} + s^t - s^{t-1} - 1)/(s - 1), \\
&\quad \text{if } Q_{2t-1} \text{ is hyperbolic.}
\end{aligned}
$$

Thus the code $\mathcal{C}(Q^o_{2t-1}(P))$ which is the linear space generated by the coordinate vectors of the points of $Q^o_{2t-2}(P)$ is a linear projective code over $GF(s)$ with $n = |Q^o_{2t-2}(P)|$ and $k = 2t - 1$.

A $(2t-3)$-flat $\mathcal{S}_{2t-3}$ contained in $\mathcal{T}_{2t-2}(P)$ but not passing through P, intersects Q_{2t-1} in a non-degenerate quadric Q_{2t-3} which is elliptic (hyperbolic) if Q_{2t-1} is elliptic (hyperbolic). Thus the intersection of such a $\mathcal{S}_{2t-3}$ and $Q^o_{2t-2}(P)$ is a non-degenerate Q_{2t-3}.

Hence if Q_{2t-3} is elliptic, the number of points on $Q^o_{2t-2}(P)$ which are not $\mathcal{S}_{2t-3}$ is

$$
\begin{aligned}
w_1(\text{ellip.}) &= (s^{2t-2} - s^t + s^{t-1} - 1)/(s - 1) - (s^{t-1} + 1)(s^{t-2} - 1)/(s - 1) \\
&= s^{2t-3} - s^{t-1} + s^{t-2}
\end{aligned}
$$

On the other hand if Q_{2t-3} is hyperbolic, the number of points on $Q^o_{2t-2}(P)$ which are not on $\mathcal{S}_{2t-3}$ is

$$
\begin{aligned}
w_1(\text{hyperbol.}) &= (s^{2t-2} + s^t - s^{t-1} - 1)/(s - 1) - (s^{t-1} - 1)(s^{t-2} + 1)/(s - 1) \\
&= s^{2t-3} + s^{t-1} - s^{t-2}.
\end{aligned}
$$

The number f_{w_1} of such flats is s^{2t-2}.

Let $\mathcal{S}^*_{2t-3}$ be one of the $(2t - 3)$-flats of $\mathcal{T}_{2t-2}(P)$, not passing through P and let the non-degenerate Q^*_{2t-3} denote the intersection of $\mathcal{S}^*_{2t-3}$ and $Q^o_{2t-2}(P)$. Let $\mathcal{S}^*_{2t-4}$ be a $(2t - 4)$-flat of $\mathcal{S}^*_{2t-3}$, which is not not a tangent to Q^*_{2t-3}. Let $\mathcal{S}_{2t-3}(P)$ be the join of P and $\mathcal{S}^*_{2t-3}$. Then $\mathcal{S}_{2t-3}(P)$ intersects $Q_{2t-2}(P)$ in a cone $Q^o_{2t-3}(P)$ of order 1 with P as its vertex and it is the join of P and a non-degenerate quadric Q^*_{2t-4} where $Q^*_{2t-4} = \mathcal{S}_{2t-4} \cap Q^*_{2t-3}$.

Now, the number of points on $Q^o_{2t-3}(P)$ is

$$
\begin{aligned}
|Q^o_{2t-3}(P)| &= 1 + s\psi(2t - 4, 0) \\
&= 1 + s(s^{2t-4} - 1/(s - 1) = (s^{2t-3} - 1)/(s - 1).
\end{aligned}
$$

Thus if Q_{2t-1} is elliptic, the number of points on $Q_{2t-2}^o(P)$ which are not on such a $S_{2t-3}(P)$ flat is

$$w_2(\text{ellip.}) = (s^{2t-2} - s^t + s^{t-1} - 1)/(s-1) - (s^{2t-3} - 1)/(s-1)$$
$$= s^{2t-3} - s^{t-1}$$

If, however, Q_{2t-1} is hyperbolic, the number of points on $Q_{2t-2}^o(P)$ which are not on such a $S_{2t-3}(P)$ flat is

$$w_2(\text{hyperbol.}) = (s^{2t-2} + s^t - s^{t-1} - 1)/(s-1) - (s^{2t-3} - 1)/(s-1)$$
$$= s^{2t-3} + s^{t-1}.$$

The number f_{w_2} of such $S_{2t-3}(P)$ flats if Q_{2t-1} is elliptic is given by

$$f_{w_2}(\text{ellip.}) = (s^{2t-2} - 1)/(s-1) - (s^{t-1} + 1)(s^{t-2} - 1)/(s-1)$$
$$= s^{2t-3} + s^{t-2}.$$

If Q_{2t-1} is hyperbolic, the number f_{w_2} of such $S_{2t-3}(P)$ flats is

$$f_{w_2}(\text{hyperbolic}) = (s^{2t-2} - 1)/(s-1) - (s^{t-1} - 1)(s^{t-2} + 1)/(s-1)$$
$$= s^{2t-3} - s^{t-2}.$$

Let $\mathcal{T}_{2t-4}(R)$ be a $(2t-4)$-flat in S_{2t-3}^* and a tangent to Q_{2t-3}^* at the point R. Then $\mathcal{T}_{2t-4}(R)$ meets Q_{2t-3}^* in a cone $Q_{2t-4}^o(R)$ of order 1 with the point R as its vertex. The join of P and $\mathcal{T}_{2t-4}(R)$ is a $(2t-3)$-flat $\mathcal{T}_{2t-3}(P,R)$ which intersects $Q_{2t-2}(P)$ in a cone $Q_{2t-3}^o(P,R)$ of order 2 and its vertex is the line joining the points P and R. It is clear that $Q_{2t-3}^o(P,R)$ is the join of the line PR and a non-degenerate quadric Q_{2t-5}.

$$\text{Number of points on } Q_{2t-3}^o(P,R)$$
$$= (s+1) + s^2\psi(2t-5,0)$$
$$= (s^{2t-3} - s^t + s^{t-1} - 1)/(s-1) \quad \text{if } Q_{2t-1} \text{ is elliptic}$$
$$= (s^{2t-3} + s^t - s^{t-1} - 1)/(s-1) \quad \text{if } Q_{2t-1} \text{ is hyperbolic.}$$

Thus the number of points on $Q_{2t-2}^o(P)$ which are not on such flats $\mathcal{T}_{2t-3}(P,R)$ is

$$w_3 = (s^{2t-2} - s^t + s^{t-1} - 1)/(s-1) - (s^{2t-3} - s^t + s^{t-1} - 1)/(s-1)$$
$$= s^{2t-3} \text{ if } Q_{2t-1} \text{ is elliptic.}$$

It is easy to check that $w_3 = s^{2t-3}$ also if Q_{2t-1} is hyperbolic. Number f_{w_3} of such $\mathcal{T}_{2t-3}(P,R)$ $(2t-3)$-flats is equal to the number of points on a non degenerate quadric Q_{2t-3}.

Thus f_{w_3} (ellip.) $= (s^{t-1} + 1)(s^{t-2} - 1)/(s-1)$ if Q_{2t-1} is elliptic, and f_{w_3} (hyperbol.) $= (s^{t-1} - 1)(s^{t-2} + 1)/(s-1)$ if Q_{2t-1} is hyperbolic.

Thus the weight-distributions of the code $\mathcal{C}(Q^o_{2t-2}(P))$ for the two cases - Q_{2t-1} elliptic and Q_{2t-1} hyperbolic are given below.

(7.2)

Q_{2t-1} elliptic		Q_{2t-1} hyperbolic	
weight	frequency	weight	frequency
0	1	0	1
$s^{2t-3} - s^{t-1} + s^{t-2}$	$(s-1)s^{2t-2}$	$s^{2t-3} + s^{t-1} - s^{t-2}$	$(s-1)s^{2t-2}$
$s^{2t-3} - s^{t-1}$	$(s-1)(s^{2t-3} + s^{t-2})$	$s^{2t-3} + s^{t-1}$	$(s-1)(s^{2t-3} - s^{t-2})$
s^{2t-3}	$s^{2t-3} - s^{t-1} + s^{t-2} - 1$	s^{2t-3}	$s^{2t-3} + s^{t-1} - s^{t-2} - 1$
	s^{2t-1}		s^{2t-1}

REFERENCES

[1] BOSE, R.C., Lecture Notes on *Combinatorial Problems of Experimental Design*, Department of Statistics, University of North Carolina at Chapel Hill (1962).

[2] BOSE, R.C., *On the application of finite projective geometry for deriving a certain series of balanced Kirkman arrangements*, Calcutta Math. Soc. Golden Jubilee Comm., Part II, 1958–59 (1963), pp. 341–356.

[3] BOSE, R.C., *Self-conjugate tetrahedra with respect to the Hermitian variety $x_0^3 + x_1^3 + x_2^3 + x_3^3 = 0$ in $PG(3, 2^2)$ and a representation of $PG(3,3)$*, Proc. Symp. on Pure Math., 19 (Amer. Math. Soc. Providence, RI) (1971), pp. 27–37.

[4] BOSE, R.C. AND CHAKRAVARTI, I.M., *Hermitian varieties in a finite projective space $PG(N, q^2)$*, Canad. J. Math., 18 (1966), pp. 1161–1182.

[5] BOSE R.C. AND MESNER, D.M., *On linear associative algebras corresponding to association schemes of partially balanced designs*, Ann. Math. Statist., 30 (1959), pp. 21–38.

[6] BROUWER, A.E., *Some new two-weight codes and strongly regular graphs*, Discrete Appl. Math., 10 (1985), pp. 111-114.

[7] CALDERBANK, R. AND KANTOR, W.M., *The geometry of two-weight codes*, Bull. London Math. Soc., 18 (1986), pp. 97–122.

[8] CHAKRAVARTI, I.M., *Some properties and applications of Hermitian varieties in $PG(N, q^2)$ in the construction of strongly regular graphs (two-class association schemes) and block designs*, Journal of Comb. Theory, Series B, 11(3) (1971), pp. 268–283.

[9] CHAKRAVARTI, I.M., *The generalized Goppa codes and related discrete designs from Hermitian varieties*, Institute of Statistics Mimeo Series 1713. Department of Statistics, University of North Carolina at Chapel Hill.

[10] DELSARTE, P., *Weights of linear codes and strongly regular normed spaces*, Discrete Math., 3 (1972), pp. 47–64.

[11] DELSARTE, P., *An algebraic approach to the association schemes of coding theory*, Philips. Res. Rep. Suppl., 19 (1973).

[12] DEMBOWSKI, P., *Finite Geometries*, Springer-Verlag, 1968.

[13] DICKSON, L.E., *Linear Groups with an Exposition of the Galois Field Theory*, Teubner, Dover Publications Inc., New York, (1901, 1958).

[14] DIEUDONNÉ, J., *La Géométrie des Groupes Classiques*, Springer-Verlag, Berlin, Troisième Edition, 1971.

[15] DOWLING, T.A., *A class of tri-weight codes*, Institute of Statistics Mimeo Series No. 600.3. University of North Carolina at Chapel Hill, Department of Statistics (1969).

[16] GAMES, R.A., *The geometry of quadrics and correlations of sequences*, IEEE Trans. Inf. Th., IT-32 (1986), pp. 423–426.

[17] HEFT, S.M., *Spreads in Projective Geometry and Associated Designs*, Ph.D. dissertation submitted to the University of North Carolina, Dept. of Statistics, Chapel Hill (1971).

[18] HIGMAN, D.J. AND MCLAUGHLIN, J.E., *Rank 3 subgroups of finite symplectic and unitary groups*, J. Reine Angew. Math., 218 (1965), pp. 174–189.

[19] HUBAUT, XAVIER L., *Strongly regular graphs*, Discrete Mathematics, 13 (357–381).

[20] JORDAN C., *Traité des Substitutions et des Équations Algébriques*, Gauthier-Villars, Paris, 1870.

[21] MacWilliams, F.J. and Sloane, N.J.A., *The Theory of Error–Correcting Codes*, North Holland, 1977.

[22] MacWilliams, F.J., Odlyzko, A.M., Sloane, N.J.A. and Ward, H.N., *Self-dual codes over $GF(4)$*, J. Comb. Th., A25 (1978), pp. 288–318.

[23] Mann. H.B., *Addition Theorems*, John Wiley & Sons, Inc., 1965.

[24] Menon, P.K., *Difference sets in Abelian groups*, Proc. Amer. Math. Soc., 11 (1960), pp. 368–376.

[25] Mesner, D.M., *A new family of partially balanced incomplete block designs with some latin square design properties*, Ann. Math. Statist., 38 (1967), pp. 571–581.

[26] Primrose, E.J.F., *Quadrics in finite geometries*, Proc. Comb. Phil. Soc., 47 (1951), pp. 299–304.

[27] Ray-Chaudhuri, D.K., *On the application of the geometry of quadrics to the construction of partially balanced incomplete block designs and error correcting codes*, Ph.D. dissertation submitted to the University of North Carolina at Chapel Hill (1959).

[28] Ray-Chaudhuri, D.K., *Some results on quadrics in finite projective geometry based on Galois fields*, Canad. J. Math., 14 (1962), pp. 129–138.

[29] Segre, B., *Forme e geometrie hermitiane, con particolare riguardo al caso finito*, Ann. Math. Pure Appl., 70 1 (1965), p. 202.

[30] Segre, B., *Introduction to Galois Geometries*, Atti della Acc. Nazionale dei, Lincei, Roma, 8(5) (1967), pp. 137–236.

[31] Wolfmann, J., *Codes projectifs à deux ou trois poids associés aux hyperquadriques d'une géométrie finie*, Discrete Mathematics, 13 (1975), pp. 185–211.

[32] Wolfmann, J., *Codes projectifs à deux poids, "caps" complets et ensembles de différences*, J. Combin. Theory, 23A (1977), pp. 208–222.

PERFECT MULTIPLE COVERINGS
IN METRIC SCHEMES

RICHARD CLAYTON*

Abstract. Perfect multiple coverings generalize the concept of perfect codes by allowing for multiplicities, much as t-designs generalize Steiner systems. A necessary and sufficient condition is found to determine when a metric scheme admits a nontrivial perfect multiple covering. Results specific to the classical Hamming and Johnson schemes are given which bear out the relationship between t-designs, orthogonal arrays, and perfect multiple coverings.

Key words. perfect multiple covering, metric scheme, perfect code, distance regular graph, t-design, orthogonal array

AMS(MOS) subject classifications. Primary 05B30, 05C50; Secondary 05C75

1. Introduction. A *symmetric association scheme* $\mathfrak{X}$ of class d consists of a finite set X and $d+1$ nonempty relations $R_0, R_1, \ldots, R_d$ on X such that

(i) $R_0 = \{(x,x) \mid x \in X\}$,

(ii) $R_0 \cup R_1 \cup \cdots \cup R_d = X \times X$ with $R_i \cap R_j = \emptyset$ if $i \neq j$,

(iii) each R_i is symmetric,

(iv) for all $x, y \in X$ with $(x,y) \in R_h$, the number of $z \in X$ such that $(x,z) \in R_i$ and $(z,y) \in R_j$ is a constant p_{ij}^h.

A metric scheme is an association scheme which can be formed from a graph having certain regularity properties. Such graphs are called distance regular graphs and were introduced by Biggs to study perfect codes in a more general setting than the Hamming spaces.

For a connected graph Γ with vertex set X, we define the distance $d(x,y)$ on X to be the length of a shortest path between x and y. The *diameter* d of Γ is the maximum value attained by the distance function d. For $0 \leq i \leq d$ and $x \in X$, we define $\Gamma_i(x) = \{y \in X \mid d(x,y) = i\}$. The connected graph Γ is *distance regular* if there exist integers $b_0, \ldots, b_{d-1}$ and $c_1, \ldots, c_d$ such that for all $x, y \in X$ with $d(x,y) = i$, $|\Gamma_{i+1}(x) \cap \Gamma_1(y)| = b_i$ and $|\Gamma_{i-1}(x) \cap \Gamma_1(y)| = c_i$. This implies that Γ is regular of degree k $(= b_0)$. Setting $b_d = c_0 = 0$, we define $a_i = k - b_i - c_i$ so that $|\Gamma_i(x) \cap \Gamma_1(y)| = a_i$. For each i, $|\Gamma_i(x)|$ is a constant k_i, independent of x, and $b_i k_i = c_{i+1} k_{i+1}$.

Every distance regular graph Γ has the more general property that for all $x, y \in X$ with $d(x,y) = h$, $|\Gamma_i(x) \cap \Gamma_j(y)| = p_{ij}^h$, an integer independent of x and y, where $0 \leq h, i, j \leq d$. Therefore $a_i = p_{1\,i}^i$, $b_i = p_{1\,i+1}^i$ and $c_i = p_{1\,i-1}^i$.

Given a distance regular graph Γ of diameter d, define relations R_i $(0 \leq i \leq d)$ by

$$R_i = \{(x,y) \in X \times X \mid d(x,y) = i\}.$$

*Department of Mathematics, Ohio State University, Columbus, Ohio 43210. This research was supported in part by the Institute for Mathematics and its Applications with funds provided by the National Science Foundation.

51

Then it follows that $\mathfrak{X} = \left(X, \{R_i\}_{0 \leq i \leq d}\right)$ is a symmetric association scheme. Association schemes defined from distance regular graphs in this way are called *metric schemes*. One can recover the distance regular graph Γ from the corresponding metric scheme via the relation R_1.

We describe briefly two important examples of metric schemes.

HAMMING SCHEMES. Let F be a set of size q, not necessarily a prime power, and $X = F^d$, the set of all d-tuples with coordinates in F. The *Hamming distance* between two elements $x = (x_1, \ldots, x_d)$ and $y = (y_1, \ldots, y_d)$ is $d_H(x, y) = \left|\{\, i \mid x_i \neq y_i,\ 1 \leq i \leq d \,\}\right|$. The relations $R_0, R_1, \ldots, R_d$ on X are defined by $R_i = \{(x, y) \in X \times X \mid d_H(x, y) = i\}$. Then $\left(X, \{R_i\}_{0 \leq i \leq d}\right)$ is a metric scheme called the *Hamming scheme $H(d, q)$*.

JOHNSON SCHEMES. Let V be a set of size v and d a positive integer with $2d \leq v$. We let $X = \binom{V}{d}$ consist of all d-element subsets of V and define the *Johnson distance* on X by $d_J(x, y) = d - |x \cap y|$. Then X together with the obvious distance relations forms a metric scheme, which is called the *Johnson scheme $J(v, d)$*.

With metric schemes one can speak of a (closed) ball of radius e centered at an element of X. Suppose there exist balls of radius e which are pairwise disjoint and have union X. Then the set of centers of these balls is called a perfect code of radius e. Perfect codes tend to be quite rare in the known metric schemes. There are numerous nonexistence results, especially for the Hamming schemes (see for example [5], [10]–[13]). The primary tool used to prove the nonexistence of perfect codes in a given scheme is the generalized Lloyd theorem, proved by Biggs [2] and Delsarte [8], independently. This result states that if a perfect code of radius e exists then the sum polynomial Ψ_e of degree e has all of its zeros among a prescribed finite set $\{z_0, z_1, \ldots, z_d\}$.

The main idea of this paper is to generalize the notion of perfect codes to that of perfect multiple coverings. A perfect multiple covering can be viewed as a collection of balls of radius e whose multiset union is $\mu \cdot X$ (i.e. each $x \in X$ occurs μ times). So a perfect code is the case $\mu = 1$. Lloyd's theorem does not generalize to perfect multiple coverings. However, a necessary and sufficient condition for a metric scheme $\mathfrak{X}$ to admit a (nontrivial) perfect multiple covering is that the polynomial Ψ_e have at least one of its zeros among $\{z_0, z_1, \ldots, z_d\}$. Naturally, perfect multiple coverings are more abundant than perfect codes. The principal goal of this paper is to show that besides being interesting combinatorial objects themselves, perfect multiple coverings, like perfect codes, are closely related to t-designs and orthogonal arrays.

In Section 2 the equivalent definition of a metric scheme as a P-polynomial scheme is described. Section 3 contains results for perfect multiple coverings in arbitrary metric schemes, and also a characterization of perfect multiple coverings using the Radon transform. In Sections 4 and 5 we give results which are particular to the Hamming and Johnson schemes. Finally in Section 6 we discuss indecomposable perfect multiple coverings.

2. Metric Schemes. In this section the notion of a P-polynomial scheme is defined. In his thesis, Delsarte introduced the concept of a P-polynomial scheme. The reader is referred to [1], [4], or [8] for more detail.

For any symmetric association scheme $\mathfrak{X} = \left(X, \{R_i\}_{0 \le i \le d}\right)$ we can define graphs Γ_i with vertex set X and edge set R_i. Let A_i be the adjacency matrix for Γ_i. We then have $A_i A_j = \sum_{h=0}^{d} p_{ij}^{h} A_h$ for all i, j. The linear span of $A_0, A_1, \ldots, A_d$ over $\mathbb{C}$ is a $(d+1)$-dimensional algebra $\mathfrak{A}$, called the Bose-Mesner algebra of $\mathfrak{X}$. There exists an algebra isomorphic to the Bose-Mesner algebra which consists of matrices of order $d+1$ and is often easier to use. For each $0 \le i \le d$, define the intersection matrices B_i by $(B_i)_{jh} = p_{ij}^{h}$, $(0 \le h, j \le d)$. Since $B_i B_j = \sum_{h=0}^{d} p_{ij}^{h} B_h$, the algebra $\mathfrak{B} = \langle B_0, B_1, \ldots, B_d \rangle$ is isomorphic to $\langle A_0, A_1, \ldots, A_d \rangle$ via the map $\varphi : \mathfrak{A} \to \mathfrak{B}$ where $\varphi(A_i) = B_i$.

Since the A_i's are pairwise commuting symmetric matrices, they can be simultaneously diagonalized. Furthermore $\mathfrak{A}$ has a unique basis over $\mathbb{C}$ consisting of primitive idempotents $E_0, E_1, \ldots, E_d$. The algebra $\mathfrak{B}$ also has a unique basis of primitive idempotents, $F_0, F_1, \ldots, F_d$, with $F_i = \varphi(E_i)$. Expressing the A_i's in terms of the E_i's, we write $A_i = \sum_{j=0}^{d} p_i(j) E_j$. Therefore the eigenvalues of A_i are $p_i(j)$, $0 \le j \le d$, with multiplicity $\mu_j = \operatorname{rank} E_j$. We can also write $E_i = \dfrac{1}{|X|} \sum_{j=0}^{d} q_i(j) A_j$.

Similarly we have $B_i = \sum_{j=0}^{d} p_i(j) F_j$ and $F_i = \dfrac{1}{|X|} \sum_{j=0}^{d} q_i(j) B_j$. Since $\operatorname{rank} F_j = 1$ for each j, the eigenvalues of B_i are $p_i(0), p_i(1), \ldots, p_i(d)$. The association scheme $\left(X, \{R_i\}_{0 \le i \le d}\right)$ is *P-polynomial* if there exist distinct real numbers $z_0, \ldots, z_d$ and polynomials $\Phi_0(z), \ldots, \Phi_d(z)$ with real coefficients such that each Φ_i is of degree i and

$$(2.1) \qquad \Phi_i(z_j) = p_i(j) \text{ for } 0 \le i, j \le d.$$

Suppose real numbers $t_0, \ldots, t_d$ with polynomials $\Theta_i(z)$ of degree i also satisfy (2.1). Then there is a linear function $f(z) = \alpha z + \beta$ such that $f(z_i) = t_i$ and $\Phi_i = \Theta_i \circ f$ for all $i = 0, \ldots, d$. For any P-polynomial scheme, one can choose $z_j = p_1(j)$ for all j, and then the corresponding polynomials Φ_i will satisfy $\Phi_i(A_1) = A_i$. In [8], Delsarte proved that an association scheme is metric if and only if it is P-polynomial.

Consider a metric association scheme $\left(X, \{R_i\}_{0 \le i \le d}\right)$. Fix some choice of z_j's and Φ_i's which satisfies (2.1). The sum polynomial Ψ_e of degree e is defined by

$$\Psi_e(z) = \sum_{i=0}^{e} \Phi_i(z).$$

We define matrices $\overline{A}_e = \sum_{i=0}^{e} A_i$ and $\overline{B}_e = \sum_{i=0}^{e} B_i$. Since the A_i's can be simultaneously diagonalized, the matrices $\overline{A}_e$ and $\overline{B}_e$ have as their eigenvalues, $\Psi_e(z_j)$,

$0 \le j \le d$. Thus $\dim(\text{nullspace } \overline{B}_e) = \left|\{i \mid \Psi_e(z_i) = 0\}\right| \le e$. In the next section we will prove that nontrivial perfect multiple coverings of radius e exist if and only if $\overline{A}_e$ is singular, i.e. Ψ_e has a zero in the set $\{z_0, \ldots, z_d\}$.

3. Perfect Multiple Coverings. Let $\mathfrak{X} = \left(X, \{R_i\}_{0 \le i \le d}\right)$ be a metric scheme. The ball of radius e centered at x is denoted by

$$\overline{\Gamma}_e(x) = \bigcup_{i=0}^{e} \Gamma_i(x) = \{x' \in X \mid d(x, x') \le e\}.$$

A *μ-fold perfect multiple covering* (PMC) of $\mathfrak{X}$ with radius e is a nonempty multiset Y from X with the property that every $x \in X$ is contained in exactly μ of the radius e balls centered at the elements of Y. Hence the multiset union of these radius e balls is $\mu \cdot X$. Equivalently, for each $x \in X$, $\overline{\Gamma}_e(x)$ contains exactly μ elements of Y. We can combine PMCs to form new PMCs. If Y_1, Y_2 are PMCs with radius e (λ-fold and μ-fold, respectively), then the multiset union $Y_1 \cup Y_2$ is a $(\lambda + \mu)$-fold PMC. Also if $Y_1 \subseteq Y_2$, then the multiset difference $Y_2 - Y_1$ is a $(\mu - \lambda)$-fold PMC. In the case $\mu = 1$ we say that Y is a *perfect code*. A necessary condition for the existence of a μ-fold PMC Y of $\mathfrak{X}$ with radius e is the sphere-packing condition:

$$(3.1) \qquad \left(\sum_{i=0}^{e} k_i\right) \cdot |Y| = \mu \cdot |X|.$$

Every metric scheme $\mathfrak{X}$ admits perfect multiple coverings simply by taking $Y = \lambda \cdot X$ for any λ. PMCs of this type are called *trivial*. We are interested in determining when a given scheme $\mathfrak{X}$ admits a nontrivial PMC .

EXAMPLE. A nontrivial 7-fold PMC in $H(10, 2)$ with $e = 2$. Set $Y = \{y \in \mathsf{F}_2^{10} \mid Hy^{\mathrm{T}} = 0\}$, where

$$H = \begin{bmatrix} 0 & 0 & 0 & 0 & 0 & 0 & 1 & 1 & 1 & 1 \\ 0 & 0 & 0 & 0 & 1 & 1 & 0 & 0 & 1 & 1 \\ 1 & 1 & 1 & 1 & 0 & 1 & 0 & 1 & 0 & 1 \end{bmatrix}.$$

One can show that Y is a 7-fold PMC by checking that every possible Hx^{T} where $x \in \mathsf{F}_2^{10}$ is the sum of at most 2 columns of H in exactly 7 different ways. We remark that Y is also an orthogonal array of strength 3.

Let $\mathfrak{X}$ be a metric scheme with diameter d and fix a radius e with $0 \le e \le d$. For an arbitrary multiset Y from X, the characteristic function of Y, χ_Y, maps X into the set of nonnegative integers, i.e. $\chi_Y(x)$ is the number of occurences of x in Y. Then Y is a trivial PMC if and only if χ_Y is constant. The *weight enumerator of Y based at x* is the $(d+1)$-dimensional column vector $w_Y(x)$ with $|\Gamma_i(x) \cap Y|$ as its ith coordinate, $0 \le i \le d$. It is convenient to view χ_Y as an $|X|$-dimensional column vector with coordinates in the same order as the labeling of the columns of the adjacency matrices A_i.

PROPOSITION 3.1. *The following are equivalent:*

(i) Y *is a μ-fold* PMC *with radius* e,

(ii) $\overline{A}_e \chi_Y = \mu \vec{j}$,

(iii) $\overline{B}_e w_Y(x) = \mu \vec{k}$ *for all* $x \in X$,

where $\vec{j} = [1\,1\cdots 1]^{\mathrm{T}}$ *and* $\vec{k} = [k_0\, k_1 \cdots k_d]^{\mathrm{T}}$.

Proof. Clearly (ii) is equivalent to the definition of a μ-fold PMC. To prove that (i) $\Rightarrow$ (iii) fix $x \in X$ and $0 \le j \le d$, and count the pairs $(y, z) \in X \times X$ where $y \in Y$, $d(x, z) = j$, and $d(y, z) \le e$ in two different ways. Conversely, the equation in (iii) implies that there are exactly μ elements of Y in the ball of radius e about x. Since this holds for all $x \in X$, we have (iii) $\Rightarrow$ (i). $\square$

THEOREM 3.2. *A metric scheme $\mathfrak{X}$ admits a nontrivial* PMC *with radius e if and only if the matrix $\overline{A}_e$ is singular.*

Proof. Suppose $\mathfrak{X}$ has a nontrivial μ-fold PMC Y. Then χ_Y and $(\mu / \sum_{i=0}^{e} k_i)\,\vec{j}$ are distinct solutions v to $\overline{A}_e v = \mu \vec{j}$, since χ_Y is nonconstant. Thus $\overline{A}_e$ is singular.

If $\overline{A}_e$ is singular, then there is a nonzero vector u with integer coordinates, necessarily not all equal, such that $\overline{A}_e u = 0$. Choose an integer λ so that all coordinates of $u + \lambda \vec{j}$ are nonnegative. Then $u + \lambda \vec{j}$ is the characteristic function of a nontrivial PMC of $\mathfrak{X}$. $\square$

Since the eigenvalues of $\overline{A}_e$ are given by the sum polynomial Ψ_e, we have

COROLLARY 3.3. *A metric scheme $\mathfrak{X}$ admits a nontrivial* PMC *with radius e if and only if the sum polynomial Ψ_e has at least one of its zeros among the set* $\{z_0, z_1, \ldots, z_d\}$.

An alternative approach to perfect multiple coverings can be given using the discrete Radon transform. In [9] Diaconis and Graham investigate the problem of inverting a certain Radon transform in $H(d, 2)$ based on translates. This is equivalent to the problem of determining whether a nontrivial PMC exists in $H(d, 2)$ with a given radius. For an arbitrary metric scheme $\mathfrak{X} = (X, \{R_i\}_{0 \le i \le d})$, fix a radius e with $0 \le e \le d$ and consider a real-valued function f defined on X. The *Radon transform* of f is defined by

$$\tilde{f}(z) = \sum_{x \in \overline{\Gamma}_e(z)} f(x),$$

for all $z \in X$. So if χ is the characteristic function of a μ-fold PMC with radius e, then $\tilde{\chi}$ is the constant function μ. The Radon transform is *one-to-one*, or *invertible*, if for all real-valued functions f and g on X, $\tilde{f} = \tilde{g}$ implies that $f = g$, i.e. if one can always recover f from $\tilde{f}$. Clearly the Radon transform is one-to-one if and only if $\overline{A}_e$ is nonsingular. That is, the Radon transform is invertible if and only if there are no nontrivial PMCs of $\mathfrak{X}$ with radius e.

We contrast Corollary 3.3 with the generalization of Lloyd's theorem, due to Biggs [2] and Delsarte [8].

THEOREM 3.4 (GENERALIZED LLOYD THEOREM). *If $\mathcal{X}$ admits a perfect code with radius e, then all the zeros of the sum polynomial Ψ_e are contained in the set $\{z_0, z_1, \ldots, z_d\}$.*

Proof. Suppose Y is a perfect code with radius e. It suffices to show that $\dim(\text{nullspace } \overline{B}_e) = e$. From Section 2, we have that $\dim(\text{nullspace } \overline{B}_e) \leq e$. To prove the reverse inequality, let $y \in Y$ and for $0 \leq i \leq e$ choose any $x_i \in X$ so that $d(x_i, y) = i$. Consider the weight enumerator $w_i = w_Y(x_i)$. Among its first $e + 1$ coordinates all entries are zero except the ith coordinate which is a one. Since $\overline{B}_e w_i = \vec{k}$ for all i, we have $\overline{B}_e(w_i - w_0) = 0$. The e vectors $w_1 - w_0, \ldots, w_e - w_0$ are linearly independent, so $\dim(\text{nullspace } \overline{B}_e) \geq e$. $\square$

For a given metric scheme $\mathcal{X}$, we say that the sum polynomial Ψ_e has *the Lloyd property* if all its zeros are contained in the set $\{z_0, z_1, \ldots, z_d\}$. In light of Corollary 3.3, it is clear that the Lloyd theorem does not hold for arbitrary PMCs. But perhaps the Lloyd theorem does extend for small values of μ, in particular, $\mu = 2$. Suppose $\mathcal{X}$ admits a 2-fold PMC Y with radius e. To prove that Ψ_e has the Lloyd property, it suffices to find elements $x_0, x_1, \ldots, x_e$ in X such that $i = d(x_i, Y) := \min\{d(x_i, y) \mid y \in Y\}$, for $i = 0, 1, \ldots, e$. Then the $e + 1$ vectors $w_Y(x_i)$ are linearly independent, and $\dim(\text{nullspace } \overline{B}_e) \geq e$, as in the proof of Lloyd's theorem. In fact, once we find an x with $d(x, Y) = e$, we are done. There exists y in Y with $d(x, y) = e$. Using any path of length e from y to x, we choose $x_0, x_1, \ldots, x_e$ so that $d(x_i, y) = i$. One easily checks that $d(x_i, Y) = i$ for each i. In the next section this is used to show that the Lloyd theorem holds for 2-fold PMCs in the Hamming schemes.

4. Hamming Schemes. Much progress has been made in determining all perfect codes in the Hamming schemes. Here is a list of the known perfect codes with $0 < e < d$:

(1) the repetition codes in $H(d, 2)$ with $d = 2e + 1$,

(2) the Hamming codes and non-linear codes in $H(d, q)$ with parameters $e = 1$, $d = \dfrac{q^m - 1}{q - 1}$, q a prime power and m arbitrary,

(3) the ternary Golay code in $H(11, 3)$ with $e = 2$, and

(4) the binary Golay code in $H(23, 2)$ with $e = 3$.

It is known that there are no other perfect codes in the Hamming schemes except possibly in the case where $e = 1$ and q is not a prime power. We conjecture that the only 2-fold PMCs in the Hamming schemes are those formed by taking the union of two perfect codes. In support of this conjecture we have the following theorem.

THEOREM 4.1. *If a 2-fold PMC with radius e exists in the Hamming scheme $H(d, q)$, then Ψ_e has the Lloyd property.*

Proof. Let Y be a 2-fold PMC of the Hamming scheme $H(d, q)$. As shown in the previous section, it suffices to find an $x \in X$ such that $d(x, Y) = e$. So choose x such that $d(x, Y)$ is maximum, and assume that $d(x, Y) < e$. Then there exist y_1 and y_2 in Y with $d(x, y_1) = d(x, Y) < e$ and $d(x, y_2) \leq e$.

If $q \geq 3$, choose a coordinate l where x and y_1 are equal, and a letter α different from both of the lth coordinates of y_1 and y_2. Let x' be the same as x except that x' has l^{th} coordinate α. Then $d(x',y_1) = d(x,y_1) + 1$, $d(x',y_2) \geq d(x,y_2)$, and for any other y in Y, $d(x',y) \geq e$. Therefore $d(x',Y) > d(x,Y)$, contradicting the choice of x.

If $q = 2$, then by the sphere-packing condition (3.1) we must have $2e + 1 \leq d$ (or $e = d$, a triviality). Then there must be a coordinate l where x, y_1, and y_2 are all equal. Let x' be the same as x except at the lth coordinate. As in the previous case, $d(x',Y) > d(x,Y)$. $\square$

REMARK. A similar argument can be used to show that if a μ-fold PMC with radius e exists in $H(d,q)$ where $\mu < q$, then Ψ_e has the Lloyd property.

Corollary 3.3 says that nontrivial PMCs with radius e exist for some μ if and only if the sum polynomial $\Psi_e(z)$ has at least one zero among $\{z_0, z_1, \ldots, z_d\}$. In the Hamming scheme case, one can choose $z_j = j$ and $\Phi_i(z) = K_i(z,q,d)$ (see [1], [8], [12]), where K_i is the Krawtchouk polynomial of degree i given by

$$K_i(z,q,d) = \sum_{j=0}^{i}(-1)^j \binom{z}{j}\binom{d-z}{i-j}(q-1)^{i-j}.$$

In fact, the sum polynomial $\Psi_e(z) = \sum_{i=0}^{e} K_i(z,q,d) = K_e(z-1,q,d-1)$ is also a Krawtchouk polynomial. Thus integral zeros of Krawtchouk polynomials correspond to nontrivial perfect multiple coverings in the Hamming schemes. In [6], [7], and [9], there are numerous results on integral zeros of Krawtchouk polynomials.

Hong [10] has proved that the sum polynomial $\Psi_e(z)$ in the Hamming scheme $H(d,q)$ has a nonintegral zero if $e \geq 3$ and $q \geq 3$, i.e. Ψ_e does not have the Lloyd property in these cases. Combining Hong's result with Theorem 4.1, we have

THEOREM 4.2. *There are no μ-fold PMCs with radius e in $H(d,q)$ if $\mu < q$, $e \geq 3$ and $q \geq 3$.*

The nontrivial PMCs constructed in the proof of Theorem 3.2 have size at least as large as the space, i.e. $|Y| \geq |X|$. We would prefer to have PMCs with $|Y| < |X|$ and no repeated elements in Y. We next give the construction of such a Y as well as a combinatorial interpretation of the integral zeros of Krawtchouk polynomials.

Consider the Hamming scheme $H(d,q)$ with alphabet $\mathbb{Z}_q$, the integers modulo q. Fix a radius $e < d$ and let m be a nonnegative integer with $m \leq d$. Define H to be the $1 \times d$ parity check matrix $[1\,1\cdots1\,0\,0\cdots0]$ where the first m coordinates are ones and all others are zeros. Set

$$Y = \{y \in \mathbb{Z}_q^d \mid Hy^{\mathrm{T}} = 0\}.$$

For $x \in \mathbb{Z}_q^d$, let $\sigma_r(x)$ denote the rth component of the weight enumerator $w_Y(x)$, $(0 \leq r \leq d)$. A counting argument shows that, for fixed r, $\sigma_r(x)$ takes on just 2 values, depending on whether $x \in Y$ or $x \notin Y$. Furthermore, for any $y \in Y$ and $x \notin Y$, $\sigma_r(y) - \sigma_r(x) = K_r(m, q, d)$. Summing over r from 0 to e, we have that if $\Psi_e(m) = 0$ then Y is a μ-fold PMC, with $\mu = q^{-1} \sum_{i=0}^{e} k_i$ by the sphere-packing condition (3.1). Also, Y is nontrivial since $|Y| = q^{d-1} < q^d$.

5. Johnson Schemes. Important examples of metric schemes are the Johnson schemes. Recall that in $J(v, d)$, we have $X = \binom{V}{d}$, the set of all d-element subsets of a set V, where $|V| = v$. A t-(v, d, λ) *design* over V is a collection of d-element subsets of V (called blocks) with the property that every t-element subset of V is contained in exactly λ blocks. We allow repeated blocks in a t-design. A design with no repeated blocks is called *simple*.

The Johnson schemes provide a natural setting for the study of design theory. The only known perfect codes in the Johnson schemes have parameters $v = 4e + 2$, $d = 2e + 1$ and $|Y| = 2$. These are analogous to the binary repetition codes of the Hamming schemes.

In the case of the Johnson scheme $J(v, d)$, one can take $z_j = j(v + 1 - j)$ and Φ_i to be the Eberlein polynomial (see [1], [8])

$$\sum_{h=0}^{i} (-1)^h \binom{x}{h} \binom{d - x}{i - h} \binom{v - d - x}{i - h}$$

of degree i in the variable $z = x(v + 1 - x)$.

EXAMPLE. A 6-fold PMC in $J(9, 4)$ with $e = 1$. Since $k_0 + k_1 = 21$ divides $\binom{9}{4} = 126$, a perfect code in $J(9, 4)$ with $e = 1$ is feasible. However it can be shown that for any μ-fold PMC ($e = 1$) of $J(9, 4)$ we must have $3 \mid \mu$ and $\mu \geq 6$. By the sphere-packing condition (3.1), a 6-fold PMC Y must have $|Y| = 36$. We prefer to list the elements of Y as characteristic functions, i.e. binary strings of length 9 having 4 nonzero coordinates. Let Y consist of the 36 elements:

$$(1111\ 00000) \qquad (1001\ \underrightarrow{11000}) \qquad (1000\ \underrightarrow{10101})$$

$$(1110\ \underrightarrow{10000}) \qquad (0101\ \underrightarrow{11000}) \qquad (0100\ \underrightarrow{10101})$$

$$(0011\ \underrightarrow{11000}) \qquad (0010\ \underrightarrow{10101})$$

where $(1001\ \underrightarrow{11000})$ represents the five elements obtained by permuting the last five coordinates cyclicly. Then it can be checked that Y is a 6-fold PMC in $J(9, 4)$. We remark that the set Y is also a 2-$(9, 4, 6)$ design. In general, a PMC with radius e in the Johnson scheme is a t-design, where $t = \max\{j \mid \Psi_e(z_i) \neq 0 \text{ for all } i \leq j\}$. We proceed with a proof of this result.

Let $\binom{V}{*}$ denote the collection of all subsets of V and extend the function d to $\binom{V}{*} \times \binom{V}{*}$ by defining

$$d(x, y) = \min\{|x|, |y|\} - |x \cap y|.$$

Now d is not a distance on $\binom{V}{*}$ since $d(x,y) = 0$ if $x \subseteq y$. Let $0 \le m \le d$ and $0 \le h, j \le m$. Then for any $y \in \binom{V}{d}$ and $x \in \binom{V}{m}$ with $d(x,y) = h$, the number of $z \in \binom{V}{d}$ such that $d(y,z) = i$ and $d(z,x) = j$ is a constant $p_{ij}^{h\,(m)}$. In fact,

$$p_{ij}^{h\,(m)} = \sum_{l=0}^{h} \binom{h}{l}\binom{m-h}{j-l}\binom{d-m+h}{l+i-j}\binom{v-d-h}{l+i-h}.$$

For each $0 \le i \le d$, define the $(m+1)\times(m+1)$ matrix $B_i^{(m)}$ by $(B_i^{(m)})_{jh} = p_{ij}^{h\,(m)}$. Also set $\overline{B}_e^{(m)} = \sum_{i=0}^{e} B_i^{(m)}$. Let Y be a multiset from $X = \binom{V}{d}$ and $x \in \binom{V}{m}$. Then define $w_Y^{(m)}(x)$ to be the $(m+1)$-dimensional vector with i^{th} coordinate equal to $\left|\{y \in Y \mid d(x,y) = i\}\right|$. The number $k_j^{(m)} := \left|\{z \in X \mid d(x,z) = j\}\right| = \binom{m}{j}\binom{v-m}{d-m+j}$ is independent of the choice of $x \in \binom{V}{m}$. Similar to Proposition 3.1, we have the following result.

PROPOSITION 5.1. *If Y is a μ-fold PMC with radius e in $J(v,d)$, then for each $m = 0, \ldots, d$ and each $x \in \binom{V}{m}$,*

$$\overline{B}_e^{(m)} w_Y^{(m)}(x) = \mu\,\vec{k}^{(m)},$$

where $\vec{k}^{(m)} = [k_0^{(m)}, k_1^{(m)}, \ldots, k_m^{(m)}]^{\text{T}}$.

Proof. To show that the jth coordinates of both sides agree, count the ordered pairs $(y,z) \in \binom{V}{d} \times \binom{V}{d}$ where $y \in Y$, $d(x,z) = j$, and $d(y,z) \le e$, in two different ways. $\square$

LEMMA 5.2. *If Y is a PMC with radius e and $\overline{B}_e^{(t)}$ is nonsingular, then Y is a t-design.*

Proof. For any $x \in \binom{V}{t}$, the initial coordinate of $w_Y^{(t)}(x)$ is the number of $y \in Y$ such that $x \subseteq y$. Since $\overline{B}_e^{(t)}$ is nonsingular, the vector $w_Y^{(t)}(x)$ is uniquely determined, independent of the choice of $x \in \binom{V}{t}$. Hence Y is a t-design. $\square$

Next we investigate the eigenvalues of $\overline{B}_e^{(m)}$.

PROPOSITION 5.3. *For all $0 \le i, j \le d$,*

$$B_i^{(m)} B_j^{(m)} = \sum_{h=0}^{d} p_{ij}^{h} B_h^{(m)}.$$

Proof. We need to show that for all $0 \le r, s \le m$,

$$\sum_{l=0}^{m} p_{ir}^{l\,(m)} p_{jl}^{s\,(m)} = \sum_{h=0}^{d} p_{ij}^{h} p_{hr}^{s\,(m)}.$$

To see this, fix $x \in \binom{V}{m}$ and $y \in \binom{V}{d}$ with $d(x,y) = s$, and count the pairs (w,z) where $w, z \in \binom{V}{d}$ and $d(x,w) = r$, $d(w,z) = i$, $d(z,y) = j$. $\square$

We can define an algebra homomorphism $\varphi_m : \langle B_0, \ldots, B_d \rangle \to \langle B_0^{(m)}, \ldots, B_d^{(m)} \rangle$ by setting $\varphi_m(B_i) = B_i^{(m)}$ and extending by linearity. We will see that the algebra $\mathfrak{B}^{(m)} = \langle B_0^{(m)}, \ldots, B_d^{(m)} \rangle$ has dimension $m + 1$. Recall that the algebra $\mathfrak{B}$ has a unique basis of primitive idempotents $F_0, F_1, \ldots, F_d$ where

$$B_i = \sum_{j=0}^{d} p_i(j) \, F_j$$

for all i. Since $I_{d+1} = B_0 = \sum_{j=0}^{d} F_j$, each F_j has rank 1. Expressing the F_i's in terms of the B_i's, we write

$$(5.1) \qquad F_i = \frac{1}{|X|} \sum_{j=0}^{d} q_i(j) \, B_j.$$

Set $F_i^{(m)} = \varphi_m(F_i)$. Then $F_0^{(m)}, F_1^{(m)}, \ldots, F_d^{(m)}$ are orthogonal idempotents with

$$(5.2) \qquad B_i^{(m)} = \sum_{j=0}^{d} p_i(j) \, F_j^{(m)}$$

for all i. If $F_j^{(m)} \neq 0$, then $p_i(j)$ is an eigenvalue of $B_i^{(m)}$.

PROPOSITION 5.4. *For $0 \le i \le m$, $F_i^{(m)} \neq 0$.*

Proof. We show that for $0 \le i \le m$ the $(0,0)$ entry of $F_i^{(m)}$ is nonzero. By (5.1), we have $F_i^{(m)} = \frac{1}{|X|} \sum_{j=0}^{d} q_i(j) \, B_j^{(m)}$. It is well-known that for the Johnson scheme $J(v,d)$, we have

$$q_i(j) = \frac{\mu_i}{k_j} \sum_{h=0}^{j} (-1)^h \binom{i}{h} \binom{d-i}{j-h} \binom{v-d-i}{j-h}$$

where $\mu_i = \dfrac{v - 2i + 1}{v - i + 1} \binom{v}{i}$ and $k_j = \binom{d}{j} \binom{v-d}{j}$. Thus the $(0,0)$ entry of $F_i^{(m)}$ equals

$$\frac{\mu_i}{|X|} \sum_{j=0}^{d} \sum_{h=0}^{j} (-1)^h \binom{i}{h} \binom{d-i}{j-h} \binom{v-d-i}{j-h} \binom{d-m}{j} \bigg/ \binom{d}{j}$$

$$= \frac{\mu_i}{|X|} \binom{d}{m}^{-1} \sum_{j=0}^{d} \sum_{l=0}^{j} (-1)^{j-l} \binom{i}{j-l} \binom{d-i}{l} \binom{v-d-i}{l} \binom{d-j}{m}.$$

60

Reverse the order of summation to get that this equals

$$\frac{\mu_i}{|X|}\binom{d}{m}^{-1}\sum_{l=0}^{d}\binom{d-i}{l}\binom{v-d-i}{l}\left(\sum_{j=l}^{d}(-1)^{j-l}\binom{i}{j-l}\binom{d-j}{m}\right)$$

$$=\frac{\mu_i}{|X|}\binom{d}{m}^{-1}\sum_{l=0}^{d}\binom{d-i}{l}\binom{v-d-i}{l}\binom{d-l-i}{m-i},$$

which is clearly positive for $0 \le i \le m$. $\square$

Since the $F_j^{(m)}$'s are orthogonal idempotents and $I_{m+1} = B_0^{(m)} = \sum_{j=0}^{d} F_j^{(m)}$, each $F_j^{(m)}$ has rank 0 or 1. Therefore $F_j^{(m)} = 0$ for $m < j \le d$ and each $B_i^{(m)}$ is diagonalizable with $\{p_i(0), p_i(1), \ldots, p_i(m)\}$ as its complete set of eigenvalues. By (5.2), the eigenvalues of $\overline{B}_e^{(m)}$ are given by $\Psi_e(z_j) = \sum_{i=0}^{e} p_i(j)$, $0 \le j \le m$. Combining this with Lemma 5.2, we have the following.

THEOREM 5.5. *Suppose Y is a PMC in $J(v, d)$ with radius e. Then Y is a t-design, where*

$$t = \max\{j \mid \Psi_e(z_i) \ne 0 \text{ for all } i \le j\}.$$

REMARK. Using similar techniques, we are able to prove an analogous result for the Hamming schemes, but instead of t-designs, PMCs are orthogonal arrays of strength t.

[The author has since found a generalization of Theorem 5.5 to arbitrary metric schemes which will appear in a later paper.]

We conclude this section by mentioning some results for the odd graph, a metric scheme closely related to the Johnson scheme. In the scheme $J(2d+1, d)$, the graph Γ_d can be shown to be distance regular. This graph is called the *odd graph* $\mathcal{O}_{d+1}$. Perfect codes of radius 1 are known to exist in $\mathcal{O}_4$ and $\mathcal{O}_6$. P. Cameron (see [3]) has proved that a perfect code with radius 1 in $\mathcal{O}_{d+1}$ is a $(d-1)$–$(2d+1, d, 1)$ design, and conversely. Cameron's result can be generalized to perfect multiple coverings.

THEOREM 5.6. *Suppose d is odd. Then a μ-fold PMC with radius 1 in $\mathcal{O}_{d+1}$ is a $(d-1)$–$(2d+1, d, \mu)$ design, and conversely.*

Proof. Let Y be a μ-fold PMC with radius 1 in $\mathcal{O}_{d+1}$ and $x \in \binom{V}{m}$ with $0 \le m \le d$. Similar to Proposition 5.1, we have

$$\left(B_0^{(m)} + B_d^{(m)}\right) w_Y^{(m)}(x) = \mu\, \vec{k}^{(m)}.$$

The eigenvalues of $B_0^{(m)} + B_d^{(m)}$ are $1 + (-1)^i(d+1-i)$, $0 \le i \le m$. Thus $B_0^{(m)} + B_d^{(m)}$ is nonsingular if $m = d - 1$, and by the same argument as in the proof of Lemma 5.2, Y is a $(d-1)$–$(2d+1, d, \mu)$ design.

Conversely, suppose Y is a $(d-1)$-$(2d+1, d, \mu)$ design and $x = \{v_1, v_2, \ldots, v_d\}$ is an arbitrary element of $\binom{V}{d}$. Let N_i denote the set of elements (i.e. blocks) in Y which contain v_i. Using inclusion-exclusion, we get that

$$\left| N_1^c \cap \cdots \cap N_d^c \right| = (-1)^d \left| N_1 \cap \cdots \cap N_d \right| + \frac{d+1+(-1)^{d+1}}{d+2}\, \mu,$$

where N_i^c is the complement of N_i in $\binom{V}{d}$. So if d is odd, the ball of radius 1 in $\mathcal{O}_{d+1}$ centered at x contains exactly μ elements of Y. Since x is arbitrary, Y is a μ-fold PMC. $\square$

REMARK. The above argument shows that for even d there are no nontrivial PMCs with radius 1 in $\mathcal{O}_{d+1}$. However nontrivial $(d-1)$-$(2d+1, d, \mu)$ designs may exist for even d.

6. Indecomposable PMCs. A PMC with radius e is called *indecomposable* if it is not the multiset union of two nonempty PMCs with radius e. We are concerned with the following problems. Do there exist indecomposable 2-fold PMCs in an arbitrary metric scheme? If a PMC does decompose, is its complete decomposition into indecomposable components unique? Also, suppose a metric scheme $\mathcal{X}$ admits a perfect code with radius e. Then does every μ-fold PMC of $\mathcal{X}$ with radius e decompose into μ perfect codes? In this section we show that for antipodal metric schemes of odd diameter d, every μ-fold PMC with radius $(d-1)/2$ decomposes into μ perfect codes. However, we show that this is not a general result for metric schemes by constructing indecomposable 3-fold PMCs with radius 1 in the Hamming schemes $H(2^m - 1, 2)$, for $m \geq 3$. These examples also show that there is no unique decomposition theorem for PMCs. The problem of finding indecomposable 2-fold PMCs in any metric scheme is open, and we conjecture that there are none.

An *antipodal scheme* $\mathcal{X}$ is a metric scheme where the graph Γ_d is a disjoint union of cliques, i.e. $R_0 \cup R_d$ is an equivalence relation. The number of vertices in each clique (or d-clique) is a constant $k_d + 1$. The Hamming schemes $H(d, 2)$, for example, are antipodal with $k_d = 1$. In any antipodal scheme with odd diameter d, the $k_d + 1$ vertices of any d-clique form a perfect code with radius $(d-1)/2$. This result is due to Biggs [3]. A slightly more general result is the following. The diameter d is not assumed to be odd.

PROPOSITION 6.1. *Let $C = \{x_1, \ldots, x_r\}$ be a d-clique of the antipodal scheme $\mathcal{X}$ of diameter d. Fix an integer j where $0 \leq j \leq (d+1)/2$. Then the collection of balls $\overline{\Gamma}_{d-j}(x_1), \overline{\Gamma}_{j-1}(x_2), \ldots, \overline{\Gamma}_{j-1}(x_r)$ are pairwise disjoint and have union X.*

Proof. Clearly these sets are pairwise disjoint. (Define $\overline{\Gamma}_{-1}(x) = \emptyset$.) To show that their union is the entire space, consider an arbitrary $x \in X$ and set $i = d(x, x_1)$. Since $p^i_{d\,d-i} > 0$, there exists $x_m \in C$ such that $d(x, x_m) = d - i$ and $d(x_1, x_m) = d$. (It must be that x_m is in the d-clique C since $d(x_1, x_m) = d$.) Now either $i \leq d - j$ or $d - i < j$, so x is contained in $\overline{\Gamma}_{d-j}(x_1) \cup \overline{\Gamma}_{j-1}(x_m)$. $\square$

PROPOSITION 6.2. *Let C be a d-clique of the antipodal scheme $\mathfrak{X}$ of diameter d, and x an arbitrary element of X. Set $i = d(x, C)$. Then for some $c \in C$, $d(x, c) = i \leq d/2$ and for all other $c' \in C$, $d(x, c') = d - i$.*

Proof. Suppose $d(x, c) = i$ for some $c \in C$. Since $p^i_{d\,d-i} > 0$, we must have $i = d(x, C) \leq d/2$. For any $c' \in C$ different from c we clearly have that $d(x, c') \geq d - i$. By Proposition 6.1 the ball $\overline{\Gamma}_{d-i}(c')$ together with the balls $\overline{\Gamma}_{i-1}(c'')$ $(c'' \in C, c'' \neq c')$ form a partition of X. Since $d(x, C) = i$, it must be that $x \in \overline{\Gamma}_{d-i}(c')$. Hence $d(x, c') = d - i$. $\square$

An *antipodal code* is a perfect code with radius $(d-1)/2$ in an antipodal scheme. Not every scheme which admits a perfect code with radius $(d-1)/2$ is antipodal. The Odd graph $\mathcal{O}_4$ is a counterexample.

THEOREM 6.3. *Let $\mathfrak{X} = (X, \{R_i\}_{0 \leq i \leq d})$ be an antipodal scheme with odd diameter d. Then every μ-fold PMC of $\mathfrak{X}$ with radius $(d-1)/2$ decomposes into μ antipodal codes.*

Proof. Suppose Y is a μ-fold PMC of $\mathfrak{X}$ with radius $e = (d-1)/2$. For $0 \leq i \leq e$, let w_i be the $(d+1)$-dimensional vector with i^{th} coordinate 1, $(d-i)^{\text{th}}$ coordinate k_d, and all other coordinates 0. Then by Proposition 6.2, w_i is the weight enumerator of an antipodal code. So for $0 \leq i \leq e$, $\overline{B}_e w_i = \vec{k}$ and thus $w_0 - w_i$ is in the nullspace of $\overline{B}_e$. Since this space has dimension $\leq e$ and the $w_0 - w_i$'s are linearly independent, the set $\{w_0 - w_i \mid i = 1, \ldots, e\}$ is a basis for the nullspace of $\overline{B}_e$.

Let $w_Y(x)$ be the weight enumerator of Y based at x. Then for some integers $\alpha_1, \ldots, \alpha_e$, we have

$$w_Y(x) = \mu w_0 + \sum_{i=1}^{e} \alpha_i(w_0 - w_i).$$

Each vector w_j has the property that its last coordinate is equal to k_d times its first coordinate. Hence $w_Y(x)$, a linear combination of the w_j's, also has this property. Choose $y \in Y$ and consider $w_Y(x)$ as x runs through the d-clique containing y. The last coordinate of any such $w_Y(x)$ is nonzero, so its first coordinate must also be nonzero. That is, if $y \in Y$, then the entire d-clique containing y is in Y. Hence Y decomposes into an antipodal code and a $(\mu - 1)$-fold PMC. Applying the same argument to this smaller PMC, we get that Y decomposes into μ antipodal codes. $\square$

We now give an example of a metric scheme $\mathfrak{X}$ which admits a perfect code of radius e yet has a μ-fold PMC with radius e which does not decompose into μ perfect codes. Consider the Hamming scheme $H(7,2)$ with $X = \mathsf{F}_2^7$. There exist perfect Hamming codes with radius 1 in $H(7,2)$. We will construct an indecomposable 3-fold PMC with radius 1.

Let $Y_1 = \{y \in \mathsf{F}_2^7 \mid Hy^{\mathrm{T}} = 0\}$, where

$$H = \begin{bmatrix} 0 & 0 & 0 & 1 & 1 & 1 & 1 \\ 0 & 1 & 1 & 0 & 0 & 1 & 1 \\ 1 & 0 & 1 & 0 & 1 & 0 & 1 \end{bmatrix}.$$

Then Y_1 is a perfect (Hamming) code with radius 1. The permutation group S_7 acts on X by permuting the 7 coordinates. For $\tau \in S_7$, let Y_τ be the image of Y_1 under the action of τ so that Y_τ is also a perfect code. It is easily seen that Y_1 is contained in $Y_{(12)} \cup Y_{(13)} \cup Y_{(14)} \cup Y_{(234)}$, the multiset union of these four perfect codes. Set

$$Y = Y_{(12)} \cup Y_{(13)} \cup Y_{(14)} \cup Y_{(234)} - Y_1.$$

Then Y is a 3-fold PMC of radius 1. To show that Y is indecomposable, we observe that the elements of weight 3 (i.e. elements having exactly 3 nonzero coordinates) in Y form a 2–$(7,3,3)$ design D consisting of the 21 blocks:

$$
\begin{array}{ccccccc}
[1\,2\,3] & [1\,3\,4] & [1\,4\,7] & [2\,3\,4] & [2\,4\,7] & [3\,4\,5] & [3\,6\,7] \\
[1\,2\,5] & [1\,3\,7] & [1\,5\,6] & [2\,3\,6] & [2\,5\,7] & [3\,5\,6] & [4\,5\,6] \\
[1\,2\,6] & [1\,4\,6] & [1\,5\,7] & [2\,4\,5] & [2\,6\,7] & [3\,5\,7] & [4\,6\,7]
\end{array}
$$

If the 3-fold PMC Y is decomposable then so is the design D. One easily checks that D is indecomposable using the fact that there are no indecomposable 2–$(7,3,2)$ designs. Therefore Y is an indecomposable 3-fold PMC of $H(7,2)$ with radius 1. (And D is an indecomposable 3-fold PMC with radius 1 in $\mathcal{O}_4$.) A similar construction can be used on binary Hamming codes with $d = 2^m - 1 > 7$. Hence we have an infinite family of indecomposable 3-fold PMCs with radius 1 in $H(2^m - 1, 2)$.

REFERENCES

[1] E. BANNAI AND T. ITO, *Algebraic Combinatorics I*, Benjamin/Cummings, Menlo Park, California, 1984.

[2] N. L. BIGGS, *Perfect Codes in graphs*, J. Combinatorial Theory, Ser. B, 15 (1973), pp. 289–296.

[3] ——————, *Perfect codes and distance-transitive graphs*, in *Combinatorics (V. C. Mavron and T. P. McDonough, eds.)*, L. M. S. Lecture Note Ser. 13, 1974, pp. 1–8.

[4] A. E. BROUWER, A. M. COHEN, AND A. NEUMAIER, *Distance Regular Graphs*, Springer-Verlag, New York, 1989.

[5] L. CHIHARA, *On the zeros of the Askey-Wilson polynomials, with applications to coding theory*, SIAM J. Math. Anal., 18 (1987), pp. 191–207.

[6] L. CHIHARA AND D. STANTON, *Zeros of generalized Krawtchouk polynomials*, J. Approx. Th. (to appear).

[7] R. CLAYTON, *Multiple packings and coverings in algebraic coding theory*, Ph.D. thesis, University of California, Los Angeles, 1987.

[8] P. DELSARTE, *An algebraic approach to the association schemes of coding theory*, Philips Research Reports Supplements no. 10, (1973).

[9] P. DIACONIS AND R. L. GRAHAM, *The Radon transform on $\mathbb{Z}_2^k$*, Pac. J. Math., 118 (1985), pp. 323–345.

[10] Y. HONG, *On the nonexistence of nontrivial perfect e-codes and tight 2e-designs in Hamming schemes $H(n,q)$ with $e \geq 3$ and $q \geq 3$*, Graphs and Combinatorics, 2 (1986), pp. 145–164.

[11] J. H. VAN LINT, *On the nonexistence of perfect 2- and 3-Hamming-error-correcting codes over $GF(q)$*, Info. and Control, 16 (1970), pp. 396–401.

[12] ——————, *Introduction to Coding Theory*, Springer-Verlag, New York, 1982.

[13] A. TIETÄVÄINEN, *On the nonexistence of perfect codes over finite fields*, SIAM J. Applied Math., 24 (1973), pp. 88–96.

NONLINEAR FEEDFORWARD SEQUENCES
OF m-SEQUENCES II

ZONGDUO DAI[1] XUNING FENG[2] MULAN LIU[3] AND ZHE-XIAN WAN[4]

Let

$$\alpha = (a_0, a_1, a_2, \dots)$$

be a given n-stage m-sequence over the binary field F_2, whose minimal polynomial will be denoted by $f(x)$. We know that $f(x)$ is primitive and of degree n. Denote $\underline{s}_i = (a_i, a_{i+1}, \dots, a_{i+n-1})$, $i \geq 0$ and call $\underline{s}_i$ the i-th state of the n-stage m-sequence α. Let

$$\phi = \sum_{i_1, i_2, \cdots, i_n = 0}^{1} a_{i_1 i_2 \cdots i_n}\, x_1^{i_1} x_2^{i_2} \cdots x_n^{i_n}, \quad a_{i_1 i_2 \cdots i_n} \in \mathsf{F}_2,$$

be a Boolean polynomial in n variables $x_1, \dots, x_n$ and of degree r. Obviously $r \leq n$. Regarding ϕ as a feedforward transformation, we obtain a feedforward sequence

$$\phi(\alpha) = (\phi(\underline{s}_0), \phi(\underline{s}_1), \phi(\underline{s}_2), \cdots)$$

Moreover, denote $\tilde{\underline{s}}_i = (a_i, a_{i+1}, \dots, a_{i+2^n-2})$, $i \geq 0$. Let ψ be any polynomial in $\mathsf{F}_2[x_0, x_1, \dots, x_{2^n-2}]$. We define

$$\psi(\alpha) = (\psi(\tilde{\underline{s}}_0), \psi(\tilde{\underline{s}}_1), \psi(\tilde{\underline{s}}_2), \dots).$$

We remarked in [1] that extending ϕ to ψ, we do not obtain new feedforward transformations in essence.

Two Boolean polynomials ϕ_1 and ϕ_2 are said to be equivalent, if they give the same feedforward sequence, i.e.

$$\phi_1(\alpha) = \phi_2(\alpha).$$

A Boolean polynomial in n variables and of degree r is said to be degenerate if it is equivalent to a Boolean polynomial in n variables and of degree less than r. In the present paper, we study the equivalence and nondegeneracy of feedforward monomial functions.

§1. Nondegeneracy of Feedforward Boolean Monomial Functions.

Let $l_1, l_2, \dots, l_r$ be r integers such that $0 \leq l_1 < l_2 < \cdots < l_r \leq 2^n - 2$. We say that the r positions $l_1, l_2, \dots, l_r$ are linearly independent, (or dependent), if the r states $\underline{s}_{l_1}, \dots, \underline{s}_{l_r}$ regarded as n-dimensional row vectors over F_2 are linearly independent (or dependent respectively). Clearly, this definition is independent of the initial states $\underline{s}_0$ chosen.

[1](Graduate School, Academia Sinica, Beijing, People's Republic of China)
[2](Institute of Mathematics, Academia Sinica, Beijing, People's Republic of China)
[3](Institute of Systems Science, Academia Sinica, Beijing, 100080, People's Republic of China)
[4](Institute of Systems Science, Academia Sinica, Beijing 100080, People's Republic of China)

LEMMA 1. *The linear relation*

$$(1) \qquad \sum_{i=1}^{r} d_i \underline{s}_{l_i} = 0, \qquad d_i \in \mathbf{F}_2$$

holds iff the congruence

$$(2) \qquad \sum_{i=1}^{r} d_i x^{l_i} \equiv 0 \qquad (\mathrm{mod}\ \tilde{f}(x))$$

holds, where $\tilde{f}(x)$ is the reciprocal polynomial of $f(x)$.

Proof. Let $f(x) = 1 + c_1 x + c_2 x^2 + \cdots + c_{n-1} x^{n-1} + x^n$ and put

$$T = \begin{pmatrix} 0 & & & & & 1 \\ 1 & 0 & & & & c_{n-1} \\ & 1 & \cdot & & & \cdot \\ & & \cdot & \cdot & & \cdot \\ & & & \cdot & 0 & c_2 \\ & & & & 1 & c_1 \end{pmatrix}$$

Then

$$\underline{s}_1 = \underline{s}_0 T,\ \underline{s}_2 = \underline{s}_0 T^2, \cdots, \underline{s}_i = \underline{s}_0 T^i, \cdots.$$

Thus (1) is equivalent to

$$(3) \qquad \sum_{i=1}^{r} d_i \underline{s}_0 T^{l_i} = \underline{s}_0 \sum_{i=1}^{r} d_i T^{l_i} = 0.$$

Since $\tilde{f}(x)$ is the minimal polynomial of T, (2) is equivalent to (3).

LEMMA 2. *Let $\underline{s}_{l_1}, \underline{s}_{l_2}, \cdots, \underline{s}_{l_r}$ be r states of the m-sequence α. Write*

$$\underline{s}_{l_i} = \sum_{j=0}^{n-1} m_{ij} \underline{s}_j, \quad i = 1, 2, \cdots, r$$

and put

$$M_{l_1 \cdots l_r} = (m_{ij})_{1 \leq i \leq r, 0 \leq j \leq n-1}$$

Then the r positions $l_1, \cdots, l_r$ are linearly independent iff rank $M_{l_1 \cdots l_r} = r$.

Proof. By hypothesis, we have

$$\begin{pmatrix} \underline{s}_{l_1} \\ \cdot \\ \cdot \\ \cdot \\ \underline{s}_{l_r} \end{pmatrix} = M_{l_1 \cdots l_r} \begin{pmatrix} \underline{s}_0 \\ \cdot \\ \cdot \\ \cdot \\ \underline{s}_{n-1} \end{pmatrix}$$

It is well-known [2] that the matrix

$$\begin{pmatrix} \underline{s}_0 \\ \cdot \\ \cdot \\ \cdot \\ \underline{s}_{n-1} \end{pmatrix}$$

is invertible, thus

$$\text{rank} \begin{pmatrix} \underline{s}_{l_1} \\ \cdot \\ \cdot \\ \cdot \\ \underline{s}_{l_r} \end{pmatrix} = \text{rank } M_{l_1\cdots l_r}.$$

Consequently, $\underline{s}_{l_1}, \cdots, \underline{s}_{l_r}$ are linearly independent, i.e. the r positions $l_1, \cdots, l_r$ are linearly independent, iff rank $M_{l_1\cdots l_r} = r$.

REMARK. The matrix $M_{l_1\cdots l_r}$ can be computed in the following manner.

Let

$$x^{l_i} \equiv \sum_{j=0}^{n-1} d_{ij}\, x^j \qquad (\text{mod } \tilde{f}(x)),$$

then

$$M_{l_1\cdots l_r} = (d_{ij})_{1\leq i\leq r, 0\leq j\leq n-1}$$

COROLLARY 1. *Assume that the r positions $l_1, l_2, \cdots, l_r$ are linearly independent. then among the r-tuples*

$$\{(a_{k+l_1}, a_{k+l_2}, \cdots, a_{k+l_r}) \mid 0 \leq k < 2^n - 1\},$$

each non-zero r-tuple appears 2^{n-r} times and the zero r-tuple $(0, 0, \cdots, 0)$ appears $2^{n-r} - 1$ times.

Proof. We may choose $n-r$ further positions $l_{r+1}, \cdots, l_n$ such that $l_1, l_2, \cdots, l_n$ are linearly independent. Then there exists an $n \times n$ invertible matrix M over $\mathbf{F}_2$ such that

(4)
$$\begin{pmatrix} \underline{s}_{l_1} \\ \underline{s}_{l_2} \\ \cdot \\ \cdot \\ \cdot \\ \underline{s}_{l_n} \end{pmatrix} = M \begin{pmatrix} \underline{s}_0 \\ \underline{s}_1 \\ \cdot \\ \cdot \\ \cdot \\ \underline{s}_{n-1} \end{pmatrix}$$

Since $\underline{s}_{i+k} = \underline{s}_i T^k$, we deduce immediately

$$\begin{pmatrix} \underline{s}_{l_1+k} \\ \underline{s}_{l_2+k} \\ \cdot \\ \cdot \\ \cdot \\ \underline{s}_{l_n+k} \end{pmatrix} = M \begin{pmatrix} \underline{s}_k \\ \underline{s}_{k+1} \\ \cdot \\ \cdot \\ \cdot \\ \underline{s}_{k+n-1} \end{pmatrix}$$

Thus

$$
(5) \qquad \begin{pmatrix} a_{l_1+k} \\ a_{l_2+k} \\ \cdot \\ \cdot \\ \cdot \\ a_{l_n+k} \end{pmatrix} = M \begin{pmatrix} a_k \\ a_{k+1} \\ \cdot \\ \cdot \\ \cdot \\ a_{k+n-1} \end{pmatrix}
$$

Denote by $V_n(\mathbf{F}_2)$ the n-dimensional row space over $\mathbf{F}_2$, then it is well-known [2] that

$$
\{(a_k, a_{k+1}, \cdots, a_{k+n-1}) \mid 0 \le k < 2^n - 1\} = V_n(\mathbf{F}_2)\backslash \underline{0},
$$

where $\underline{0}$ is the zero n-tuple. Thus

$$
\{(a_{k+l_1}, a_{k+l_2}, \cdots, a_{k+l_n}) \mid 0 \le k < 2^n - 1\} = V_n(\mathbf{F}_2)\backslash \underline{0}.
$$

from which the conclusion of the corollary follows immediately.

The following corollary is a generalization of Theorem 1 (ii) of [1].

COROLLARY 2. *Let* $l_1, l_2, \cdots, l_n$ *be* n *linearly independent positions. Set*

$$
B_1'(r) = \{x_{l_{i_1}} x_{l_{i_2}} \cdots x_{l_{i_j}}(\alpha) \mid 1 \le i_1 < \cdots < i_j \le n, 1 \le j \le r\},
$$

Then $B_1'(r)$ *is a basis of* $\mathcal{S}_r$, *where* $\mathcal{S}_r$ *is the vector space of all feedforward sequences obtained by feedforward transformations of degree* $\le r$.

Proof. In case $(l_1, l_2, \cdots, l_n) = (0, 1, \cdots, n-1)$, this corollary is Theorem 1 (ii) of [1]. Thus to prove this corollary it is sufficient to prove that any feedforward sequence obtained by a monic polynomial $x_{t_1} \cdots x_{t_r} (0 \le t_1 < t_2 < \cdots < t_r \le n)$ of degree r is a linear combination of feedforward sequences in $B_1'(r)$.

Define M by (4), and put

$$
M^{-1} = (\beta_{ij})_{0 \le i \le n-1, 1 \le j \le n}
$$

From (5), we deduce

$$
a_{k+i} = \sum_{j=1}^{n} \beta_{ij}\, a_{k+l_j} \qquad i = 0, 1, \cdots, n-1
$$

and then

$$
\prod_{\tau=1}^{r} a_{k+t_\tau} = \prod_{\tau=1}^{r} \sum_{j=1}^{n} \beta_{t_\tau j} a_{k+l_j}
$$

$$
= \sum_{j_1, \cdots, j_r = 1}^{n} \prod_{\tau=1}^{r} \beta_{t_\tau j_\tau} a_{k+l_{j_\tau}}
$$

Thus $x_{t_1} \cdots x_{t_r}(\alpha)$ is a linear combination of feedforward sequences in $B_1'(r)$.

Now we come to the main result of the present section.

THEOREM 1. *(i) The feedforward monomial $x_{l_1} x_{l_2} \cdots x_{l_r}$ of degree r is nondegenerate iff the r positions $l_1, l_2, \ldots, l_r$ are linearly independent.*

(ii) In case $x_{l_1} x_{l_2} \cdots x_{l_r}$ is nondegenerate, then in a period of length $2^n - 1$, the number of 1's in the feedforward sequences $x_{l_1} x_{l_2} \cdots x_{l_r}(\alpha)$ is 2^{n-r}.

(iii) In case $x_{l_1} x_{l_2} \cdots x_{l_r}$ is degenerate, assume $\underline{s}_{l_1}, \underline{s}_{l_2}, \cdots, \underline{s}_{l_s}$ is a maximal linearly independent set in $\underline{s}_{l_1}, \underline{s}_{l_2}, \cdots \underline{s}_{l_r}$. If among $\underline{s}_{l_{s+1}}, \cdots, \underline{s}_{l_r}$ there is a state which is the sum of an even number of states in $\underline{s}_{l_1}, \cdots \underline{s}_{l_s}$, then the feedforward sequence $x_{l_1} x_{l_2} \cdots x_{l_r}(\alpha)$ is the all-zero sequence. Otherwise, $x_{l_1} x_{l_2} \cdots x_{l_r}(\alpha) = x_{l_1} x_{l_2} \cdots x_{l_s}(\alpha)$.

Proof. (i) The "only if" part is trivial, and the "if" part is a consequence of Corollary 2 to Lemma 2,

(ii) This is a consequence of Corollary 1 to Lemma 2.

(iii) Suppose one of $\underline{s}_{l_{s+1}}, \cdots, \underline{s}_{l_r}$ is a sum of an even number of states in $\underline{s}_{l_1}, \cdots, \underline{s}_{l_s}$, then there is an odd number of states in $\underline{s}_{l_1} \cdots, \underline{s}_{l_r}$ whose sum is the zero state. Thus in each of the r-tuples

$$(6) \qquad (a_{l_1+k},\ a_{l_2+k}, \cdots, a_{l_r+k}),\quad 0 \le k < 2^n - 1,$$

the sum of their components of the corresponding positions is zero. Hence the all 1 r-tuple $(1, 1, \cdots, 1)$ cannot appear among the r-tuples (6). Consequently, $x_{l_1} x_{l_2} \cdots x_{l_r}(\alpha)$ is the zero sequence.

Now suppose that one of the states $\underline{s}_{l_{s+1}}, \cdots, \underline{s}_{l_r}$, say $\underline{s}_{l_r}$, is a sum of an odd number of the states from $\underline{s}_{l_1}, \cdots, \underline{s}_{l_s}$. It can be proved that $x_{l_1} x_{l_2} \ldots x_{l_r}(\alpha) = x_{l_1} x_{l_2} \cdots x_{l_{r-1}}(\alpha)$. In fact, it is sufficient to prove that $(a_{l_1+k}, \cdots, a_{l_r+k}) = (1, \cdots, 1)$ iff $(a_{l_1+k}, \cdots, a_{l_r-1+k}) = (1, \cdots, 1)$. The "only if" part is obvious. For the "if" part, since $\underline{s}_{l_r}$ is an odd number of states from $\underline{s}_{l_1}, \cdots, \underline{s}_{l_s}, a_{l_r+k}$ is the sum of the corresponding components, which are all 1, we have necessarily $a_{l_r+k} = 1$. Then the second statement of (iii) follows immediately.

§2. Equivalence of Feedforward Boolean Monomial Functions.

THEOREM 2. *(i) Two feedforward nondegenerate monomial functions $x_{l_1} x_{l_2} \ldots x_{l_r}$ and $x_{l'_1} x_{l'_2} \cdots x_{l'_r}$ $(0 \le l_1, l_2, \cdots, l_r, l'_1 \cdots, l'_r < 2^n - 1)$ of degree r are equivalent iff there exists an $r \times r$ invertible matrix Q over $\mathbf{F}_2$ with odd weight rows (i.e. the number of 1's in each row is odd) such that*

$$(7) \qquad \begin{pmatrix} \underline{s}_{l'_1} \\ \underline{s}_{l'_2} \\ \cdot \\ \cdot \\ \cdot \\ \underline{s}_{l'_r} \end{pmatrix} = Q \begin{pmatrix} \underline{s}_{l_1} \\ \underline{s}_{l_2} \\ \cdot \\ \cdot \\ \cdot \\ \underline{s}_{l_r} \end{pmatrix}$$

(ii) Let E_r be the number of feedforward nondegenerate monomial functions in r variables chosen from $x_0, x_1, \cdots, x_{2^n-2}$ equivalent to a given one. Then

$$(8) \qquad E_r = \frac{2^{\frac{r(r-1)}{2}} \prod_{i=1}^{r-1} (2^i - 1)}{r!}$$

Proof. (i) We prove the "only if" part first. Suppose

$$(9) \qquad x_{l_1} x_{l_2} \ldots x_{l_r}(\alpha) = x_{l'_1} x_{l'_2} \cdots x_{l'_r}(\alpha)$$

We are going to prove each $\underline{s}_{l'_i} (1 \le i \le r)$ is a linear combination of $\underline{s}_{l_1}, \cdots, \underline{s}_{l_r}$. Suppose $\underline{s}_{l'_i}$ is not a linear combination of $\underline{s}_{l_1}, \cdots, \underline{s}_{l_r}$, then $(1'_i, l_1 \cdots, l_r)$ are $r+1$ linearly independent positions. By Corollary 1 to Lemma 2, there is a k_0 such that

$$(a_{k_0+l'_i}, a_{k_0+l_1}, \cdots, a_{k_0+l_r}) = (0, 1, \ldots, 1).$$

Then

$$x_{l_1} x_{l_2} \cdots x_{l_r}(\underline{s}_{k_0}) = 1, \quad x_{l'_1} x_{l'_2} \cdots x_{l'_r}(\underline{s}_{k_0}) = 0,$$

which contradicts (9).

Therefore there is an $r \times r$ matrix Q such that (7) holds. Since $l'_1, \cdots, l'_r$ are linearly independent positions, Q is invertible.

Furthermore, we have to prove that the row weight is odd for each row of Q. Suppose this is not true. Without loss of generality we may assume that the weight of the first row of Q is even. Let k_0 be such that

$$(a_{k_0+l_1}, a_{k_0+l_2}, \cdots, a_{k_0+l_r}) = (1, 1, \ldots, 1),$$

then $a_{k_0+l'_1} = 0$. Thus

$$x_{l_1} x_{l_2} \cdots x_{l_r}(\underline{s}_{k_0}) = 1, \quad x_{l'_1} x_{l'_2} \cdots x_{l'_r}(\underline{s}_{k_0}) = 0,$$

which contradicts (9).

Let us come to the "if" part now. Suppose Q is an $r \times r$ invertible matrix with odd weight rows such that (7) holds. Then for some k

$$(a_{k+l_1}, a_{k+l_2}, \cdots, a_{k+l_r}) = (1, 1, \ldots, 1)$$

iff

$$(a_{k+l'_1}, a_{k+l'_2}, \cdots, a_{k+l'_r}) = (1, 1, \ldots, 1)$$

Thus

$$x_{l_1} x_{l_2} \cdots x_{l_r}(\underline{s}_k) = 1 \quad \text{iff} \quad x_{l'_1} x_{l'_2} \cdots x_{l'_r}(\underline{s}_k) = 1.$$

But by Corollary 1 to Lemma 2, the number of $1's$ in the feedforward sequences

$$x_{l_1} x_{l_2} \cdots x_{l_r}(\alpha) \quad \text{and} \quad x_{l'_1} x_{l'_2} \cdots x_{l'_r}(a)$$

given by nondegenerate Boolean monomials $x_{l_1} x_{l_2} \cdots x_{l_r}$ and $x_{l'_1} x_{l'_2} \cdots x_{l'_r}$ of degree r are all equal to 2^{n-r}. It follows that

$$x_{l_1} x_{l_2} \cdots x_{l_r}(\underline{s}_k) = 0 \quad \text{iff} \quad x_{l'_1} x_{l'_2} \cdots x_{l'_r}(\underline{s}_k) = 0.$$

Therefore

$$x_{l_1} x_{l_2} \cdots x_{l_r}(\alpha) = x_{l'_1} x_{l'_2} \cdots x_{l'_r}(\alpha).$$

(ii) Let Q_1 and Q_2 be $r \times r$ invertible matrices with odd weight rows.
Put

$$\begin{pmatrix} \underline{s}_{l'_1} \\ \underline{s}_{l'_2} \\ \cdot \\ \cdot \\ \cdot \\ \underline{s}_{l'_r} \end{pmatrix} = Q_1 \begin{pmatrix} \underline{s}_{l_1} \\ \underline{s}_{l_2} \\ \cdot \\ \cdot \\ \cdot \\ \underline{s}_{l_r} \end{pmatrix}, \quad \begin{pmatrix} \underline{s}_{l''_1} \\ \underline{s}_{l''_2} \\ \cdot \\ \cdot \\ \cdot \\ \underline{s}_{l''_r} \end{pmatrix} = Q_2 \begin{pmatrix} \underline{s}_{l_1} \\ \underline{s}_{l_2} \\ \cdot \\ \cdot \\ \cdot \\ \underline{s}_{l_r} \end{pmatrix}$$

Clearly, $x_{l'_1} x_{l'_2} \cdots x_{l'_r} = x_{l''_1} \cdots x_{l''_r}$ iff there is a permutation matrix P such that $Q_2 = PQ_1$. Therefore E_r is equal to the number of $r \times r$ invertible matrices over $\mathbf{F}_2$ with odd weight rows divided by $r!$.

We need the following lemma.

LEMMA 3. *Let V be a subspace of $V_n(\mathbf{F}_2)$. If V has a vector of odd weight, then the number of vectors of odd weight in V is equal to the number of vectors of even weight in V.*

Proof. Let $\underline{v}$ be a vector of odd weight in V and let V_e be the subspace formed by all even weight vectors in V. Then the vectors in the coset $V_e + \underline{v}$ are all of odd weight and V is decomposed into the disjoint union of cosets V_e and $V_e + \underline{v}$. Lemma 3 follows immediately.

Now let us enumerate the number of $r \times r$ invertible matrices with odd weight rows. We may choose any row vector of odd weight to be the first row of an $r \times r$ invertible matrix with odd weight rows; by Lemma 3 there are 2^{r-1} choices. Once the first row is chosen, we may choose the second row to be any row vector of odd weight different from the first row; there are $2^{r-1} - 1$ choices. Once the first two rows are chosen, we may choose the third row to be any row vector of odd weight but not contained in the linear span of the first two rows; again by Lemma 3 there are $2^{r-1} - 2$ choices. Proceeding in this way, we obtain finally that the number of $r \times r$ invertible matrices with odd weight rows is equal to

$$2^{r-1} \prod_{i=0}^{r-2} (2^{r-1} - 2^i) = 2^{\frac{r(r-1)}{2}} \prod_{i=1}^{r-1} (2^i - 1)$$

Dividing this number by $r!$, we obtain the expression (8) for E_r.

REFERENCES

[1] DAI, Z., FENG, X., LIU, M. AND WAN, Z., *Nonlinear feedforward sequences of m-sequences*, Proc. of 1988 Beijing International Workshop on Information Theory, July 4–7 (1988), A–2.1–A–2.8.

[2] ZIERLER, N., *Linear recurring sequences*, J. Soc. Indust. Appl. Math., 7 (1959) 31–48.

LOOPS OF CLUTTERS*.

MICHEL MARIE DEZA† AND KOMEI FUKUDA‡

Abstract. For a clutter $\mathcal{C}$ on a finite set E, let $f(\mathcal{C})$ be the clutter of maximal subsets of E not containing any member of $\mathcal{C}$. The *loop* $L(\mathcal{C})$ of a clutter $\mathcal{C}$ is the finite sequence of clutters $\mathcal{C}, f(\mathcal{C}), f^2(\mathcal{C}), \ldots, f^t(\mathcal{C})$, where t (the *length* of the loop) is the minimum positive integer with $f^t(\mathcal{C}) = \mathcal{C}$. Our motivation of the study of the loop lies on the fact that when $\mathcal{C}$ is the set of circuits of a matroid, the loop contains other critical information associated with the matroid, e.g., the set of bases $f(\mathcal{C})$ and the set of hyperplanes $f^2(\mathcal{C})$. We investigate various properties of the loops, in particular, the possible lengths for fixed $|E|$, the dualities and the symmetries. Our preliminary investigations indicate that there are many interesting problems on the loops whose resolution may provide us with a new insight into Sperner Theory, Matroid Theory and Extremal Set Theory.

1. Introduction. Let E be a finite set of n elements. A *clutter* or *Sperner family* on E is a family of noncomparable subsets of E, i.e.,

$$C, C' \in \mathcal{C} \quad \text{and} \quad C \neq C' \Rightarrow \quad C \nsubseteq C'.$$

For any clutter $\mathcal{C}$, let $f(\mathcal{C})$ be the clutter of all maximal subsets of E containing no member of $\mathcal{C}$. The operator f is much used in matroid theory: f is the operator to obtain the family of bases from the family of circuits of a matroid, and f is the operator to obtain the family of hyperplanes from the family of bases. The importance of this operator often relies on the fact that it has an inverse. For any clutter $\mathcal{C}$, the inverse $f^{-1}(\mathcal{C})$ is simply the family of all minimal subsets of E contained in no member of C. By virtue of this fact one can define matroids in terms of circuits, bases or hyperplanes, or even their complementary sets cohyperplanes, cobases or cocircuits.

In this paper we study the operator f from the following point of view. For any given $\mathcal{C}$, we consider the sequence

$$\mathcal{C},\ f(\mathcal{C}), f^2(\mathcal{C}),\ f^3(\mathcal{C}), \ldots$$

Because f has an inverse and there are finitely many clutters on E, this sequence must come back to the original clutter $\mathcal{C}$ to form the loop:

$$L = L(\mathcal{C}) = \mathcal{C}_0, \mathcal{C}_1, \mathcal{C}_2, \ldots, \mathcal{C}_{t-1},\ \mathcal{C}_t = \mathcal{C},$$

where $C_i = f^i(\mathcal{C})$ and $t = t(L) > 1$ is the smallest number with $f^t(\mathcal{C}) = \mathcal{C}$, called the *length* of L. Whenever we do not have to specify the first clutter (that is almost always the case in the present paper), we consider the loop L as a cyclically ordered

---

*This work was partially supported by C.N.R.S. (France)/ J.S.P.S. (Japan) joint research program

†17, Passage de L' Industrie 75010 Paris, France

‡Department of Information Sciences, Tokyo Institute of Technology, Oh–okayama, Meguro–ku, Tokyo, Japan

set $\{\mathcal{C}_0, \mathcal{C}_1, \mathcal{C}_2, \ldots, \mathcal{C}_{t-1}\}$. So the cardinality $|L|$ of L is its length $t(L)$, and the equality $L = L'$ will be used to mean that the loops L and L' are equal as cyclically ordered sets.

If $\mathcal{C}$ is the family of circuits of a matroid (or a graph), $\mathcal{C}_1$ is the family of bases (spanning trees) and $\mathcal{C}_2$ is the family of hyperplanes (complements of minimal cutsets). The families $\mathcal{C}_3, \mathcal{C}_4, \ldots, \mathcal{C}_{t-1}$ have never been studied in spite of the fact that they have exactly the same information as the circuits, the bases and the hyperplanes.

The realizable lengths of loops have been studied by Duchet [Du], Brouwer and Shrijver [B-So], and Brouwer [B]. Some related research considering similar loops or operators are [E–Fu], [S], [V].

The main purpose of the present paper is to study two fundamental problems on loops of clutters:

Problem A. For fixed n, (or more generally, a given class of clutters), determine the realizable lengths of loops, in particular the minimum and maximum length.

Problem B. For a given operator h (different from f) associating a clutter to some clutter, find the relationship between $L(\mathcal{C})$ and $L(h(\mathcal{C}))$.

Problem A was first investigated by Duchet [Du] for the particular case of length 2, and more generally by Brouwer and Shrijver [B-Sc]. By an exhaustive search one can easily check that the set of realizable lengths of loops is $\{3\}$ for $n = 1$, $\{2,4\}$ for $n = 2$, $\{5\}$ for $n = 3$, $\{2, 3, 6\}$ for $n = 4$. It was shown in [B-Sc] that the set of realizable lengths for $n = 5$ is $\{2, 3, 7, 16, 27\}$. On the other hand, in general, one can easily verify that the length $n + 2$ is always realizable for any n (e.g., the loop of the clutter $\{E\}$), and that the minimum length is greater than 1. Duchet [Du] proved that for every even n, there always exists a loop of length 2. Separately, Brouwer [B] proved that a loop of length 2 exists for every $n \neq 1$, 3. This settled the problem of determining the minimum lengths for each n. The maximum length appears to be difficult to determine. By computer experiments, we found that the maximum length is at least 1032 for $n = 6$ and 3791 for $n = 7$.

For Problem B, we investigate essentially two choices of h. The first one is the duality operator $^{-}$:

$$\overline{\mathcal{C}} = \{\overline{C} : C \in \mathcal{C}\},$$

where $\overline{C} = E \backslash C$. It turns out that $L(\mathcal{C})$ and $L(\overline{\mathcal{C}})$ have the same length t, and there is a natural one-to-one correspondence between $L(\mathcal{C})$ and $L(\overline{\mathcal{C}})$:

$$\overline{\mathcal{C}}_i = \mathcal{D}_{t-i} \quad \text{for all } i,$$

where $\mathcal{D} = \overline{\mathcal{C}}$. The implication is obvious: the dual loop is obtained from the original loop $L(\mathcal{C})$ by taking the dual of each clutter $\mathcal{C}_i$ and reversing the order. Consequently, for any loop L, the loop $L(\overline{\mathcal{C}})$ does not depend on the choice of $\mathcal{C} \in L$, and hence there is a uniquely defined loop, the *dual* loop $\overline{L}$ of L. Clearly the dual pair $L, \overline{L}$ of loops have the same sum of sizes of clutters:

$$\|L\| = \|\overline{L}\|$$

where $\|L\| = \Sigma\{|\mathcal{C}| : \mathcal{C} \in L\}$. It should be noted that for the "blocker" operator $b = \overline{f}$ (see Section 2 for definition), $L(\overline{\mathcal{C}}) = L(b(\mathcal{C}))$.

The second operator is what we call the reflection operator. This operator associates each k-uniform clutter with another k-uniform clutter:

$$\widetilde{\mathcal{C}} = \{D \subseteq E : |D| = k \quad \text{and} \quad D \notin \mathcal{C}\}.$$

Like the duality operator, this operator is idempotent: $\widetilde{\widetilde{\mathcal{C}}} = \mathcal{C}$. However the analysis of the relationship between $L(\mathcal{C})$ and $L(\widetilde{\mathcal{C}})$ appears to be much more difficult. For all of the uniform clutters $\mathcal{C}$ we investigated, the following surprising properties hold:

(1.1) $\qquad$ (a) $\quad$ for any uniform clutter $\mathcal{D}$,
$$D \in L(\mathcal{C}) \quad \text{iff} \quad \widetilde{D} \in L(\widetilde{\mathcal{C}});$$
$\qquad\qquad\qquad (b)$ $\quad L(\mathcal{C})$ $\quad$ and $L(\widetilde{\mathcal{C}})$ have the same length;
$\qquad\qquad\qquad (c)$ $\quad \|L(\mathcal{C})\| = \|L(\widetilde{\mathcal{C}})\|$.

We conjecture that these properties hold for every uniform clutter $\mathcal{C}$ (the *reflection conjecture*). The property (a) is important because this implies that the pair $L(\mathcal{C})$ and $L(\widetilde{\mathcal{C}})$ do not depend on the choice of $\mathcal{C}$: for any loop L containing a uniform clutter, there exists a unique loop $\widetilde{L}$, the *reflection* loop, satisfying $\widetilde{L} = L(\widetilde{\mathcal{D}})$ for all uniform clutters $\mathcal{D} \in L$. It should be remarked that the properties (b) and (c) seem to come from some nontrivial reasons, since the reflection pair L and $\widetilde{L}$ can have very different characteristics. For example, the distributions of clutter sizes $(|\mathcal{D}| : \mathcal{D} \in L)$ and $(|\mathcal{D}| : \mathcal{D} \in \widetilde{L})$ can be completely different. In this paper we prove this conjecture for many special classes of clutters and, in particular, for all singleton clutters $\{F\}, F \subseteq E$.

Finally, we investigate "symmetry" of loops. The notion of symmetry comes from our observation that many loops L satisfy some of the following strong properties:

(1.2) $\qquad$ (a) L $\quad$ is self-dual : $\quad L = \overline{L}$;
$\qquad\qquad\qquad (b)$ L $\quad$ is self-reflective : $\quad L = \widetilde{L}$;
$\qquad\qquad\qquad (c)$ L $\quad$ is self-dual-reflective : $\quad \widetilde{L} = \overline{L}$;

or, more generally,

(1.3) $\qquad$ (a) L $\quad$ p-self-dual : $\quad L = \overline{L}^p$;
$\qquad\qquad\qquad (b)$ L $\quad$ p-self-reflective : $\quad L = \widetilde{L}^p$;
$\qquad\qquad\qquad (c)$ L $\quad$ p-self-dual-reflective : $\quad \widetilde{L} = \overline{L}^p$;

for some permutation p of E (where L^p is the image of L under the action of the permutation p). We will show how these properties restrict certain structural properties of loops. For instance, having either the $(p-)$ self-reflection or the $(p-)$

self-dual-reflection immediately implies that the loop satisfies the reflection conjecture (1.1).

Finally, we conjecture that for a fixed n the average size of clutter $\|L\| \, / \, |L|$ in any loop L is at least $2^n/(n+2)$, which is attained by the *complete uniform loop* $L(\{E\})$. Also, we conjecture that the average size is at most $\binom{n}{\lfloor \frac{n}{2} \rfloor} /2$ for all $n \geq 4$, which is attained by the Brouwer-Duchet loop of length 2. These conjectures are true for all classes of loops for which we could derive an explicit expression of the average size and for many randomly generated loops on few elements. If these conjectures are true, then these expressions provide us with a lower bound and an upper bound of the (universal) average size of clutters on E, which are trivially computable.

For readers unfamiliar with Matroid Theory or Sperner Theory, good references are [W], and [En–G], [G–K].

2. Clutter Operators. Let E be a finite set of cardinality n. For any set $\mathcal{D}$ of subsets of E, let $\min(\mathcal{D})$ and $\max(\mathcal{D})$ denote the family of minimal and maximal sets in $\mathcal{D}$, respectively. For any clutter $\mathcal{C}$ on E, let

$$f(\mathcal{C}) = \max\{D \subseteq E : C \nsubseteq D \quad \text{for all} \quad C \in \mathcal{C}\},$$
$$g(\mathcal{C}) = \min\{D \subseteq E : C \nsubseteq D \quad \text{for all} \quad C \in \mathcal{C}\}.$$

The first result is very elementary but important.

LEMMA 2.1 ([D-F1]). *g is the inverse of f.*

Proof. We will show $g(f(\mathcal{C})) = \mathcal{C}$. If $C \in \mathcal{C}$ then there exists $C' \in g(f(\mathcal{C}))$ with $C' \subseteq C$ by the definition of f and g. Next we take any $C' \in g(f(\mathcal{C}))$. Suppose $C \nsubseteq C'$ for all $C \in \mathcal{C}$. Then, by the definition of f, there exists $D \in f(\mathcal{C})$ such that $C' \subseteq D$, contradicting $C' \in g(f(C))$. Thus there exists $C \in \mathcal{C}$ with $C \subseteq C'$. Since $g(f(\mathcal{C})$ and $\mathcal{C}$ are clutters, they are equal. $\square$

We introduce two operators of clutters closely related to f and g. For a clutter $\mathcal{C}$, let

$$a(\mathcal{C}) = \max\{D \subseteq E : \quad D \cup C \neq E \quad \text{for all} \quad C \in \mathcal{C}\},$$
$$b(\mathcal{C}) = \min\{D \subseteq E : \quad D \cap C \neq \phi \quad \text{for all} \quad C \in \mathcal{C}\}.$$

Note that the operator b is often called the *blocker* operator. Also, define

$$\overline{\mathcal{C}} = \{\overline{C} : C \in \mathcal{C}\},$$

which is the clutter of complements $\overline{C} = E \backslash C$. Clearly, we have

$$(2.1) \qquad\qquad a(\mathcal{C}) = \overline{g}(\mathcal{C}) \quad \text{and} \quad b(\mathcal{C}) = \overline{f}(\mathcal{C}).$$

More interesting relationships can be obtained by using the well-known equality

LEMMA 2.2 ([E–Fu]). $b^2(\mathcal{C}) = \mathcal{C}$.

LEMMA 2.3.

(a) $\overline{f}(\mathcal{C}) = g(\overline{\mathcal{C}})$;

(b) $a(\mathcal{C}) = f(\overline{\mathcal{C}})$;

(c) $b(\mathcal{C}) = g(\overline{\mathcal{C}})$.

Proof. Using Lemma 2.2 and (2.1), we have $f(\overline{f}(\mathcal{C})) = \overline{\mathcal{C}}$. Applying f^{-1} to both sides, we obtain (a) $\overline{f}(\mathcal{C}) = g(\overline{\mathcal{C}})$. The equalities (b) and (c) immediately follow from (2.1) and (a). $\square$

COROLLARY 2.4. $a^2(\mathcal{C}) = \mathcal{C}$.

Proof. Using Lemma 2.3(b) and Lemma 2.2, $a(a(\mathcal{C})) = a(f(\overline{\mathcal{C}}))f(\overline{f}(\overline{\mathcal{C}})) = \mathcal{C}$. $\square$

The following diagram shows the relations among the five operators $f, g, a, b, ^-$. Observe that in the diagram there are two loops, the loop $L = L(\mathcal{C})$ of $\mathcal{C}$ and the *dual* loop $\overline{L} = L(\overline{\mathcal{C}})$, and the operators a, b and $^-$ send a clutter in one loop to another in the other (its dual) loop while f and $g = f^{-1}$ send a clutter to another in the same loop.

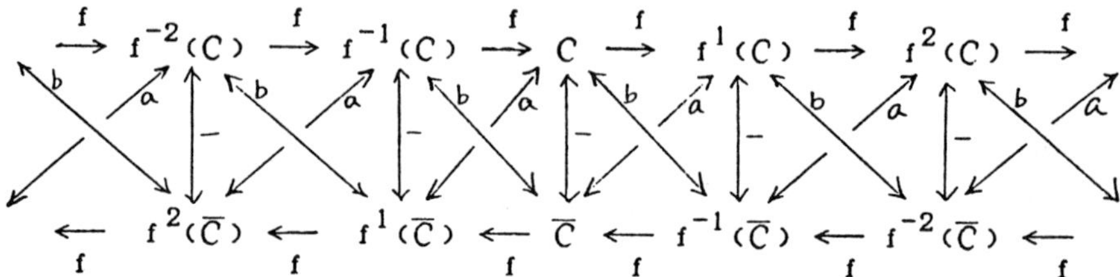

One can easily show:

PROPOSITION 2.5. *Let $\mathcal{C}$ be a clutter on E, and let $L = L(\mathcal{C})$ and $\overline{L} = L(\overline{\mathcal{C}})$. Then*

(a) L *and* $\overline{L}$ *have the same length;*

(b) $\mathcal{C}_i = \overline{\mathcal{D}}_{t-i}$ *for all i, where $\mathcal{D} = \overline{\mathcal{C}}$;*

(c) L *and* $\overline{L}$ *have the same sum of sizes:* $\|L\| = \|\overline{L}\|$.

A clutter is called *maximal* if it is not extendable to a larger clutter, i.e., for each $D \subseteq E$ there is $C \in \mathcal{C}$ such that either $D \subseteq C$ or $C \subseteq D$. Let

$$f'(\mathcal{C}) = \{D \in f(\mathcal{C}) : D \nsubseteq C \quad \text{for all} \quad C \in \mathcal{C}\}$$
$$f''(\mathcal{C}) = \{D \in f(\mathcal{C}) : D \subseteq C \quad \text{for some} \quad C \in \mathcal{C}\}$$
$$g'(\mathcal{C}) = \{D \in g(\mathcal{C}) : D \nsubseteq C \quad \text{for all} \quad C \in \mathcal{C}\}$$
$$g''(\mathcal{C}) = \{D \in g(\mathcal{C}) : D \subseteq C \quad \text{for some} \quad C \in \mathcal{C}\}.$$

Thus, $f(\mathcal{C}) = f'(\mathcal{C}) \cup f''(\mathcal{C})$ and $g(\mathcal{C}) = g'(\mathcal{C}) \cup g''(\mathcal{C})$. Actually, $f''(\mathcal{C})$ consists of sets of form $C \backslash \{a\}$ where $a \in C \in \mathcal{C}$. Clearly,

LEMMA 2.6. $\mathcal{C} \cup f'(\mathcal{C})$ and $\mathcal{C} \cup g'(\mathcal{C})$ are maximal clutters.

Using Lemma 2.3, we can easily show

LEMMA 2.7.

(a) $\overline{f}'(\mathcal{C}) = g'(\overline{\mathcal{C}})$;

(b) $\overline{f}''(\mathcal{C}) = g''(\overline{\mathcal{C}})$.

PROPOSITION 2.8. *The following statements are equivalent:*

$$
\begin{array}{ll}
(a)\ \mathcal{C} \text{ maximal}; & (d)\ \overline{\mathcal{C}} \text{ is maximal}; \\
(b)\ f'(\mathcal{C}) = \emptyset; & (e)\ f'(\overline{\mathcal{C}}) = \emptyset; \\
(c)\ g'(\mathcal{C}) = \emptyset; & (f)\ g'(\overline{\mathcal{C}}) = \emptyset.
\end{array}
$$

Proof. Since (a) and (d) are clearly equivalent, by Lemma 2.7, it is left to show the equivalence of (a) and (b). Assume (a) and take any $D \in f(\mathcal{C})$. Since $\mathcal{C}$ is maximal, there is $C \in \mathcal{C}$ such that either $D \subseteq C$ or $C \subseteq D$, but the latter cannot hold, because $D \in f(\mathcal{C})$. Thus $D \in f''(\mathcal{C})$, and (b) holds. Now suppose $\mathcal{C}$ is not maximal. Then there is $D \subseteq E$ such that $\mathcal{C} \cup \{D\}$ is a clutter. It follows that there is $D' \supseteq D$ such that $D' \in f(\mathcal{C})$. Clearly $D' \in f'(\mathcal{C})$ and (b) is false. $\square$

It should be noted that an analog of Proposition 2.8 for f'', g'' does not hold: $f''(\overline{\mathcal{C}}) = \emptyset$ is equivalent to $g''(\overline{\mathcal{C}}) = \emptyset$ but not equivalent to $f''(\overline{\mathcal{C}}) = \emptyset$ (i.e., $\mathcal{C} \cup f(\mathcal{C})$ and $\mathcal{C} \cup f(\mathcal{C})$ and $\mathcal{C} \cup g(\mathcal{C})$ do not necessarily form clutters simultaneously).

3. Theorem of Alternatives on Loops. Edmonds and Fulkerson [E–F] observed that the following alternative property holds for clutters:

PROPOSITION 3.1. *Let $\mathcal{C}$ be a clutter on E. Then for any $F \subseteq E$, exactly one of the following alternatives holds:*

(a) $\quad \exists\, A \in \mathcal{C}$ such that $A \subseteq F$;

(b) $\quad \exists\, B \in f(\mathcal{C})$ such that $F \subseteq B$.

Proof. Immediate from the definition of f. $\square$

Recall that $\mathcal{C}_j = f^j(\mathcal{C})$ for any clutter $\mathcal{C}$ and each j.

PROPOSITION 3.2. *Let $\mathcal{C}$ be a clutter on E. Fix indices i, j with $i < j$, and $F \subseteq E$. Then if $F \notin \mathcal{C}_k$ for $k = i+1, \ldots, j-1$ then at least one of the following alternative holds:*

(a_i) $\quad \exists\, A \in \mathcal{C}_j$ such that $A \subseteq F$;

(b_j) $\quad \exists\, B \in \mathcal{C}_j$ such that $F \subseteq B$.

Proof. By Proposition 3.1, we know that one of the statements always holds:

(a_{k-1}) $\exists\, A \in \mathcal{C}_{k-1}$ such that $A \subseteq F$;

(b_k) $\exists\, B \in \mathcal{C}_k$ such that $F \subseteq B$.

Similarly, one of the following statements holds:

(a_k) $\exists\, A \in \mathcal{C}_k$ such that $A \subseteq F$;

(b_{k+1}) $\exists\, B \in \mathcal{C}_{k+1}$ such that $F \subseteq B$.

Since $\mathcal{C}_k$ is a clutter, both (b_k) and (a_k) hold iff $F \in \mathcal{C}_k$. So if $F \notin \mathcal{C}_k$ then at least one of (a_{k-1}) and (b_{k+1}) hold. By inductive argument the result follows. $\square$

Proposition 3.2 has some interesting corollaries. For instance, if we set $j = t + i$ (i.e., $\mathcal{C}_j = \mathcal{C}_i$), where t is the length of the loop $L(\mathcal{C})$, then we immediately obtain:

COROLLARY 3.3. *Let $\mathcal{C}$ be a clutter on E and let $F \subseteq E$. If F is comparable with no member of $\mathcal{C}$ then $F \in \mathcal{C}_j$ for some j.*

The next two corollaries follow naturally.

COROLLARY 3.4. *Let $\mathcal{C}$ be a k-uniform clutter on E. Then every k-subset of E appears (in some clutter) in the loop $L(\mathcal{C})$.*

COROLLARY 3.5. *Every r-subset of E appears in the loop of any matroid of rank r.*

Corollary 3.3 gives a sufficient condition for a subset of E to appear in the loop $L(\mathcal{C})$. It is easy to see that this is not a necessary condition. However, we have:

PROPOSITION 3.6. *Let $\mathcal{C}$ be a clutter on E. Then a subset F of E is a member of $\mathcal{C}_k$ for some k if and only if there exists j such that no member of $\mathcal{C}_j$ is comparable with F.*

Proof. It is enough to show the "only if" part. Without loss of generality we may assume $F \in \mathcal{C}_0$. Suppose that for each j there exists some member of $\mathcal{C}_j$ which is comparable with F. This implies that there is $C \in \mathcal{C}_1$ such that $C \subseteq F$. So there is $C' \in \mathcal{C}_2$ such that $C' \subseteq F$, and so on. Consequently some $C'' \in \mathcal{C}_{t-1}$ must be contained in F, contradicting the assumption. $\square$

4. Group of Permutations Preserving a Clutter. For a given clutter $\mathcal{C}$ on E, define $G = G(\mathcal{C}) = \mathrm{Aut}\ \mathcal{C}$, the group of all permutations of E preserving $\mathcal{C}$.

Obviously, we have $G(\mathcal{C}) = G(\overline{\mathcal{C}})$. The following is less trivial.

LEMMA 4.1. $G(\mathcal{C}) = G(f(\mathcal{C}))$.

Proof. Since the clutters $f^i(\mathcal{C})$ form a loop, it is enough to show $G(f(\mathcal{C})) \supseteq G(\mathcal{C})$. We must show that $g(b) \in f(\mathcal{C})$ for any fixed $b \in f(\mathcal{C})$ and $g \in G \backslash \{1\}$ where $G = G(\mathcal{C})$. In fact, otherwise, we must have either (i) $g(b) \supseteq a$ for some $a \in \mathcal{C}$

(impossible since then $b \supseteq g^{-1}(a) \in \mathcal{C}$) or (ii) $g(b) \subsetneq b'$ for some $b' \in f(\mathcal{C})$. We prove the impossibility of case (ii) by induction for decreasing $|b|$. For maximal $|b|$, say m, it is impossible since $|b'| \leq |b|$. For $|b| = m - 1$ (if any), $g(b) \subsetneq b'$ would imply $b \subsetneq g^{-1}(b')$, contradicting $f(\mathcal{C})$ being a clutter, for $g^{-1}(b') \in f(\mathcal{C})$ by induction. $\square$

COROLLARY 4.2. $G(\mathcal{C}) = G(g(\mathcal{C})) = G(a(\mathcal{C})) = G(b(\mathcal{C}))$.

Proof. Follows from Lemmas 2.3, 4.1 and the equality $G(\mathcal{C}) = G(\overline{\mathcal{C}})$. $\square$

Lemma 4.1 implies that every clutter in a loop has the same group G. But it is possible to have different loop with the same G. For example, $\mathcal{C}$ and $\overline{\mathcal{C}}$ may produce different loops, but $G(\mathcal{C}) = G(\overline{\mathcal{C}})$. Other examples will be given in the next section (Example 5.3).

We denote by S_E the group all permutations of E. For a subgroup G of $S_{E'}$ a clutter $\mathcal{C}$ is called *G-clutter* if $G(\mathcal{C}) = G$, and the loop L associated with G-clutter is called a *G-loop*.

It is not difficult to see that there are some subgroups G not admitting a G-clutter. For example, for $E = \{1, 2, 3\}$, the trivial group $G = \langle 1 \rangle$ does not admit a G-clutter (i.e., every clutter on E is preserved by some nontrivial permutation).

Problem 4.3. Characterize subgroups $G \leq S_E$ admitting a G-clutter.

More general treatment of automorphism groups and of symmetries of loops will be in [D–F2].

5. The Reflection Conjecture and Examples. In this section we shall introduce many interesting examples of loops which can be analyzed. In particular, we emphasize showing what types of symmetry each loop has, and showing the validity of the reflection conjecture (1.1) for each loop. Let us recall some important definitions.

The reflection operator $\sim$ is the mapping which associates each k-uniform clutter with another k-uniform clutter:

$$\widetilde{\mathcal{C}} = \{D \subseteq E : |D| = k \quad \text{and} \quad D \notin \mathcal{C}\}.$$

For each loop L containing a uniform clutter, if $L(\widetilde{\mathcal{D}})$ does not depend on the choice of uniform clutters $\mathcal{D} \in L$, then we call this unique loop the *reflection loop* of L and denote it by $\widetilde{L}$.

The reflection conjecture says that for each loop L containing a uniform clutter,

(a)   the reflection loop $\widetilde{L}$ exists;

(b) $|L| = |\widetilde{L}|$ (the same length);

(c) $\|L\| = \|\widetilde{L}\|$ (the same sum of sizes).

Recall that we defined the following three notions of symmetries:

(a)   *self-dual*: $L = \overline{L}$;

(b)   *self-reflective*: $L = \widetilde{L}$;

(c)   *self-dual-reflective*: $\widetilde{L} = \overline{L}$;

and the following more general notions:

(a)   *p-self dual*: $L = \overline{L}^p$;

(b)   *p-self-reflective*: $L = \tilde{L}^p$;

(c)   *p-self-dual-reflective*: $\tilde{L} = \overline{L}^p$;

where p is a permutation p of E (and L^p is the image of L under the action of the permutation p). So we have trivially

PROPOSITION 5.1. *If a loop L is either $(p-)$ self-reflection or $(p-)$ self-dual-reflection, then it satisfies the reflection conjecture (1.1).*

Example 5.2. The complete uniform loop

We call a clutter $\mathcal{C}$ *uniform* or *k-uniform* if every member C of $\mathcal{C}$ has the same cardinality k. The k-uniform clutter $(E; k) := \{C \subseteq E : |C| = k\}$ is called the *complete k-uniform* clutter, for $k \geq 0$. For convenience, we define $(E; -1) = \emptyset$, the empty clutter. Note that the empty clutter $(E; -1)$ is different from $(E; 0) = \{\emptyset\}$, and can be considered as a k-uniform clutter for any $0 \leq k \leq n$.

PROPOSITION 5.2.1. *The S_E-clutters are exactly the complete uniform clutters $(E; k)$, $-1 \leq k \leq n$, and form the loop of length $n + 2$:*

$$L((E; n)) = (E; n),\ (E; n - 1), \ldots, (E; 1),\ (E; 0),\ (E; -1),\ (E; n),$$

which will be called the complete uniform loop.

Since every subset of E appears exactly once in the loop, the sum of sizes $\|L((E; n))\| = 2^n$, and the average size of clutters in the loop is $2^n/(n + 2)$. Observing that $\overline{(E; k)} = (E; n - k)$ and $\widetilde{(E; k)} = (E; -1)$ for all $0 \leq k \leq n$, we see that the complete uniform loop is both self-dual and self-reflection, hence the reflection conjecture is satisfied.

Example 5.3. Two $S_{E-\{1\}}$-loops

For $n \geq 2$, let

$$\mathcal{C} = \{\{1\}\}$$
$$\mathcal{C}' = \{\{1\}, E - \{1\}\}.$$

While the clutters $\mathcal{C}$ and $\mathcal{C}'$ (on E) have the same automorphism group $S_{E-\{1\}}$, they produce different loops. Both loops $L(\mathcal{C})$ and $L(\mathcal{C}')$ have the same length $(n + 2)$, the same sum of sizes 2^n, and have exactly four uniform clutters. The first loop $L(\mathcal{C})$ contains two 1-uniform clutters and two $(n-1)$-uniform clutters. On the other hand, the second loop $L(\mathcal{C}')$ contains two 2-uniform clutters and two $(n-2)$-uniform clutters. Both loops are self-dual and self-reflective, and hence satisfy the reflection conjecture. These facts can be easily verified using some technique for splittable clutters developed in the next section.

Example 5.4. Loops of rigid clutters

A clutter $\mathcal{C}$ (or its loop) is *rigid* if $G(\mathcal{C}) = \langle 1 \rangle$. The simplest rigid clutter is $\{1\}$ on $E = \{1, 2\}$, and its loop $\{1\}$, $\{2\}$ is obviously self-dual and self-reflective. There are no rigid clutters on E with $n = 3$ or 4. For $n = 5$, we have the following example.

Let $\mathcal{C} = \{13, 14, 23, 345\}$. Here we employ a simplified notation for clutters: 13 and 345, say, mean the sets $\{1, 3\}$ and $\{3, 4, 5\}$. In the sequel, whenever there are no ambiguities, we use this notation. Then $\mathcal{C}$ is a rigid loop on $\{1, 2, 3, 4, 5\}$. The loop $L(\mathcal{C})$ has length 7 and contains no uniform clutters.

Example 5.5. Brouwer-Duchet loops [Du], [B]

Let $|E| = n = 2k$. Let

$$\mathcal{C}_i = \{C \subseteq E : |C| = k \quad \text{and}$$
$$| \{1, 2, \ldots k\} \cap C | = i \quad (\text{mod } 2)\}$$

for $i = 0, 1$. Then it is easy to see that $L(\mathcal{C}) = \{\mathcal{C}_0, \mathcal{C}_1\}$. The average size of clutters is $\binom{n}{\frac{n}{2}} / 2$.

When k is odd, $\mathcal{C}_0 = \overline{\mathcal{C}}_1$, and when k is even $\mathcal{C}_0 = \overline{\mathcal{C}}_0$. This implies that the loop is self-dual. Moreover, we have $\mathcal{C}_0 = \widetilde{\mathcal{C}}_1$, hence it is self-reflective and thus satisfies the reflection conjecture.

Brouwer [B] constructed loops of length 2 for every odd $n \neq 1, 3$ also but here we omit the description of his construction because it is a little complicated.

Example 5.6. Loops of stars

For $1 \leq s \leq k \leq n$, let

$$\text{Star}(s, k, n) = \{C \subseteq E : \{1, 2, \ldots, s\} \in C, \quad |C| = k\}.$$

Set $\mathcal{C} = \text{Star}(1, k, 2k)$. Then one can verify that the length of the loop $L(\mathcal{C})$ is $k + 1$, the sum of sizes is 2^{2k+1}, and the average size of clutters is $2^n / (n + 2)$. This loop contains exactly two uniform clutters, $\mathcal{C}$ and $\overline{\mathcal{C}} \equiv \widetilde{\mathcal{C}}$, hence it is self-dual and self-reflective.

Example 5.7. Loops of the Fano matroid and Steiner systems

Let $\mathcal{C}$ be the set of circuits of the Fano matroid M on $E = \{1, 2, \ldots, 7\}$, i.e., $\mathcal{C} = \{126, 135, 147, 234, 257, 367, 456, 1237, 1245, 1347, 1567, 2356, 2467, 3457\}$. Then the loop $L(\mathcal{C})$ is

$$
\begin{aligned}
\mathcal{C}_0 &= \quad \text{the set of circuits} = \mathcal{C}_2 \cup \mathcal{C}_3 \\
\mathcal{C}_1 &= \quad \text{the set of bases} = S_4(2, 3, 7) \\
\mathcal{C}_2 &= \quad \text{the set of of hyperplanes (lines)} = S(2, 3, 7) = \widetilde{\mathcal{C}}_1 \\
\mathcal{C}_3 &= \quad \text{the set of cocircuits} = S_2(2, 4, 7) \\
\mathcal{C}_4 &= \quad \text{the set of cobases} = S_8(2, 4, 7) = \widetilde{\mathcal{C}}_3 \\
\mathcal{C}_5 &= \quad \text{the set of cohyperplanes} = \mathcal{C}_0.
\end{aligned}
$$

Clearly it is self-dual and its length is 5. All known examples of loops for $n = 7$ have longer lengths. Except for $\mathcal{C}_0$, all clutters are uniform and $\mathcal{C}_1 = \tilde{\mathcal{C}}_2$ and $\mathcal{C}_3 = \tilde{\mathcal{C}}_4$. Thus it is self-reflective as well.

More general loops with self-reflective property can be obtained as follows. For $0 \leq s < k \leq n$, a clutter $\mathcal{C}$ is called an s-design $S_\lambda(s, k, n)$ if it is a k-uniform clutter such that every s-subset of E is contained in exactly λ members of $\mathcal{C}$. In particular, an s-design $S_1(s, k, n)$, denoted by $S(s, k, n)$, is called a *Steiner system*, and an s-design $S(s, 3, n)$ is called a Steiner *triple* system. The (set of hyperplanes $\mathcal{C}_2$ of the) Fano matroid is the Steiner triple system $S(2, 3, 7)$.

PROPOSITION 5.7.1. *Let* $\mathcal{C}$ *be a design* $S_\lambda(s, k, n)$. *Then* $s + 1 \leq |D| \leq s + \lambda$ *for all* $D \in f^{-1}(\mathcal{C})$. *In particular,* $f^{-1}(\mathcal{C})$ *is* $(s + 1)$-*uniform if* $\mathcal{C}$ *is a Steiner system (i.e.* $\lambda = 1$*) and* $f^{-1}(\mathcal{C}) = \tilde{\mathcal{C}}$ *if, in addition,* $s = k - 1$.

Proof. Let $D \in f^{-1}(\mathcal{C})$. By Lemma 2.1, D is a minimal set not contained in any member of $\mathcal{C}$. Suppose $|D| > s + \lambda$ and let $a_1, a_2, \ldots, a_{\lambda+1}$ be distinct members of D. Consider $\lambda + 1$ sets $D_i = D \backslash \{a_i\}$. Each of them is contained in some member of $\mathcal{C}$ (because of minimality of D) but in a different one (because, otherwise, it will contain D). Fix a s-subset T of $D \backslash \{a_1, a_2, \ldots, a_{\lambda+1}\}$ (it is possible since $|D| > s + \lambda$ by the assumption). So, we have $\lambda + 1$ different members of $\mathcal{C}$ (blocks) containing s-set T, but $S_\lambda(s, k, n)$ has exactly λ such blocks. $\square$

Both bounds of Proposition 5.7.1 are not best possible. For example, for $\mathcal{C} = S_{12}(2, 4, 9)$ (respectively, $S_8(2, 4, 7)$) we have $f^{-1}(\mathcal{C}) = \tilde{\mathcal{C}}$ and so $3 < |D| = 4 < 14$ (respectively, $3 < |D| = 4 < 10$).

We observe that the loop of the Steiner system $S(2, 3, 9)$:

$$\mathcal{C} = \{123, 147, 159, 168, 249, 258, 267, 348, 357, 369, 456, 789\}$$

is very similar to that of the Fano matroid: it has length 5, contains four uniform clutters, and is self-reflection:

$$\mathcal{C}_0 = \tilde{\mathcal{C}}_4 \quad \text{(3-uniform)},$$
$$\mathcal{C}_1 = \tilde{\mathcal{C}}_2 \quad \text{(4-uniform)}.$$

However, the loop is not self-dual.

There is a following striking analogy among the loops of the affine plane $AG(2, 3) = S(2, 3, 9)$, of the projective plane $PG(2, 2) = S(2, 3, 7)$ (Fano loop), and the loop $L3 - 2$ (the loop of $\{1\}$ on $\{1, 2, 3\}$)

Loop	$\mathcal{C}_0$	$\mathcal{C}_1 = \tilde{\mathcal{C}}_0$	$\mathcal{C}_2$	$\mathcal{C}_3 = \tilde{\mathcal{C}}_4$	$\mathcal{C}_4$
$AG(2, 3)$	$S_9(2, 4, 9)$	$S_{12}(2, 4, 9)$	$\mathcal{C}_0 \cup \mathcal{C}_4$	$S_6(2, 3, 9)$	$S(2, 3, 9)$
$PG(2, 2)$	$S_2(2, 4, 7)$	$S_8(2, 4, 7)$	$\mathcal{C}_0 \cup \mathcal{C}_4$	$S_4(2, 3, 7)$	$S(2, 3, 7)$
$L3 - 2$	$\{23\}$	$\{12, 13\}$	$\mathcal{C}_0 \cup \mathcal{C}_4$	$\{2, 3\}$	$\{1\}$

In each of the three cases, the clutter $\mathcal{C}_2$ can be considered as the set of circuits of some matroid, $\mathcal{C}_3$ is the set of bases, $\mathcal{C}_2$ is the set of hyperplanes, and except for $AG(2,3)$, $\mathcal{C}_0$ is the set of cocircuits and $\mathcal{C}_1$ is the set of cobases. All those three loops and the dual to $AG(2,3)$ are loops of length 5 satisfying the "loop equations" $\mathcal{C}_1 = \widetilde{\mathcal{C}}_0$, $\mathcal{C}_3 = \widetilde{\mathcal{C}}_4$, $\mathcal{C}_2 = \mathcal{C}_0 \cup \mathcal{C}_4$. It would be interesting to know if there exist other such loops.

Observe that, in general, if $\mathcal{C} = S_\lambda(s,k,n)$, then $\mathcal{C} = S_{\binom{n-s}{k-s}-\lambda}(s,k,n)$.

Example 5.8. Isometric clutters $\mathcal{C}$, $f(\mathcal{C})$

For any two sets A and B, the Hamming distance $d(A,B)$ between them is defined as the cardinality of the symmetric difference, i.e., $|A \cup B| - |A \cup B|$. We call two clutters $\mathcal{C}$, $\mathcal{C}'$ *isometric* if there is a bijection α between them such that for any $A, B \in \mathcal{C}$, $d(A,B) = d(\alpha(A),\alpha(B))$.

(a)   Two isometric "open snakes" for $n = 4$

$\mathcal{C}$	$f(\mathcal{C})$
12	1 3
23	1 4
34	2 4

(b)   Two isometric "closed snakes" for $n = 5$

$\mathcal{C}$	$f(\mathcal{C})$
12	1 3
23	1 4
34	2 4
45	2 5
1 5	3 5

In both cases (a) and (b), $f(\mathcal{C}) = \widetilde{\mathcal{C}}$ and it consists of all pairs which are not in $\mathcal{C}$, because any 3-set contains a set from $\mathcal{C}$. (Any 3-subset of a 4-set consists of 3 consecutive points in cyclic order. Any 3-subset of a 5-set is either three consecutive points in cyclic order or of form 1 34.) Moreover $f^2(\mathcal{C}) = \mathcal{C}$, i.e., (a) and (b) are loops of length 2, since any 3-set contains a set from $f(\mathcal{C})$. These examples are quite exceptional.

Both snakes above and the Brouwer-Duchet loops (Example 5.6) satisfy the loop equations $\mathcal{C}_0 = \widetilde{\mathcal{C}}_1 = \mathcal{C}_2$. Another example (due to A. Blokhuis) is the closed snake (2 Fano planes) for $n = 7$, $\mathcal{C} = \{124, 235, 346, 457, 561, 672, 713, 764, 653, 542, 431, 327, 216, 175\}$.

Another example of a k-uniform clutter such that $f(\mathcal{C})$ consists of all remaining k-subsets, satisfying $f(\mathcal{C}) = \widetilde{\mathcal{C}}$, is

$$
\begin{array}{ccc}
12 & 4 & \\
12 & 5 & \\
23 & 5 & \\
23 & & 6 \\
 & 34 & 6 \\
1 & 34 & \\
1 & & 45 \\
 & 2 & 45 \\
 & 2 & 56 \\
 & 3 & 56 \\
\end{array}
$$

because any 4-subset of a 6-set contains a triplet from this clutter. (Check three cases for 4-sets: 1234, 123 5, 12 45.) But $f^2(\mathcal{C}) \neq \mathcal{C}$ in this case, because it contains 1245, 2356, 1346.

(c)   A general example of an isometric $\mathcal{C}$ satisfying $f(\mathcal{C}) = \overline{\mathcal{C}}$

Case 1. $|E| = 2k - 1$

$$\mathcal{C} = (E;\ k), \quad f(\mathcal{C}) = (E;\ k-1), \text{ so } f(\mathcal{C}) = \overline{\mathcal{C}}.$$

Case 2. $|E| = 2k$

$$\mathcal{C} = (E - \{2k\}; k), \quad f(\mathcal{C}) = \overline{\overline{\mathcal{C}}} \qquad .$$

6. Splittable Clutters. For a given clutter $\mathcal{C}$, it is in general very hard to compute $f(\mathcal{C})$: the computational complexity is clearly exponential in the size of $\mathcal{C}$ and n since the output size can be exponential in n. In this section, we shall introduce some classes of clutters for which the computation $f(\mathcal{C})$ is easy.

Let (E_1, E_2) be a given partition of E, and let

$$(p, q) = (E_1; p) \times (E_2; q),$$

i.e., the $(p+q)$-uniform clutter of sets consisting of some p-set from E_1 and some q-set from E_2. A clutter $\mathcal{C}$ is called *splittable* if there is a nontrivial partition (E_1, E_2) of E such that

$$\mathcal{C} = (p_1, q_1) \cup (p_2, q_2) \cup \cdots \cup (p_h, q_h),$$

for some p_i's and q_i's. In the expression above, since $\mathcal{C}$ is a clutter, we may suppose

$$s \geq p_1 > p_2 > \cdots > p_h \geq 0 \quad \text{and}$$
$$0 \leq q_1 < q_2 < \cdots < q_h \leq n - s,$$

where $s = |E_1|$. Clearly $h \leq \min\{s, n-s\} + 1$, and hence splittable clutters have a compact representation. The automorphism group Aut $\mathcal{C}$ is $S_{E_1} \times S_{E_2}$.

First we note that some of the examples in the previous section are splittable. For $|E| = n = 2k$, letting $E_1 = \{1, \ldots, k\}$ and $E_2 = \{k+1, \ldots n\}$, the Brouwer-Duchet clutters (Example 5.5) can be written as

$$\mathcal{C}_0 = (k'', k - k'') \cup \cdots \cup (4, k-4) \cup (2, k-2) \cup (0, k) \quad \text{and}$$
$$\mathcal{C}_1 = (k', k - k') \cup \cdots \cup (3, k-3) \cup (1, k-1),$$

where k' and k'' are the largest odd and even number not greater than k, respectively. One can easily see that the two $S_{E-\{1\}}$-clutters (Example 5.3) and the star families $\mathrm{Star}(s, k, n)$ (Example 5.6) are also splittable.

PROPOSITION 6.1. *Let (E_1, E_2) be a nontrivial partition of E with $s|E_1| \leq |E_2|$. Then the total number of (E_1, E_2)-splittable clutters is*

$$\sum_{h=1}^{s+1} \binom{s+1}{h} \binom{n-s+1}{h}.$$

PROPOSITION 6.2. *If $\mathcal{C}$ is (E_1, E_2)-splittable then $f(\mathcal{C})$ is also (E_1, E_2)-splittable and*

$$f(\mathcal{C}) = (s, q_1 - 1) \cup (p_1 - 1, q_2 - 1) \cup$$
$$(p_2 - 1, q_3 - 1) \cup \cdots \cup (p_{h-1} - 1, q_h - 1) \cup (p_h - 1, n - s).$$

We omit the proofs as they are quite straightforward. Note that in the expression of $f(\mathcal{C})$ above the first term and/or the last term may be empty, because $q_1 - 1$ and $p_h - 1$ can be negative.

THEOREM 6.3. *The loop $L(\mathcal{C})$ of any 1-uniform clutter $\mathcal{C}$ is self-dual reflective, and hence satisfies the reflection conjecture.*

Proof. Let $\mathcal{C}$ be a 1-uniform clutter. Since the result is true for the complete uniform clutter, we assume $\mathcal{C}$ is not complete. Clearly, $\mathcal{C}$ is splittable and can be written as $(1, 0)$ for some nontrivial partition (E_1, E_2). Now using Proposition 6.2, we have

$$\mathcal{C} = \mathcal{C}_0 = (1, 0) \qquad : 1 - \text{uniform clutter}$$
$$\mathcal{C}_1 = (0, n - s) \qquad : (n - s) - \text{uniform clutter}$$
$$\mathcal{C}_2 = (s, n - s - 1) : (n - 1) - \text{uniform clutter}$$
$$\mathcal{C}_3 = (s, n - s - 2) \cup (s - 1, n - s)$$
$$\mathcal{C}_4 = (s, n - s - 3) \cup (s - 1, n - s - 1) \cup (s - 2, n - s)$$
$$\vdots$$
$$\mathcal{C}_j = (s, n - s - (j-1)) \cup (s-1, n - s - (j-3)) \cup \cdots \cup (s - (j-2), n - s),$$
$$(j \leq \min\{n - s + 1, s + 2\})$$

Now consider the case $s+2 < n-s+1$ (the cases $s+2 = n-s+1$ and $s+2 > n-s+1$ can be treated similarly). Then

$$\mathcal{C}_{s+2} = (s, n-2s-1) \cup (s-1, n-2s+1) \cup \cdots \cup (0, n-s)$$
$$\mathcal{C}_{s+3} = (s, n-2s-2) \cup (s-1, n-2s) \cup \cdots \cup (0, n-s-1)$$
$$\vdots$$
$$\mathcal{C}_{n-s+1} = (s, 0) \cup (s-1, 2) \cup \cdots \cup (0, s+1)$$
$$\mathcal{C}_{n-s+2} = (s-1, 1) \cup \cdots \cup (0, s) \qquad : s - \text{uniform clutter}$$
$$\mathcal{C}_{n-s+3} = (s, 0) \cup (s-2, 1) \cup \cdots \cup (0, s-1)$$
$$\mathcal{C}_{n-s+4} = (s-1, 0) \cup \ldots U(0, s-2)$$
$$\vdots$$
$$\mathcal{C}_{n-s+(s+1)} = (2, 0) \cup (0, 1)$$
$$\mathcal{C}_{n-s+(s+2)} = (1, 0) = \mathcal{C}_0.$$

It follows that the loop L has length $n - s + (s + 2) = n + 2$, and has exactly four uniform clutters, $\mathcal{C}_0 = (1,0)$, $\mathcal{C}_1 = (0, n - s), \mathcal{C}_2 = (s, n - s - 1)$, $\mathcal{C}_{n-s+2} = (s - 1, 1) \cup \cdots \cup (0, s)$. Since

$$\widetilde{\mathcal{C}}_0 = \overline{\mathcal{C}}_2$$
$$\widetilde{\mathcal{C}}_1 = \overline{\mathcal{C}}_{n-s+2},$$

the loops $L(\widetilde{\mathcal{D}})$, $\mathcal{D} = \mathcal{C}_0, \mathcal{C}_1, \mathcal{C}_2, \mathcal{C}_{n-s+2}$ are all the same, and equal to the dual loop $\overline{L}$. This implies that the reflection loop $\widetilde{L}$ exists and the loop L is self-dual-reflection. The proof is complete. □

As we see in the proof, any singleton clutter $\mathcal{C} = \{F\}, F \subseteq E$, appears (as $\mathcal{C}_1$) in the loop of some 1-uniform clutter. Thus,

COROLLARY 6.4. *The reflection conjecture (1.1) is true for all singleton clutters.*

7. Catalog of Loops and Some Experimental Results. At present we don't have strong techniques for analyzing loops of clutters. So, it will be helpful for us to employ some enumerative approaches or computer experiments.

7.1. Catalog of loops for $n \leq 4$. First we give a complete catalog of loops for $1 \leq n \leq 4$. For enumeration, of course we identify isomorphic loops. Here we say that two loops L and L' on E are *isomorphic* if there is a permutation p of E such that $L' = L^p$.

Table 1 contains all nonisomorphic loops for $n \leq 4$. For each loop L, we tried to associate a graph whose set of circuits generates L. There is only one loop, the open snake L4–1, for which this is impossible ("nongraphic loop"). One can easily observe that all loops are (p–) self-dual and (p–)-self-reflection. So the reflection conjecture is true for $n \leq 4$.

TABLE 1. Complete catalogue of loops for $n \leq 4$

(n = 1)

Loop	$|L|$	$\|L\|$	C_0	Symmetry	Comment
L1-1	3	$2=2^n$	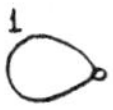	SD, SR	CU

(n = 2)

Loop	$|L|$	$\|L\|$	C_0	Symmetry	Comment
L2-1	2	2	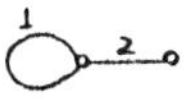	SD, SR	Sp, Ri, Du, St
L2-2	4	$4=2^n$	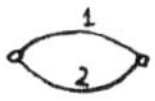	SD, SR	CU

(n = 3)

Loop	$|L|$	$\|L\|$	C_0	Symmetry	Comment
L3-1	5	$8=2^n$	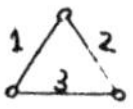	SD, SR	CU
L3-2	5	8	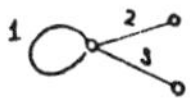	SD, SR	Sp

(n = 4)

Loop	$|L|$	$\|L\|$	C_0	Symmetry	Comment
L4-1	2	6	(12, 23, 34)	SD, p-SR, p=(2 3)	open snake
L4-2	2	6	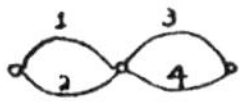	SD, SR	Sp, Du
L4-3	3	8	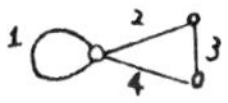	SD, SR	Sp, St
L4-4	6	$16=2^n$	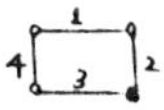	SD, SR	CU
L4-5	6	16	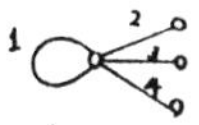	SD, SR	Sp
L4-6	6	16	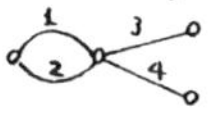	p-SD, p-SR, p=(1 3)(2 4)	Sp
L4-7	6	16	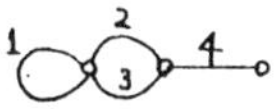	p-SD, p-SR, p=(1 4)	

Abbreviations: CU = Complete Uniform, Sp = Splittable, Ri = Rigid
Du = Duchet clutter, St = Star clutter Star(1,k,2k)
SD = Self-Dual, SR = Self-Reflection

For example for the case $n = 2$ we have two loops

$$L2 - 1 = \{12\}, \quad \{1,2\}, \quad \{\emptyset\}, \quad \emptyset \quad \text{and} \quad L2 - 2 = \{1\}, \{2\}$$

In the case $n = 3$, there are exactly 19 clutters, including 2 "nonproper" clutters: $\{123\}, \{\emptyset\}$. This set of 19 clutters is partitioned by the following 4 loops of clutters:

$$L3 - 1 = \{123\}, \quad \{12, 23, 13\}, \{1, 2, 3\}, \quad \{\emptyset\}, \quad \emptyset$$

and three loops of the type

$$L3 - 2 = \{1\}, \{23\}, \quad \{12, 13\}, \quad \{1, 23\}, \quad \{2, 3\}.$$

The maximal (i.e., nonextendable) clutters are the four clutters of the first loop and the clutters

$$\{1, 23\}, \quad \{2, 13\}, \quad \{3, 12\}$$

i.e., one from each of the three remaining loops.

We should also note that the loop L3–2 is isomorphic to the loop of the Fano matroid, $L(S(2, 3, 7))$, up to the equivalence on subsets of E induced by G-orbits on 2^E, where G is the corresponding automorphism groups $\langle(23)\rangle$ and $\langle(145)(276), (26)(45)\rangle$ (details in [D-F2]). Each of these 3 loops has form $\mathcal{C}_0, \mathcal{C}_1, \mathcal{C}_0 \cup \mathcal{C}_1, \widetilde{\mathcal{C}}_0$ with $\mathcal{C}_0 = \{1\}, S(2, 3, 7), \; S(2, 3, 9)$ and $\mathcal{C}_1 = \overline{\mathcal{C}}_0$ for the first two cases

7.2 Computer experiments. Limited computer experiments have been performed to investigate realizable lengths of loops for small n. For each $5 \leq n \leq 8$, clutters were randomly generated and their loops were computed. The number of clutters generated are different for each n: more than 200 loops for $n = 5$, 6, less than 100 for $n = 7$, and one for $n = 8$. Table 2 contains this result. It seems that for $n = 5$, 2, 7 and 16 are the only realizable lengths. As n increases, the maximal length of loops grows rapidly. Also the number of different realizable lengths seems to grow fast. For $n = 6$, all the generated lengths are even except for one loop of length 87.

TABLE 2.   Lengths of known examples of loops

n	Lengths
1	$\underline{3}$
2	2, $\underline{4}$
3	$\underline{5}$
4	2, 3, $\underline{6}$
5	2, $\underline{7}$, 16
6	2, 4, 6, $\underline{8}$, 10, 12, 14, 16, 18, 24, 28, 32, 34, 40, 46, 48, 52, 54, 56, 60, 64, 66, 68, 70, 76, 78, 82, 87, 90, 92, 94, 102, 104, 124, 128, 132, 134, 252, 380, 414, 616, 1026, 1032
7	5, 8, $\underline{9}$, 22, 27, 36, 43, 45, 46, 65, 124, 144, 170, 277, 396, 444, 923, 1083, 1229, 1331, 2685, 3025, 3791
8	2, 5, $\underline{10}$, 186
9	2, 5, $\underline{11}$

Note: The table contains all realizable lengths for $n \leq 4$. The underlined length $n + 2$ is always realizable.

Table 3 contains some realizable lengths up to $(n + 2)$ for $n \leq 9$. The lengths 3 and 4 seem to be quite exceptional, because excluding the complete uniform loops, there is only one loop for each length.

TABLE 3. Lengths (up to $n+2$) of known examples of loops of k-uniform clutters

n	k	Lengths	Attained by
1	1	3	
2	1	2 4	Duchet (1)
3	1	5	
4	1	6	
	2	2 3 6	closed snake (12, 23, 31)
			Duchet (13, 14, 23, 24) and open snake (12, 23, 34)
5	1	7	
	2	2 7	closed snake (12, 23, 34, 45, 51)
6	1	8	
	2	8	
	3	2 4 6 8	Star (1, 3, 6)
			Duchet (123, 145, 146, 156, 245, 246, 256, 345, 346, 356)
7	1	9	
	2	8 9	
	3	5 8 9	closed snake (12, 23, 34, 45, 56, 67, 71)
			Fano=S(2, 3, 7)
8	1	10	
	2	10	
	3	10	
	4	2 5 10	Star (1, 4, 8)
			Duchet
9	1	11	
	2	11	
	3	2 5 11	S(2, 3, 9)
			Ex. 4.5 in (Du).

Table 4 shows average sizes of loops $\|L\| / |L|$. It is remarkable that average sizes are quite close to each other. We observed that the complete uniform loop attains the minimum. We conjecture that this is true in general.

TABLE 4. Average size of clutters ($\|L\|/|L|$)

n	$2^n/(n+2)$ (lower bound?)	Experiments			$\binom{n}{\lfloor n/2 \rfloor}/2$ (Upper bound?)
		Min	Aver	Max	
2	1.00	(1.00	= 1.00	= 1.00)	1.00
3	1.60	(1.60	= 1.60	= 1.60)	1.60
4	8/3	($8/3$	$< A_4$	< 3.00)	3.00 (Duchet)
5	4.57	4.57	< 4.67	< 5.00	5.00 (closed snake)
6	8.00	8.00	< 8.26	< 10.00	10.00 (Duchet)
7	14.22	14.22	< 14.69	< 15.77	17.50 (Fano gives only 16.80)
8	25.60				35.00 (Duchet)
9	46.55				63.00 (Ex. 4.5 (Du) gives 42.00, S(2, 3, 9) gives 55.20)

Note: The experiments were done for $n = 5, 6, 7$, and the values in brackets for $n = 2, 3, 4$ are exact. The average value A_4, for $n = 4$, is

$$(3a + (8/3)b)/(a + b),$$

where a is the number of loops of length 2 (types L4–1, L4–2 from Table 1) and b is the number of all other loops (all remaining 5 types).

8. Final Remarks. We have described many interesting problems on loops of clutters. Among them, the reflection conjecture is certainly the most challenging problem. In fact, conjecture (1.1)(a) can be strengthened. That is, for any loop L containing a uniform clutter:

(8.1) The reflection loop $\widetilde{L}$ exists, and furthermore for $\mathcal{C} \in L$ and $\mathcal{D} \in \widetilde{L}$, there is an integer M such that the correspondence between the k-uniform clutters of L and the k-uniform clutters of $\widetilde{L}$ is explicitly written as:

$$\widetilde{\mathcal{C}}_i = \mathcal{D}_{m-k-i},$$

for each k.

We verified this conjecture for most examples in Section 5.

In all known examples of p-self-dual-reflection $\widetilde{L} = \overline{L}^p$ (see definition in Section 5) we have, for some integer m, $\mathcal{C}_i = \widetilde{\overline{\mathcal{C}}}{}^p_{m+k+i}$ for any k-uniform $\mathcal{C}_i \in L$. Denote by $\pi(= |\langle p^2 \rangle|)$ the order of permutations p^2, i.e., the smallest integer with $(p^2)^\pi = \langle 1 \rangle$. Then, in such case, the length $t(L)$ of the loop divides $\pi(n + 2m)$, because

$$
\begin{aligned}
\mathcal{C}_i = \widetilde{\overline{\mathcal{C}}}{}^p_{m+k+i} &= \overline{\widetilde{\overline{\mathcal{C}}}{}^p_{m+(n-k)+(m+k+i)}}{}^p \\
&= \mathcal{C}^{p^2}_{(n+2m)+i} = \mathcal{C}^{(p^2)^\pi}_{\pi(n+2m)+i} \\
&= \mathcal{C}^{\langle 1 \rangle}_{\pi(n+2m)+i}
\end{aligned}
$$

It is an example of what is called in [D–F2] a partial (on k-uniform clutters only) rotation.

REFERENCES

[B]   A.E. BROUWER, *On dual pairs of antichains*, Math. Centrum report ZW 40/74, Amsterdam, (1975).

[B–Sc]   A.E. BROUWER AND SCHRIJVER, *On the period of an operator defined on antichains*, Math. Centrum report ZW 24/74, Amsterdam (1974).

[D–F1]   M. DEZA AND K. FUKUDA, *On bouqets of matroids and orientations*, Pub. R.I.M.S., Kyoto Univ. (1986), 110–129.

[D–F2]   M. DEZA AND K. FUKUDA, *Loops of clutters II*, in preparation.

[Du]   P. DUCHET, *Sur les hypergraphes invariants*, Discrete Mathematics 8 (1974), 269–280.

[E–Fu]   J. EDMONDS AND D.R. FULKERSON, *Bottleneck extrema*, J. Combin. Theory 8 (1970), 299–306.

[En–G]   K. ENGEL AND H. -D. O.F. GRONAU, *Sperner theory in partially ordered sets*, Leipzig (1985).

[G–K]   C. GREEN AND D.J. KLEITMAN, *Proof techniques in the theory of finite sets*, in Studies in Combinatorics, MAA Studies in Math. 17 (G.–C. Rota, Ed.), 22–79, Washington, D.C. (1978).

[S]   P. SEYMOUR, *Forbidden minors of binary clutters*, J. London Math. Soc. 12 (1976), 356–360.

[V]   P. VADERLIND, *Clutters and semimatroids*, Europ. J. Combinatorics 7 (1986), 271–282.

[W]   D. WELSH, *Matroid Theory*, Academic Press, New York (1976).

POSITIVE INDEPENDENCE AND ENUMERATION OF CODES WITH A GIVEN DISTANCE PATTERN*

M. DEZA†, D.K. RAY-CHAUDHURI‡ AND N.M. SINGHI#

Abstract. A concept of P-independent sets is defined for **Z**-modules or convex sets. P-independence gives a convex analogue of usual independence. It is used for codes. A quasi-polynomial type theorem is proved for the number of inequivalent codes with a given distance pattern and length. The relationships with the classical coding problem and the design problem are discussed.

1. Number of Codes. Let Q and X be two finite sets with $|Q| = q$ and $|X| = l$. Any multiset C whose elements are from the set Q^X is called a *code* of length l over the alphabet Q. We denote by $|C|$ the sum of multiplicities of all elements of Q^X in C. When C is a subset of Q^X, $|C|$ is clearly the cardinality of C. $|C|$ is called the size of the code.

We shall also think of C as a matrix of order $|C| \times l$ by stacking elements of C as rows. A column of C is a column in this matrix. Let C_1 and C_2 be any two codes. We will write $C_1 \sim C_2$ if C_2 can be obtained from C_1 by applying a sequence of pormutation of columns or a permutation of Q to any column of C or by deleting or adding any column whose elements are equal.

For any code C let d_C be the $|C| \times |C|$ matrix whose rows and columns are indexed by elements of C and the entry in the uth row vth column is $d(u, v)$ where $d(u, v)$ is the Hamming distance between u and v (= number of $x \in X$ for which $u(x) \neq v(x)$). In particular $d(u, v) = 0$ if $u = v$. d_C is called the distance-pattern of C. If $C \sim C_1$, it can be easily seen that d_{C_1} is equal to d_C.

For any $m \times m$ matrix d we will say that a code C is a realization of d if $d_C = d$ and in this case d will be called a *realizable* matrix. Define

$$D_m = D_m(Q) = \{d \mid d \text{ is an } m \times m \text{ matrix and } d = d_C \text{ for some code } C\}.$$

Elements of D_m have clearly nonnegative integral entries. If $d_1, d_2 \in D_m$ are realized by the codes C_1 and C_2 then the matrix $d_1 + d_2$ is realized by the code $C_1 \vee C_2$, by putting the matrix of C_2 alongside that of C_1. Also clearly the zero-matrix $0 \in D_m$. Thus D_m is a semigroup under addition contained in the semigroup of all $m \times m$ nonnegative integral matrices with all diagonal entries equal to 0.

The aim of this paper is to describe some results about this semigroup which are essentially analogues of similar results on the number of distinct t-designs or

---

*The results of this paper were proved when the authors were visiting the Institute for Mathematics and its application at Minneapolis, USA with support from IMA . The second author also received support from NSA grant MDA 904-88-H-2034.

†C.N.R.S. UA 212, Université Paris 7, France.

‡Department of Mathematics, Ohio State University, Columbus, Ohio, 43210.

#School of Mathematics, Tata Institute of Fundamental Research, Colaba, Bombay, 400005, India.

orthogonal arrays obtained in [SS, RS_1, RS_2]. This will be done in this section. We also give in this process a few general results on **Z**-modules or convex sets as was pointed out in [DS] and discuss analogues of some results of [DS] for a general alphabet. This will be done in the next section.

We note that the classical coding problem for a given r and m asks for constructing a code C with minimum possible length such that $|C| = m$ and the minimum nonzero entry in d_C is r. The following proposition whose proof is easy [D_1] shows that this is equivalent to asking for minimum N such that $\bar{d} \in D_{m+1}$ for some matrix d with all off-diagonal entries $\geq r$ and $\bar{d}$ is as defined in the proposition below.

PROPOSITION 1.1. *Let* $d = (d_{ij})$ *be any nonnegative integral-matrix and* N *be a nonnegative integer. Define*

$$
\bar{d} =
\begin{pmatrix}
 & & & N \\
 & & & N - d_{12} \\
 & d & & \vdots \\
 & & & N - d_{1m} \\
N & N - d_{12} \cdots N - d_{1m} & & 0
\end{pmatrix}
$$

Then

(a) *if d is realizable by a code of length l, then $\bar{d} \in D_{m+1}$ for all $N \geq l$*

(b) *if $n <$ Minimum $\{l|$ there is a realization of d of length $l\}$,*

   then $\bar{d} \notin D_{m+1}$.

Now let Q^m denote the set of columns of length m with entries from Q. We will consider each element of Q^m as a code of length 1. We choose one representative from each class of these codes of length 1 except the class consisting of columns in which all entries are equal. Let E_m be the set of all these representatives. Let $e \in E_m$. Then $d_e, e \in E_m$, will be called a q-tomy. Clearly $d_e \in D_m$. Now let C be any code, $|C| = m$. Define $f_C : E_m \longrightarrow \mathbf{Z}$, (the ring of integers) by

$$f_C(e) = |\{e_1|e_1 \text{ is a column of } C \text{ and } e_1 = e\}|$$

The function f_C will be called the frequency vector of the code C. Note that

(i) *$C \sim C_1$ if and only if $f_{C_1} = f_C$,*

(ii) *$d_C = \sum f_C(e)d_e$ where the sum is over all $e \in E_m$ and $f_C(e) \geq 0$ for all $e \in E_m$.*

   and

(iii) *$l = \sum f_C(e)$ where the sum is over all $e \in E_m$.*

The following proposition is now clear.

PROPOSITION 1.2. *(i) D_m is generated by all q-tomies $d_e, e \in D_m$, i.e. for each $d \in D_m$ we have a function $f_d : E_m \longrightarrow \mathbf{Z}$ such that $f_d(e) \geq 0$ and $d = \sum f_d(e)d_e$ where the sum is over all $e \in E_m$.*

(ii) The code C whose frequency vector is the function f_d is a realization of d.

Now any integral function $f : E_m \longrightarrow \mathbf{Z}$ will be called a signed code over the alphabet Q. The length of the signed code is $\sum f(e)$, where the sum is over all $e \in E_m$ and the matrix $\sum f(e)d_e$ is its distance - pattern. Define $|f| = m$. A signed code is a code (frequency vector of a code) if and only if $f(e) \geq 0$ for all $e \in E_m$. The following theorems have been proved in $[\mathrm{D_1}]$, $[\mathrm{AD}]$ and $[\mathrm{A}]$.

THEOREM 1.3. *Let $|Q| = 2$ and let $d = (d_{ij})$ be any $m \times m$ integral matrix. Then d is a distance pattern for a signed code if and only if $d_{ij} + d_{ik} + d_{jk}$ is even for all $1 \leq i, j, k \leq m, i \neq j \neq k$.*

THEOREM 1.4. *Let $|Q| = 2$ and let $d = (d_{ij})$ be any $m \times m$ nonnegative rational matrix. Then for some integer λ, λd is the distance pattern of a code C over Q if and only if d is the distance-pattern of a set of m L^1-integrable functions.*

Let J denote the unique code (up to equivalence) whose frequency vector f_J is defined by $f_J(e) = 1$ for all $e \in E_m$. Let d_J be the distance-pattern of J. Using theorem 1.3 we get the following theorem.

THEOREM 1.5. *Let $Q = 2$ and $d = (d_{ij})$ be an $m \times m$ integral matrix. Then $d + \lambda d_J$ is realizable for all large integers $\lambda \geq \lambda_0(d)$ for some sufficiently large number $\lambda_0 = \lambda_0(d)$ if and only if $d_{ij} + d_{ik} + d_{jk}$ is even for all $1 \leq i, j, k \leq m, i \neq j \neq k$. (Note that d realizable means that there is a code C with $d_C = d$).*

Let $\mathbf{N}$ denote the set of all nonnegative integers. Any function $f : \mathbf{N} \longrightarrow \mathbf{C}$ (or $f : \mathbf{Z} \longrightarrow \mathbf{C}$) is said to be a quasipolynomial of degree t if and only if there exists an integer $M > 0$ and polynomials $f_0, f_1, \ldots, f_{M-1}$ such that

$$f(x) = f_i(x) \text{ if } x = i(\bmod M), 0 \leq i \leq M - 1$$

and $\max\{$ degree $f_i, 0 \leq i \leq M - 1\} = t$. The integer M will be called a period of f and f_i's will be called polynomials associated with f which are essentially unique. By using the above equations the domain of any quasipolynomial $f : \mathbf{N} \longrightarrow \mathbf{C}$ can be uniquely extended to $\mathbf{Z}$. Quasipolynomials occur naturally in counting combinatorial objects (see [S], [SS], $[\mathrm{RS_1}]$).

Now let $\mathbf{N}(m)$ denote the set of all $m \times m$ matrices with entries from $\mathbf{N}$. We define a map

$N_m : \mathbf{N} \times \mathbf{N}(m) \longrightarrow \mathbf{N}$ by

$N_m(l, d) = $ *the number of inequivalent codes C with $d_C = d$ and length l.*

Note that $N_m(l, d)$ is also equal to the number of distinct functions $f : E_m \longrightarrow \mathbf{N}$ such that $\sum f(e)d_e = d$ and $\sum f(e) = l$ where the sum is over all $e \in E_m$. Also note that if any diagonal entry in d is $\neq 0$, then $N_m(l, d) = 0$.

Let $\mu_1 = (\mu_{ij}, 1 \leq i, j \leq m)$ be an ordered set of m^2 variables. Let μ_0 be another variable and let $\mu = (\mu_1, \mu_0)$. For any $(l, d) \in \mathbf{N} \times \mathbf{N}(m)$ define

$$\mu^{(l,d)} = \mu_0^l (\Pi \mu_{ij}^{d_{ij}})$$

where the product is over all $1 \leq i, j \leq m$ and $d = (d_{ij})$.

Now define

$$F_m(\mu) = \sum N_m(l, d) \mu^{(l,d)}$$

where the sum is over all $(l, d) \in \mathbb{N} \times \mathbb{N}(m)$. $F_m(\mu)$ is the generating function for the numbers $N_m(l, d)$.

The rest of this section is devoted to describing how $F_m(\mu)$ can be considered as a Poincare series for a graded algebra of a toroidal monoid and obtaining some information on $N_m(l, d)$ as was done for the case of designs in [SS] and for orthogonal arrays in [RS$_1$] . For more details of terms described here, see [S] or [SS] . In particular we show that a counting function related to $N_m(l, d)$'s is quasipolynomial.

Let $Y = (Y_e, e \in E_m)$ be an ordered set of $|E_m|$ variables and $W = (W_{ij}, 1 \leq i \leq j \leq m)$ be another set of m^2 variables. Let

$$\phi = \{t_{ij}(Y, W) | 1 \leq i, j \leq m\}$$

be a set of m^2 linear forms in the variables YUW defined by

$$t_{ij}(Y, W) = \left(\sum (d_e)_{ij} Y_e\right) - W_{ij}$$

where $d_e = ((d_e)_{ij})$ is the distance pattern of the code $e \in E_m$ of length 1 and the sum is over all $e \in E_m$. Let E_ϕ be the set of all pairs $(f, d), f : E_m \longrightarrow \mathbb{N}$ and $d \in \mathbb{N}(m), d = (d_{ij})$ such that $t_{ij}(f, d) = 0$ for all $1 \leq i, j \leq m$. Thus E_ϕ is the monoid of all solutions to the equations in ϕ. E_ϕ is a toroidal monoid (see [SS]). Note that if f is the frequency vector of a code C and $(f, d) \in E_\phi$, then $d = d_C$. Thus E_ϕ is also the set of all pairs $(\bar{C}, d)$ where $\bar{C}$ is the equivalence class of a code C with $d_C = d$. In particular,

$$N_m(l, d) = \text{ the number of elements } (f, d) \in E_\phi$$

with $\sum f(e) = l$ where the sum is over all $e \in E_m$. Now take some more new variables $\nu_e, e \in E_m$. Let $\nu = (\nu_e | e \in E_m)$ be the ordered set of these variables. Define

$$F'_m(\nu, \mu_1) = \sum (\nu, \mu_1)^{(f,d)}$$

where the sum is over all $(f, d) \in E_\phi$ and $(\nu, \mu_1) = \pi(\nu_e^{f(e)}) \, \pi(\mu_{ij}^{d_{ij}})$ where the first product is over all $e \in E_m$ and the second is over all $1 \leq i, j \leq m$. Note that if $\nu_e = \mu_0$ for all $e \in E_m, F'_m(\nu, \mu_1) = F_m(\mu)$. $F'_m(\nu, \mu_1)$ is actually the Poincare series for the graded subring R of the ring of all polynomials over a field K in variables YUW for which the monomials $(\Pi y_e^{f(e)})(\Pi w_{ij}^{d_{ij}})$ form a basis, where $(f, d) \in E_\phi, d = (d_{ij})$. For more details, see [S] or [SS] .

An element $\beta \in E_\phi$ is said to be *completely fundamental* if whenever for any integer $n > 0, n\beta = \gamma + \delta$, for some $\gamma, \delta \in E_\phi$, then $\gamma = n_1\beta$ for an integer $n_1, 0 \leq n_1 \leq n$. It can be easily seen that completely fundamental elements of E_ϕ are precisely (δ_e, d_e) where $\delta_e : E_m \longrightarrow \mathbb{N}$ is defined by $\delta_e(e') = 1$ or 0 according as $e' = e$ or $e' \neq e$. The following two theorems follow from general results about *graded rings and theorems of Hochster and Stanley (see [S] or [SS]). Theorem 1.6 below can also be proved directly.*

THEOREM 1.6. *$F'_m(\nu, \mu_1) = \frac{1}{Q(\nu, \mu_1)}$ where $Q(\nu, \mu_1)$ is a polynomial in the variables in the sets ν and μ_1 given by*

$$Q(\nu, \mu_1) = \Pi(1 - (\nu, \mu_1)^{(\delta_e, d_e)})$$

where the product is over all $e \in E_m$.

THEOREM 1.7.

(a) *R is a Cohen-Macaulay integral domain.*

(b) *Define $F''_m(\mu_0) = F_m(\mu)$ with all $\mu_{ij} = \mu_0, 1 \le i, j \le m$.*

Then

$$F''_m(\mu_0) = \frac{P_1(\mu_0)}{Q_1(\mu_0)}$$

where P_1 and Q_1 are polynomials in μ_0 with degree $P_1 <$ degree Q_1.

The part (a) of the theorem below follows by taking $\nu_e = \mu_0$ for all $e \in E_m$ and the part (b) of theorem 1.7 from the same ideas as used in the proof of theorem 1.1 in [SS].

THEOREM 1.8.

(a) *$F_m(\mu) = \frac{P'(\mu)}{Q'(\mu)}$ where $P'(\mu)$ and $Q'(\mu)$ are polynomials in μ with no common factor and $Q'(\mu) = \Pi(1 - \mu_0 \mu_{ij}^{(d_e)_{ij}})$ where the product is over all $e \in E_m$ and $d_e = ((d_e)_{ij})$.*

(b) *The function $M_m : \mathsf{N} \longrightarrow \mathsf{N}$ defined by $M_m(s) = \sum N_m(l, d)$ where the sum is over all $(l, d) \in \mathsf{N} \times \mathsf{N}(m)$ satisfying $\sum_{1 \le i,j \le m} d_{ij} = s, d = (d_{ij})$ is a quasipolynomial.*

We conclude this section with some remarks. One can get more information on the function $F'_m(\nu, \mu)$ or $N_m(l, d)$ using commutative algebra. In particular, a reciprocity theorem can be obtained. Some of these results will be discussed in a subsequent communication. We also observe that the function $N_m(l, d)$ has close connection with the classical coding problem. In fact $\sum N_m(l, d)$ where the sum is over all $m \times m$ matrices d with all off diagonal entries $\ge r$ is precisely the number of codes C of length l with $|C| = m$ and minimum distance $\ge r$.

We also note that in [D$_1$] and [D$_3$] for all distance patterns on $m \le 4$ points all realizations up to equivalence were described. In particular they prove that $N_m(l, d) = 1$ for $m \le 4, |Q| = 2$ and any $m \times m$ matrix d. Some classification was also obtained for the case $m = 5$ when d is on any facet of the convex cone generated by E_5. But if d is in the interior of this cone, $N_m(l, d)$ may be > 1.

2. Positive independence. In this section we will develop a concept of positive independence (hereafter called P-independence) for any Z-module or any

convex set. The particular case of this phenomenon for binary codes was studied in
[D_5].

Let M be a $\mathbb{Z}$-module. Let $E = \{\underline{e}_1, \underline{e}_2, \ldots, \underline{e}_s\} \subseteq M$. Our interest is in studying the abelian semigroup $N_E \subseteq M$ generated by E. Thus $N_E = \{x_1\underline{e}_1 + x_2\underline{e}_2 + \cdots + x_s\underline{e}_s | x_i \in \mathbb{N}\}$.

Interest in this study is motivated by the fact that existence questions of many combinatorial objects amount to studying such semigroups. For example, as seen in the previous section existence question of codes is related to studying the semigroup D_m generated by q-tomies, $d_e, e \in E_m$. Existence question of designs or orthogonal arrays also correspond to similar pairs (E, N_E) (see [SS], [RS_j]).

A vector $\underline{x} \in \mathbb{Z}^s, \underline{x} = (x_1, x_2, \cdots, x_s)$ will be called a *linear dependency* on E if $\sum x_i\underline{e}_i = 0$ where the sum is over all $i = 1, 2, \cdots, s$. The set $N'_E = \{\underline{x} \in \mathbb{Z}^s | \underline{x}$ a linear dependency on $E\}$ is clearly a submodule of $\mathbb{Z}^s$. For any $\underline{x} \in \mathbb{Z}^s$ define

> (i) $\operatorname{supp} \underline{x} = \{i | 1 \leq i \leq s, x_i \neq o\}$
>
> (ii) $\quad \underline{x}_+ = (y_1, y_2, \cdots y_s), y_i = x_i$ if $x_i > 0$ and $y_i = 0$, otherwise $, 1 \leq i \leq s$
>
> (iii) $\quad \underline{x}_- = \underline{x}_+ - \underline{x}$
>
> (iv) $\operatorname{supp}_p \underline{x} = \{i | 1 \leq i \leq s, x_i > 0\}$.

Note that $\operatorname{supp}_p \underline{x} = \operatorname{supp} \underline{x}_+$ and

$$(\operatorname{supp} \underline{x}_+) \cap (\operatorname{supp} \underline{x}_-) = \phi$$

We will say that $\underline{y} \in N_E$ is *weakly rigid* if $\underline{y} = x_1\underline{e}_1 + \underline{x}_2\underline{e}_2 + \cdots + x_s\underline{e}_s = w_1\underline{e}_1 + w_2\underline{e}_2 + \cdots + w_s\underline{e}_s$ x_i, w_i's nonnegative integers implies that $x_i = w_i, 1 \leq i \leq s$, i.e. $\underline{y}$ has a unique expression in terms of $\underline{e}_i$'s. An element $\underline{y} \in N_E$ will be called *rigid* if $\lambda\underline{y}$ is weakly rigid for all $\lambda \in \mathbb{N}$. Note that completely fundamental elements defined in the previous section are always rigid. The concept of rigidity has been studied in [DR] and [DS] for the convex cone of distance patterns of all binary codes of size m. Note that a distance pattern $d \in D_m(Q)$ is weakly rigid if and only if $\sum N_m(l, d) = 1$ where the sum is over all $l \geq 0$. We now show how rigid elements can be found by using linear dependencies and a naturally associated simplicial complex.

For $\underline{x} = (x_1, x_2, \cdots x_s)$ and $\underline{w} = (w_1, w_2, \cdots, w_s)$ write $\underline{x} \geq \underline{w}$ if and only if $x_i \geq w_i$ for $1 \leq i \leq s$. Consider any $\underline{y} \in N_E$. Suppose that $\underline{y} = x_1\underline{e}_1 + x_2\underline{e}_2 + \cdots + x_s\underline{e}_s, x_i \in \mathbb{N}$. Let $\underline{x} = (x_1, x_2, \cdots, x_s)$. Suppose that $\underline{x} \geq \underline{w}$ for some $\underline{w} \in N'_E, \underline{x} \neq \underline{w}$ and $\underline{w} \neq \underline{0}$. Clearly

$$\underline{y} = x_1\underline{e}_1 + x_2\underline{e}_2 + \cdots + x_s\underline{e}_s - (w_1\underline{e}_1 + w_2\underline{e}_2 + \cdots + w_s\underline{e}_s)$$
$$= (x_1 - w_1)\underline{e}_1 + (x_2 - w_2)\underline{e}_2 + \cdots + (x_s - w_s)\underline{e}_s.$$

Thus $\underline{y}$ is not weakly rigid. Conversely if $\underline{y} = x_1\underline{e}_1 + x_2\underline{e}_2 + \cdots + x_s\underline{e}_s$ is not weakly rigid by reversing the above steps we have a $\underline{w} \in N'_E$ such that $\underline{x} \geq \underline{w}$. The part (a) of the following theorem is now clear and part (b) follows by the same argument by considering $\lambda\underline{y}$ for sufficiently large λ.

98

THEOREM 2.1. *Let* $\underline{y} = x_1\underline{e}_1 + x_2\underline{e}_2 + \cdots + x_s\underline{e}_s \in N_E, x_i \in \mathbf{N}, \ \underline{x} = (x_1, x_2, \cdots, x_s)$. *Then*

(a) $\underline{y}$ *is weakly rigid if and only if* $\underline{x} \not\geq \underline{w}$ *for all* $\underline{w} \in N'_E, \underline{w} \neq \underline{x}, \underline{w} \neq \underline{0}$.

(b) $\underline{y}$ *is rigid if and only if* $\mathrm{supp}_p\underline{y}$ *does not contain* $\mathrm{supp}_p\underline{w}$ *for any* $\underline{w} \in N'_E$

For each $\underline{y} \in N_E, \underline{y}$ *weakly rigid,* $\underline{y} = x_1\underline{e}_1 + x_2\underline{e}_2 + \cdots + x_s\underline{e}_s$, *define* $\mathrm{supp}\ \underline{y} = \{i | x_i \neq 0, \ 1 \leq i \leq s\}$. *Note that from the definition of weak rigidity it is clear that* $\mathrm{supp}\ \underline{y}$ *is uniquely defined. Let*

$$R_E = \{X \subseteq \{1, 2, \cdots, s\} | \text{ for some } \underline{y} \in N_E, \underline{y} \text{ rigid }, \text{ supp } \underline{y} = X\}.$$

The following corollary is immediate from the above theorem.

COROLLARY 2.2. *The set* R_E *is a simplicial complex such that* $X \in R_E$ *if and only if* X *does not contain* $\mathrm{supp}_p\underline{x}$ *for any linear dependency* $\underline{x} \in N'_E$.

Remark 2.3. From the corollary it is clear that the simplicial complex R_E depends only on the module N'_E and not on E. Thus for any submodule $N' \subseteq \mathbf{Z}^s$, we define $R_{N'} = \{Y \subseteq \{1, 2, \cdots, s\} | Y \not\supseteq \mathrm{supp}_p\underline{x} \text{ for any } \underline{x} \in N'\}$. Clearly $R_E = R_{N_{E'}}$.

Now let $N' \subseteq \mathbf{Z}^s$ be a $\mathbf{Z}$-module. Clearly the simplicial complex $R_{N'}$ describes much of the combinatorial structure of the module N'. Note that $R_{N'}$ consists of precisely the subsets $Y \subseteq \{1, 2, \cdots, s\}$ which are not contained in the positive parts of the circuits of the oriented matroid of supports of elements of N'. With this analogy we define a set $Y \subseteq \{1, 2, \cdots, s\}$ to be P-*independent* if and only if $Y \in R_{N'}$; i.e. Y does not contain $\mathrm{supp}_p\underline{x}$ for any $\underline{x} \in N'$. The objects equivalent to circuits for P-independence are the minimal nonempty $\mathrm{supp}_p\underline{x}$'s , $\underline{x} \in N'$. Hence we define a subset $Y \subseteq \{1, 2, \cdots, s\}$ to be a P-*circuit* if and only if $Y \neq \phi$ and $Y = \mathrm{supp}_p\underline{x}$ for some $\underline{x} \in N'$ and if $Y \supseteq \mathrm{supp}_p\underline{y}$ for any $\underline{y} \in N'$, then $\underline{y} = 0$ or $Y = \mathrm{supp}_p\underline{y}$. An element $\underline{y} \in N'$ will be called *elementary* if for all $\underline{x} \in N'$ with $\underline{y}_+ \geq \underline{x}_+$, either $\underline{x} = 0$ or $\underline{y}_+ = \underline{x}_+$. Thus elementary elements are precisely atoms in the preorder $\geq$ defined on N' by $\underline{y} \geq \underline{x}$ if and only if $\underline{y}_+ \geq \underline{x}_+$.

Note that for weak rigidity we need to verify condition (a) of theorem 2.1 only for elementary $\underline{w}$ and similarly for rigidity we need to verify in condition (b) only the fact that $\mathrm{supp}\ \underline{y}$ does not contain any P-circuits. It is also clear that for any P-circuit Y there exists an elementary $\underline{y} \in N'$ such that $Y = \mathrm{supp}_p\underline{y}$. However $\mathrm{supp}_p\underline{y}$ for an elementary $\underline{y}$ in general may not be a P-circuit.

Problem 1: Describe all P-circuits or P-independent sets or elementary elements for the $\mathbf{Z}$-module of all linear dependencies of q-tomies $d_e, e \in E_m$. Describe all weakly rigid or rigid codes $C, |C| = m, C \subseteq Q^X$.

For $m \leq 5$ and $|Q| = 2$ this problem was solved in [D$_2$] (see also [DS]). It will also be interesting to describe all rigid objects for the analogous semigroups considered for t-designs, orthogonal array or their q-analogues in [SS], [RS$_1$] and [RS$_2$].

In [D$_2$] it was also shown that all elementary elements generate the $\mathbf{Z}$-module of all linear dependencies of q-tomies $d_e, e \in E_m$ for $m \leq 5, |Q| = 2$. Note that this implies that for this case given any two codes C_1 and C_2 with the same distance pattern we have a sequence $C_1 = C_1', C_2', \cdots, C_g' = C_2$ such that $C_i', 1 \leq i \leq g$, has the same distance pattern as C_1 and C_{i+1}' is obtained from C_i' by adding an elementary element of the above $\mathbf{Z}$-module. The module of $n \times m$ integral matrices in which all row sums and column sums are equal to 0 is also generated by elementary elements. In fact in this case the elementary elements are precisely $n \times m$ matrices

$$A = (a_{ij}) \text{ where}$$
$$a_{ij} = \begin{cases} 1 & \text{if } (i,j) = (s,t) \text{ or } (s',t') \\ -1 & \text{if } (i,j) = (s,t') \text{ or } (s',t) \end{cases}$$
$$\text{and } 0, \text{ otherwise}$$

where $s \neq s', t \neq t', 1 \leq s, s' \leq n, 1 \leq t, t' \leq m$. This follows essentially from Ryser's Theorem [R] or by direct observation. This leads to the following problem.

Problem 2: When do elementary elements generate the whole module? In particular, is it true for all modules described in problem 1?

We do not know of any example of modules for which it is not true. The interest in this question arises from the fact that in general the numbers of elementary elements in a $\mathbf{Z}$-module may be much less than the number of circuits of the corresponding matroids. Thus these may be better as a set of generators.

We conclude this paper with some remarks on analogues for the convex sets. Let C be a convex cone in $\mathbf{R}^m$ generated by $E = \{e_1, e_2, \cdots, e_s\}$. Thus every element of C can be expressed in the form $x_1 e_1 + x_2 e_2 + \cdots + x_s e_s, x_i \geq 0, x_i \in \mathbf{R}$. It is clear that all the above definitions can be formulated for this case with $\mathbf{Z}$ replaced by $\mathbf{R}$, module replaced by vector space etc. Note that in this case weakly rigid implies rigid. We define one more term here. A facet F of the convex cone C will be called rigid if and only if each element of F is rigid. Support of F is defined by supp $F = \{i | 1 \leq i \leq s, e_i \in F\}$. Clearly F is generated by $\{e_i | i \in \text{supp } F\}$. The following theorem follows immediately from the analogue of theorem 2.1 for this case. Note that this theorem in particular implies that a rigid face is also simplicial.

THEOREM 2.4. *A face F of a convex cone $C \subseteq \mathbf{R}^m$ generated by $E = \{e_1, e_2, \cdots, e_s\}$ is rigid if and only if supp $F \in R_E$, where R_E is the simplicial complex of P-independent subsets of $\{1, 2, \ldots, s\}$ with respect to the vector space $\subseteq \mathbf{R}^s$ of all linear dependencies of $\{e_1, e_2, \cdots, e_s\}$.*

All rigid faces for the convex cone generated by distance patterns of binary codes with $|C| = 5$ were found in [DS] . We note that with slight modifications these ideas can also be extended to convex sets of sets of nonnegative integral solutions of nonhomogeneous equations by considering affine dependencies in place of linear dependencies.

REFERENCES

[A] ASSOUAD, P., *Sous espaces de l' et inequalités hypermetriques*, C.R. Acad. Sci., Paris 294, Series A (1982), pp. 439-442.

[AD]   ASSOUAD, P. AND DEZA, M., *Metric subspaces of L^1*, Publ. Math. d'Orsay, Universite, Paris-Sud (1982).

[D$_1$]   DEZA, M. (TYLKIN), *Realizability of matrices of distance in unitary cubes (in Russian)*, Prol. Kibern, 7 (1962), pp. 31-42.

[D$_2$]   DEZA, M., *Isometries of the hypergraphs*, Proc. Int. Conference on Theory of Graphs, Calcutta, (ed. A.R. Rao) (1977); McMillan, India (1979), pp. 174-189.

[D$_3$]   DEZA, M., *Small Pentagonal spaces*, Rendiconti del Seminario Matematico di' brescia, Volume settino (1984), pp. 269-282.

[DR]   DEZA, M. AND ROSENBERG, I.G., *Intersections and distance patterns*, Util. Math., 25 (1984), pp. 191-212.

[DS]   DEZA, M. AND SINGHI N.M., *Rigid Pentagons in Hypercubes*, Graphs and Combinaterics, 4 (1988), pp. 31-42.

[R]   RYSER, H., *Combinaterial Mathematics*, the Carus Mathematical Monographs, no. 14, The Mathematical Association of America.

[RS$_1$]   RAY-CHAUDHURI, D.K. AND SINGHI, N.M., *On existence and number of orthogonal arrays*, J. of Combinatorial Theory A, 47 (1988), pp. 28-36.

[RS$_2$]   RAY-CHAUDHURI, D.K. AND SINGHI, N.M., *q-analogues of t-designs and their existence*, Linear Algebra And Its Applications, 114/115 (1989), pp. 57-68.

[S]   STANLEY, R., *Combinatorics and Commutative Algebra*, Birkhäuser, Boston (1983).

[SS]   SINGHI, N.M., AND SHRIKHANDE, S.S., *A reciprocity relation for t-designs*, Europ. J. Combinatorics, 8 (1987), pp. 59-68.

BOUNDS ON THE NUMBER OF PAIRS OF
UNJOINED POINTS IN A PARTIAL PLANE

DAVID A. DRAKE† AND PAUL ERDÖS‡

Abstract. We prove two theorems which bound the number of pairs of unjoined points in a partial plane Σ defined on a finite number v of points. The bounds are obtained under assumptions on the number of lines in Σ together with the assumption that no line contains more than $v - 3$ points.

Key words. linear space, partial plane, projective plane

AMS(MOS) subject classifications. Primary 05B30, 51E30; Secondary 51E15

1. Introduction. A *partial plane* is a pair $\Sigma = (S, C)$ where S is a finite set (of elements called *points*) and C is a collection of subsets of S (called *lines*) such that no two points of Σ lie in more than one common line. Throughout the paper, D (for *deficit*) denotes the number of pairs of unjoined points in Σ, $v = |S|$, $b = |C|$, and k is the largest cardinality of a line of Σ. Our principal result is the following

THEOREM A. *Let n be an integer, $n \geq 29$, $n^2 - n + 3 \leq v \leq n^2 + n - 1$, $b < v$, $k \leq v - 3$. Then $2D > 3v - 13v^{3/4}$.*

A *linear space* is a partial plane whose deficit D is zero. Our interest in the case $b < v$ arises from the following theorem of de Bruijn and Erdös [2]: in every linear space Σ, the inequality $b \geq v$ holds; and b equals v if and only if Σ is a proper or degenerate projective plane. The de Bruijn-Erdös theorem immediately yields $D \geq 1$ if $b < v$.

An improvement of the inequality $D \geq 1$ can be obtained from Totten's classification [5] of "restricted" linear spaces; i.e., spaces with $(b - v)^2 \leq v$. See also [4] for a shorter proof of the Totten classification. A consequence of this classification is that every linear space with $n^2 + 2 \leq v$ has $b \geq n^2 + n + 1$. Therefore, if Σ is a partial plane with $b < v$ lines and $v = n^2 + t$ points where $2 \leq t \leq n$, then $D \geq n - t + 2$: for, otherwise, the addition of D lines of cardinality 2 would yield a linear space with $b \leq n^2 + n$.

Theorem A treats all values of v except those of the form $n^2 + n + 1 + \epsilon$ where ϵ is one of -1, 0 or 1. Whenever n is the order of a projective plane Π, these three exclusions are necessary. One can form Σ from Π in these cases by removing one point and two lines, by removing one line, or by adjoining one point and extending one line of Π to include the new point. One obtains $2D < v$ for $\epsilon = 0$ and $2D < 2v$ for $\epsilon = \pm 1$. A similar construction with $\epsilon = -2$ gives a deficit D for which $2D$

---

†Department of Mathematics, University of Florida, Gainesville, Florida 32611. This author's contribution to the paper was supported in part by the Institute for Mathematics and its Applications with funds provided by the National Science Foundation.

‡Mathematical Institute, Hungarian Academy of Sciences, Budapest H-1364, Hungary.

is approximately $3v - 8\sqrt{v}$. Thus, there is no hope of sharpening the bound to $2D > 3v$ unless the value $v = n^2 + n - 1$ is also excluded.

If there is a partial plane Σ with $n^2 + n + 3$ points and $n^2 + n + 2$ lines, all of size n + 1, the deficit D will satisfy $2D = 3n^2 + 3n + 6$ which is also less than $3v$. At least in the cases $n = 2, 3, 4$, such Σ do exist. They can be constructed as follows. Let $L = \{g_0, g_1, ..., g_n\}$ be a subset of the additively written cyclic group G of order $n^2 + n + 3$ so that the $n^2 + n$ differences $g_i - g_j$ are distinct. Then the translates $L + g$ with $g \in G$ give a partial plane Σ' with $b = v = n^2 + n + 3$ and all lines of size $n + 1$. One obtains Σ by discarding one of the lines of Σ'. The desired "near difference sets" can be obtained from $(n^2 + n + 1, n + 1, 1)$-difference sets $L = \{g_0, ..., g_n\}$ whenever $0 = g_0 < g_1 < ... < g_n < (n^2 + n + 3)/2$. One simply interprets L as a subset of the cyclic group of order $n^2 + n + 3$. For $n = 2, 3, 4$, for example, one may take L to be $\{0, 1, 3\}, \{0, 4, 5, 7\}, \{0, 3, 4, 9, 11\}$.

The considerations of the two preceding paragraphs indicate that, if $b < v = n^2 + n + 1 + \epsilon$, then the best one can hope for is a D-bound somewhat less than $v(|\epsilon| + 1)/2$. Theorem A treats the case $\epsilon = 2$. Rather than attempting to generalize this result to $\epsilon > 2$, however, we have taken a different tack; namely, that of permitting b to be greater than v. Our main result is

THEOREM B. *Let β be a real number with $4 \leq \beta \leq 12$ and n be an integer with $n \geq \max(19, (13\beta + 16)/6)$. Suppose also that $n^2 + \frac{n}{2} \leq v \leq n^2 + n$, $b \leq n^2 + n + 1 - \beta$, $k \leq v - 3$. Then $2D > (\beta/4)v - 4v^{3/4}$.*

We do not claim that Theorem B is the best possible result. We have included it for two reasons: firstly, it demonstrates that $b < v$ is not a necessary condition to force a large D; and, secondly, much of the proof of Theorem A can be used in the proof of Theorem B. En route to proving Theorem B, we obtain the following two results.

PROPOSITION C. *Let $4 \leq \beta < 8n^2 + 4n - 4$, $6n \geq 13\beta + 16$, $k \leq n + 1$, $n^2 + \frac{n}{2} \leq v \leq n^2 + n$, $b \leq n^2 + n + 1 - \beta$. Then $D > \beta v/8$.*

For a line L, the *L-deficit D_L* is defined to be the number of point pairs P, Q with P a point on L and Q a point off L which is unjoined to P.

PROPOSITION D. *Let $n \geq 19$ be an integer, $\frac{2}{3}n^2 + \frac{2}{3}n + 10 \leq v \leq n^2 + n$, $n + 3 \leq k \leq v - 3$, $b \leq n^2 + n + 1$. Then $2D_L > 3v$ for each k-line L.*

All four results stated above can be reworded to read as follows: if a partial plane Σ has a small deficit, then b is large relative to v. With such rewording, one observes their connection to two other recent theorems. One is a theorem of Erdös, Fowler, Sòs and Wilson [5] which reads as follows: if Σ has deficit 0 and v is of the form $n^2 + n + 1$, then either Σ is a projective plane or $b \geq n^2 + 2n + 1$. The second is a recent improvement due to Blokhuis, Schmitt and Wilbrink [1] which reads: if Σ has deficit 0, v is of the form $n^2 + n + 1$ and Σ is not obtained from a projective plane by "breaking up" a line, then $b > n^2 + 3n - 4\sqrt{n}$.

2. The small line case. Throughout the paper, Σ denotes a partial plane on v points with b lines, the largest of which consist of k points. The deficit (the number of pairs of unjoined points) in Σ is denoted by D. A line of Σ of cardinality i is called an *i-line*.

LEMMA 2.1. *When $k = n$ and $b < v$, the following statements hold:*

(1) *if $v \geq n^2 - n + 4$, then $2D > 3v$;*
(2) *if $v = n^2 - n + 3$, then $2D \geq 3n^2 - 3n + 6$.*

Proof. An easy calculation, using the fact that

$$D \geq \binom{v}{2} - b\binom{n}{2} \geq \binom{v}{2} - (v-1)\binom{n}{2},$$

yields the asserted conclusions. $\square$

In the rest of Section 2, we consider the case $k = n + 1$. When $k = n + 1$, clearly

$$(2.1) \qquad D \geq \binom{v}{2} - b_{n+1}\binom{n+1}{2} - (b - b_{n+1})\binom{n}{2},$$

and thus

$$(2.2) \qquad 2nb_{n+1} \geq v^2 - v - bn^2 + bn - 2D.$$

In Lemmas 2.2 through 2.5 below, we attempt to force the existence of a point P which lies in R lines, r of which are $(n+1)$-lines, where R and r are large. Each pair of $(n+1)$-lines L, K through P contains n^2 pairs of points not joined by any of the R lines through P. Thus, there are at least $n^2 - (b - R)$ pairs of unjoined points on $L \cup K$. Altogether, the number of pairs of unjoined points on the $(n+1)$-lines through P will be at least $(n^2 - b + R)(r^2 - r)/2$, so this number is a lower bound for D.

LEMMA 2.2. *Let $k = n + 1$, $v = n^2 + y$, $1 \leq y \leq n$; and suppose that $D \leq \delta v$ for some real number δ. Suppose also that no point of Σ lies in $n + 1$ or more lines, $y + 1$ or more of which are $(n+1)$-lines. Then $f \leq 0$ where f is defined to be*

$$y^3(-n+1) + y^2(2n^2 - 2) + y(n^5 + n^4 - n^3 - 3n^2 + n + 1) + (-n^5 - n^4 + n^3 + n^2)$$
$$+ \delta\big(y^2(2n - 2) + y(2n^3 - 6n^2 + 2n + 2) + (-4n^4 + 2n^3 + 2n^2)\big)$$
$$+ b\big(y(-n^3 + n) + (n^3 - n)\big).$$

Proof. Let w denote the number of points of Σ which lie in $y + 1$ or more $(n+1)$-lines. Each of these w points P is joined to at most n^2 points of $\Sigma \backslash \{P\}$, so

$$(2.3) \qquad 2D \geq w(y - 1).$$

104

Count flags (P, L) such that L is an $(n+1)$-line of Σ. Since $y \leq n$, one obtains

$$(2.4) \qquad (n+1)b_{n+1} \leq wn + (v-w)y.$$

Inequality (2.4) yields $2w(n-y) \geq 2(n+1)b_{n+1} - 2vy$, whence inequality (2.2) gives

$$(2.5) \qquad 2nw(n-y) \geq v^2 n + v^2 - vn - v - bn^3 + bn - 2Dn - 2D - 2vny.$$

Inequality (2.3) gives $4Dn(n-y) \geq 2nw(n-y)(y-1)$. Combine the last inequality with (2.5) to obtain

$$(2.6) \quad D(4n^2 - 2ny + 2y - 2n - 2) \geq (v^2 n + v^2 - vn - v - bn^3 + bn - 2vny)(y-1).$$

Since $D \leq \delta v$ and $y \leq n \leq 2n + 1$, one may replace D by δv in (2.6). If one also replaces v by $n^2 + y$, the conclusion of Lemma 2.2 ensues. $\square$

LEMMA 2.3. *For integers n and y, let $k = n + 1$, $v = n^2 + y$, $b < v$. Then*

(1) $2D > 3v$ *if* $2\sqrt{n} \leq y \leq n - 2$ *and* $n \geq 29$;

(2) $2D > 3n^2 - 9n + 8$ *if* $y = n - 1$ *and* $n \geq 7$.

Proof. Without loss of generality, one may assume that $b = v - 1$. Assume, by way of contradiction, that $2D \leq 3v$ and that Σ has no point that is incident with $n + 1$ or more lines, $y + 1$ or more of which are $(n+1)$-lines. Apply Lemma 2.2 with $\delta = 3/2$ and $b = n^2 + y - 1$. Then $f \leq 0$ where

$$f = y^3(-n+1) + y^2(-n^3 + 2n^2 + 4n - 5) + y(n^4 + 5n^3 - 12n^2 + 2n + 4) + (-7n^4 + 2n^3 + 4n^2 + n).$$

Regarding $f = f(y)$ as a function of y and using $n \geq 21$, one obtains $0 < f(8)$, $f(n-2)$. Since, the second derivative $f''(y)$ is negative for positive y, $f(y) > 0$ for all y in the interval $[8, n-2]$. This contradiction proves the existence of a point P with at least $n + 1$ incident lines, at least $y + 1$ of which are $(n+1)$-lines. Each of the pairs of $(n+1)$-lines incident with P contains at least $n^2 - (b - n - 1) = n - y + 2$ unjoined pairs of points. Thus, $(y+1)y(n-y+2) \leq 2D \leq 3v = 3n^2 + 3y$. Then $3n^2 - n(y^2 + y) + (y^3 - y^2 + y) \geq 0$. This inequality fails, however, for all n and y with $2\sqrt{n} \leq y \leq n - 2$, $n \geq 29$. The contradiction gives $2D > 3v$, and completes the proof of assertion (1).

The proof of assertion (2) is similar. One applies Lemma 2.2 with $y = n - 1$, $b = n^2 + y - 1 = n^2 + n - 2$ and $\delta = (3n^2 - 9n + 8)/2v = (3n^2 - 9n + 8)/(2n^2 + 2n - 2)$ to obtain $0 \geq f = 2n^2 - 14n + 12$. This contradiction yields a point P which lies on $n + 1$ or more lines, at least n of which are $(n+1)$-lines. Arguing as above, one obtains $2D \geq 3n^2 - 3n$, a contradiction which completes the proofs of assertion (2). $\square$

LEMMA 2.4. *Let n be an integer, β and δ be positive real numbers. Suppose that $k = n + 1$, $v = n^2 + y$, $n/2 \leq y \leq n$, $b = n^2 + n + 1 - \beta$, $D \leq \delta v$, $\beta \geq 6\delta + 1$, $3n \geq 52\delta + 8$. Then some point P of Σ lies in $n + 1$ or more lines, $y + 1$ or more of which are $(n + 1)$-lines.*

Proof. Assume, by way of contradiction, that there is no such point P. Apply Lemma 2.2 with $b = n^2 + n + 1 - \beta$. One obtains $f \leq 0$ where

$$
\begin{aligned}
f =\; & y^3(-n + 1) + y^2(2n^2 + 2\delta n - 2\delta - 2) \\
& + y(\beta n^3 + 2\delta n^3 - n^3 - 6\delta n^2 - 2n^2 - \beta n + 2\delta n + 2n + 2\delta + 1) \\
& + (-4\delta n^4 - \beta n^3 + 2\delta n^3 + n^3 + 2\delta n^2 + \beta n - n)
\end{aligned}
$$

Regarding $f = f(y)$ as a function of y, one computes

$$
\begin{aligned}
8f(n/2) =\; & n^4(4\beta - 24\delta - 1) + n^3(-8\beta - 4\delta + 1) \\
& n^2(-4\beta + 20\delta + 4) + n(8\beta + 8\delta - 4)
\end{aligned}
$$

Since $n \geq 2$, the preceding expression is increasing in β. Thus,

$$
8f(n/2) \geq 3n^4 - (52\delta + 7)n^3 - 4\delta n^2 + (56\delta + 4)n.
$$

Use $3n \geq 52\delta + 8$ to obtain

$$
8f(n/2) \geq n^3 - 4\delta n^2 + (56\delta + 4)n > 0.
$$

Thus, $f(n/2)$ is positive. Computation reveals that $f(n)$ and the second derivative $f''(n/2)$ are also positive. Consequently $f(y) > 0$ for all y in the interval $[n/2, n]$, a contradiction which proves Lemma 2.4. $\square$

LEMMA 2.5. *Let n be an integer, β and δ be positive real numbers. Suppose that $k = n + 1$, $v = n^2 + y$, $n/2 \leq y \leq n$, $b = n^2 + n + 1 - \beta$, $\beta \geq \max(6\delta + 1, 8\delta)$, $3n \geq 52\delta + 8$. Then $D > \delta v$.*

Proof. Assume $D \leq \delta v$. Let P be a point given by Lemma 2.4. Each pair of $(n + 1)$-lines which is incident with P must contain at least $n^2 - (b - n - 1) = \beta$ unjoined pairs of points. Thus, $(y + 1)y\beta \leq 2D \leq 2\delta v = 2\delta n^2 + 2\delta y$. Then $g(y) := y^2\beta - y(2\delta - \beta) - 2\delta n^2 \leq 0$. A computation shows that the larger root of $g(y)$ is less than $n/2$ when $\beta \geq 8\delta \geq 0$. Thus, $g(y) > 0$ for $n/2 \leq y$, a contradiction which proves Lemma 2.5. $\square$

Proof of Proposition C. Apply Lemma 2.5 with $\delta = \beta/8$ to obtain the asserted conclusion when $k = n + 1$. Thus, assume that $k \leq n$. Then $D \geq \binom{v}{2} - b\binom{n}{2}$. Using $b = n^2 + n + 1 - \beta$ gives $8D - \beta v \geq 4v^2 - 4v - 4(n^2 + n + 1 - \beta)(n^2 - n) - \beta v =: h(v)$. One calculates $h(n^2 + \frac{n}{2}) > 0$, and $h'(n^2 + \frac{n}{2}) > 0$ if $\beta < 8n^2 + 4n - 4$. $\square$

LEMMA 2.6. *Let $k = n + 1, v = n^2 + y, b < v$. Then $2D > 3v$ if either of the following two sets of conditions holds:*

(1) $0 \leq y \leq n/2$, and $n \geq 24$;

(2) $-n + 4\sqrt{n} \leq y \leq 0$, and $n \geq 28$.

Proof. Again, without loss of generality, we take b to be $v - 1$. Assume, by way of contradiction, that $2D \leq 3v$. Let A denote the average number of $(n + 1)$-lines incident with a given point of Σ. In inequality (2.2), replace $2D$ by $3v$ and b by $v - 1$; then replace v by $n^2 + y$ to obtain

$$(2.7) \qquad 2A = \frac{2(n + 1)}{n^2 + y} b_{n+1} \geq n + y - 2 + \frac{y}{n} - \frac{4}{n} - \frac{y + 1}{n^2 + y}.$$

If $|y| \leq n$ and $n \geq 6$, inequality (2.7) yields $2A > n + y - 4$, hence

$$(2.8) \qquad A \geq \frac{(n + y - 3)}{2} =: B.$$

Then some point P of Σ lies in at least B $(n + 1)$-lines. Suppose that P lies in a total of $B + x$ lines. Then P is unjoined to at least $v - 1 - (B + x)n$ other points. In addition, each pair of $(n + 1)$-lines incident with P contains at least $n^2 - (b - B - x) = (n - y - 1 + 2x)/2$ pairs of unjoined points. Thus

$$(2.9) \qquad D \geq n^2 + y - 1 - (B + x)n + \binom{B}{2}(n - y - 1 + 2x)/2.$$

Define

$$f(y) = 2y^2 + 4ny - 16y + 2n^2 - 32n + 30,$$
$$g(y) = -y^3 - y^2(n - 7) + y(n^2 - 10n + 9) + (n^3 - n^2 + 47n - 31).$$

Using the definition of B, inequality (2.9) becomes

$$(2.10) \qquad 16D \geq xf(y) + g(y).$$

For $n \geq 12$, computation shows that $f(y) > 0$ for all $y > -n + 4\sqrt{n}$. Thus (2.10) implies

$$(2.11) \qquad 16D \geq g(y).$$

Define $h(y)$ to be $24v - g(y)$. Inequality (2.11) and the assumption on D yield

$$(2.12) \quad 0 \leq h(y) = y^3 + y^2(n - 7) - y(n^2 - 10n - 15) - (n^3 - 25n^2 + 47n - 31).$$

If $n \geq 17$, the smaller root of the derivative $h'(y)$ is less than $-n + 7$. Thus, the maximum values achieved by $h(y)$ on the intervals $[0, n/2], [-n + 4\sqrt{n}, 0]$ must occur at end points. If $n \geq 24$, both $h(0)$ and $h(n/2)$ are negative. This contradiction of (2.12) proves conclusion (1). If $n \geq 28$, then $h(-n + 4\sqrt{n})$ is also negative. Again (2.12) is contradicted, so conclusion (2) has been proved. $\square$

LEMMA 2.7. *Whenever $b < v$ and $n \geq 29$, each of the following statements holds:*

(1) $k \leq n, n^2 - n + 3 = v$ implies $2D \geq 3n^2 - 3n + 6$;
(2) $k \leq n, n^2 - n + 4 \leq v$ implies $2D > 3v$;
(3) $k \leq n + 1, n^2 - n + 4\sqrt{n} \leq v \leq n^2 + n - 2$ implies $2D > 3v$;
(4) $k \leq n + 1, n^2 + n - 1 = v$ implies $2D \geq 3n^2 - 9n + 10$.

Proof. Apply Lemmas 2.1, 2.3 and 2.6.

3. A linear programming problem. Throughout Section 3, we assume that Σ is a partial plane on v points and b lines whose largest lines are k-lines. For a particular k-line L, write b_i to denote the number of i-lines which are different from L and which contain a point of L. (Observe that the b_i's had a different definition in Section 2.) Clearly,

$$(3.1) \qquad\qquad b_i \geq 0 \text{ for } 2 \leq i \leq k, \text{ and}$$

$$(3.2) \qquad\qquad B_L := b_2 + b_3 + \ldots + b_k \leq b - 1.$$

Let C_L denote the number of pairs of points of Σ not on L which are joined by lines that intersect L. Let D_L denote the $L - deficit$; i.e., the number of pairs of points (P, Q) with P in L and Q not in L such that P and Q are joined by no line of Σ. Then

$$(3.3) \qquad\qquad C_L = \sum_{i=2}^{k} \binom{i-1}{2} b_i \leq \binom{v-k}{2}, \text{ and}$$

$$(3.4) \qquad\qquad D_L = k(v - k) - \sum_{i=2}^{k} (i-1)b_i.$$

Consider the following

(3.5) **Linear Programming Problem.** Given integers v, k, b with $v > k > 1$, $b > 1$, minimize D_L (i.e., maximize $\sum_{i=2}^{k}(i-1)b_i$) over all real vectors $(b_2, \ldots, b_k)$ which satisfy the inequalities (3.1), (3.2), (3.3).

Clearly, an optimal solution to (3.5) gives a value D_L^* of D_L which is a lower bound for the actual values D_L which arise from partial planes Σ. We consider also the linear programming problem which is dual to (3.5).

(3.6) **Dual Linear Programming Problem.** Given integers v, k, b with $v > k > 1$, $b > 1$, minimize $(b-1)x + \binom{v-k}{2}y$ over all real pairs (x, y) with $x \geq 0, y \geq 0$, subject to the conditions $x + \binom{i-1}{2}y \geq i - 1$ for $2 \leq i \leq k$.

LEMMA 3.1. *Suppose that $(t-1)(t-2) \leq (v-k)(v-k-1)/(b-1) \leq t(t-1)$ holds for some t with $2 \leq t \leq k - 1$. Then, an optimal solution D_L^* to (3.5) is obtained by putting $b_i = 0$ for $i \neq t, t+1$ and setting*

(1) $2b_t = (b-1)t - (v-k)(v-k-1)/(t-1) =: 2b_t^*$,
(2) $2b_{t+1} = (v-k)(v-k-1)/(t-1) - (b-1)(t-2) =: 2b_{t+1}^*$.

Proof. Calculations reveal that the specified b_i's are a feasible solution to (3.5). A feasible solution to (3.6) is given by $x = t/2, y = 1/(t-1)$. Next, one checks that

$$(t-1)b_t + tb_{t+1} = (b-1)\frac{t}{2} + \binom{v-k}{2}\frac{1}{t-1}.$$

The duality theorem now guarantees the optimality of both of these solutions. ∎

LEMMA 3.2. *The inequality* $2D_L \geq 2k(v-k)-(b-1)t-(v-k)(v-k-1)/(t-1)$ *is valid whenever the assumptions of Lemma 3.1 hold.*

Proof. Lemma 3.1 gives $D_L \geq D_L^* = k(v-k) - (t-1)b_t^* - tb_{t+1}^*$. ∎

LEMMA 3.3. *Define* T *to be the positive real number which satisfies* $T(T-1) = (v-k)(v-k-1)/(b-1)$. *Then* $D_L \geq k(v-k) - T(b-1)$.

Proof. Let t be the integer which satisfies $t-1 < T \leq t$. Since Lemma 3.1 gives $D_L \geq D_L^* = k(v-k) - (t-1)b_t^* - tb_{t+1}^*$, it suffices to verify that

$$(3.7) \qquad\qquad T \geq S := \left((t-1)b_t^* + tb_{t+1}^*\right)/(b-1);$$

i.e., to prove that

$$(3.8) \qquad\qquad T(T-1)(b-1) \geq S(S-1)(b-1).$$

By the theorem of complementary slackness, the optimal solution of Lemma 3.1 satisfies (3.3) with equality. Thus, the left hand side of inequality (3.8) is

$$(v-k)(v-k-1) = (t-1)(t-2)b_t^* + t(t-1)b_{t+1}^*.$$

The definition of S in (3.7) now yields (3.8) and, thus, completes the proof of Lemma 3.3 ∎

LEMMA 3.4.

(1) $2D_L \geq 2k(v-k)-b+1-\sqrt{(b-1)^2 + 4(v-k)(v-k-1)(b-1)} =: g(k,v)$;
(2) *If* $b \leq 8v - 8k + 2$, *then* $2D_L \geq 2k(v-k) - b + 1 - (2v - 2k + 1)\sqrt{b-1}$.

Proof. Apply Lemma 3.3 to obtain conclusion (1). Conclusion (2) follows from conclusion (1) if $(b-1)^2 + 4(v-k)(v-k-1)(b-1) \leq (2v-2k+1)^2(b-1)$. The last inequality holds whenever $b \leq 8v - 8k + 2$. ∎

4. The large line case. Throughout Section 4, we assume that Σ is a partial plane on v points and b lines, the largest of which consist of k points. As in Section 3, L denotes a fixed k-line. In contrast to Section 2, we treat the case that k is large relative to v.

LEMMA 4.1. *Let n be a positive integer, $\frac{1}{2}n^2 + 4n + 9 < v, n + 3 \le k \le \frac{3}{4}v$, $b \le n^2 + n + 1$. Then $2D_L > 3v$ for each k-line L.*

Proof. Assume, by way of contradiction, that $3v \ge 2D_L$. Apply Lemma 3.4 (2), replacing $2D_L$ by $3v$ and $b - 1$ by $n^2 + n$ to obtain

$$3v \ge 2kv - 2k^2 - n^2 - n - 2v\sqrt{n^2 + n} + (2k - 1)\sqrt{n^2 + n}.$$

Replace the first occurrence of $\sqrt{n^2 + n}$ by $n + \frac{1}{2}$, the second occurrence by n to obtain

$$f(k) := 2k^2 - k(2v + 2n) + (2nv + 4v + n^2 + 2n) \ge 0.$$

One now computes $f(n + 3) = f(v - 3) = -2v + n^2 + 8n + 18$ which is negative in view of the lower bound assumed for v. Thus, $f(k) < 0$ for all k in the interval $[n + 3, v - 3]$. Since $\frac{3}{4}v \le v - 3$ when $n \ge 1$, this is a contradiction for all k which satisfy the hypotheses of Lemma 4.1. $\square$

LEMMA 4.2. *Let $n \ge 5$ be an integer, $\frac{2}{3}n^2 + \frac{2}{3}n + 10 \le v \le n^2 + n, \frac{3}{4}v \le k \le v - 3, b \le n^2 + n + 1$. Then $2D_L > 3v$ for each k-line L.*

Proof. Once again, it is no loss of generality to assume that $b = n^2 + n + 1$. We apply Lemma 3.4 (1) with $b = n^2 + n + 1$. It suffices to prove that $g(v - 3, v) > 3v$ and that $g(k - 1, v) \ge g(k, v)$ for $\frac{3}{4}v + 1 \le k \le v - 3$. We leave the proof of the first of these two inequalities to the reader. To prove the second, it helps to write l for $v - k$. The inequality to be established is equivalent to

$$\sqrt{(n^2 + n)^2 + 4(l^2 + l)(n^2 + n)} - \sqrt{(n^2 + n)^2 + 4(l^2 - l)(n^2 + n)} \le 2v - 2 - 4l.$$

It suffices to prove the inequality which is obtained from the preceding inequality by omitting the terms $(n^2 + n)^2$ inside both radicals. The remaining details are left to the reader. $\square$

Proof of Proposition D. Apply Lemmas 4.1 and 4.2.

LEMMA 4.3. *Let $n \ge 13, k = n + 2, v \ge n^2 - n, b \le n^2 + n + 1$. Then each k-line L satisfies $D_L > v - 4\sqrt{v}$.*

Proof. Assume, by way of contradiction, that $v - 4\sqrt{v} \ge D_L$. Apply Lemma 3.4 (2), replacing D_L by $v - 4\sqrt{v}$, k by $n + 2$, and $b - 1$ by $n^2 + n$ to obtain

$$2v - 8\sqrt{v} \ge (2n + 4)v - 3n^2 - 9n - 8 - 2v\sqrt{n^2 + n} + (2n + 3)\sqrt{n^2 + n}.$$

Replace the first occurrence of $\sqrt{n^2 + n}$ by $n + \frac{1}{2}$, the second by n, to obtain

$$0 \ge v + 8\sqrt{v} - n^2 - 6n - 8.$$

Since $v \ge n^2 - n$, one obtains $0 \ge 8\sqrt{n^2 - n} - 7n - 8$ which leads to the contradiction $n < 13$. $\square$

LEMMA 4.4. *Let* $n \geq 25, k = n + 1, n^2 - n + 3 \leq v \leq n^2 - n + 4\sqrt{n}, b < v$. *Then* $D_L > v - 2v^{3/4}$ *for every k-line L.*

Proof. Apply Lemma 3.2 with $k = n+1, t = n, b = v-1$. Utilize the assumption $D_L \leq v - 2v^{3/4}$ to reach a contradiction for all v and n in the given intervals. This is a routine but unpleasant calculation. $\square$

LEMMA 4.5. *Suppose that Σ has three k-lines, not all incident with a common point. Under the hypotheses of Lemmas 4.3 and 4.4, respectively, the following inequalities hold:* $2D > 3v - 12\sqrt{v} - 3k + 6, 2D > 3v - 6v^{3/4} - 3k + 6$.

Proof. Let E denote $v - 4\sqrt{v}$ or $v - 2v^{3/4}$, depending upon the set of assumptions made for the parameters. Let J, K, L be three k-lines with no common point. Then there are more than $3E$ triples (P, Q, G) where G is one of J, K, L; P is a point on G; and Q is a point unjoined to P. An unjoined point pair $\{P, Q\}$ can count in three triples only if one of P or Q lies in two of J, K, L while the second point lies in the third line. Thus, if J, K, L are mutually disjoint, there are more than $3E/2$ unjoined point pairs $\{P, Q\}$ occurring among the triples; so $D > 3E/2$.

At the other extreme, assume that J, K, L intersect each other in pairs in three distinct points. Then, at most $3(k - 2)$ point pairs are counted three times among the triples (P, Q, G). Thus, $D > (3k - 6) + \left(3E - 3(3k - 6)\right)/2 = \frac{3}{2}E - \frac{3}{2}k + 3$. Since $k \geq 4$, the other intersection patterns for J, K, L yield larger lower bounds for D. $\square$

LEMMA 4.6. *Suppose that* $n \geq 13, k = n + 2, n^2 - n \leq v \leq n^2 + n + 1 \geq b$. *Suppose that the number of k-lines in Σ is r for some $r \geq \sqrt{3n}$. Then* $2D > 3v - 12\sqrt{v} - 3k + 6$.

Proof. By Lemma 4.5, one may assume that all k-lines are incident with a common point P. Each pair of k-lines through P accounts for at least $n^2 + 2n + 1 - b + r$ unjoined point pairs. Thus, it suffices to verify that $(r^2 - r)(n^2 + 2n + 1 - b + r) > 3v$. $\square$

LEMMA 4.7. *Suppose that* $n \geq 25, k = n + 1, n^2 - n + 3 \leq v \leq n^2 - n + 4\sqrt{n}, b < v$. *Suppose that the number of k-lines in Σ is r for some $r \geq \sqrt{3n}$. Then* $2D > 3v - 9v^{3/4}$.

Proof. By Lemma 4.5, one may assume that all k-lines are incident with a common point P. Each pair of k-lines through P accounts for at least $n^2 - b + r$ unjoined point pairs. Thus, it suffices to verify that $(r^2 - r)(n^2 - b + r) > 3v - 9v^{3/4}$. This is a rather tedious calculation. $\square$

LEMMA 4.8. *Suppose that* $4 \leq \beta < 8n^2 + 4n - 4, 6n \geq 13\beta + 16, k = n + 2, n^2 + \frac{n}{2} \leq v \leq n^2 + n, b \leq n^2 + n + 1 - \beta$. *Suppose also that the number of k-lines in Σ is r for some $r < \sqrt{3n}$. Then* $2D > (\beta/4)v - 4v^{3/4}$.

Proof. Form a new partial plane Σ' on the same points and lines as Σ. Detach one point from each of the k-lines, but retain all other incidences. Then Σ' has

v points and b lines, satisfies $k' = n + 1$, and has deficit $D' = D + r(n + 1)$. By Proposition C, $D' > \beta v/8$; so $D > (\beta v/8) - r(n + 1)$. $\square$

LEMMA 4.9. *Let* $n \geq 9, k = n + 1, n^2 - n + 3 \leq v, b < v$. *Suppose that the number of k-lines of Σ is r for some $r < \sqrt{3n}$. Then* $2D > 3v - 4v^{3/4}$.

Proof. Form Σ' by detaching one point from each k-line. Then $D' = D + rn$. By Lemma 2.1, $2D > 3v - 3 - 2rn$. $\square$

LEMMA 4.10. *Let* $n \geq 29, k = n+1, n^2 - n + 3 \leq v \leq n^2 + n - 1, b < v$. *Then* $2D > 3v - 9v^{3/4}$.

Proof. Apply Lemmas 2.7, 4.7, 4.9. $\square$

LEMMA 4.11. *Let* $n \geq 29, k = n+2, n^2 - n + 3 \leq v \leq n^2 + n - 1, b < v$. *Then* $2D > 3v - 13v^{3/4}$.

Proof. If the number of k-lines is $r \geq \sqrt{3n}$, apply Lemma 4.6. Otherwise, form Σ' as in the proofs of Lemmas 4.8 and 4.9. Then $D' = D + r(n + 1)$. By Lemma 4.10, $2D' > 3v - 9v^{3/4}$. Computation completes the proof. $\square$

Proof of Theorem A. Apply Lemmas 2.1, 4.10, 4.11 and Proposition D, respectively, to handle the cases $k \leq n, k = n + 1, k = n + 2, k \geq n + 3$. $\square$

Proof of Theorem B. The conclusion follows from Proposition C if $k \leq n + 1$, from Lemmas 4.6 and 4.8 if $k = n + 2$, and from Proposition D when $k \geq n + 3$. $\square$

REFERENCES

[1] A. BLOKHUIS, R. J. M. SCHMITT AND H. A. WILBRINK, *On the number of lines in a linear space on $p^2 + p + 1$ points*, Proceedings of Combinatorics '88, Ravello, Italy (to appear) (1988).

[2] N. G. DE BRUIJN AND P. ERDÖS, *On a combinatorial problem*, Indagationes Math., 10 (1948), pp. 421–423.

[3] P. ERDÖS, J. C. FOWLER, V. T. SÒS AND R. M. WILSON, *On 2-designs*, J. Combinatorial Theory, Series A, 38 (1985), pp. 131–142.

[4] J. C. FOWLER, *A short proof of Totten's classification of restricted linear spaces*, Geometriae Dedicata, 15 (1984), pp. 413–422.

[5] J. TOTTEN, *Classification of restricted linear spaces*, Canadian J. Math., 28 (1976), pp. 321–333.

INSIDE EUCLID'S ALGORITHM

Willard L. Eastman†

Abstract. The polynomial version of Euclid's algorithm is expanded to remove the inherent polynomial division. The expanded algorithm exhibits a two loop structure. The choice of which loop to execute at a given iteration depends on whether the iteration completes, or does not complete, a polynomial division. It is shown that one of the loops can be deleted, producing a clean version of the algorithm suitable for implementation in VLSI. The new version of Euclid's algorithm is computationally equivalent to the standard long division version, but is more efficient in terms of hardware. Processing cells are presented for a two-dimensional systolic array architecture capable, with pipelining, of computing polynomial gcd's in constant time. The new version of Euclid's algorithm bears a strong resemblance to the Berlekamp-Massey algorithm.

Key words. Euclid's algorithm, polynomial division, greatest common divisor, VLSI implementation

1. Introduction. In Book VII, Proposition 2 of his Elements [1], Euclid gave his famous algorithm for finding the greatest common divisor $\gcd(s, t)$ of two integers s and t. Euclid's algorithm can be immediately adapted to find the greatest common divisor $\gcd(f(x), g(x))$ of two polynomials $f(x)$ and $g(x)$ over a field F, with $\deg(f(x)) \geq \deg(g(x))$. In the extended version, the algorithm also produces a pair of polynomials $a(x)$ and $b(x)$ satisfying

$$\gcd(f(x), g(x)) = a(x)f(x) + b(x)g(x).$$

Many applications for the polynomial version of Euclid's algorithm have appeared in recent years. Sugiyama *et al.* [2] used Euclid's algorithm to solve the key equation in decoding Goppa codes. Mills [3] developed a continued fraction algorithm equivalent to Euclid's algorithm for finding the linear recurrence of lowest degree satisfied by a given sequence. Welch and Scholtz [4] studied the relationship between Mills' algorithm and the Berlekamp-Massey algorithm [5–6]. McEliece and Shearer [7] extended the work of Sugiyama *et al.* and gave an application to finding Padé approximants. Brent *et al.* [8] applied Euclid's algorithm to the inversion of Toeplitz matrices. Sugiyama [9] extended his earlier work further to the solution of Wiener-Hopf equations. This work implies that an extended version of Euclid's algorithm can be used to solve Toeplitz or Hankel systems of equations (with arbitrary right-hand-sides). A number of important signal processing applications require the solution of Toeplitz systems of equations. Finally, Shao *et al.* [10] used Euclid's algorithm in their design of a decoder for deep space telemetry.

In view of the large number of important applications for the computation of polynomial gcd's, versions of the algorithm especially suited for very large scale integrated (VLSI) circuit implementation are of interest. Brent and Kung [11]

---

†The MITRE Corporation, Bedford, Massachusetts 01730. This work was supported by the Rome Air Development Center, U.S. Air Force Electronic Systems Division, Griffiss Air Force Base, NY.

113

have given a linear array design based on the conventional long division version of Euclid's algorithm, capable of computing polynomial gcd's in time proportional to the sum of the degrees of the polynomials. In section 4 we present cells for a two-dimensional systolic array capable of computing a sequence of polynomial gcd's in constant time. This design is based upon a modified version of Euclid's algorithm developed in section 3. The modified version is computationally equivalent to the standard long division version of the algorithm, but realizes a significant saving in hardware. This modified version could also be used to improve the design of Brent and Kung [11], as well as the Reed-Solomon decoder design of Shao *et al.* [10], which is based on [11].

For brevity, we shall work with the original version of Euclid's algorithm rather than with the extended version which obtains $a(x)$ and $b(x)$. Euclid's algorithm and its properties are well known. See, for example, Knuth [12]. At the jth iteration of Euclid's algorithm a new remainder polynomial $r^{(j)}(x)$ is defined by

$$r^{(j)}(x) \leftarrow r^{(j-2)}(x) - \lfloor r^{(j-2)}(x)/r^{(j-1)}(x) \rfloor r^{(j-1)}(x) \, ,$$

where $\lfloor s(x)/t(x) \rfloor$ denotes the quotient polynomial obtained when $s(x)$ is divided by $t(x)$. The algorithm is initialized by setting

$$r^{(-1)}(x) \leftarrow f(x)$$
$$r^{(0)}(x) \leftarrow g(x)$$

and terminates at the first j for which $r^{(j)}(x) = 0$, at which time

$$\gcd(f(x), g(x)) = r^{(j-1)}(x).$$

We state the algorithm in the form of a program using Iverson's notation [13] and employing four polynomials: a quotient polynomial $q(x)$, an 'old' remainder polynomial $r^O(x)$, a 'new' remainder polynomial $r^N(x)$, and a 'temporary' remainder polynomial $r^T(x)$. Program 1 is divided into two sections or boxes: an initialization box consisting of two statements which initialize the 'old' remainder polynomial $r^O(x)$ by $f(x)$ and the 'new' remainder polynomial $r^N(x)$ by $g(x)$, and a recursion box consisting of four specification statements followed by a comparison of $r^N(x)$ against 0. The program terminates when the comparison is satisfied by equality; otherwise the entire loop contained in the box is repeated. Thus, an iteration consists of the execution one time of all statements in the recursion box. At the beginning of the jth iteration, $r^O(x)$ is $r^{j-2}(x)$, the remainder polynomial obtained at the $j-2$nd iteration, and $r^N(x)$ is $r^{j-1}(x)$, the remainder obtained at the $j-1$st iteration; at the conclusion of the jth iteration, $r^O(x)$ is $r^{j-1}(x)$, and $r^N(x)$ is $r^j(x)$. The initialization box thus defines $r^{-1}(x)$ and $r^0(x)$. At termination the $\gcd(f(x), g(x))$ is given by $\gamma r^O(x)$ for the field element γ which renders the gcd monic.

Our objective is parallel scalar computation in an array of computing elements involving only local communication among elements. Such an array is sometimes called a systolic array because information (input data and partial results) flows, or is pumped, through cells of the array. For a discussion of systolic array fundamentals see, for example, Kung [14]. In order to implement the algorithm in hardware it is important first to eliminate the polynomial division of line 1 (and the polynomial multiplication of line 2) in the recursion box. In the next section each polynomial division is replaced by a sequence of partial divisions, where each partial division consists of a field element inversion, a multiplication of a polynomial by a scalar, and a subtraction of aligned polynomials. (The field element inversion can be avoided by employing Burton's stratagem [15].) This replacement leads to an equivalent algorithm with a more complicated structure. Simplification of this algorithm in turn results in an improved algorithm presented in section 3. This version forms the basis for the computational cell designs of section 4.

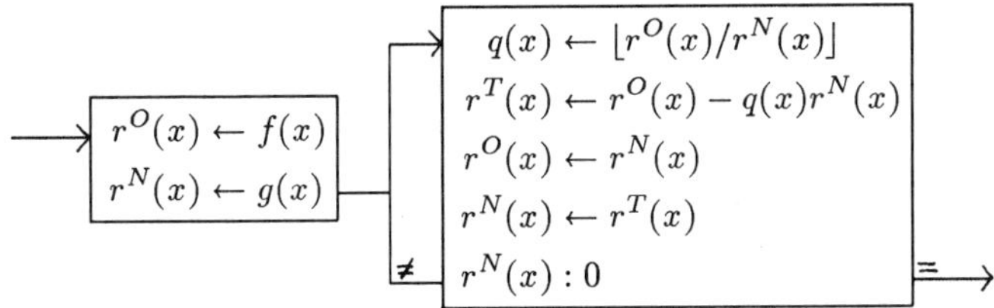

Input : polynomials $f(x), g(x)$

$$\deg(f(x)) \geq \deg(g(x)) \geq 0$$

Output : $\gcd(f(x), g(x)) = \gamma r^O(x)$

Program 1: Euclid's Algorithm

2. The long division version of Euclid's algorithm. In this section we expand Euclid's algorithm in order to take apart the polynomial division defined in the first step of the recursion

$$(1) \qquad\qquad q(x) \leftarrow \lfloor r^O(x)/r^N(x) \rfloor \ .$$

This expansion is simply the conventional long division form of Euclid's algorithm. Henceforth we make the assumption that $\deg(f(x)) > \deg(g(x)) \geq 0$. This assumption facilitates the expansion of the algorithm and is made without loss of generality. When the assumption does not hold, we can replace $f(x)$ by $g(x)$ and $g(x)$ by $f(x)$ mod $g(x)$. We wish to replace the polynomial division of (1) by a sequence of $k+1$ partial divisions, where k is an integer defined by

$$(2) \qquad\qquad k = \deg(r^O(x)) - \deg(r^N(x)) = \deg(q(x)).$$

We have $k > 0$ for all polynomial divisions (1).

In performing the sequence of $k + 1$ partial divisions it is necessary to align the polynomials $r^O(x)$ and $r^N(x)$ in order to perform the subtractions. Initially,

115

alignment can be achieved by shifting $r^O(x)$ k places to the right, where a right-shift is equivalent to dividing by x. When initial alignment has been obtained, we do not want to redefine the divisor $r^N(x)$ until the polynomial division, i.e. the $k+1$st partial division, is completed. Until that time, the new remainder, say $r^T(x)$, becomes the next numerator $r^O(x)$, and the divisor $r^N(x)$ is unaltered (except for shifting right to maintain proper alignment with $r^O(x)$). On the other hand, when the polynomial division is complete, the new remainder becomes the next divisor, while the old divisor becomes the next numerator. Thus, we have

$$r^N(x) \leftarrow x^{-1} r^N(x)$$
$$(3) \qquad r^O(x) \leftarrow r^O(x) - q r^N(x)$$

if not completing a polynomial division (k times), and

$$r^N(x) \leftarrow r^O(x) - q r^N(x)$$
$$r^O(x) \leftarrow x^{-1} r^N(x)$$

if completing a polynomial division ($k+1$st time), where q is a scalar defined as the ratio of the leading coefficient of $r^O(x)$ to the leading coefficient of $r^N(x)$.

This specification of q is imprecise. For implementation it is necessary to state exactly where the coefficients defining q are to be found. For this reason we turn the polynomials around and align the trailing coefficients. At the jth iteration q can then be defined by r^O_j / r^N_j if $r^N_j \neq 0$. While reversing the polynomials may seem needlessly confusing, it simplifies the implementation of the algorithm. As will be seen in section 4, a single left shift at each iteration places the required coefficients in the leftmost column of the computing array when they are needed.

In program 2 we initialize $r^O(x)$ by the reciprocal $\overline{f}(x)$ of $f(x)$. If

$$p(x) = \sum_{j=0}^{n} p_j x^j$$

is a polynomial of degree n over some field, then the reciprocal of $p(x)$, denoted by $\overline{p}(x)$, is defined by

$$\overline{p}(x) = \sum_{j=0}^{n} p_{n-j} x^j = x^n p(1/x),$$

i.e. $\overline{p}(x)$ has the same coefficients as $p(x)$ but in reverse order. It is easily shown that

$$\overline{a(x)b(x)} = \overline{a}(x)\overline{b}(x).$$

From this it immediately follows that

$$(4) \qquad \gcd(\overline{f}(x), \overline{g}(x)) = \gamma \, \overline{\gcd(f(x), g(x))}$$

for the field element γ that makes the right-hand-side monic.

To properly align $r^O(x)$ and $r^N(x)$ as $f(x)$ and $g(x)$ are initially aligned, we initialize $r^N(x)$ by $x^d \overline{g}(x)$, where $d = \deg(f(x)) - \deg(g(x))$ is assumed to be strictly positive. Program 2 is a representation of Euclid's algorithm for polynomials (in the unextended version) when each polynomial division is replaced by a sequence of $k + 1$ partial divisions, where k is defined by (2). The polynomials $r^O(x)$ and $r^N(x)$ have been initialized by $\overline{f}(x)$ and $x^d \overline{g}(x)$, respectively. Correspondingly, at termination, the $\gcd(\overline{f}(x), \overline{g}(x))$ is given by a scalar multiple of $r^O(x)$, so that, using (4), the $\gcd(f(x), g(x))$ is given by a scalar multiple of $\overline{r^O}(x)$.

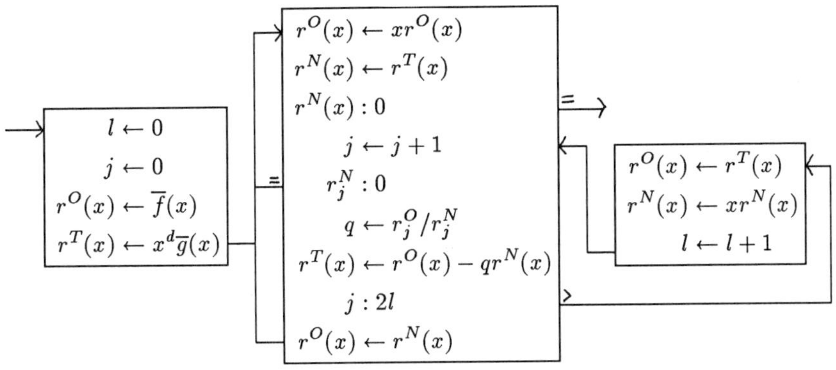

Input : polynomials $f(x), g(x)$; integer $d = \deg(f(x)) - \deg(g(x)) > 0$

Output : $\gcd(f(x), g(x)) = \gamma \overline{r^O}(x)$

Note : r_j^N is the coefficient of x^j in $r^N(x)$, etc.

$\quad 0 < d < \infty$ is assumed.

Program 2: Long Division Version of Euclid's Algorithm

Program 2 is the conventional long division version of program 1 (but with all polynomials reversed), showing explicitly what is implied by (1). The recursion is divided into two loops. The left one, consisting of the nine statements in the center box, is used for completing a polynomial division. The right loop, consisting of the three statements in the right box together with statements 4-8 of the center box, is used for continuation of the division. Choice of which loop to follow is determined by the integer variable l.

Assume that as we complete one polynomial division and initiate its successor we have $j = 2l$. (Observe that j can never be less than $2l$, for l is incremented only when $j > 2l$, and j is incremented at the same time; on the other hand, if $j > 2l$, we stay in the continuation loop.) If $\deg(r^O(x)) = \deg(r^N(x)) + k$ in program 1, then we want to execute the right-hand loop of program 2 k times, followed by one execution of the completion loop. Before the initial incrementation of j we have $r_j^O = 0$, $r_{j+1}^O \neq 0$, and $r_{j+i}^N = 0$ for $i = 0, \ldots, k - 1$ and $r_{j+k}^N \neq 0$. After the initial incrementation of j, $r_j^O \neq 0$. The upper part of the completion loop is first executed k times; each iteration increments j and shifts $r^O(x)$ left one place, so that r_j^O is unchanged as j increases. After k executions, $r_j^N \neq 0$, so that we enter the continuation loop with $j = 2l + k$. In the continuation loop, $r^N(x)$ is shifted left one place at each iteration, so that r_j^N now remains fixed and nonzero. We remain in the continuation loop for k executions, incrementing both j and l, after which we return to the completion loop with $j = 2l$. The final remainder $r^T(x)$ becomes the divisor in the next polynomial division, while the current divisor $r^N(x)$ becomes the numerator for the next polynomial division. Termination occurs when the new divisor $r^N(x) = 0$ after completion of a polynomial division. Observe, however, that $2 \deg(f(x))$ iterations (counted by incrementations of j) always suffice in program 2 to obtain the gcd. Each iteration i of program 1 has been replaced by $2d_i$ iterations in program 2, where d_i denotes the difference k between the degrees of $r^N(x)$ and $r^O(x)$ at the beginning of the ith iteration in program 1. The sum of the d_i over all i cannot exceed $\deg(f(x))$.

The two-loop structure of program 2 is an inherent problem of the long division version of Euclid's algorithm. It causes difficulty in implementation, requiring test-and-branch instructions and duplication of hardware. The linear array design of Brent and Kung [11] employs a computational cell that operates differently in each of three different states: an initial state, and two computing states — reduceA and reduceB, corresponding to the two different loops in program 2. Shao *et al.* [10] improved on this design by physically switching the numerator and denominator polynomials when required, thus avoiding the need to mechanize two distinct states or loops, but still requiring tests to determine when to switch. A better solution is provided by our second requirement: Eliminate the continuation loop in program 2.

3. An alternative version. In program 2 two different loops are followed according as we are completing or simply continuing a polynomial division. Both loops contain some statements in common, namely, lines 4–8 in the completion box. Both loops define a new polynomial $r^T(x)$ at line 7, and retain this new polynomial together with one of the pair $(r^N(x), r^O(x))$. In the continuation loop $r^T(x)$ becomes the new numerator, while the other retained polynomial (shifted) becomes the divisor; in the completion loop the assignments are reversed: $r^T(x)$ becomes the new divisor, while the other retained polynomial (shifted) becomes the numerator. Surprisingly, all that really matters is that the correct pair of polynomials be retained. It does not matter which polynomial is assigned to be the numerator and which the divisor. We can take advantage of this fact to design an improved algorithm for VLSI implementation.

First observe that it is permissible to multiply either $r^O(x)$ or $r^N(x)$ by an arbitrary scalar β. For if

$$R^O(x) = \beta r^O(x)$$

and

$$R^N(x) = \gamma r^N(x)$$

for some scalars β and γ, then

$$Q = R_j^O / R_j^N = (\beta/\gamma)q$$

and

$$\begin{aligned}
R^T(x) &= R^O(x) - QR^N(x) \\
&= \beta r^O(x) - (\beta/\gamma)q\gamma r^N(x) \\
&= \beta r^T(x).
\end{aligned}$$

Thus the only effect produced by multiplying $r^O(x)$ or $r^N(x)$ by a scalar is to multiply future values of $r^O(x)$ and $r^N(x)$ by some scalar.

Next, consider the effect of swapping roles. If the assignments of polynomials to $r^O(x)$ and $r^N(x)$ are reversed at some stage, then we shall calculate a new $R^T(x)$, say, at line 7 by

$$R^T(x) = r^N(x) - (r_j^N/r_j^O)r^O(x)$$

so that

$$-qR^T(x) = -qr^N(x) + r^O(x) = r^T(x),$$

or

$$R^T(x) = -q^{-1}r^T(x).$$

Thus, reversing the roles of numerator and divisor has no effect on the algorithm other than a multiplication of the result by a scalar so long as we take care to retain the correct pair of polynomials at each iteration.

We are now in a position to eliminate the continuation loop from program 2. We shall still replace each polynomial division by a sequence of $k+1$ partial divisions. After the initial determination of $r^T(x)$ (in a given polynomial division) we omit the branch to the continuation loop, define $r^O(x)$ by the old divisor in the last line, and let $r^T(x)$ become the divisor at line 2, thus reversing the roles played by $r^O(x)$ and $r^N(x)$.

Having once defined $r^O(x)$ at line 9 of the completion loop, however, we must not redefine it (except for shifts in line 1) until the polynomial division is completed. This we can ensure by adding the statement $l \leftarrow j - l$ to the end of the completion box, and replacing the branch from the test $j : 2l$ with a branch to the first line whenever the relation is satisfied by $\leq$. The first time through we have $j = 2l + k$. At the new last line of the box, l is redefined as $l' = j - l = l + k$. Thereafter, the branch test will succeed for the next k iterations, until $j = 2l + 2k = 2l'$, when the polynomial division is finally completed. During these k iterations, the roles of $r^O(x)$ and $r^N(x)$ remain reversed. The divisor polynomials of program 2 are now numerators, and scalar multiples of the numerators of program 2 are now divisors. The variable l, which is used to determine completion of a polynomial division, is analogous to the shift-register length variable in the Berlekamp-Massey algorithm. The Berlekamp-Massey shift-register length is increased every time a new polynomial division is inaugurated.

There is one more point to be made. During the k iterations with reversed roles, r_j^O is fixed and nonzero (as r_j^N was fixed and nonzero in program 2). However, it is possible that at some one of these k iterations r_j^N is zero, causing a branch to line 1 from line 5. This is more efficient than the longer path taken in program 2, where q is defined as 0, $r^T(x)$ as $r^O(x)$, followed by a branch to the continuation loop which redefines $r^O(x)$ as $r^T(x)$, *i.e.* as itself. The result is the same; the path taken is longer in program 2.

Our third version of Euclid's algorithm is given by program 3. As with program 2, at most $2\deg(f(x))$ iterations are required in program 3 to obtain the gcd.

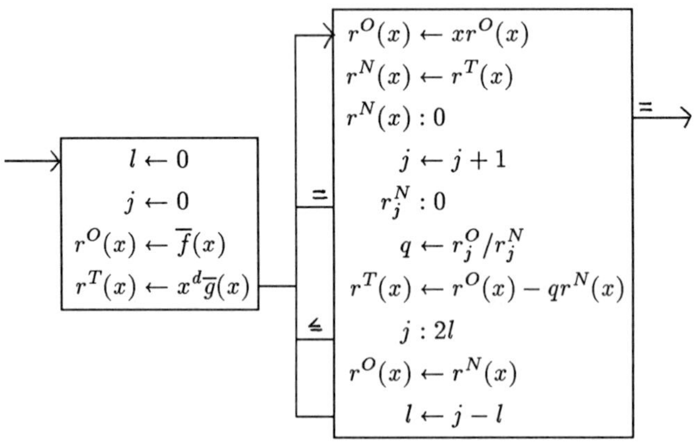

Input : polynomials $f(x), g(x)$; integer $d = \deg(f(x)) - \deg(g(x))$

Output : $\gcd(f(x), g(x)) = \gamma \overline{r^O}(x)$

Note : r_j^N is the coefficient of x^j in $r^N(x)$, *etc.*

$0 < d < \infty$ is assumed.

Program 3: Alternative Long Division Algorithm

Program 2 is an exact translation of Euclid's algorithm for polynomials when polynomial division is broken down. Program 3 is better suited for parallel computation than program 2. Both the implementations of Brent and Kung [11] and of Shao *et al.* [10] could be improved by basing them on program 3 instead of program 2. It is of course true that program 3 is computationally equivalent to program 2. Both programs require the same number of field element multiplications, subtractions, and divisions, and all intermediate results are identical except for multiplication by a scalar. But when implemented in hardware, the two programs are different. Program 3 avoids a costly duplication of hardware.

Program 3 closely parallels Berlekamp's decoding algorithm [5–6] and, in effect, shows why hardware implementations of the Berlekamp-Massey algorithm are more efficient than those based on the long division version of Euclid's algorithm. If the changes made in program 2 to obtain program 3 are introduced into the algorithm of Welch and Scholtz [4] based on Mills' continued fraction expansion [3], they convert it to an algorithm strikingly similar to the Berlekamp-Massey algorithm, as shown in [16]. In the next section we present a two-dimensional array of computational cells based on a modified version of program 3. With suitable pipelining, this array provides constant time solution of polynomial gcd's.

4. Implementation. Our objective remains parallel scalar computation involving only local communication between processing elements. In this section we present two cell designs for implementation of program 3. In preparation for this we first make two further alterations in program 3. We employ Burton's stratagem [15] to remove scalar division, and we introduce a logical variable to eliminate all branching.

First, we remove the division at line 6 of the recursion box of program 3. We delete line 6 and multiply line 7 by r_j^N, obtaining

$$r_j^N r^T(x) \leftarrow r_j^N r^O(x) - r_j^O r^N(x).$$

Following Burton, we now accept $r_j^N r^T(x)$ as $r^T(x)$ in the program. The only effect this has is to multiply the final result by some scalar, which causes no harm since we have to normalize in any case. We also replace the termination test on the remainder $r^N(x) : 0$ by a test on the iteration counter $j : 2 \deg(f(x))$, resulting in program 4. As noted previously, $2 \deg(f(x))$ iterations always suffice to obtain the gcd; if $r^N(x)$ becomes 0 before execution of $2 \deg(f(x))$ iterations, no further changes are made to $r^N(x)$ by the program, and shifts of $r^O(x)$ at line 1 of the recursion do not affect the gcd, which is obtained from its reciprocal $\overline{r^O(x)}$).

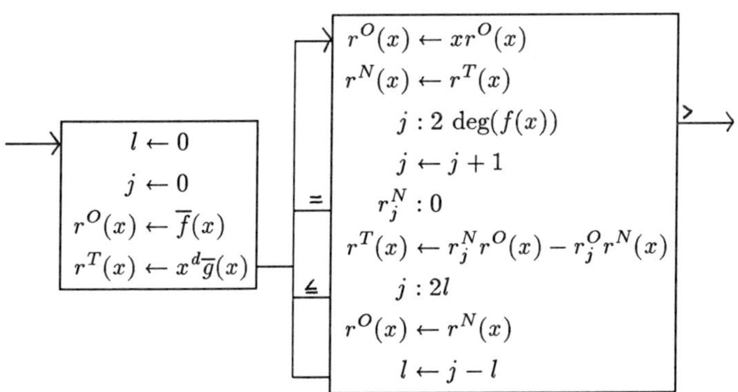

Input : polynomials $f(x), g(x)$; integer $d = \deg(f(x)) - \deg(g(x))$

Output : $\gcd(f(x), g(x)) = \gamma \overline{r^O}(x)$

Note : r_j^N is the coefficient of x^j in $r^N(x)$, *etc.*

$0 < d < \infty$ is assumed.

Program 4: Division-Free Euclid's Algorithm

121

Next, we want to remove the three test-and-branch lines from the recursion box of the program. The first test $j : 2 \deg(f(x))$ is rendered superfluous by providing $2 \deg(f(x))$ levels in the array. No test for termination is then required. At the appropriate time, the coefficients of $\gcd(f(x), g(x)) = \gamma \bar{r}^O(x)$ become available in successive time units in the last row (*i.e.* row $2 \deg(f(x))$) of the array.

The second test $r_j^N : 0$ is postponed and combined with the third test $j : 2l$. No harm results if the intervening specification statement is executed when $r_j^N = 0$. Its only effect is to multiply $r^T(x)$ by a scalar. To eliminate the combined tests we introduce a logical variable e, specified by

$$ e \leftarrow (r_j^N = 0) \vee (j \leq 2l), $$

where $(r_j^N = 0)$ is a logical variable whose value is defined to be 1 if the statement '$r_j^N = 0$' is true, and 0 otherwise, *etc.* The need for branching is then eliminated: $r^O(x)$ can be updated by $er^O(x) + \bar{e}r^N(x)$, and the variable l by $el + \bar{e}(j - l)$, where $\bar{e} = 1 - e$.

Program 4 can now be implemented using a two-dimensional systolic array of computationally simple cells of two types: a first-column cell (figure 1) and a general cell (figure 2). Each first column cell receives as inputs the array level j, the variable l (from the cell above), and coefficients r_j^O and r_j^N of the remainder polynomial (from the cell in the second column of the level above). Each first column cell computes two variables: the logical variable e defined in (3) and the integer variable l. (The computed l is distinguished from the incoming l in figure 2 by the appendage of a tilde.) The computed $\tilde{l}$ is passed down to the first cell in the next level. For correct timing, a unit delay (not shown) must be inserted between the successive cells in the first column for holding l one time unit before passing it down to the next cell. The variable e and two copies of the variables r_j^O and r_j^N are passed to the cell on the right. The computation of $\tilde{l}$ is merely a selection of the incoming l or $j - l$ (which is computed by a scalar subtraction), determined by the computed value of e. The computation of e requires two scalar comparisons.

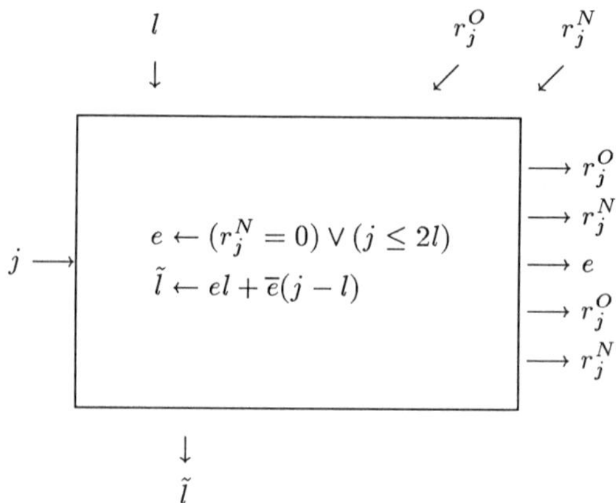

FIG. 1. *First Column Cell at Level j*

Figure 2 shows the cell comprising the rest of the array (all except for the first column). Each cell receives the variables r^O_{k-1}, r^N_{k-1}, e, r^O_j, and r^N_j from the cell to its left, and passes the last three on unaltered to the cell on its right. Each cell receives the coefficients $r^O_k(t)$ and $r^N_k(t)$ from the cell diagonally above and one column to the right, passes them to the cell on its right, and computes new values $r^O_k(t+1)$ and $r^N_k(t+1)$ which are passed down to the cell diagonally below and one column to the left. (The computed values of r^N_k and r^O_k are distinguished from the incoming values by tildes in figure 2.) All cells on any diagonal through $((j+1,k),(j,k+2),(j-1,k+4))$ can compute simultaneously for a given pair of input polynomials. The computation of $r^O_k(t+1)$ in each cell is simply a selection of $r^O_k(t)$ or $r^N_k(t)$ depending on e; the computation of $r^N_k(t+1)$ requires the evaluation of two scalar products and one scalar difference.

There is a built-in shift in the array. In each successive row the cell computing r^O_k and r^N_k is shifted one column to the left. In this way the second-column cell at level $j-1$ always computes the inputs r^O_j and r^N_j needed by the first-column cell at the next level j. (This feature has been facilitated by the reversal of the input polynomials.) As a result of the shift, the outputs r^O_k and r^N_k subsequently become the inputs r^O_{k-1} and r^N_{k-1} from the left for the cell directly below in the array (*i.e.*, k is incremented as one descends in a given column of the array).

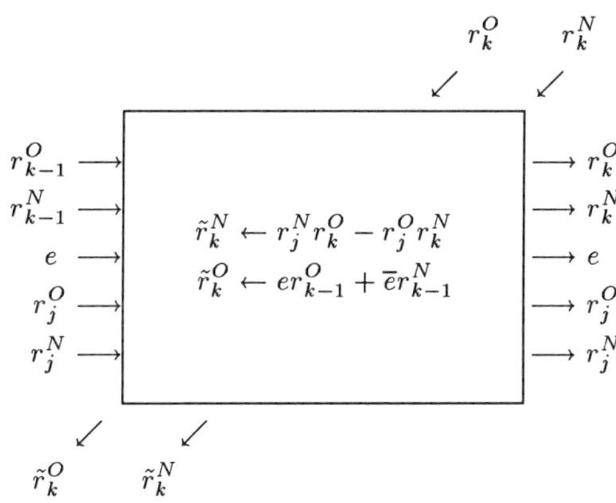

FIG. 2. *General Cell at Level j*

The first row of the array requires $\deg(f(x))$ of the cells of figure 2 in addition to the first column cell of figure 1. A total of $2\deg(f(x))$ rows are required to obtain the $\gcd(f(x), g(x))$. The $\deg(f(x))+1$ cells of the first row receive the $\deg(f(x))+1$ coefficients of $f(x)$ (in reverse order) as inputs for r^N_k. The first $\deg(g(x))+1$ cells of the first row receive the $\deg(g(x))+1$ coefficients of $g(x)$ (in reverse order) as inputs for $r^O(x)$. In the last row (*i.e.* row $2\deg(f(x))$) of the array cell 1 supplies the variable l; the $\deg(\gcd)$ is given by $\deg(f(x))-l$. Cells 2 to $\deg(\gcd)+1$ contain the unnormalized reciprocal of $\gcd(f(x), g(x))$. The normalization scalar is given by r^O_0, which is found in cell 2. Figure 3 illustrates this process over time for example 1:

Example 1

$$\left.\begin{aligned} f(x) &= x^5 + 3x^4 + 3x^2 + 5x + 10 \\ g(x) &= 2x^2 + 7x + 3 \end{aligned}\right\} \ \text{over GF(11)}$$

Clearly the array is fully pipelineable for high throughput. The upperleftmost cell is ready to begin processing a pair of polynomials at time $t = 0$. The cell to its right can begin at time $t = 1$, at which time the upperleftmost cell is ready to begin processing a second pair of polynomials. The cells in row 1 column 3 and row 2 column 1 are ready to begin processing the first pair of polynomials at time $t = 2$, at which time it is appropriate to continue processing the second pair in cell 2 and to begin processing a third pair in the first (leftmost) cell of row 1. If a sequence of pairs of polynomials is presented in timely fashion, the upperleftmost cell is ready to begin processing a new pair at every time unit, and, after the array is filled, a new polynomial gcd is provided at every unit of time. Arrangement of the input data for this pipelining is illustrated in figure 4. For this figure, $r_j^O(t)$ denotes the coefficient of x^j in the reciprocal of the tth input polynomial $f(x)$, and $r_j^N(t)$ denotes the corresponding coefficient of the shifted reciprocal of the tth input polynomial $g(x)$. While the time required for filling the array (latency) depends linearly on the degrees of the input polynomials $f(x)$, *i.e.* on the number of rows in the array, with pipelining this architecture provides for constant time computation of polynomial gcd's.

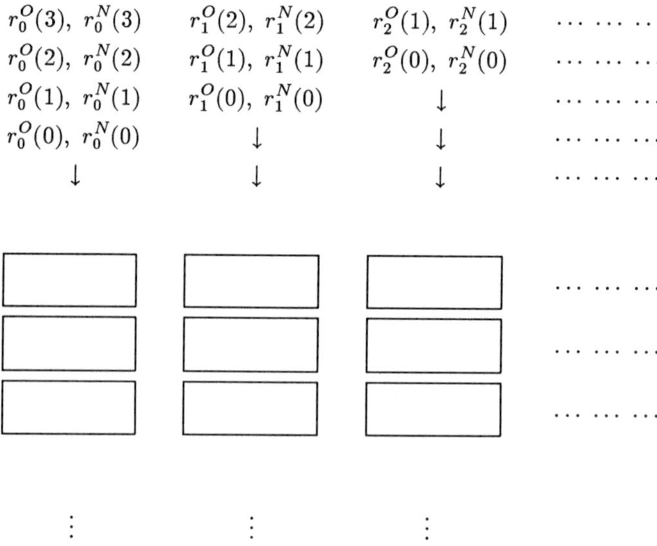

FIG. 4. *Data Input to Array for Pipelined Operation*

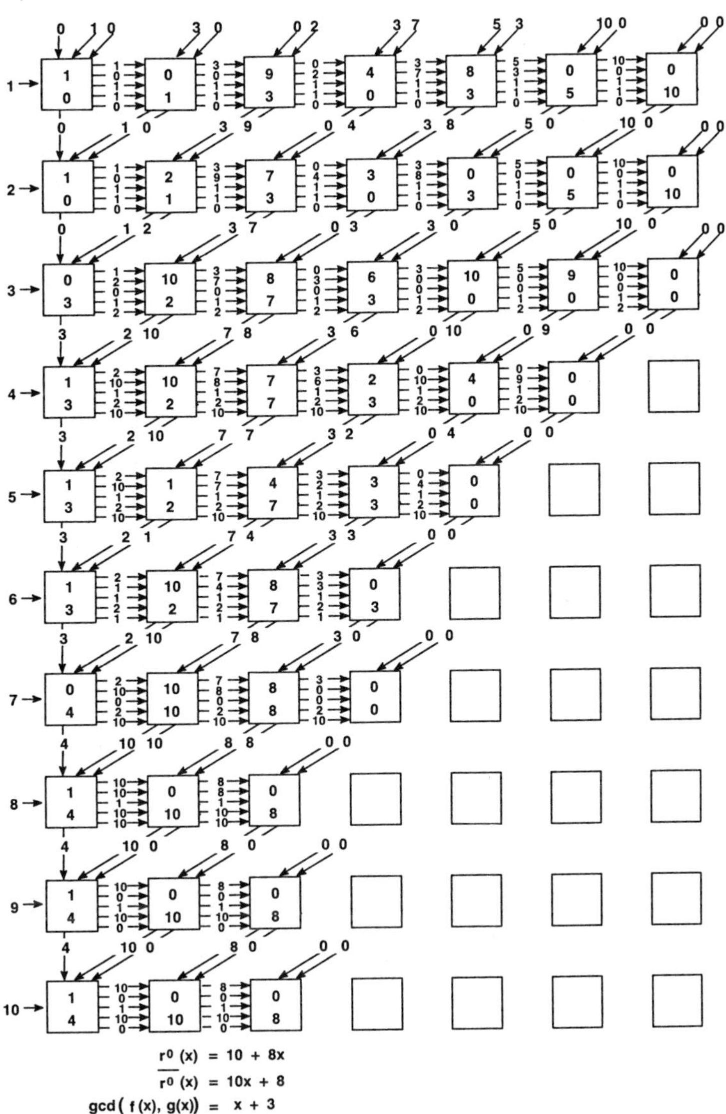

FIG. 3. *Data Flow Through Systolic Array*

If the degrees are unknown or very large, then a two-dimensional array implementation becomes uneconomical. However, a linear array design may still be of interest. By feeding outputs from the general cell of figure 2 back to the cell on its left instead of down to the next level, it is possible to implement program 4 using just a single row from the two-dimensional array just described, but with loss of constant time processing. The suggestion for converting the two-dimensional array design into a linear array was made by Vaccaro [17].

5. Summary. Cell designs have been presented for a two-dimensional systolic array implementation of Euclid's polynomial gcd algorithm. This array, when fully pipelined, can begin processing a new pair of input polynomials at every unit of time and can output a new polynomial gcd at every unit of time. In a BCH decoding application, for example, the array can begin the processing of a new syndrome polynomial at every unit of time and can output a new error locator polynomial (and error evaluator polynomial) at every unit of time, permitting very fast real-time decoding. To map Euclid's algorithm into a version suitable for implementation in a systolic array we have taken four steps:

    (1) breaking down polynomial division

    (2) elimination of the continuation loop

    (3) elimination of scalar division

    (4) elimination of branching.

The second step has been overlooked in previous implementations of Euclid's algorithm, leading to unnecessarily complicated solutions requiring multi-phase computational cells [11] or needless switching of numerator and denominator polynomials [10]. The alternative version of Euclid's algorithm proposed in this paper is computationally equivalent to the standard long division version, but is more economical of hardware. This new version bears a strong resemblance to the Berlekamp-Massey algorithm, and the computational cell designs presented in section 4 are almost identical to those proposed in [18] for implementing the Berlekamp-Massey algorithm.

ACKNOWLEDGMENT

The author thanks colleagues Bruce L. Johnson, Richard A. Games, and John J. Vaccaro for stimulating discussions and helpful criticism and suggestions.

REFERENCES

[1]   HEATH, T.L.(ED. AND TRANSL.), *The Thirteen Books of Euclid's Elements*, Dover, New York, 1956.

[2]   SUGIYAMA, Y., M. KASAHARA, S. HIRASAWA, AND T. NAMEKAWA, *A Method for Solving Key Equation for Decoding Goppa Codes*, Information and Control, 27 (1975), pp. 87–99.

[3]   MILLS, W.H., *Continued Fractions and Linear Recurrences*, Mathematics of Computation, 29 (1975), pp. 173–180.

[4]   WELCH, L.R. AND R.A. SCHOLTZ, *Continued Fractions and Berlekamp's Algorithm*, IEEE Trans. on Information Theory, IT-25 (1979), pp. 19–27.

[5]   BERLEKAMP, E.R., *Algebraic Decoding Theory*, McGraw-Hill, New York, 1968.

[6]   MASSEY, J.L., *Shift-Register Synthesis and BCH Decoding*, IEEE Trans. on Information Theory, IT-15 (1969), pp. 122–127.

[7]   MCELIECE, R.J. AND J.B. SHEARER, *A Property of Euclid's Algorithm and an Application to Padé Approximation*, SIAM J. Appl. Math., 34 (1978), pp. 611–615.

[8]   BRENT, R.P., F.G. GUSTAVSON, AND D.Y.Y. YUN, *Fast Solution of Toeplitz Systems of Equations and Computation of Padé Approximants*, Jour. of Algorithms, 1 (1980), pp. 259–295.

[9]   SUGIYAMA, Y., *An Algorithm for Solving Discrete-Time Wiener-Hopf Equations Based upon Euclid's Algorithm*, IEEE Trans. on Information Theory, IT-32 (1986), pp. 394–409.

126

[10] SHAO, H.M., T.K. TRUONG, L.J. DEUTSCH, J.H. YUEN, AND I.S. REED, *A VLSI Design of a Pipeline Reed-Solomon Decoder*, IEEE Trans. on Computers, C-34 (1985), pp. 393–403.

[11] BRENT, R.P. AND H.T. KUNG, *Systolic VLSI Arrays for Linear-Time GCD Computation*, in *VLSI '83*, F. Anceau and E.J. Aas, eds., Elsevier (North-Holland), 1983.

[12] KNUTH, D.E., *The Art of Computer Programming*, Addison-Wesley, Reading, MA, 1969.

[13] IVERSON, K.E., *A Programming Language*, Wiley, New York, 1962.

[14] KUNG, H.T., *Why Systolic Architectures*, Computer Magazine, 15-1 (1982), pp. 37–46.

[15] BURTON, H.O., *Inversionless Decoding of Binary BCH Codes*, IEEE Trans. on Information Theory, IT-17 (1971), pp. 464–466.

[16] EASTMAN, W.L., *Euclidean Decoders for BCH Codes*, Rome Air Development Center Technical Report RADC-TR-88-44.

[17] VACCARO, J.J., private communication.

[18] EASTMAN, W.L., *Euclideanization of the Berlekamp-Massey Algorithm*, presented at the 1988 Tactical Communications Conference.

CONSTRUCTION OF DESIGNS

MARSHALL HALL JR.*

1. Introduction. Gold is where you find it. The same is true of designs. There are many ways to construct designs all of which work some of the time. The most valuable tool is a group G of automorphisms. If the order of G is large this can make the construction easy. We can start with some part of the incidence matrix, say rows or columns, or with a subdesign.

Section 2 deals with the matrices associated with a design, the incidence matrix A, the intersection matrix $S = A^T A$, and the projection matrix $C = r(r - \lambda)I + \lambda k J - rS$. Section 3 deals with Codes and their relation to designs. Section 4 deals with the construction of a symmetric (41, 16, 6) design. Its code over F_2 suggests that there might be a collineation of order 5 fixing just one point and one block. This does in fact lead to a design. Section 5 gives some material on the plane of order 10, where the binary code has been the chief tool. A design (22, 33, 12, 8, 4) is treated in section 6. This is the smallest number of points for which the existence of the design is in doubt. In Section 7 a possible start on a symmetric design (81, 16, 3) is given.

Section 8 gives the construction of a (28, 42, 15, 10, 5) design made recently by van Lint and Tonchev. No prime greater than 3 divides the order of a collineation group. Their construction depends on a collineation of order 3 with one fixed point and 12 fixed blocks.

2. Associated matrices. If $D = (v, b, r, k, \lambda)$ is a balanced incomplete block design (briefly design) then trivially

$$(2.1) \qquad bk = vr, \qquad r(b - 1) = \lambda(v - 1)$$

The *incidence matrix* $A = [a_{ij}]$ $i = 1, \ldots v$, $j = 1, \ldots b$ where $a_{ij} = 1$ if the ith point is on the jth block. Here

$$(2.2) \qquad AA^T = (r - \lambda)I_v + \lambda\, J_{v,v}$$

with I_v the identity matrix of size v and $J_{m,n}$ the m by n matrix of all 1's. Also

$$(2.3) \qquad AJ_{b,v} = r\, J_{v,v}\,, \quad J_{b,v}\, A = k\, J_{b,b}.$$

We define the *intersection matrix* $S = A^T A = [s_{ij}]$ where $s_{ij} = |B_i \cap B_j|$. Here

$$(2.4) \qquad S^2 = (r - \lambda)S + \lambda k^2 J_{b,b}$$

---

*Department of Mathematics, Emory University, Atlanta, Georgia 30322

The *projection matrix* C is defined by $C = (r - \lambda)I_b + \lambda k J_{bb} - rS$, Here

(2.5)
$$C^2 = r(r - \lambda)C$$

S and C are symmetric matrices. C corresponds to a positive semi–definite quadratic form. The eigenvalues of C are 0 and $r(r - \lambda)$. Finally

(2.6)
$$AC = O \; .$$

Hence if S (and so C) is known, this gives a method for recovering A and so the design.

Since the eigenvalues of C are 0 and $r(r - \lambda)$, no principal minor of C can have a negative determinant. This excludes certain choices of initial blocks. The eigenvalues of S are rk of multiplicity 1 and $(r - \lambda)$ of multiplicity $v - 1$ and $b - v$ eigenvalues 0. Thus no principal minor of S could have a negative eigenvalue or eigenvalues greater than $(r - \lambda)$. But I have not come across any such example.

3. Codes. The Mac Williams Identity. For a design $D : (v, b, r, k, \lambda)$ let A be its incidence matrix. For a finite field $F_q = G_F(q), q = k^s, k$ prime, the code C of D is the subspace of $F_q^b = \{(x_1, \ldots x_v) x_i \in F_q\}$ spanned by the rows of A. The orthogonal dual code $C^\perp$ is defined by $C^\perp = \{u | (u, v) = 0 \; \forall v \in C\}$ where the inner product $(u, v) = u_1 v_1 + u_2 v_2 + \cdots + u_v v_v$.

THEOREM 3.1. *Suppose that* $q = p^s$ p, *prime and that* $p | r - \lambda$. *Then* $C \cap C^\perp$ *is of codimension at most 1 in* C.

Proof. Let r_i, r_j, r_m be three rows of A. Then $(r_i, r_i) = r$ $(r_i, r_j) = \lambda$ if $i \neq j$. Then $(r_m, r_i - r_j) = \lambda - \lambda = 0$ in F_q. Hence $r_i - r_j \in C^\perp$, proving the theorem.

The *weight distribution* of C is $A_0, A_1 \ldots, A_i, \cdots A_b$ if there are A_i words of weight i in C. The *weight enumerator* of C is $W_C(x, y) = A_0 x^b + A_1 x^{b-1} y + \cdots + A_i x^{b-i} y^i + \cdots A_b y^b$ There is a famous identity of Jesse Mac Williams giving the weight distribution of $C^\perp$ in terms of that of C. This is

$$W_C^\perp(x, y) = \frac{1}{|C|} W_C(x + (q - 1) \, y, x - y)$$

The theorem and the Mac Williams identity give valuable information about the code and in turn about the design.

4. The (41, 16, 6) Design. For a symmetric design $(41, 16, 6)$ it is conceivable that there may be an automorphism of order 5 fixing exactly one point x and one block B. There will be 8 other point cycles $R_2, \cdots R_9$ and 8 other block cycles $S_2, \cdots S_9$. We construct an orbit matrix $M = [m_{ij}] i, j = 1, \cdots cm$. Here m_{ij} is the number of points in cycle R_i lying in a representative block of S_j. One such matrix is

(4.1)

	S_0	S_2	S_3	S_4	S_5	S_6	S_7	S_8	S_9
X	1	1	1	1	0	0	0	0	0
R_2	5	1	2	2	0	3	3	2	2
R_3	5	2	1	2	3	0	3	2	2
R_4	5	2	2	1	3	3	0	I	2
R_5	0	1	4	1	2	1	2	3	2
R_6	0	1	1	4	2	2	1	3	2
R_7	0	4	1	1	1	2	2	3	2
R_8	0	2	2	2	3	3	3	1	0
R_9	0	2	2	2	2	2	2	0	4

This suggests the possibility of a further automorphism of order 3 permuting (R_2, R_3, R_4) (R_5, R_6, R_7). Fortunately this works, yielding a design. The point automorphisms and representative blocks are given here.

$$(4.2) \quad \alpha = (x)\,(1,2,3,4,5)(6,7,8,9,10)(11,12,13,14,15)(16,17,18,19,20)(21,22,23,24,$$
$$(26,27,28,29,30)(31,32,33,34,35)(36,37,38,39,40)$$

$$B = (x)(1,6,11)(2,7,12)(3,8,13)(4,9,14)(5,10,15)(16,21,26)(21,22,27)$$
$$(18,23,28)(19,24,29)(20,25,30)(31)(32)(33)(34)(35)(36)(37)(38)(39)(40)$$

$$(4.3) \qquad
\begin{aligned}
B_0 &= x, 1, 2, 3, 4, 5, 6, 7, 8, 9, 10, 11, 12, 13, 14, 15 \\
B_1 &= x, 4, 6, 7, 13, 15, 16, 21, 27, 28, 29, 30, 31, 32, 36, 38 \\
B_6 &= x, 3, 5, 9, 11, 12, 17, 18, 19, 20, 21, 26, 31, 32, 36, 38 \\
B_{11} &= x, 1, 2, 8, 10, 14, 16, 22, 23, 24, 25, 26, 31, 32, 36, 38 \\
B_{16} &= 6, 7, 9, 13, 14, 15, 18, 19, 22, 25, 26, 31, 32, 34, 39, 40 \\
B_{21} &= 3, 4, 5, 11, 12, 14, 16, 23, 24, 27, 30, 31, 32, 34, 39, 40 \\
B_{26} &= 1, 2, 4, 8, 9, 10, 17, 20, 21, 28, 29, 31, 32, 34, 39, 40 \\
B_{31} &= 1, 3, 6, 8, 11, 13, 18, 19, 20, 23, 24, 25, 28, 29, 30, 32 \\
B_{36} &= 1, 2, 6, 7, 11, 12, 17, 20, 22, 25, 27, 30, 36, 38, 39, 40
\end{aligned}$$

5. The projective Plane of Order 10. The projective plane of order 10 is a symmetric (111, 11, 1) design. As yet its existence has not been settled.

In a major work [3] in 1973, Jessie Mac Williams, Neil Sloane, and John Thompson applied coding theory to the problem of the existence of the plane. Since 2 divides 11-1=10 to exactly the first power, even the dimension of the binary code C is known. This dimension is 56 and the words of even weight form the orthogonal dual $C^{\perp}$ of dimension 55. $C^{\perp}$ is a "doubly even" code, with all the weights multiples of 4. Also as the all 1 vector is in the code, $A_{111} = 1$ and $A_{111-i} = A_i$. It is easy to show that $A_o = 1$, $A_i = 0, i = 1, \ldots 10$ and $A_{11} = 111$ as a word of weight 11 is necessarily one of the lines. Using this and the Mac William identity, it is easy to see that the complete weight enumerator can be expressed in terms of A_{12}, A_{15}, and A_{16}.

For a word of weight 15 (on points) it is not difficult to show that up to isomorphism, points $1, \cdots 15$ must lie on lines in the following way

$$
\begin{array}{l}
1,2,3,4,5 \\
1,6,7,8,9 \\
2,6,10,11,12 \\
3,7,10,13,14 \\
4,8,11,13,15 \\
5,9,12,14,15
\end{array}
$$

(5.1)

$$
\begin{array}{ll}
1,10,15 & \quad 4\ 6\ 14 \\
1,11,14 & \quad 4\ 7\ 12 \\
1,12,13 & \quad 4\ 9\ 10 \\
2\ 7\ 15 & \quad 5\ 6\ 13 \\
2\ 8\ 14 & \quad 5\ 7\ 11 \\
2\ 9\ 13 & \quad 5\ 8\ 10 \\
3\ 6\ 15 \\
3\ 8\ 12 \\
3\ 9\ 11
\end{array}
$$

Using a computer it was possible to show that this configuration cannot be completed to a full plane. We conclude that $A_{15} = 0$.

In a similar but much more complicated way Clement Lam has shown that $A_{12} = 0$ and $A_{16} = 0$. The weight distribution is now completely determined and in particular $A_{19} = 24,675$.

A word of weight 19 gives a configuration of the 19 points on lines. There will be 6 lines with 5 points, 37 lines with 3 points and 68 with 1 point. Up to isomorphism there are 64 choices of the 6 5–point lines. All but the 3 hardest cases have been eliminated and these are being tested on the CRAY at the Institute for Defense Analyses. It seems likely to me that these three cases will also be eliminated and we can conclude that the plane of order 10 does not exist.

6. The (22, 33, 12, 8, 4) Design. The smallest number of points for which the existence of a design is not known is 22 and the parameters are (22,33,12,8,4). Such a design could be the residual of a symmetric (34,12,4) design, but such a design does not exist since 34 is even and 12-4=8 is not a square.

This has been studied in detail in [1].

The binary code C of D will be doubly even with weights 0,4,8,12,16,20,24,28. The weight 32 is impossible since if there were, in the remaining 33rd column there will be 8 1's and a row of A with 1 of these will have 11 further 1's. But two words of C must have an even number of 1's in common. If $C_0, C_1, \cdots C_{33}$ is the weight distribution of $C^{\perp}$ it will follow that $C_0 = 1$, $C_1 = 0$ and $C_2 = 0$ Here $C_1 = 0$ since no column is empty. If we had $C_2 \neq 0$, there would be two identical columns, which can be shown impossible. The principal minor in the projection matrix would be $\begin{bmatrix} 32 & -64 \\ -64 & 32 \end{bmatrix}$ whose determinant is $32^2(-3)$. With $C_1 = C_2 = 0$ we get equations expressing all weights in terms of $2^s = |C|, A_4, A_8, A_{24}, A_{28}$.

In particular we have

$$(6.1) \qquad 2^{s-9}C_4 = -45 \cdot 2^{s-9} + 90 + 28A_4 + 5A_8 + 3A_{24} + 20A_{25}$$
$$2^{s-9}C_5 = -39 \cdot 2^{s-9} + 474 + 92A_4 + 5A_8 + 3A_{24} - 44A_{28}$$

From this

$$(6.2) \qquad 2^{s-9}C_5 = 2^{s-9}C_4 + 6 \cdot 2^{s-9} + 384 + 64A_4 - 64\,A_{28}$$

Now $C_{33} = 1$ and $C_{33-i} = C_i$. Thus $C_5 = C_{28} \geq A_{28}$. Hence if $A_{28} \geq 6$ then $C_5 \geq 6$. But if $A_{28} < 6$ then from 6.2) $2^{s-9}C_5 > 6.2^{s-9}$ and $C_5 > 6$. In any even $C_5 \geq 6$.

A word in C_5 corresponds to 5 columns of A in which every row was 0,2, or $4\ 1\frac{1}{2}$ in these 5 columns. Up to isomorphism there are 108 ways in which 5 such columns can be found.

For example Case 6 corresponds to the following principal minor in S

$$(6.3) \qquad \begin{bmatrix} 8 & 3 & 3 & 1 & 1 \\ 3 & 8 & 1 & 2 & 2 \\ 3 & 1 & 8 & 2 & 2 \\ 1 & 2 & 2 & 8 & 3 \\ 1 & 2 & 2 & 3 & 8 \end{bmatrix}$$

The corresponding minor of the projection matrix C has $45(-3888)$ as its determinant excluding Case 6. By various arguments all but 13 of the 108 cases have been excluded.

$$\begin{array}{cccc}
1 & 38 & 55 & 64 \\[4pt]
\begin{bmatrix} 8 & 2 & 2 & 2 & 2 \\ 2 & 8 & 2 & 2 & 2 \\ 2 & 2 & 8 & 2 & 2 \\ 2 & 2 & 2 & 8 & 2 \\ 2 & 2 & 2 & 2 & 8 \end{bmatrix} &
\begin{bmatrix} 8 & 3 & 3 & 2 & 2 \\ 3 & 8 & 2 & 3 & 2 \\ 3 & 2 & 8 & 3 & 2 \\ 2 & 3 & 3 & 8 & 2 \\ 2 & 2 & 2 & 2 & 8 \end{bmatrix} &
\begin{bmatrix} 8 & 2 & 2 & 3 & 3 \\ 2 & 8 & 3 & 3 & 2 \\ 2 & 3 & 8 & 3 & 2 \\ 3 & 3 & 3 & 8 & 1 \\ 3 & 2 & 2 & 1 & 8 \end{bmatrix} &
\begin{bmatrix} 8 & 4 & 4 & 2 & 2 \\ 4 & 8 & 2 & 4 & 2 \\ 4 & 2 & 8 & 4 & 2 \\ 2 & 4 & 4 & 8 & 2 \\ 2 & 2 & 2 & 2 & 8 \end{bmatrix}
\end{array}$$

$$(6.4)$$

$$\begin{array}{cccc}
65 & 74 & 78 & 80 \\[4pt]
\begin{bmatrix} 8 & 4 & 3 & 3 & 2 \\ 4 & 8 & 3 & 3 & 2 \\ 3 & 3 & 4 & 4 & 2 \\ 3 & 3 & 4 & 8 & 2 \\ 2 & 2 & 2 & 2 & 8 \end{bmatrix} &
\begin{bmatrix} 8 & 3 & 3 & 3 & 3 \\ 3 & 8 & 3 & 3 & 3 \\ 3 & 3 & 8 & 3 & 3 \\ 3 & 3 & 3 & 8 & 1 \\ 3 & 3 & 3 & 1 & 8 \end{bmatrix} &
\begin{bmatrix} 8 & 2 & 3 & 4 & 3 \\ 2 & 8 & 4 & 3 & 3 \\ 3 & 4 & 8 & 2 & 3 \\ 4 & 3 & 2 & 8 & 1 \\ 3 & 3 & 3 & 1 & 8 \end{bmatrix} &
\begin{bmatrix} 8 & 4 & 2 & 3 & 3 \\ 4 & 8 & 4 & 3 & 1 \\ 2 & 4 & 8 & 2 & 4 \\ 3 & 3 & 2 & 8 & 2 \\ 3 & 1 & 4 & 2 & 8 \end{bmatrix}
\end{array}$$

$$
81 \qquad
\begin{bmatrix}
8 & 3 & 3 & 3 & 3 \\
3 & 8 & 4 & 3 & 2 \\
3 & 4 & 8 & 2 & 3 \\
3 & 3 & 2 & 8 & 2 \\
3 & 2 & 3 & 2 & 8
\end{bmatrix}
\qquad 82 \qquad
\begin{bmatrix}
8 & 2 & 4 & 3 & 3 \\
2 & 8 & 4 & 3 & 3 \\
4 & 4 & 8 & 2 & 2 \\
3 & 3 & 2 & 8 & 2 \\
3 & 3 & 2 & 2 & 8
\end{bmatrix}
\qquad 88 \qquad
\begin{bmatrix}
8 & 3 & 3 & 4 & 2 \\
3 & 8 & 4 & 2 & 3 \\
3 & 4 & 8 & 2 & 3 \\
4 & 2 & 2 & 8 & 2 \\
2 & 3 & 3 & 2 & 8
\end{bmatrix}
\qquad 89 \qquad
\begin{bmatrix}
8 & 3 & 4 & 3 & 2 \\
3 & 8 & 4 & 3 & 2 \\
4 & 4 & 8 & 1 & 3 \\
3 & 3 & 1 & 8 & 3 \\
2 & 2 & 3 & 3 & 8
\end{bmatrix}
$$

$$
91 \qquad
\begin{bmatrix}
8 & 3 & 4 & 3 & 2 \\
3 & 8 & 4 & 2 & 3 \\
4 & 4 & 8 & 2 & 2 \\
3 & 2 & 2 & 3 & 3 \\
2 & 3 & 2 & 3 & 8
\end{bmatrix}
$$

We know that

$$(6.5) \qquad S^2 = 8S + 2565$$

Hamada and Kobayashi [2] have shown that the rows of S are of the following types

$$
(6.6) \qquad
\begin{aligned}
&8\,4\,4\,4\,4 \quad .2^{12}.\,3^{16} \\
&8\,4\,4\,4\,1 \quad .2^{9}.\,3^{19} \\
&8\,4\,4\,1\,1 \quad .2^{6}.\,3^{22} \\
&8\,4\,4\,0 \;.2^{6}.\,3^{25}
\end{aligned}
$$

Using 6.5) and 6.4) it will be possible to construct S from the 13 starts of 6.4). But the number of cases is prohibitively large.

If there is a C_3 then the first 3 columns of A can be taken as 1,2,3,4,5,6,7,8; 1,2,3,4,9,10,11,12; and 5,6,7,8,9,10,11,12. Every further column will have 4 1's in the top 12 rows and 4 1's in the top 12 rows and 4 1's in the bottom rows. Excluding the first 3 zero columns the bottom 10 rows will be a (10,30,12,4,4) design. One such choices is the 3 design obtained by adjoining a 10th point to the Steiner triple system on 9 points.

The 30 columns are:

(6.7)														
1	1	2	3	10		13	1	2	4	8		25	2	6	8	9
2	4	5	6	10		14	1	2	5	6		26	3	4	7	9
3	7	8	9	10		15	1	2	7	9		27	3	5	6	8
4	1	4	7	10		16	1	3	4	5		28	4	5	8	9
5	2	5	8	10		17	1	3	6	7		29	4	6	7	8
6	3	6	9	10		18	1	3	8	9		30	5	6	7	9
7	1	5	9	10		19	1	4	6	9						
8	2	6	7	10		20	1	5	7	8						
9	3	4	8	10		21	2	3	4	6						
10	1	6	8	10		22	2	3	5	9						
11	2	4	9	10		23	2	3	7	8						
12	3	5	7	10		24	2	4	5	7						

One of the top 12 rows of A will have 2 1's is the first 3 columns and 10 more in these 30 columns. to have inner product 4 with each of the last 10 rows we much choose its 1's in 10 columns which together have each of $1, \cdots 10$ exactly 4 times. This can be done in 900 ways. The automorphism group of the above array is of order 1440, and the 900 choices fall into 8 orbits under this group. Using a computer G.H. John van Rees at the University of Manitoba was able to show that no combination completes these 10 rows to a full design. Thus excludes 6.7) as a possible (10,30,12,4,4) design. But there are many designs with these parameters.

7. A Possible (81,16,3) Design. For a symmetric (81,16,3) design there may be a collineation of order 13 with 3 fixed points X, Y, Z and 6 orbits of length 13. The following table gives the distribution of points in block orbits.

a_0	a_1	a_2	a_3	a_4	a_5	a_6	a_1	a_8	a_9	a_{10}	a_{11}	a_{12}	X	Y	Z
b_0	b_1	b_2	b_3	b_4	b_5	b_6	b_7	b_8	b_9	b_{10}	b_{11}	b_{12}	X	Y	Z
c_0	c_1	c_2	c_3	c_4	c_5	c_6	c_7	c_8	c_9	c_{10}	c_{11}	c_{12}	X	Y	Z
X	a	a	b	b	c	c	d	d	d	e	e	e	f	f	f
Y	a	a	b	b	c	c	d	d	d	e	e	e	f	f	f
Z	a	a	b	b	c	c	d	d	d	e	e	e	f	f	f
a	a	a	b	b	b	c	c	c	d	d	d	d	e	e	e
a	a	a	b	b	b	c	c	c	e	e	e	e	f	f	f
a	a	a	b	b	b	c	c	c	f	f	f	f	d	d	d

This suggests the possibility of a further collineation of order 3.

8. The Tonchev–van Lint Construction. Recently van Lint and Tonchev have constructed a (28,42,15,10,5) design. No collineation of prime order greater than 3 can exist. They assume one fixed point and largest possible number of fixed blocks, 12, for a collineation of order 3. This gives certain restrictions on the structure and with further assumptions the full design was constructed. The following is a listing of the blocks. The point collineation is (P) (1,2,3) (4,5,6) (7,8,9)

(10,11,12) (13,14,15) (16,17,18) (19,20,21) (22,23,24) (25,26,27)

$$(28, 42, 15, 10, 5)$$

P	1	2	3	4	5	6	7	8	9
P	10	11	12	13	14	15	16	17	18
P	19	20	21	22	23	24	25	26	27
P	1	2	3	10	11	12	19	20	21
P	4	5	6	13	14	15	22	23	24
P	7	8	9	16	17	18	25	26	27
P	1	2	3	13	14	15	25	26	27
P	4	5	6	16	17	18	19	20	21
P	7	8	9	10	11	12	22	23	24
P	1	2	3	16	17	18	22	23	24
P	4	5	6	10	11	12	25	26	27
P	7	8	9	13	14	15	19	20	21

P	1	6	9	11	14	17	20	24	27
P	2	4	7	12	15	18	21	22	25
P	3	5	8	10	13	16	19	23	26
2	3	6	7	11	18	17	19	24	25
3	1	4	8	12	14	18	20	22	26
1	2	5	9	10	15	16	21	23	27
3	5	6	7	12	15	17	20	23	26
1	6	4	8	10	13	18	21	24	27
2	4	5	9	11	14	16	19	22	25
1	4	8	9	12	13	17	19	23	25
2	5	9	7	10	14	18	20	24	26
3	6	7	8	11	15	16	21	22	27
2	6	9	11	12	13	18	21	23	26
3	4	7	12	10	14	16	19	24	27
1	5	8	10	11	15	17	20	22	25
1	6	7	10	14	15	18	19	23	25
2	4	8	11	15	13	16	20	24	26
3	5	9	12	13	14	11	21	22	27
2	5	8	12	15	17	18	19	24	27
3	6	9	10	13	15	16	20	22	25
1	4	7	11	14	16	17	21	23	26
1	5	7	12	13	16	20	21	24	25
2	6	8	10	14	17	21	19	22	26
3	4	9	11	15	18	19	20	23	27
3	5	8	11	14	18	21	23	24	25
1	6	9	12	15	16	19	24	22	26
2	4	7	10	13	17	20	22	23	27
1	5	7	11	13	18	19	22	26	27
2	6	8	12	14	16	20	23	27	25
3	4	9	18	15	17	21	24	25	26

REFERENCES

[1] M. HALL JR, R. ROTH, G.H. JOHN VAN REES, AND S.A. VANSTONE, "On Designs (22,23,12,8,4)", J. Conbinatorial Theory (Series A) 47 (1988), 157–175.

[2] N. HAMADA AND Y. KOBAYASHI, "On the block structure of B1B designs with parameters $v = 22, b = 33, r = 12, k = 8$ and $\lambda = 4$", J. Combinatorial Theory (Series A) 24 (1978) 75–83.

[3] F.J. MAC WILLIAMS, N.J.A. SLOANE, AND J.G. THOMPSON, "On the existence of a projective plane of order 10", J. Combinatorial Theory (Series A) 14 (1973) 66–78.

ALGEBRAIC GEOMETRIC CODES

JACOBUS H.VAN LINT*

1. Introduction. The most important development in the theory of error-correcting codes in recent years is the introduction of methods from algebraic geometry to construct *good* codes. The ideas are based on generalizations of so-called *Goppa codes* . The (by now) "classical" Goppa codes (1970, cf.[6]) were already a great improvement on codes known at that time. The algebraic geometric codes were also inspired by ideas of Goppa but the most sensational development was a paper by Tsfasman, Vlădut and Zink (1982,cf.[15]). In this paper the idea of codes from algebraic curves was combined with certain recent deep results from algebraic geometry to produce a sequence of error-correcting codes that led to a new lower bound on the information rate of good codes that is better than the Gilbert-Varshamov bound. The novice reader should realize that the G-V-bound (1952) was never improved (until 1982) and believed by many to be best possible. Actually, the improvement is only achieved for alphabets of size at least 49 and several binary coding experts still have hope that no improvement of the G-V-bound for F_2 will be possible; (this author is not one of them).

The aim of the present tutorial paper (notes of five 90-minute lectures held at the workshop) is to introduce combinatorialists with some knowledge of coding theory to the new ideas. (In Sections 1 to 3 (= lecture 1) the necessary coding theory is reviewed.) In the fall of 1987 Gerard van der Geer and I gave a (quite intensive and strenuous) course in Düsseldorf (a DMV- Seminar) on this topic. I will borrow heavily from the notes the two of us wrote for that course (to appear as DMV-Lecture Notes [5]). Much of the algebraic geometry that is necessary to understand the new codes is treated considerably better in Van der Geer's notes than I can do here (partly due to lack of time; mostly because it is not my field). Nevertheless I hope that this paper will make it possible for many readers to introduce themselves to this fascinating area. The serious student should start by reading Fulton's book on Algebraic Curves [4]. There are several good survey papers and introductions to our subject. We mention only a few : Beth [2] ; for those who read French, Driencourt and Michon [3] is excellent ; also recommended is Lachaud [8] ; the survey by Tsfasman himself [14] is good ; there is a quite elementary introduction to the topic by Springer and Van Lint [10] ; for the readers that prefer German the master's thesis by M.Wirtz (University of Münster, [16]) is definitely "gründlich".

This paper is structured as follows. In Section 2 we introduce the terminology from coding theory and the Gilbert-Varshamov bound. Section 3 is devoted to cyclic codes , the BCH-bound and to Reed-Solomon codes. These codes are the first natural introduction to algebraic geometric codes (cf. [10]). Section 4 is an introduction to the geometric terminology of the second half of the paper. In Section

---

*Department of Mathematics and Computing Science, Eindhoven University of Technology, Eindhoven, Netherlands

5 we treat classical Goppa codes and also show that there is a strong connection between the two classes of codes (i.e. R S and Goppa). For a more detailed treatment of Sections 2 to 5 we refer to [9]. Section 6 is an introduction to algebraic curves, the related function fields and it treats two examples that reappear in the remaining sections. Two concepts that will be new to several readers, namely *divisors* and *differentials* are the topics of Sections 7 and 8. These two sections are the main part of the prerequisite knowledge for the algebraic geometric codes. The key to understanding the algebraic geometric codes is the famous Riemann-Roch theorem, treated in Section 9. Then in Section 10 we (finally) introduce the codes $C(D, G)$ and $C^*(D, G)$ and calculate the parameters of these codes. Section 11 treats several examples. As stated earlier, the improvement of the Gilbert-Varshamov bound was considered sensational. In Section 12 we sketch how this was done.

Until a few months ago practically nothing was known about (efficient) decoding of these new codes. Presently there are some interesting schemes, due to Justesen et al [7] , Skorobogatov and Tsfasman [14] and to Pellikaan. These are treated in Section 13.

The whole area of this paper is extremely exciting and it has been quite a challenge to explain these ideas (many of which I have only learned recently) to such a distinguished audience. I sincerely hope that these notes will stimulate many readers to *seriously* study this fascinating area of mathematics. It provides a new proof of the fact that *all* mathematics is applicable.

2. Error-correcting codes. In block coding one starts by choosing a so-called alphabet Q that is a set of q distinct symbols (usually q will be a power of a prime and Q the finite field $\mathbf{F}_q$). A *code C* with *word length n* is a subset of Q^n. Elements of Q^n are called *words* , those of C *codewords* .

In Q^n we introduce so-called *Hamming-distance* by

$$(2.1) \qquad d(\mathbf{x}, \mathbf{y}) := |\{i : 1 \leqq i \leqq n, x_i \neq y_i\}|.$$

For a code C we define the *minimum distance d* by

$$(2.2) \qquad d := \min\{d(\mathbf{x}, \mathbf{y}) : \mathbf{x} \in C, \mathbf{y} \in C, \mathbf{x} \neq \mathbf{y}\}.$$

If C has word length n, M words, and minimum distance d, then we call C an (n, M, d) code. If $d = 2e + 1$ then C is an e-error- correcting code.

One of the most important parameters of a code C is its so-called *information rate R* defined by

$$(2.3) \qquad R := n^{-1} \log_q |C|.$$

To see that this is a natural concept, note that if we wished to encode four words in a binary alphabet, it would suffice to use $00, 01, 10, 11$. If, however, we use a code C with four words of length 3, then by (2.3) our information rate is 2/3.

A *linear code* is a linear subspace of $\mathbf{F}_q^n$. We use the notation $[n,k]$ code if the code has dimension k and $[n,k,d]$ code if the minimum distance is d. For such a code we have $R = k/n$.

For any alphabet containing the symbol 0, we define the weight $w(\mathbf{x})$ of a word $\mathbf{x}$ to be the number of nonzero symbols of $\mathbf{x}$. The *minimum weight* of a linear code is the minimum of $w(\mathbf{c})$ over all nonzero codewords $\mathbf{c}$ and because of linearity, this is equal to the minimum distance of the code. Any matrix G that has as its rows k basis vectors of C is called a *generator matrix* of C. We call two codes equivalent if one is obtained from the other by a permutation of the positions in the words. So w.l.o.g. we can assume that a generator matrix G of C has the so-called standard form $(I_k \quad P)$, where P is a k by $n-k$ matrix.

DEFINITION 2.1. If C is an $[n,k]$ code then we define the dual code $C^\perp$ by

$$C^\perp := \left\{ \mathbf{y} \in \mathbf{F}_q^n : \forall_{\mathbf{x} \in C}[< \mathbf{x}, \mathbf{y} >= 0] \right\},$$

where $< \mathbf{x}, \mathbf{y} >$ denotes the usual inner product.

We shall need a few more definitions.

DEFINITION 2.2. If C is a code of length n, then the *extended* code $\overline{C}$ is defined by

$$\overline{C} := \left\{ (c_1, c_2, \ldots, c_n, c_{n+1}) : (c_1, c_2, \ldots, c_n) \in C, \sum_{i=1}^{n+1} c_i = 0 \right\}.$$

DEFINITION 2.3. Let C be linear code over $\mathbf{F}_{q^s}$. The *subfield subcode* over $\mathbf{F}_q$ consists of all words of C that have all coordinates in the subfield.

We shall often be interested in sequences of codes with increasing word length n and either a fixed rate R or a fixed error-correcting capability. To clarify the latter situation we consider communication over a channel with error probability p_e (i.e. each transmitted symbol has probability p_e of being received incorrectly). In a received word the expected number of errors is np_e and in order to correct these we need d to be at least $2np_e + 1$. So d/n should exceed $2p_e$ if we are to use these codes successfully for error-correction on the given channel. This makes it clear why we introduce the parameter $\delta := d/n$. We use the notation $A_q(n,d)$ for the maximal value of M for which an (n, M, d) code exists.

DEFINITION 2.4. $\qquad \alpha(\delta) := \limsup_{n \to \infty} n^{-1} \log_q A_q(n, \lfloor \delta n \rfloor).$

This function tells us the information rate of good long codes for which $d/n = \delta$

For thirty years the best lower bound on $\alpha(\delta)$ was the so-called *Gilbert-Varshamov* bound that we now derive. The cardinality $V_q(n,d)$ of the set of words in $\mathbf{F}_q^n$ that have distance at most d to a given word is given by

$$(2.4) \qquad V_q(n,d) = \sum_{i=0}^{d} \binom{n}{i} (q-1)^i.$$

We define the entropy function H_q on $[0, (q-1)/q]$ by

$$H_q(0) := 0,$$
(2.5)
$$H_q(x) := x \log_q(q-1) - x \log_q x - (1-x) \log_q(1-x) \qquad \text{for} \quad 0 < x < (q-1)/q.$$

Using Stirling's formula it is not difficult to prove that

$$\text{(2.6)} \qquad \limsup_{n \to \infty} n^{-1} \log_q V_q(n, \lfloor \delta n \rfloor) = H_q(\delta).$$

If C has minimum distance d and minimum cardinality for this distance , then all words in $\mathbf{F}_q^n$ have distance less than d to some codeword. Therefore $|C| \cdot V_q(n, d-1) \geq q^n$. From (2.4), (2.5), (2.6), and Definition 2.4 we find :

> **THEOREM 2.1.** *(Gilbert-Varshamov bound).* $\qquad \alpha(\delta) \geq 1 - H_q(\delta)$.

In Theorem 12.2 we shall find a new lower bound for $\alpha(\delta)$ that is better than Theorem 2.1 for all $q \geq 49$ in a subinterval of $[0, (q-1)/q]$.

For later reference we mention one upper bound for $A_q(n, d)$.

> **THEOREM 2.2.** *(Singleton bound).* $\qquad A_q(n, d) \leq q^{n-d+1}$.

Proof. If C is a code with length n and distance d, then deleting the last $d-1$ coordinates of each word yields a code of length $n-d+1$ in which all the codewords are still different. $\square$

As a corollary we find that for an $[n, k, d]$ code we have

$$\text{(2.7)} \qquad d \leq n - k + 1.$$

Codes for which equality holds in (2.7) are called *MDS-codes* (*maximum distance seperable codes*). If G is the generator matrix of an MDS code, then any k columns of G are linearly independent. Since G is a parity check matrix for the dual code, the dual code has minimum distance larger than k. Since the dual code has dimension $n - k$, it follows from (2.7) that its minimum distance cannot exceed $k + 1$. Hence the dual of an MDS code is also an MDS code.

3. Cyclic codes. We now introduce more algebraic structure.

> **DEFINITION 3.1.** A linear code C is called *cyclic* if

$$\forall_{(c_0, c_1, \ldots, c_{n-1}) \in C} \quad [(c_{n-1}, c_0, \ldots, c_{n-2}) \in C].$$

From now on we make the convention $(n, q) = 1$. We identify words $(a_0, a_1, \ldots, a_{n-1})$ in $\mathbf{F}_q^n$ with polynomials $a_0 + a_1 x + \cdots + a_{n-1} x^{n-1}$ in the algebra $\mathbf{F}_q[x]/(x^n - 1)$. Multiplication by x in this algebra amounts to a cyclic shift of the words. Therefore the following theorem is a direct consequence of Definition 3.1.

THEOREM 3.1. *A cyclic code corresponds to an ideal in* $\mathsf{F}_q[x]/(x^n - 1)$.

Since the algebra is a principal ideal ring, a cyclic code is completely described by a *generator* $g(x)$ of the corresponding ideal (which we simply identify with the code). If the decomposition of $x^n - 1$ into irreducible factors (over F_q) is $x^n - 1 = f_1(x)\dots f_r(x)$ then we find 2^r (not necessarily inequivalent) cyclic codes of length n since $g(x)$ must be a divisor of $x^n - 1$. If $x^n - 1 = g(x)h(x)$ and $g(x) = g_0 + g_1 x + \cdots + g_{n-k}x^{n-k}$, $h(x) = h_0 + h_1 x + \cdots + h_k x^k$, then a generator matrix G of the cyclic code C with generator $g(x)$ has k cyclic shifts of $(g_0, g_1, \dots, g_{n-k}, 0, 0, \dots, 0)$ as its rows and a parity check matrix H has $n - k$ cyclic shifts of $(0, 0, \dots, 0, h_k, h_{k-1}, \dots, h_0)$ as its rows. It follows that the cyclic code with generator $h(x)$ is equivalent to $C^{\perp}$.

Let C be a cyclic code with generator $g(x) = f_1(x)\dots f_t(x)$. For $1 \leq i \leq t$ let β_i be a zero of $f_i(x)$ in the field F_{q^m}. The code C is completely determined by this set of zeros. Any such set Z determining the code is called a *zero set* of C. We have

$$(3.1) \quad \mathbf{c} = (c_0, c_1, \dots, c_{n-1}) \in C \iff \forall_{\beta \in Z} \ [c_0 + c_1\beta + \cdots + c_{n-1}\beta^{n-1} = 0].$$

Since elements of F_{q^m} can be represented as column vectors in F_q^m, the t by n matrix H with rows $(1, \beta_i, \beta_i^2, \dots, \beta_i^{n-1})$ can be interpreted as a tm by n matrix over F_q and we see from (3.1) that $\mathbf{c}$ is a codeword if and only if $\mathbf{c}H^{\top} = 0$. If the rows of H are not linearly independent, then a parity check matrix for the code can be obtained by deleting some rows of H.

DEFINITION 3.2. Let β be a primitive n^{th} root of unity in an extension field of F_q. The cyclic code defined by the zero set $Z := \{\beta^l, \beta^{l+1}, \dots, \beta^{l+s-2}\}$ is called a *BCH code with designed distance* s. We usually take $s = 1$ (narrow sense BCH code).

THEOREM 3.2. *The minimum distance of a BCH code with designed distance s is at least s.(This is called the BCH bound).*

Proof. If we take any $s - 1$ columns of the matrix H defined by Z as shown above, the resulting matrix is a Vandermonde matrix, and hence nonsingular. Since $\mathbf{c}H^{\top} = 0$ for a codeword $\mathbf{c}$, it follows that $\mathbf{c}$ has weight at least s. $\square$

We now come to a class of codes that form the starting point of our description of algebraic geometric codes, the so-called Reed-Solomon codes.

DEFINITION 3.3. A *Reed-Solomon* code (RS code) is a BCH code of length $n = q - 1$ over F_q. The generator of an RS code has the form $g(x) = \prod_{i=1}^{d-1}(x - \alpha^i)$, where α is a primitive element of F_q and d is the designed distance.

Since the dimension of an RS code with designed distance d is $n - d + 1$, the minimum distance is exactly d by (2.7), i.e. an RS code is an MDS code. In this case the fact that the dual is also MDS is not surprising since the dual code has generator $\prod_{i=0}^{n-d+1}(x - \alpha^i)$; (it is also an RS code).

Consider the code of Definition 3.3. We extend the code (cf. Definition 2.2) to a code of length q. Codewords with $c_{n+1} = 0$ have $x = 1$ as a zero and hence they have weight at least $d+1$ by Theorem 3.2. Hence the extended code is also an MDS code.

We now give a different description of the same codes. Again, let $n = q$. Number the elements of $\mathbf{F}_q$ as follows : $\alpha_i = \alpha^i$ $(0 \leq i \leq q-2)$, $\alpha_{q-1} = 0$. Let L denote the set of polynomials of degree less than k in $\mathbf{F}_q[x]$. The code C is defined by

$$(3.2) \qquad C := \{(f(\alpha_0), f(\alpha_1), \ldots, f(\alpha_{q-1})) : f \in L\}.$$

Since a polynomial of degree less than k can have at most $k-1$ zeros, the minimum weight of C is at least $n - k + 1$. From (2.7) it follows that C is an MDS code. Consider a codeword $\mathbf{c}$ with $c_i = f(\alpha_i)$, where $f(x) = \sum_{j=0}^{k-1} a_j x^j$. Then, if $1 \leq l \leq q - k - 1$ we have $\sum_{i=0}^{q-2} c_i(\alpha^l)^i = \sum_{j=0}^{k-1} a_j \sum_{i=0}^{q-2}(\alpha^{l+j})^i = 0$, because the inner sum is 0 since $1 \leq l + j \leq q - 2$. From Definition 3.3 it follows that $\mathbf{c}$ is a codeword in the extension of the RS code with distance $n - k$. Hence (3.2) defines the same code as Definition 3.3 (with $d = n - k + 1$).

The second representation of Reed-Solomon codes allows us to generalize the idea. We now consider $\mathbf{F}_{q^m}$ as alphabet and choose n distinct elements from this field, say $\alpha_1, \alpha_2, \ldots, \alpha_n$. Let $\mathbf{v} = (v_1, v_2, \ldots, v_n)$ be a vector from $\mathbf{F}_{q^m}^n$ with no zero coordinates and write $\mathbf{a} := (\alpha_1, \alpha_2, \ldots, \alpha_n)$.

DEFINITION 3.4. The *generalized Reed-Solomon code* $\mathrm{GRS}_k(\mathbf{a}, \mathbf{v})$ has as codewords all $(v_1 f(\alpha_1), v_2 f(\alpha_2), \ldots, v_n f(\alpha_n))$, where f runs through the set of polynomials of degree less than k in $\mathbf{F}_{q^m}[x]$.

In the same way as above we see that a generalized Reed-Solomon code and its dual are MDS codes.

4. Geometric description of RS codes. This section is a preparation for the description of codes from algebraic curves. We consider the field $\mathbf{F}_q$ and denote its algebraic closure by $\mathbf{F}$. Projective N- dimensional space $\mathbf{P}^N$ consists of all $(x_1, x_2, \ldots, x_{N+1})$ in $\mathbf{F}^{N+1} \setminus \{0\}$. The points $(x_1, x_2, \ldots, x_{N+1})$ and $(cx_1, cx_2, \ldots, cx_{N+1})$, where $c \in \mathbf{F}^*$ are defined to be the same. In particular, $\mathbf{P}^1$ is the projective line. We denote points as (x, y). A *rational function* on $\mathbf{P}^1$ is a quotient $a(x,y)/b(x,y)$ where a and b are homogeneous polynomials of the same degree. (Without this restriction the quotient would not be well defined on $\mathbf{P}^1$.) A point on $\mathbf{P}^1$ is called a *pole* of a rational function $a(x,y)/b(x,y)$ if $b(x,y)$ is zero in this point (and $a(x,y)$ is not zero). Let Q be the point $(1,0)$. We define $\mathcal{L}$ to be the vector space of all rational functions $a(x,y)/b(x,y)$, where a and b have coefficients in $\mathbf{F}_q$, with the property that these functions do not have poles anywhere on $\mathbf{P}^1$ except possibly in Q. In case there is a pole in Q, we require the order of this pole (defined in the usual way) to be less than k. A code C is now defined as follows. We consider the so-called *rational points* on $\mathbf{P}^1$, i.e. those points for which the coordinates are in $\mathbf{F}_q$; (these points are Q and the points $(\alpha_i, 1)$ where α_i runs through $\mathbf{F}_q$). Let $P_1, P_2, \ldots, P_n$ be the points $\neq Q$. Then

$$(4.1) \qquad C := \{(f(P_1), f(P_2), \ldots, f(P_n)) : f \in \mathcal{L}\}.$$

Summarizing, we have taken the projective line, a set of n points on this line and a vector space of functions and then the code consisted of the set of n-tuples of function values. The only difference in the following treatment of algebraic geometric codes is that the line will be replaced by a curve. To see the connection with the previous section observe that since $\mathbf{F}$ is closed, the restriction on the poles of $a(x,y)/b(x,y)$ forces us to take $b(x,y) = y^l$ with $l \leq k$. Then $a(x,y)$ is homogeneous of degree l and C is nothing other than the code of (3.2).

5. Classical Goppa codes. Consider the BCH code of Definition 3.2 with $Z = \{\beta^j : 1 \leq j < d\}$. Let $(c_0, c_1, \ldots, c_{n-1})$ be a codeword. Then we have

$$
(z^n - 1) \sum_{i=0}^{n-1} \frac{c_i}{z - \beta^{-i}} = \sum_{i=0}^{n-1} c_i \sum_{l=0}^{n-1} z^l (\beta^{-i})^{n-1-l} =
$$

$$
= \sum_{l=0}^{n-1} z^l \sum_{i=0}^{n-1} c_i (\beta^{l+1})^i = z^{d-1} p(z),
$$

i.e.

$$
(5.1) \qquad \sum_{i=0}^{n-1} \frac{c_i}{z - \beta^{-i}} = \frac{z^{d-1} p(z)}{z^n - 1},
$$

for some polynomial $p(z)$ and in fact this condition defines the code. We generalize this definition by replacing Z by some other set and z^{d-1} by another polynomial.

DEFINITION 5.1. Let $L := \{\gamma_0, \gamma_1, \ldots, \gamma_{n-1}\}$ be an n-element subset of $\mathbf{F}_{q^m}$ and let $g(z)$ be a monic polynomial in $\mathbf{F}_{q^m}[z]$ such that $g(\gamma_i) \neq 0$ for $0 \leq i \leq n-1$. The *Goppa code* $\Gamma(L, g)$ with Goppa polynomial $g(z)$ is the set of words $(c_0, c_1, \ldots, c_{n-1})$ in $\mathbf{F}_q^n$ for which

$$
(5.2) \qquad \sum_{i=0}^{n-1} \frac{c_i}{z - \gamma_i} \equiv 0 \qquad (\text{mod } g(z)).
$$

Before we study some properties of these codes, we reformulate the definition, again to make the generalization to algebraic curves in the following sections more natural. Start with the field $\mathbf{F}_{q^m}$. Consider the vector space of all rational functions $f(z)$ with the following properties :

(i) $f(z)$ has zeros in all the points where $g(z)$ has zeros, each with at least the same multiplicity as the zero of $g(z)$,

(ii) $f(z)$ has no poles, except possibly in some of the points $\gamma_0, \gamma_1, \ldots, \gamma_{n-1}$ and in that case poles of order 1.

A code over $\mathbf{F}_{q^m}$ is defined by taking as codewords the n-tuples

$$
(\mathrm{Res}_{\gamma_0} f, \mathrm{Res}_{\gamma_1} f, \ldots, \mathrm{Res}_{\gamma_{n-1}} f),
$$

where the residue of $f(z)$ in a point γ_i is defined in the usual way. The Goppa code $\Gamma(L, g)$ is the subfield subcode (over $\mathbf{F}_q$) of this code.

A parity check matrix for $\Gamma(L, g)$ is found as follows. Let $g(z) = \sum_{i=0}^{t} g_i z^i$. Then the polynomial

$$\phi(z) = \frac{g(z) - g(x)}{z - x} = \sum_{l+j \leq t-1} g_{l+j+1} x^j z^l$$

is a polynomial of degree less than t in z (for any x). Since $(z - x)\phi(z) \equiv -g(x) \pmod{g(z)}$ we can rewrite (5.2) as follows, with $h_j := 1/g(\gamma_j)$:

$$(5.3) \qquad \sum_{i=0}^{n-1} c_i h_i \sum_{l+j \leq t-1} g_{l+j+1} (\gamma_i)^j z^l = 0.$$

In (5.3) the coefficient of z^l is 0 for $0 \leq l \leq t - 1$. This means that if $\mathbf{c} = (c_0, c_1, \ldots, c_{n-1})$ is a codeword, then it has inner product 0 with the rows of a matrix that has the entry $h_i(g_{t-l} + g_{t-l+1}\gamma_i + \cdots + g_t \gamma_i^l)$ in row l ($0 \leq l \leq t-1$) and column i. Using elementary row operations this yields the following parity check matrix for $\Gamma(L, g)$:

$$(5.4) \qquad H = \begin{pmatrix} h_0 & h_1 & \cdots & h_{n-1} \\ h_0\gamma_0 & h_1\gamma_1 & \cdots & h_{n-1}\gamma_{n-1} \\ \vdots & \vdots & \ddots & \vdots \\ h_0\gamma_0^{t-1} & h_1\gamma_1^{t-1} & \cdots & h_{n-1}\gamma_{n-1}^{t-1} \end{pmatrix}.$$

Now compare this with Definition 3.4 where we take $\mathbf{v} := (h_0, h_1, \ldots, h_{n-1})$ and $\mathbf{a} := (\gamma_0, \gamma_1, \ldots, \gamma_{n-1})$, $k = t$. We see that H is the generator matrix of the code $\mathrm{GRS}_k(\mathbf{a}, \mathbf{v})$. So the Goppa code $\Gamma(L, g)$ is a subfield subcode of the dual of a generalized Reed-Solomon code.

The lesson we learn, that shall repeat itself later, is that the codes defined using polynomials as in Definition 3.4 and the codes defined using residues in first order poles, as we did above, are dual codes (in other words : it is sufficient to treat only one of the classes).

For the sake of completeness we point out that we have also found the following theorem.

THEOREM 5.1. *The Goppa code $\Gamma(L, g)$ of Definition 5.1, where g has degree t, has dimension at least $n - mt$ and minimum distance at least $t + 1$.*

Proof. The statement about the dimension follows from (5.4) and the fact that a codeword has weight $> t$ follows from (5.2). $\square$

6. Algebraic curves. In the following, k is an algebraically closed field. In our applications k will be the algebraic closure of a finite field $\mathbf{F}_q$ but in this introduction the reader can think of $\mathbf{C}$ if that is easier to grasp. $\mathbf{A}^n$ will denote affine n-dimensional space over k with coordinates $x_1, \ldots, x_n$. Similarly $\mathbf{P}^n$ will be n-dimensional projective space with homogeneous coordinates $x_0, x_1, \ldots, x_n$. We shall first discuss the affine case. The situation for projective spaces is slightly more complicated.

In the space A^n we introduce a topology, the so-called Zariski topology. The closed sets B are the sets of zeros of ideals a of $k[x_1, x_2, \ldots, x_n]$, i.e.

$$B = V(a) := \{(x_1, x_2, \ldots, x_n) \in A^n \; : \; f(x_1, x_2, \ldots, x_n) = 0 \text{ for all } f \in a\}.$$

We always assume that a is maximal, i.e. a consists of all polynomials that vanish on B. A closed subset B is called *irreducible* if B cannot be written as the union of two proper closed subsets of B. The set $V(a)$ is irreducible if and only if a is a prime ideal.

For example, consider in A^2 (with coordinates x, y) the principal ideal generated by $x^2 - y^2$. It is the union of two straight lines with equations $y = x$ resp. $y = -x$. Each of these lines is an irreducible closed set in A^2. In this section we shall study curves in affine and projective spaces and we shall always require these to be irreducible.

Consider a prime ideal p in the ring $k[x_1, x_2, \ldots, x_n]$. The set X of zeros of p is called an affine variety. (For example, if $n = 3$ and p is the ideal in $k[x, y, z]$ generated by the polynomial $x^2 + y^2 + z^2 - 1$, then X is the unit sphere in A^3.) Two polynomials that differ by an element of p will have the same value in each point of X. So we introduce a new ring :

DEFINITION 6.1. The *coordinate ring $k[X]$* of the variety X is the ring $k[x_1, \ldots, x_n]/p$.

(The reader should keep in mind that X denotes the curve and not a variable.)

DEFINITION 6.2. The field of quotients of $k[X]$ is denoted by $k(X)$ and it is called the *function field* of X.

The transcendence degree of $k(X)$ over k is called the *dimension* of X. If this dimension is 1 then X is called an *algebraic curve*.

EXAMPLE 6.1. If X is the parabola with equation $y^2 = x$ in the affine plane (over k), then $k(X)$ is an algebraic extension of degree 2 of the field $k(x)$, obtained by adjoining an element y with $y^2 = x$. The coordinate ring $k[X]$ consists of all $A + By$, where A and B are in $k[x]$ and again $y^2 = x$.

For projective spaces the situation is complicated by the homogeneous coordinates. As we saw before, it only makes sense to study rational functions for which numerator and denominator are homogeneous polynomials of the same degree. As a consequence (using the fact that k is algebraically closed) there are no regular functions on X except constant functions.

In projective space P^n with homogeneous coordinates $x_0, x_1, \ldots x_n$ we can start in the same way as above, using homogeneous polynomials, thus defining projective varieties. Now, let X be an affine or projective variety. Let P be a point of X and let U be a neighborhood of P. A function ϕ defined on U is called *regular* in P if $\phi = f/g$, where $g(P) \neq 0$ and f and g are polynomials, resp. homogeneous polynomials of the same degree. The functions that are regular in every point of U form a ring denoted by $O(U)$. Two functions that are regular in P are called equivalent if they are equal in some neighborhood of P.

DEFINITION 6.3. The *local ring O_P* (sometimes $O_P(X)$) of the point P on X is the set of equivalence classes of regular functions.

This is indeed a "local ring" in the algebraic sense, i.e. it has a unique maximal ideal m_P consisting of the classes of functions that have a zero at P.

For a projective variety X we again define a *function field $k(X)$* with "rational functions" as elements. To do this we consider pairs (U, f) with $f \in O(U)$, U a nonempty open set in X, and define equivalence of pairs $(U, f), (V, g)$ by $f = g$ on $U \cap V$. The equivalence classes are the "rational functions".

In the following we shall only consider curves X. The curve X is completely characterized by the field $k(X)$ and some authors actually define curves by starting with the function fields.

Consider a curve in $\mathbb{A}^2$ defined by an equation $F(x, y) = 0$ and let $P = (a, b)$ be a point on the curve. If at least one of the derivatives F_x or F_y is not zero in P, then P is called a *simple* point (or *nonsingular* point). In this case the curve has a tangent at P with equation $F_x(P)(x - a) + F_y(P)(y - b) = 0$. In general, one can define a simple point of a curve X by requiring that m_P/m_P^2 (as k-vector space) has dimension 1; (we do not prove this). From now on we shall restrict our attention to *nonsingular curves* (or *smooth* curves), i.e. curves for which all points are nonsingular. This restriction has the following consequence. Let P be a point of X. As we saw above, the maximal ideal m_P of the local ring O_P consists of the functions that are 0 in P. The other elements of O_P are units. Since m_P/m_P^2 has dimension 1, there is a generating element t for this space. We also use t for the corresponding element in m_P. It then follows that every element z of O_P can be written in a unique way as $z = ut^m$, where u is a unit and $m \in \mathbb{N}$. The function t is called a *local parameter* (local coordinate) or *uniformizing parameter*. If $m > 0$ then P is a zero of multiplicity m of z. We write $m = \mathrm{ord}_P(z) = v_P(z)$. (For readers familiar with the terminology : O_P is a discrete valuation ring, elements t with $v_P(t) = 1$ are local parameters). We then extend the order function to $k(X)$ by defining $v_P(f/g) := v_P(f) - v_P(g)$. If $v_P(z) = -m > 0$ then we say that z has a *pole* of order m in P.

EXAMPLE 6.2. (A trivial example to clarify the situation). Let X be the circle in $\mathbb{A}^2$ with equation $x^2 + y^2 = 1$ and let $P = (1, 0)$. Let $z = z(x, y) = 1 - x$. This function is 0 in P, so it is in m_P. We claim that z has order 2. To see this, observe that y is a local parameter in P because the line $y = 0$ intersects X with multiplicity 1 in P. Furthermore, on X we have $1 - x = y^2/(1 + x)$ and the function $(1 + x)^{-1}$ is a unit in O_P. Everything can be done similarly for $\mathbb{P}^2$. Then X is given by $x^2 + y^2 - z^2 = 0$, $P = (1, 0, 1)$. We consider $(z - x)/z$ in O_P, again an element of m_P. A local parameter in P is $t = y/z$. We have $(z - x)/z = t^2 \cdot (z/(z + x))$, where the second factor on the right is a unit in O_P. So $v_P((z - x)/z) = 2$.

Remark : We often consider $\mathbb{P}^2$ as the union of three overlapping affine spaces, defined by $x = 1$, resp. $y = 1$, resp. $z = 1$.

EXAMPLE 6.3. Let $F(x, y, z) = xz - y^2$. In $\mathbb{P}^2$ we consider the curve X given by $F(x, y, z) = 0$. The affine part is the parabola of Example 6.1 and there is one point $Q = (1, 0, 0)$ on the "line at infinity". The expressions $f = (A_l + B_{l-1}y)/(C_l + D_{l-1}y)$, where A_l denotes a homogeneous polynomial of degree l in x and z (or zero) and $y^2 = xz$, form the field $k(X)$. The function f is regular in Q if the coefficient of x^l in C_l is not zero. One easily sees that y/x is a local parameter in Q. Suppose we wish to study the behavior of $g = (z^3 + xyz)/x^3$ in Q. Take affine coordinates with $x = 1$. The curve now has equation $z = y^2$ (note that the line $y = 0$ intersects the curve once in Q) and one easily sees that the curve $z^3 + yz = 0$ intersects X three times in $(0,0)$. Now that we know that g has a zero with multiplicity 3 in Q, this is easily shown in homogeneous coordinates : on X we have

$$\frac{z^3 + xyz}{x^3} = \left(\frac{y}{x}\right)^3 \left(\frac{x^2 + yz}{x^2}\right)$$

and the second factor on the right is regular in Q.

DEFINITION 6.4. If k is the algebraic closure of F_q and X is a curve, then points on X with coordinates in F_q are called *rational* over F_q.

We end this section with a few more examples.

EXAMPLE 6.4. Let P^1 be the projective line over k. A local parameter in the point $P = (1, 0)$ is y/x. The rational function $(x^2 - y^2)/y^2$ has a pole of order 2 in P. If k does not have characteristic 2, then $(1,1)$ and $(-1,1)$ are zeros with multiplicity 1.

EXAMPLE 6.5. (The *Klein quartic*) Consider the plane curve defined by the equation $f(x, y, z) = x^3y + y^3z + z^3x = 0$. (Note that this curve is singular over F_7 in the point $(1,2,4)$). We consider the curve over the algebraic closure of F_2. Over F_2 there are three rational points : $(1,0,0)$, $(0,1,0)$, and $(0,0,1)$. If we go to F_4, we find two new points, namely $(1, \omega, 1 + \omega)$ and $(1, 1 + \omega, \omega)$, where $\mathsf{F}_4 = \{0, 1, \omega, 1 + \omega\}$, $(\omega^2 = 1 + \omega)$. In later sections we shall use this curve over F_8. Let $\mathsf{F}_8 = \mathsf{F}_2(\xi)$, where $\xi^3 = \xi + 1$. Besides the three points over F_2, we have points (x, y, z) with $xyz \neq 0$. Take $z = 1$, $y = \xi^i$ $(0 \leq i \leq 6)$ and write $x = \xi^{3i}\eta$. It follows that $\eta^3 = \eta + 1 = 0$, i.e. η is one of the elements ξ, ξ^2, ξ^4. Therefore the curve has $3 + 7 \times 3 = 24$ rational points over F_8.

EXAMPLE 6.6. Let X be the plane curve with equation $x^3 + y^3 + z^3 = 0$ over the closure of F_4. There are nine rational points, namely the cyclic shifts of $(0, \alpha, 1)$, where $\alpha \in \{1, \omega, 1 + \omega\}$. In $Q = (0, 0, 1)$ we have the local parameter $t = x/z$. The function $\phi = x/(y + z)$ cannot be represented by this expression in Q. On the curve X we have

$$\frac{x}{y + z} = \frac{x(y^2 + yz + z^2)}{y^3 + z^3} = t^{-2} \cdot \frac{y^2 + yz + z^2}{z^2} \quad ,$$

where the last factor on the right is regular in Q. Therefore we say that ϕ has a pole of order 2 in Q. Similarly $y/(y + z)$ has a pole of order 3 in Q.

As an exercise the reader can consider the curve of Example 6.3 over F_4. It has five points. The function g has a zero of multiplicity 3 in Q, three zeros of multiplicity 1 and a pole of order 6 in $(0,0,1)$.

7. Divisors. In the following, X is a smooth projective curve over k.

DEFINITION 7.1.

(1) A *divisor* is a formal sum $D = \sum_{P \in X} n_P P$, with $n_P \in \mathbb{Z}$ and $n_P = 0$ for all but a finite number of points P ;

(2) $\mathrm{Div}(X)$ is the additive group of divisors with formal addition (the free abelian group on X) ;

(3) A divisor D is called *effective* if all n_P are non-negative (notation $D \succ 0$) ;

(4) The *degree* $\deg(D)$ of a divisor is $\sum n_P$.

Let $v_P = \mathrm{ord}_P$ be the discrete valuation (for functions on X) defined in Section 6.

DEFINITION 7.2. If f is a rational function on X, not identically 0, we define the divisor of f to be

$$(f) := \sum_{P \in X} v_P(f) P.$$

So, in a sense, the divisor of f is a bookkeeping device that tells us where the zeros and poles of f are and their multiplicities and orders. Since f is a rational function for which the numerator and denominator have the same degree, and since k is algebraically closed, it is intuitively clear that f has the same number of zeros as poles, if counted properly. We do not give a proof. The following theorem is a consequence.

THEOREM 7.1. *The degree of a divisor of a rational function is 0.*

We shall call two divisors D and D' linearly equivalent if and only if $D - D'$ is the divisor of a rational function; notation $D \equiv D'$. This is indeed an equivalence relation. Although we shall not really use it, we mention for the sake of completeness that the group of equivalence classes, known as the *Picard group* of the curve, plays a very important rôle in the theory of algebraic curves.

DEFINITION 7.3. $\mathrm{Pic}(X) := \mathrm{Div}(X) / \{(f) : f \in k(X)^*\}$.

The group $\mathrm{Pic}(X)$ is also called the *divisor class group*.

Recall that in Section 5 following Definition 5.1 we gave a reformulation involving a vector space of rational functions for which certain zeros were prescribed and furthermore all points where poles would be allowed (but not required) were specified. We now have a mechanism available to do this same thing on curves.

DEFINITION 7.4. Let D be a divisor on a curve X. We define a vector space $\mathcal{L}(D)$ over k by

$$\mathcal{L}(D) := \{f \in k(X)^* : (f) + D \succ 0\} \cup \{0\} \,.$$

Note that if $D = \sum_{i=1}^{r} n_i P_i - \sum_{j=1}^{s} m_j Q_j$ with all $n_i,\ m_j > 0$, then $\mathcal{L}(D)$ consists of 0 and the functions in the function field that have zeros of multiplicity at least m_j at Q_j ($1 \le j \le s$) and that have no poles except possibly at the points

P_i, with order at most n_i $(1 \leq i \leq r)$. We shall show that this vector space has finite dimension. First we note that if $D \equiv D'$ and g is a rational function with $(g) = D - D'$, then the mapping $f \to fg$ shows that $\mathcal{L}(D)$ and $\mathcal{L}(D')$ are isomorphic.

THEOREM 7.2.

(i) $\mathcal{L}(D) = \{0\}$ if $\deg(D) < 0$;

(ii) $\dim_k \mathcal{L}(D) \leq 1 + \deg(D)$.

Proof. (i) If $\deg(D) < 0$ then for any function $f \in k(X)^*$ we have $\deg((f)+D) < 0$, i.e. $f \notin \mathcal{L}(D)$.

(ii) If f is not 0 and $f \in \mathcal{L}(D)$, then $D' := D + (f)$ is an effective divisor for which $\mathcal{L}(D')$ has the same dimension as $\mathcal{L}(D)$ by our observation above. So w.l.o.g. D is effective, say $D = \sum_{i=1}^{r} n_i P_i$. Again, assume that f is not 0 and $f \in \mathcal{L}(D)$. In the point P_i we map f onto the corresponding element of the n_i-dimensional vector space $t_i^{-n_i} O_{P_i}/O_{P_i}$, where t_i is a local parameter at P_i. We thus obtain a mapping of f onto the direct sum of these r vector spaces ; (map the 0-function onto 0). This is a linear mapping. Suppose f is in the kernel. This means that f does not have a pole in any of the P_i, i.e. f is a constant function. It follows that

$$\dim_k \mathcal{L}(D) \leq 1 + \sum_{i=1}^{r} n_i = 1 + \deg(D). \quad \square$$

EXAMPLE 7.1. Consider again the curve X of Example 6.6. We saw that $\phi = x/(y+z)$ has a pole of order 2 in $Q = (0, 1, 1)$. The function has two zeros, each with multiplicity 1, namely $P_1 = (0, \omega, 1)$, $P_2 = (0, 1 + \omega, 1)$. From the representation $\phi = (y^2 + yz + z^2)/x^2$ we see that Q is the only pole. So $(\phi) = P_1 + P_2 - 2Q$ and $\deg(\phi) = 0$ in accordance with Theorem 7.1. It is not trivial but one can show that there cannot be a function in $k(X)$ that has a pole of order 1 in Q and no other poles. (The reader might be tempted to try a fraction in which numerator and denominator are both products of three linear functions, and hence both have nine zeros on X, in such a way that eight zeros coincide. Then the function would have one zero and one pole. However, a well known theorem on cubic curves (cf.[4] p.124) says that this cannot happen (all nine zeros would coincide)). It follows that in this case the space $\mathcal{L}(2Q)$ has dimension 2. A basis consists of ϕ and the function that is identically 1. (Similarly $\mathcal{L}(Q) = k$).

DEFINITION 7.5. We denote $\dim_k \mathcal{L}(D)$ by $l(D)$.

In Section 9 we shall state the main theorem that we need concerning $l(D)$.

8. Differentials on a curve. Consider an affine curve X in $\mathbb{A}^2$ defined by the equation $F(x, y) = 0$ and let $P = (a, b)$ be a point on X. The tangent T_P at P is defined by $d_P F = 0$, where we define

$$d_P F := F_x(a, b)(x - a) + F_y(a, b)(y - b).$$

149

If $G \in k[X]$ it would not make sense to define $d_P G$ in the same way because G is only defined modulo multiples of F. However, on T_P the linear function $d_P G = G_x(a,b)(x-a) + G_y(a,b)(y-b)$ is well defined. Given P, the mapping d_P maps an element of $k[X]$ to a linear function defined on the tangent T_P, i.e. an element of T_P^*. For a fixed function G, the mapping $d_P G$ associates with each point P of X an element of T_P^*. Let $\Phi[X]$ denote the set of all mappings that associate with each point P of X an element of T_P^*. We are now in a position to give a definition for any affine or projective curve.

DEFINITION 8.1. An element $\phi \in \Phi[X]$ is called a *regular differential form* (on the curve X) if every point P of X has a neighborhood U such that in this neighborhood ϕ can be represented as $\phi = \sum_{i=1}^{m} f_i dg_i$, where all f_i and g_i are regular in U.

So, the regular differential forms on X form a $k[X]$-module , which we call $\Omega[X]$, that is generated by elements df, where $f \in k[X]$,with the relations $d(f+g) = df + dg$ and $d(fg) = fdg + gdf$ and $da = 0$ for $a \in k$. The extension to *rational differential forms* is made in the same way as was done for rational functions in Section 6. We now have the well known rule $d(f/g) = (gdf - fdg)/g^2$.

The following example shows that on a projective curve we cannot associate differential forms on X with functions on X.

EXAMPLE 8.1. Once again consider the curve X (char$(k)\neq 3$) in $\mathbf{P}^2$ given by $x^3 + y^3 + z^3 = 0$. We define the open set U_x by $U_x := \{(x,y,z) : y \neq 0, z \neq 0\}$ and similarly U_y, U_z. Since $x^2 dx + y^2 dy + z^2 dz = 0$ on X, it is easy to check that a regular differential ω is defined by the representations

$$\left(\frac{y}{z}\right) d\left(\frac{x}{y}\right) = \frac{ydx - xdy}{z^2} \text{ on } U_x, \frac{zdy - ydz}{x^2} \text{ on } U_y, \frac{xdz - zdx}{y^2} \text{ on } U_z.$$

(Note that there is no point on X where two coordinates are 0.) There are no regular functions on X, so there is no representation of ω as gdf.

From now on we call the rational differential forms on X *differentials* and denote the space of differentials by $\Omega(X)$. One can show that $\Omega(X)$ is of dimension 1 over $k(X)$; in a neighborhood of a point P with local parameter t a differential ω can be represented as $\omega = fdt$, where f is a rational function. This makes the following definition possible.

DEFINITION 8.2. The divisor (ω) of the differential ω is defined by

$$(\omega) := \sum_{P \in X} v_P(f_P)P,$$

where $\omega = f_P dt_P$ is the local representation of ω and v_P is the valuation on O_P (extended to $k(X)$).

(One has to show that this does not depend on the choice of the local parameters and also that only finitely many coefficients are not 0.)

Let ω be a differential and $W = (\omega)$. W is called a *canonical divisor* . If ω' is another nonzero differential, then $\omega' = f\omega$ for some rational function f. So $(\omega') = W' \equiv W$ and therefore the canonical divisors form one class in $\mathrm{Pic}(X)$. This class is also denoted by W (often the letter K is used). Now consider the space $\mathcal{L}(W)$. This space (which by Definition 7.4 consists of rational functions) can be mapped onto an isomorphic space of differential forms by $f \to f\omega$. By the definition of $\mathcal{L}(W)$ the image of f under the mapping is a regular differential form, i.e. $\mathcal{L}(W)$ is isomorphic to $\Omega[X]$.

DEFINITION 8.3. Let X be a smooth projective curve over k. We define the *genus g* of X by $g := l(W)$.

The genus of a curve will play an important rôle in the following sections. It would therefore be useful to have ways of determining the genus of a curve. For most of the methods we must refer to textbooks on algebraic geometry. We mention one simple formula without proof, namely the so-called *Plücker formula* :

THEOREM 8.1. *If X is a nonsingular projective curve of degree d in $\mathbf{P}^2$, then*

$$g = \frac{1}{2}(d-1)(d-2).$$

So the curve of Example 8.1 has genus 1 and by the definition of genus, $\mathcal{L}(W) = k$, so regular differentials on X are multiples of the differential ω of Example 8.1.

For the construction of Goppa codes over algebraic curves we shall need the concept of "residue" of a differential at a point P. This is defined in accordance with our treatment of local behavior of a differential ω. Let P be a point on X, t a local parameter at P and $\omega = f dt$ the local representation of ω. The function f can be written as $\sum_i a_i t^i$. We define the residue $\mathrm{Res}_P(\omega)$ of ω in the point P to be a_{-1} (as was to be expected).

One of the basic results in the theory of algebraic curves is known as the "residue theorem". We only state the theorem.

THEOREM 8.2. *If ω is a differential on a smooth projective curve X, then*

$$\sum_{P \in X} \mathrm{Res}_P(\omega) = 0.$$

9. The Riemann-Roch theorem. The following famous theorem, known as the *Riemann-Roch* theorem is not only a central result in algebraic geometry with applications in many different areas (e.g. various parts of number theory) but it is also the key to the new sensational results in coding theory.

THEOREM 9.1. *Let D be a divisor on a smooth projective curve of genus g. Then, for any canonical divisor W*

$$l(D) - l(W - D) = \deg(D) - g + 1.$$

There are several proofs of this theorem. Each one would take more time to treat than all of the present survey is taking. The theorem allows us to determine the degree of canonical divisors.

COROLLARY 9.1. *For a canonical divisor W we have $deg(W) = 2g - 2$.*

Proof. Everywhere regular functions on a projective curve are constant, i.e. $\mathcal{L}(0) = k$, i.e. $l(0) = 1$. Substitute $D = W$ in Theorem 9.1 and the result follows from Definition 8.3. $\square$

It is now clear why in Example 7.1 the space $\mathcal{L}(2Q)$ only had dimension 2. By Theorem 8.1 the curve X has genus 1, the degree of $W - 2Q$ is negative, so $l(W - 2Q) = 0$. By Theorem 9.1 we have $l(2Q) = 1$.

At first, Theorem 9.1 does not look too useful. However, Corollary 9.1 provides us with a means to use it successfully.

COROLLARY 9.2. *Let D be a divisor on a smooth projective curve of genus g and let $deg(D) > 2g - 2$. Then*

$$l(D) = deg(D) - g + 1.$$

Proof. By Corollary 9.1 $\deg(W - D) < 0$, so by Theorem 7.2(i) $l(W - D) = 0$. $\square$

The term $l(W - D)$ in Theorem 9.1 can be interpreted in terms of differentials. We introduce a generalization of Definitions 7.4 and 7.5 for differentials.

DEFINITION 9.1. Let D be a divisor on a curve X. We define

$$\Omega(D) := \{\omega \in \Omega(X) : (\omega) - D \succ 0\}$$

and we denote $\dim_k \Omega(D)$ by $\delta(D)$, called the *index* of D.

The connection with functions is established by the following theorem.

THEOREM 9.2. $\delta(D) = l(W - D).$

Proof. If $W = (\omega)$ we define a linear map $\phi : \mathcal{L}(W - D) \to \Omega(D)$ by $\phi(f) := f\omega$. This is clearly an isomorphism. $\square$

EXAMPLE 9.1. If we take $D = 0$, then by Definition 8.3 there are exactly g linearly independent regular differentials on a curve X. So the differential of Example 8.1 is the only regular differential on X (up to a constant factor) as was already observed after Theorem 8.1.

In the following sections we return to coding theory. Our alphabet will again be $\mathbf{F}_q$. We shall apply the theorems of the previous sections. In order to do this a few adaptations are necessary. E.g. the space $\mathcal{L}(D)$ of Definition 7.4 will be considered over $\mathbf{F}_q$. All that we need to know is that Theorem 9.1 remains true. In a number of examples this will be obvious from the basis of $\mathcal{L}(D)$ (a basis over k with polynomials over $\mathbf{F}_q$, where k is again the closure).

10. Codes from algebraic curves. Let X be a non-singular projective curve over F_q. We shall define two kinds of "geometric" codes from X. The first kind generalizes the definition of Section 4, the second kind generalizes the codes of Section 5. In the following, $P_1, P_2, \ldots, P_n$ are rational points on X and D is the divisor $P_1 + P_2 + \cdots + P_n$. Furthermore G is some other divisor that has support disjoint from D. Although it is not necessary, we shall make more restrictions on G, namely that the support of G consists of rational points and furthermore

$$(10.1) \qquad\qquad 2g - 2 < \deg(G) < n.$$

DEFINITION 10.1. The linear code $C(D, G)$ of length n over F_q is the image of the linear map $\alpha : \mathcal{L}(G) \to \mathsf{F}_q^n$ defined by $\alpha(f) := (f(P_1), f(P_2), \ldots, f(P_n))$.

We shall call such a code a "geometric generalized RS code".

THEOREM 10.1. *The code $C(D, G)$ has dimension $k = \deg(G) - g + 1$ and minimum distance $d \geq n - \deg(G)$.*

Proof. (i) If f belongs to the kernel of α, then $f \in \mathcal{L}(G - D)$ and by (10.1) and Theorem 7.2 this implies $f = 0$. The result follows from (10.1) and Corollary 9.2.

(ii) If $\alpha(f)$ has weight d then there are $n - d$ points P_i, say $P_{i_1}, P_{i_2}, \ldots, P_{i_{n-d}}$, for which $f(P_i) = 0$. Therefore $f \in \mathcal{L}(G - E)$, where $E = P_{i_1} + \cdots + P_{i_{n-d}}$. Hence $\deg(G) - n - d \geq 0$. $\square$

EXAMPLE 10.1. Let $X := \mathsf{P}^1$ over F_q. Take $G = mQ$ where Q is the point $(1, 0)$, $n = q$, $P_i = (\alpha_i, 1)$, where $\mathsf{F}_q = \{\alpha_1, \alpha_2, \ldots, \alpha_q\}$. Then, if $m = k - 1$ we see that $C(D, G)$ is the extended RS code as described in Section 4.

EXAMPLE 10.2. Let X be the curve of Examples 6.6 and 7.1, $G = 2Q$, where $Q = (0, 1, 1)$. We take $n = 8$ (so D is the sum of the remaining rational points). The coordinates are given by

	P_1	P_2	P_3	P_4	P_5	P_6	P_7	P_8	Q
x	1	1	1	1	1	1	0	0	0
y	0	0	0	$\overline{\omega}$	ω	1	$\overline{\omega}$	ω	1
z	$\overline{\omega}$	ω	1	0	0	0	1	1	1

where $\overline{\omega} = 1 + \omega$. We saw in Example 7.1 that 1 and $x/(y + z)$ are a basis of $\mathcal{L}(2Q)$ over k and hence also over F_q. This leads to the following generator matrix for $C(D, G)$:

$$\begin{pmatrix} 1 & 1 & 1 & 1 & 1 & 1 & 1 & 1 \\ \omega & \overline{\omega} & 1 & \omega & \overline{\omega} & 1 & 0 & 0 \end{pmatrix}.$$

Of course it is trivial to see that $d = 6$ in this case.

We now come to the second class of geometric codes. We shall call them "geometric Goppa codes".

DEFINITION 10.2. The linear code $C^*(D, G)$ of length n over $\mathbf{F}_q$ is the image of the linear map $\alpha^* : \Omega(G - D) \to \mathbf{F}_q^n$ defined by

$$\alpha^*(\eta) := (\operatorname{Res}_{P_1}(\eta), \operatorname{Res}_{P_2}(\eta), \ldots, \operatorname{Res}_{P_n}(\eta)).$$

The parameters are given by the following theorem.

THEOREM 10.2. *The code $C^*(D, G)$ has dimension $k^* = n - \deg(G) + g - 1$ and minimum distance $d^* \geq \deg(G) - 2g + 2$.*

Proof. Just as in Theorem 10.1 these assertions are direct consequences of Theorem 9.1 (Riemann-Roch). ☐

EXAMPLE 10.3. We use the notation of Section 5. Let $D = P_0 + P_1 + \cdots + P_{n-1}$, where $P_i := (\gamma_i, 1)$ on the projective line $\mathbf{P}^1$ over $\mathbf{F}_{q^m}$. Let $G := (g)$ where $g(x, y)$ is the homogeneous form of the Goppa polynomial. Then the Goppa code $\Gamma(L, g)$ is the subfield subcode over $\mathbf{F}_q$ of $C^*(D, G)$.

We saw in Section 5 that Goppa codes could be defined as (subcodes of) duals of generalized Reed-Solomon codes. Therefore the following theorem should not be surprising.

THEOREM 10.3. *The codes $C(D, G)$ and $C^*(D, G)$ are dual codes.*

Proof. From Theorem 10.1 and Theorem 10.2 we know that $k + k^* = n$. So it suffices to take a word from each code and show that the inner product of the two words is zero. Let $f \in \mathcal{L}(G)$, $\eta \in \Omega(G - D)$. By Definitions 10.1 and 10.2 the differential $f\eta$ has no poles except possibly poles of order 1 in the points $P_1, P_2, \ldots, P_n$. The residue of $f\eta$ in P_i is equal to $f(P_i)\operatorname{Res}_{P_i}(\eta)$. By Theorem 8.2 the sum of the residues of $f\eta$ (over all the poles, i.e. over the P_i) is equal to zero. Hence we have

$$0 = \sum_{i=1}^{n} f(P_i)\operatorname{Res}_{P_i}(\eta) = <\alpha(f), \alpha^*(\eta)> . \quad ☐$$

Several authors prefer the codes $C^*(D, G)$ over geometric RS codes but the non-experts in algebraic geometry probably feel more at home with polynomials than with differentials. If one is willing to drop the condition that D and G have disjoint supports, then the codes $C(D, G)$ suffice to get all the codes (cf. [5]).

In the next section we shall treat several more examples of geometric codes. The reader should already have noticed that we have defined a class of *good* codes. E.g. Theorem 10.1 implies that all geometric codes over a curve of genus 0 (i.e. over $\mathbf{P}^1$) are MDS codes! In fact, Theorem 1 says that $d \geq n - k + 1 - g$, so if g is small, we are close to the Singleton bound

11. Examples of geometric codes. In Section 2 we made it clear that, for a given alphabet $\mathbf{F}_q$, we are interested in *long* codes. The approach of Section 10 makes it necessary to find rational points on a given curve and the number of these points determines the length of our codes. A central problem in algebraic geometry is finding bounds for the number of rational points on a curve. In order to appreciate some of our examples, we mention without proof the famous *Weil bound*.

THEOREM 11.1. *Let X be a curve of genus g over $\mathbf{F}_q$. If $N_q(X)$ denotes the number of rational points on X, then*

$$|N_q(X) - (q+1)| \leq 2g\sqrt{q}.$$

EXAMPLE 11.1. Let $X = \mathbf{P}^1$ over $\mathbf{F}_{q^m}$. We define $P_0 := (0,1)$, $P_\infty := (1,0)$ and we define the divisor D as $\sum_{j=1}^{n} P_j$, where $P_j := (\beta^j, 1)$, $1 \leq j \leq n$. We define $G := aP_0 + bP_\infty$, $a \geq 0$, $b \geq 0$. (Here β is a primitive n^{th} root of unity.) By Theorem 9.1 $\mathcal{L}(G)$ has dimension $a + b + 1$ and one immediately sees that the functions $(x/y)^i$, $-a \leq i \leq b$ form a basis of $\mathcal{L}(G)$. Consider the code $C(D,G)$. A generator matrix for this code has as rows $(\beta^i, \beta^{2i}, \ldots, \beta^{ni})$ with $-a \leq i \leq b$. So $(c_1, c_2, \ldots, c_n)$ is a codeword in $C(D,G)$ if and only if $\sum_{j=1}^{n} c_j(\beta^l)^j = 0$ for all l with $a < l < n - b$. It follows that $C(D,G)$ is a Reed-Solomon code. The subfield subcode with coordinates in $\mathbf{F}_q$ is a BCH code.

EXAMPLE 11.2. In this example we consider codes from *Hermitean* curves. Let $q = r^2 = 2^l$. A Hermitean curve X in $\mathbf{P}^2$ over $\mathbf{F}_q$ is defined by the equation

$$(11.1) \qquad x^{r+1} + y^{r+1} + z^{r+1} = 0.$$

By Theorem 8.1 the genus is $g = \frac{1}{2}r(r-1) = \frac{1}{2}(q - \sqrt{q})$. We shall first show that X has the maximal number of rational points, i.e. by Theorem 11.1 exactly $1 + q\sqrt{q}$ rational points. If in (11.1) one of the coordinates is 0, then w.l.o.g. one of the others is 1 and the third one is one of the solutions of $\xi^{r+1} = 1$, which has $r + 1$ solutions in $\mathbf{F}_q$. This shows that X has $3(r+1)$ points with $xyz = 0$. If $xyz \neq 0$, we may take $z = 1$ and y any element $\neq 0$ in $\mathbf{F}_q$ such that $y^{r+1} \neq 1$. For each choice of y there are $r + 1$ solutions x. This yields $(r - 2)(r + 1)^2$ pairs (x, y). It follows that X has $3(r+1) + (r-2)(r+1)^2 = 1 + q\sqrt{q}$ rational points. We take $G := mQ$, where $Q := (0, 1, 1)$ and $q - \sqrt{q} < m < q\sqrt{q}$. The code $C(D,G)$ over $\mathbf{F}_q$ has length $n = q\sqrt{q}$, dimension $k = m - g + 1$ and distance $d \geq n - m$. In order to see how good these codes are, we take as example $q = 16$. A basis for $\mathcal{L}(G)$ is easily found. The functions $f_{i,j}(x,y,z) = x^i y^j / (y + z)^{i+j}$, $0 \leq i \leq 4$, $j \geq 0$, $4i + 5j \leq m$ will do the job. First, observe that there are $m - 5 = m - g + 1$ pairs (i, j) satisfying these conditions. In the same way as in Example 6.4 we see that $f_{i,j}$ has a pole of order $4i + 5j$ in Q, and so the functions are independent. Therefore the code is easily constructed but decoding is another question! For the moment we only try to get some idea of the quality of the code. Suppose that we intend to send a long message (say 10^9 bits) over a channel with an error probability $p_e = 0.01$. We compare encoding using a rate $\frac{1}{2}$ Reed-Solomon code over $\mathbf{F}_{16}$ with the use of $C(D,G)$, where we take $m = 37$ to also get rate $\frac{1}{2}$. In this case $C(D,G)$ has distance 27. The RS code has word length 16 (64 bits) and distance 9. If a word is received incorrectly, we assume that all the bits are wrong (when counting the number of errors). For the RS code the error probability after decoding is roughly $3 \cdot 10^{-4}$; for the code $C(D,G)$ it is less than $2 \cdot 10^{-7}$. In this example it is important to keep in mind that we are fixing the alphabet (in this case $\mathbf{F}_{16}$). If we compare the code $C(D,G)$, for which the words are strings of 256 bits, with a rate $\frac{1}{2}$ RS code over $\mathbf{F}_{2^5}$, (words are 160 bits long), the latter code will come close in performance (error probability $2 \cdot 10^{-6}$) and a rate $\frac{1}{2}$ RS code over $\mathbf{F}_{2^6}$ (words are 384 bits long) performs better (roughly 10^{-7}). We remark that if one also compares with a binary BCH code of length 255 and rate about $\frac{1}{2}$, then the BCH code wins. However, this is not a fair comparison either because codes over larger alphabets (such as $\mathbf{F}_{16}$) are used to handle burst errors. E.g. our code $C(D, G)$ can handle a burst of length 46 bits (this influences at most 13 letters of a codeword) and the BCH code would fail completely on such a burst.

EXAMPLE 11.3. Let X be the Klein quartic over $\mathbf{F}_8$ of Example 6.5. By Theorem 8.1 the genus is 3. By Theorem 11.1 X can have at most 25 rational points and as we saw in Example 6.3, it has 24 rational points; (in fact this is optimal by an improvement of Theorem 11.2 due to J.-P.Serre [12]). Let $Q := (0, 0, 1)$ and let D be the sum of the other 23 rational points, $G = 10Q$. From Theorem 10.1 we find that $C(D, G)$ has dimension $10 - g + 1 = 8$ and minimum distance $d \geq 23 - 10 = 13$. We now concatenate this code with the $[4, 3, 2]$ single parity check code as follows. The symbols in codewords of $C(D, G)$ are elements of $\mathbf{F}_8$ which we interpret as column vectors of length 3 over $\mathbf{F}_2$ and then we adjoin the parity check. The resulting code C is a $[92, 24, 26]$ binary code. The punctured code, a $[91, 24, 25]$ code (constructed in 1987 by Barg et al [1]) set a new world record for codes with $n = 91$, $d = 25$. Several other codes of this kind are given in the same paper.

For the reader interested in the actual construction of the code in this example, we give the details. Define $P_1 := (1, 0, 0)$, $P_2 := (0, 1, 0)$, $P_3 := (0, 0, 1) = Q$. The remaining 21 rational points have coordinates $\neq 0$ by Example 6.5. To show that y/z is a local parameter in Q we observe that in affine coordinates we have $x^3 y + y^3 + x = 0$ and the line $y = 0$ meets this curve with multiplicity 1 in $(0,0)$. Therefore we also have local parameters in P_1, resp. P_2, namely z/x resp. x/y. We analyze the behavior of y/z in P_1 and P_2 : we have

(i) in P_1 : $\quad \frac{y}{z} = \left(\frac{z}{x}\right)^2 \cdot \frac{x^3}{x^3 + y^2 z}$, so P_1 is a zero of multiplicity 2,

(ii) in P_2 : $\quad \frac{y}{z} = \left(\frac{y}{x}\right)^3 \cdot \frac{y^3 + z^2 x}{y^3}$, so P_2 is a pole of order 3.

Hence $\left(\frac{y}{z}\right) = 2P_1 - 3P_2 + P_3$, $\left(\frac{z}{x}\right) = P_1 + 2P_2 - 3P_3$, and $\left(\frac{x}{y}\right) = -3P_1 + P_2 + 2P_3$, i.e. $\left(\frac{y}{x}\right) = 3P_1 - P_2 - 2P_3$.

It follows that the functions $(z/x)^i (y/x)^j$ with $0 \leq 3i + 2j \leq 10$, $0 \leq j \leq 2i$ are in $\mathcal{L}(10Q)$. We find solutions with poles of order 0,3,4,5,6,7,8,9,10 respectively; clearly eight independent elements, i.e. a basis since $l(10Q) = 8$. So, we can give a generator matrix for the code explicitly.

Remark : From this example we see that $l(3Q) = 2$ although Riemann-Roch only promises $l(3Q) \geq 1$.

EXAMPLE 11.4. Consider the curve X over $\mathbf{F}_4$ given by $x^2 y + \omega y^2 z + \overline{\omega} z^2 x = 0$.

This is a nonsingular curve with genus 1. Its rational points are given by

	P_1	P_2	P_3	P_4	P_5	P_6	Q_1	Q_2	Q_3
x	1	0	0	1	1	1	ω	1	1
y	0	1	0	ω	$\overline{\omega}$	1	1	ω	1
z	0	0	1	$\overline{\omega}$	ω	1	1	1	ω

Let $D := P_1 + P_2 + \cdots + P_6$, $G := 2Q_1 + Q_2$. We claim that the functions $x/(x + y + \overline{\omega}z)$, $y/(x + y + \overline{\omega}z)$, $z/(x + y + \overline{\omega}z)$ are a basis of $\mathcal{L}(G)$. To see this, note that the numerators are not 0 in Q_1 and Q_2 and observe that the line with equation $x + y + \overline{\omega}z = 0$ meets X in Q_2 and is tangent to X at Q_1. By Theorem 10.1 the code $C(D, G)$ of length 6 has minimum distance at least 3. However, the code is in fact an MDS code, namely the well known $[6, 3, 4]$ "hexacode" with generator $\begin{pmatrix} 1 & 0 & 0 & 1 & \omega & \omega \\ 0 & 1 & 0 & \omega & 1 & \omega \\ 0 & 0 & 1 & \omega & \omega & 1 \end{pmatrix}$. (This code is used in Conway's construction of the Golay code.) It was proved by Driencourt and Michon that the known $[q + 2, q - 1, 4]$ MDS codes are not geometric codes if $q > 4$ (see [3]).

EXAMPLE 11.5. We mention one slightly more complicated example. Let X be the curve over $\mathbf{F}_{2^4}$ with equation $x^5 + y^2z^3 + yz^4 + z^5 = 0$. (The affine part has equation $y^2 + y = x^5 + 1$.) It is now more difficult to find the genus. The curve in the plane is singular but there is a nonsingular (nonplanar) curve (a so-called nonsingular model) that has the same function field. The reader interested in more detail is referred to [5] Example 2.15 and Example 3.15. One could of course find a canonical divisor by trial and error and use Corollary 9.1 to find g. The genus is in fact 2. X has one point with $z = 0$, namely $(0, 1, 0) = Q$. If $z = 1$ and x is arbitrary, then $x^5 + 1 = \xi$ is in $\mathbf{F}_4$ and for each possible value of ξ, the equation $y^2 + y = \xi$ has two solutions in $\mathbf{F}_{2^4}$. So there are 32 other rational points. Again we have equality in Theorem 11.1. Let D be the sum of the rational points $\neq Q$ and choose $G = mQ$. The codes $C(D, G)$ found in this way are $[32, m - 1, 32 - m]$ codes. The idea of Example 11.3 again works. In [11] we find that the best known code with $n = 159$ and $d = 29$ is a 63-dimensional classical Goppa code. By concatenating $C(D, G)$ with $m = 17$ with the even-weight code of length 5 and puncturing, we find a $[159, 64, 29]$ binary code. The code $C(D, G)$ has another interesting property, namely that it is formally self-dual. For a definition of these codes and applications see [11] Ch.19.

12. Improvement of the Gilbert-Varshamov bound. We return to the point of view of Section 2. We fix an alphabet $\mathbf{F}_q$. We consider codes $C(D, G)$ as defined in Definition 10.1, where X has $n + 1$ rational points $P_1, P_2, \ldots, P_n, Q$, and $G = mQ$ with $2g - 2 < m < n$. We define $\gamma(X) := g/n$. It was shown by Tsfasman, Vlǎdut and Zink [15] that there exists a sequence of curves X such that the corresponding geometric codes are a sequence of codes that will yield an improvement of the bound of Theorem 2.1. To be precise, they proved :

THEOREM 12.1. *Let q be a prime power and a square. There exists a sequence of curves X_i over $\mathbf{F}_q$ ($i \in \mathbf{N}$) such that X_i has $n_i + 1$ rational points, genus g_i, where $n_i \to \infty$ as $i \to \infty$, $\gamma(X_i) \to (q^{\frac{1}{2}} - 1)^{-1} =: \overline{\gamma}$ for $i \to \infty$.*

As we saw in Theorem 10.1, the corresponding codes $C_i := C(D, G)$ over X_i have rate $R_i = (m_i - g_i + 1)/n_i$ and distance d_i with $d_i \geq n_i - m_i$. So, with the notation of Section 2 we have $R_i + \delta_i \geq 1 - \gamma(X_i)$. It follows that from Theorem 12.1 we find the following result.

THEOREM 12.2. $\delta + \alpha(\delta) \geq 1 - \bar{\gamma}$.

It is an elementary calculus exercise to determine whether or not the straight line (in the (δ, α) plane) defined by Theorem 12.2 intersects the curve of Theorem 2.1. For intersection one finds $q \geq 43$ but since q must be a square, $q = 49$ is the smallest example.

13. The decoding of algebraic geometric codes. This section reports on very recent work about which I learned just before the workshop. In April 1988 J.Justesen and a group of collaborators [7] published a report on construction and decoding of algebraic geometric codes (using more elementary methods than we do). Their ideas were picked up and generalized by Skorobogatov and Vlǎdut [13] in Moscow (after a lecture by Justesen). These generalizations are presented below (with some modifications). My group in Eindhoven also learned about these ideas through lectures. In the meantime (May 1988) the methods have been improved by R.Pellikaan (Eindhoven). We can only give some indication of the principles of his improvement.

In the following we use the notation of Section 10. As before, X is a curve of genus g, $D = P_1 + P_2 + \cdots + P_n$, G and D have disjoint supports and $\deg(G) > 2g - 2$. We consider the code $C^*(D, G)$. Let $r := \deg(G) - g + 1$ and let $f_1, f_2, \ldots, f_r$ be a basis of $\mathcal{L}(G)$. Then

$$H := \begin{pmatrix} f_1(P_1) & f_1(P_2) & \cdots & f_1(P_n) \\ \vdots & \vdots & \ddots & \vdots \\ f_r(P_1) & f_r(P_2) & \cdots & f_r(P_n) \end{pmatrix}$$

is a parity check matrix for $C^*(D, G)$.

In the following we will denote a received word by $\mathbf{u}$.

We define for $f \in \mathcal{L}(G)$:

$$(13.1) \qquad\qquad S(\mathbf{u}, f) :=< \mathbf{u}, \alpha f > = \sum_{i=1}^{n} u_i f(P_i).$$

(As we saw in Section 2 : $\mathbf{u} \in C^*(D, G) \iff S(\mathbf{u}, f) = 0$.) The syndrome of the received word $\mathbf{u}$ is $H\mathbf{u}^\mathsf{T} = (S(\mathbf{u}, f_1), \ldots, S(\mathbf{u}, f_r))^\mathsf{T}$. We shall write $\mathbf{u}$ as $\mathbf{u} = \mathbf{c} + \mathbf{e}$, where $\mathbf{c} \in C^*(D, G)$ and $\mathbf{e}$ is the error vector. Let there be t errors, so $wt(\mathbf{e}) = t$, and let the errors occur at the locations $Q_1, Q_2, \ldots, Q_t$ (a subset of $P_1, P_2, \ldots, P_n$). We remind the reader who is familiar with Berlekamp-Massey decoding of BCH codes of the so-called error-locator polynomial $\sigma(z) := \prod_{i=1}^{t}(z - \beta_i)$, where the error locations are $Q_i = (\beta_i, 1)$ in the notation of Example 11.1.We shall do something analogous to finding this error-locator.

The first step in our decoding algorithm consists of the choice (if possible) of a divisor F such that

$$
\text{(13.2)} \qquad
\begin{aligned}
&(a) \quad F \text{ is effective and } G - F \text{ is effective,}\\
&(b) \quad t < l(F) =: l,\\
&(c) \quad t + 2g - 2 < \deg(G - F).
\end{aligned}
$$

We introduce functions g_i and h_j as follows :

$$
\text{(13.3)} \qquad
\begin{aligned}
&(a) \quad g_1, g_2, \ldots, g_l \text{ are a basis of } \mathcal{L}(F),\\
&(b) \quad h_1, h_2, \ldots h_m \text{ are a basis of } \mathcal{L}(G - F).
\end{aligned}
$$

We now consider the system of linear equations in the variables $x_1, x_2, \ldots, x_l$ given by

$$
\text{(13.4)} \qquad \sum_{i=1}^{l} s_{ij}(\mathbf{u}) x_i = 0 \qquad (j = 1, 2, \ldots, m),
$$

where $s_{ij}(\mathbf{u}) := S(\mathbf{u}, g_i h_j)$. Note that $s_{ij}(\mathbf{u}) = s_{ij}(\mathbf{e})$ because for codewords $\mathbf{c}$ we have $s_{ij}(\mathbf{c}) = 0$ since $g_i h_j \in \mathcal{L}(G)$.

In the following we use the fact that if $x_1, x_2, \ldots, x_l$ is a solution of (13.4), and if we define g by $g := \sum_{i=1}^{l} x_i g_i$, then (13.4) can be written as

$$
\forall_{h \in \mathcal{L}(G-F)} [< \mathbf{u}, \alpha(gh) > = 0].
$$

For a given $\mathbf{u}$ and any $g \in \mathcal{L}(F)$ the expression $< \mathbf{u}, \alpha(gh) >$ is a linear function on $\mathcal{L}(G-F)$. So we have (for fixed $\mathbf{u}$) a mapping (again linear) from $\mathcal{L}(F)$ to $\mathcal{L}(G-F)^*$ and equation (13.4) amounts to finding an element in the kernel of this mapping. We claim that the space $\mathcal{L}(F - Q_1 - Q_2 - \cdots - Q_t)$ is in this kernel. This is fairly obvious since $< \mathbf{u}, \alpha(gh) > = < \mathbf{e}, \alpha(gh) >$, so if g is a non-zero function in $\mathcal{L}(G)$ that is zero in each Q_i, then by the definition of the points Q_i, the inner product is 0. By the condition (13.2)(b) the space $\mathcal{L}(F - Q_1 - Q_2 - \cdots - Q_t)$ contains nonzero functions. We formulate this as a lemma.

LEMMA 13.1. *If $g \neq 0$, $g \in \mathcal{L}(F - Q_1 - Q_2 - \cdots - Q_t)$ and $g = \sum_{i=1}^{l} x_i g_i$, then the x_i are a solution of (13.4).*

Now we show a converse to this statement.

LEMMA 13.2. *Let $y_1, y_2, \ldots, y_l$ be a nontrivial solution of the system of equations (13.4). Define $g \in \mathcal{L}(F)$ by $g := \sum_{i=1}^{l} y_i g_i$. Then $g(Q_j) = 0$ for $1 \leq j \leq t$.*

Proof. We define a mapping $\beta : \mathcal{L}(G - F) \to \mathbf{F}_q^t$ by $\beta(f) := (f(Q_1), \ldots, f(Q_t))$. The kernel of this mapping is $\mathcal{L}(G - F - \sum_{i=1}^{t} Q_i)$. By (13.2)(c) and Corollary 9.2 the two function spaces have dimensions that differ by t, so the image of β is all of $\mathbf{F}_q^t$. Therefore we can choose a new basis $h_1', \ldots, h_m'$ of $\mathcal{L}(G - F)$ such that $h_j'(Q_k) = \delta_{jk}$. We have

$$
0 = < \mathbf{u}, \alpha(g h_j') > = e(Q_j) g(Q_j) \quad, \text{ so } \quad g(Q_j) = 0. \qquad \square
$$

The system (13.4) can be obtained from the received word $\mathbf{u}$ and subsequently solved. From a solution we can obtain g as in Lemma 13.2 and by substitution of $P_1, P_2, \ldots, P_n$ find a set of zeros, say $Q_1, Q_2, \ldots, Q_s$ that apparently contains the error locations. (We have chosen a convenient numbering of the points Q_j.) By (13.1) the system of linear equations

$$(13.5) \qquad \sum_{i=1}^{s} f_j(Q_i) z_i = S(\mathbf{u}, f_j) \qquad j = 1, 2, \ldots, r$$

has the solution $(e(Q_1), e(Q_2), \ldots, e(Q_t), 0, 0, \ldots, 0)$. This system cannot have another solution because the difference of two solutions would yield a codeword of weight $\leq s$. However, by Theorem 7.2(i) we have $s \leq \deg(F)$ and by (13.2)(c) we have $\deg(F) < \deg(G) - t - 2g + 2 < d^*$.

We therefore have the following decoding algorithm:

ALGORITHM 13.1.

(1) Choose F as in (13.2);
(2) Solve the linear equations (13.4);
(3) Find the zeros of g as defined in Lemma 13.2;
(4) Solve the linear equations (13.5).

All the operations are easily executed but especially the systems of linear equations are time-consuming.

In many of our examples of algebraic geometric codes we took $G = aQ$. In that case (13.2) implies $F = bQ$ and we must have $\deg(G - F) = a - b > t + 2g - 2$. Assume $l(F) = b - g + 1$. Then (13.2)(a) states that $t < b - g + 1$ and we find $t \leq \lfloor \frac{1}{2}(a - 3g + 1) \rfloor$ whereas $d^* \geq a - 2g + 2$. Therefore the best choice for b is $\lfloor \frac{1}{2}(a - g + 1) \rfloor$ and then we can correct up to $\lfloor \frac{1}{2}(d^* - 1 - g) \rfloor$ errors, i.e. *less* than what one would wish!

EXAMPLE 13.1. Consider once again the curve $x^3 + y^3 + z^3 = 0$ over $\mathbf{F}_4$, $Q = (0, 1, 1)$, $G = 4Q$. For the functions f_i we can take $1, x/(y + z), y/(y + z)$ and $x^2/(y^2 + z^2)$. We find

$$H = \begin{pmatrix} 1 & 1 & 1 & 1 & 1 & 1 & 1 & 1 \\ \omega & \overline{\omega} & 1 & \omega & \overline{\omega} & 1 & 0 & 0 \\ 0 & 0 & 0 & 1 & 1 & 1 & \overline{\omega} & \omega \\ \overline{\omega} & \omega & 1 & \overline{\omega} & \omega & 1 & 0 & 0 \end{pmatrix}.$$

If $\mathbf{u}$ is received, let $H\mathbf{u}^\mathsf{T} = (s_1, s_2, s_3, s_4)^\mathsf{T}$ be the (usual) syndrome. Note (from H) that $s_1 s_4 = s_2^2$ if $t = 1$. In Algorithm 13.1 we must take $F = 2Q$. As we saw above, we can correct one error (which is in fact trivial : the syndrome is a multiple of a column of H). In the algorithm the bases of (13.3) are both $\{1, x/(y + z)\}$ and the s_{ij} of (13.4) are $s_{11} = s_1$, $s_{12} = s_{21} = s_2$, $s_{22} = s_4$. So (13.4) becomes $\begin{pmatrix} s_1 & s_2 \\ s_2 & s_4 \end{pmatrix} \begin{pmatrix} x_1 \\ x_2 \end{pmatrix} = \begin{pmatrix} 0 \\ 0 \end{pmatrix}$. (If $s_1 s_4 \neq s_2^2$ we know that more than one error occurred.)

If $s_1 s_4 = s_2^2$ a solution of (13.4) is $x_1 = s_2$, $x_2 = s_1$. For g we find $s_2 g_1 + s_1 g_2 = \dfrac{s_2(y+z) + s_1 x}{y+z}$. So g has two zeros among the P_i and the error is located by solving (13.5). Note that in the usual trivial decoding scheme s_1 and s_2 also determine two columns of H and then we need s_3 to find which one it is.

EXAMPLE 13.2. If $C^*(D, G)$ is an RS code then the equations (13.4) are the well known relations between the syndromes s_i and the coefficients $\sigma_i = x_{l-i}$ of the error-locator $\sigma(z)$. In Berlekamp- Massey decoding step (4) of Algorithm 13.1 is done more efficiently.

EXAMPLE 13.3. As in Example 11.2 take $q = 16$ and consider the $[64, 32, 27]$ code $C^*(D, G)$ with $G = 37Q$. We can correct $\lfloor \frac{1}{2}(d^* - g - 1)\rfloor = 10$ errors (instead of 13).

EXAMPLE 13.4. Consider the Klein quartic over $\mathbf{F}_8$, take $P_1 = (1, 0, 0)$, $P_2 = (0, 1, 0)$, $P_3 = (0, 0, 1)$ and $G = 5(P_1 + P_2 + P_3)$ and let D be the sum of the other 21 rational points. The code $C^*(D, G)$ has $k^* = 8$, $d^* \geq 11$. Algorithm 13.1 will correct three errors if we take $F = aP_1 + bP_2 + cP_3$ with $a + b + c = 6$ or 7. Now suppose that there are $t = 5$ errors. Take $F = aP_1 + bP_2 + cP_3$ with $a + b + c = 8$; (there are 27 solutions (a, b, c)). The reader should reread Section 13 and check what can go wrong. Only (13.2)(c) is not satisfied. We needed this in the proof of Lemma 13.2. In the present case $\mathcal{L}(G - F)$ and $\mathbf{F}_q^t$ both have dimension 5 but β maybe does not map one onto the other. Using deep results from algebraic geometry R.Pellikaan showed that this cannot happen for all the choices of F. So one of them does indeed correct five errors but the workload has increased tremendously. More details on these ideas are to be expected soon.

REFERENCES

[1] A.M.BARG, S.L.KATSMAN AND M.A.TSFASMAN, *Algebraic Geometric Codes from Curves of Small Genus*, Probl.of Information Transmission, 23 (1987), pp. 34–38.

[2] T.BETH, *Some aspects of coding theory between probability, algebra, combinatorics and complexity theory*, in Combinatorial Theory, Lecture Notes in Mathematics 969, Springer Verlag, New York.

[3] Y.DRIENCOURT AND J.F.MICHON, *Rapport sur les Codes Géométriques*, Univ.Aix-Marseille II et Université Paris 7.

[4] W.FULTON, *Algebraic Curves*, Benjamin Cummings, Reading, 1969.

[5] G.VAN DER GEER AND J.H.VAN LINT, *Introduction to Coding Theory and Algebraic Geometry*, DMV Lecture Notes (to appear).

[6] V.D.GOPPA, *A new class of linear error-correcting codes*, Probl.of Information Transmission, 6 (1970), pp. 207–212.

[7] J.JUSTESEN,K.J.LARSEN,H.ELBRØND JENSEN,A.HAVEMOSE AND T.HØHOLDT, *Construction and decoding of a class of algebraic geometry codes*, MAT.Rep.No.1988-10, Danmarks Tekniske Højskole.

[8] G.LACHAUD, *Les codes géométriques de Goppa*, Séminaire Bourbaki, no.641.

[9] J.H.VAN LINT, *Introduction to Coding Theory*, Springer Verlag, New York, 1982.

[10] J.H.VAN LINT AND T.A.SPRINGER, *Generalized Reed-Solomon Codes from Algebraic Geometry*, IEEE Trans.on Information Theory, IT-33 (1987), pp. 305–309.

[11] F.J.MAC WILLIAMS AND N.J.A.SLOANE, *The Theory of Error-Correcting Codes*, North Holland, Amsterdam, 1977.

161

[12]   J.-P.SERRE, *Sur le nombre des points rationnels d'une courbe algébrique sur un corps fini*, C.R. Acad. Sc. Paris, 296 (1983), pp. 397–402.

[13]   A.N.SKOROBOGATOV AND S.G.VLĂDUT, *On the Decoding of Algebraic-Geometric Codes*, preprint.

[14]   M.A.TSFASMAN, *Goppa codes that are better than the Varshamov-Gilbert bound*, Probl.of Information Transmission, 18 (1982), pp. 163–165.

[15]   M.A.TSFASMAN, S.G.VLĂDUT AND T.ZINK, *Modular curves, Shimura curves and Goppa codes better than the Varshamov- Gilbert bound*, Math.Nachr., 109 (1982), pp. 21–28.

[16]   M.WIRTZ, *Verallgemeinerte Goppa-Codes*, Diplomarbeit University of Münster (W.Germany).

COMBINATORIAL CHARACTERS OF QUASIGROUPS

JONATHAN D.H. SMITH†

CONTENTS

1. Introduction. Over a century ago, when the character theory of finite abelian groups had become established, Dedekind began the programme of extending the theory to finite non–abelian groups. Having made little headway a decade later, he proposed the task to Frobenius. Developments progressed rapidly in Frobenius' hands, along both Dedekind's original group determinant approach and Frobenius' new approach that is now considered part of the theory of association schemes. Shortly afterwards, representation theory methods using matrices took over, and have dominated ever since.

The motivation behind the present survey is a continuation of Dedekind's programme, passing from abelian groups beyond non–commutative groups to "non-associative groups" or quasigroups. Since quasigroups (in the form of Latin squares) pre–date groups by several decades, Dedekind might conceivably have formulated his programme in these terms (but did not, as far as the records seem to indicate). In particular, his group determinant may be equally well considered as a quasigroup determinant. The three approaches–quasigroup determinants, association schemes, and representation theory–turn out to give three distinct theories when applied to quasigroups. The current survey focuses on the combinatorial character theory of quasigroups, which results from the association scheme approach.

It is possible to take a narrow view of the theory, regarding it merely as an example in or application of the theory of association schemes. From that point of view the fourth section presents the example, replacing the standard association scheme notation (i.e. that of [BI], [De]) with notation better adapted to the example. As usual when a mathematical theory finds an application, though, the application begins to suggest developments of the theory itself. This is illustrated here by the

---

†Department of Mathematics, Iowa State University, Ames, IA 50011, USA

concepts of induction and superschemes. (See also [So] for new primitive schemes discovered by analogy with simple quasigroup schemes.)

The main aim of this survey, however, is to go beyond the narrow view and to present the theory in its proper context. This context comprises the historical background of Dedekind's programme and its continuation, presented in the second section, and the general algebraic theory of quasigroups, sketched in the third section. It is this background which motivates the formulations of the fourth section, and the developments of the theory discussed in the fifth section. Space considerations have precluded giving full details or proofs of theorems. The historical background in Section 2 makes use of Hawkins' excellent guides [H1–2]. References for quasigroup theory include Bruck's works such as [B1–3], the forthcoming [Ch], and parts of [S3–4]. The emphasis in the survey is on the various underlying ideas, following the quirks of the subject as it vacillates from direct generalisation given correct definitions to a perverse confounding of naive intuition.

2. Dedekind's programme–extending abelian characters. A *quasigroup* $(Q,.)$ is a set Q equipped with a binary operation $Q \times Q \longrightarrow Q; (x,y) \longmapsto x.y = xy$ called *multiplication*, such that in the equation

$$(2.1) \qquad x.y = z \, ,$$

knowledge of any two of x, y, z in Q specifies the third uniquely. Immediate examples are provided by groups, for which the multiplication satisfies the associative law $xy.z = x.yz$ (written here using the convention that multiplications denoted by juxtaposition are to be carried out before multiplications denoted by a dot). Thus quasigroups may be considered as non–associative (i.e. not necessarily associative) generalisations of groups. Groups in turn may be considered as non–commutative (i.e. not necessarily commutative) generalisations of abelian groups.

Character theory originated in Fourier analysis and Gauss' "Disquisitiones Arithmeticae" (cf. [Ga, §230] for introduction of the term "character"). It was developed for finite abelian groups by Dedekind in the late 1870's (published in his supplement to [Di]) and in further detail by Weber shortly after ([W1]–W4]). The methods of finite Fourier transforms belong to this stage of the theory. In the language of 20-th century algebra, the essence of the theory may be summarised as follows. Let Q be an abelian group of finite order s. Then the complex group algebra CQ, being semisimple and commutative, decomposes as the (internal) direct sum

$$(2.2) \qquad CQ = \bigoplus_{i=1}^{s} C\epsilon_i$$

of 1–dimensional subalgebras $C\epsilon_i$ that consist of all scalar multiples of an idempotent ϵ_i. Conventionally, $\epsilon_1 = \dfrac{1}{|Q|} \sum_{q \in Q} q$. Under (2.2), each element q of Q is written as a linear combination

$$(2.3) \qquad q = \sum_{i=1}^{s} \chi_i(q)\epsilon_i \, .$$

The coefficients in these linear combinations yield functions

$$(2.4) \qquad\qquad \chi_i : Q \longrightarrow \mathbf{C}; q \longmapsto \chi_i(q)$$

that are the *irreducible characters* $\chi_1 = 1, \chi_2, \ldots, \chi_s$ of the abelian group Q. These functions satisfy

PROPOSITION 2.5. *The set* $X = \{\chi_1 = 1, \chi_2, \ldots, \chi_s\}$ *under multiplication is the group* $Hom(Q, \mathbf{C}^*)$ *of homomorphisms of* Q *into the multiplicative group* $\mathbf{C}^*$ *of non–zero complex numbers.* $\square$

At Dedekind's instigation [Fr, pp. 2,38], Frobenius worked in the mid–1890's to extend this elegant and useful theory from abelian groups to general finite groups. His initial approach considered Dedekind's concept of a "group determinant". In the current context it is perhaps more appropriate to use the term "(associative) quasigroup determinant". Consider the (unbordered) multiplication table of a finite group $Q = \{q_1 = 1, q_2, \ldots, q_n\}$ as an $(n \times n)$–matrix. For each $i = 1, \ldots, n$, replace each matrix entry q_i by a variable X_i. The determinant of the new matrix obtained thus is an element $\Delta(X_1, \ldots, X_n)$ of the polynomial ring $\mathbf{C}[X_1, \ldots, X_n]$. This homogeneous polynomial is a product

$$(2.6) \qquad\qquad \Delta(X_1, \ldots, X_n) = \pm \prod_{i=1}^{s} p_i(X_1, \ldots, X_n)^{d_i}$$

of irreducible factors $p_i(X_1, \ldots, X_n)$, monic as elements of $(\mathbf{C}[X_2, \ldots, X_n])\,[X_1]$, whose degrees are equal to the powers d_i to which they appear in the factorisation. In modern language, each irreducible factor p_i corresponds to an irreducible character χ_i, and the degree $d_i = \deg p_i$ of the irreducible polynomial p_i is equal to the degree $\chi_i(1)$ of the corresponding irreducible character χ_i. (See [H1, Th. 7.1] for the precise correspondence, and [H1, §§1–5] [H2] for a detailed history.) If Q is abelian, then

$$(2.7) \qquad\qquad p_i(X_1, \ldots, X_n) = \sum_{j=1}^{n} \chi_i(q_j) X_j \ .$$

In general, however, the quasigroup determinant proved extremely intractable, even to an algebraist as skilled as Frobenius [H2, §4]. What emerged as a more fruitful way of extending the abelian theory was consideration of the centre ZCQ of the group algebra $\mathbf{C}Q$. This centre is a commutative, associative semisimple complex algebra spanned by the sums $c_i = \sum_{q \in C_i(1)} q$ of the elements in the various group conjugacy classes $C_1(1) = \{1\}, C_2(1), \ldots, C_s(1)$. It has a direct decomposition

$$(2.8) \qquad\qquad ZCQ = \bigoplus_{i=1}^{s} \mathbf{C}\epsilon_i$$

into a sum of sets $C\epsilon_i$ of scalar multiples of idempotents ϵ_i, directly generalising (2.2). The corresponding analogue of (2.3) is the expression

$$(2.9) \qquad c_j = \sum_{i=1}^{s} \frac{1}{d_i} \left(\sum_{q \in C_j(1)} \chi_i(q) \right) \epsilon_i \quad .$$

Up to this point, everything carries over nicely from the abelian case. Proposition 2.5, however, breaks down drastically. All that remains may be summarised in Proposition 2.10 below. Recall that a *complex–valued group class function f* on Q is a function $f : Q \longrightarrow \mathbf{C}$ whose restriction to each group conjugacy class $C_i(1)$ is constant. A homomorphism $f \in Hom(Q, \mathbf{C}^*)$ is a class function, but the converse is false. Denote the set of all complex–valued group class functions on Q by $\mathbf{C}gc(Q)$. The set $\mathbf{C}gc(Q)$ of functions inherits a C–algebra structure from the domain $\mathbf{C}$ of its elements.

PROPOSITION 2.10. *(i)   The set $X = \{\chi_1 = 1, \chi_2, \ldots, \chi_s\}$ is a basis for the underlying C–vector space of $\mathbf{C}gc(Q)$.*
(ii).   The set $\mathbf{N}X$ of sums of irreducible characters is a submonoid of the monoid $(\mathbf{C}gc(Q), .)$.
(iii)   The set $\{\chi \in X | \chi(1) = 1\}$ is the subgroup $Hom(Q, \mathbf{C}^*)$ of the monoid $(\mathbf{C}gc(Q), .)$. $\square$

With his understanding of the centre of the group algebra, Frobenius was able to prove parts (i) [Fr, p. 8, (8.)], [H2, §4] and (iii) [Fr, pp. 42–4], [H1; Th. 4.1, (7.4)] of Proposition 2.10. Part (ii), however, did not lie within the scope of either of his two approaches to the characters of general finite groups. It needed the third approach, which subsumed character theory under representation theory by regarding characters from $\mathbf{N}X$ as traces of complex matrix representations. Inspired by [Mo], Frobenius proved (ii) [Fr, p. 119] by observing that the product of a pair of characters is the trace of the tensor product of the representations of which the factors are traces [H2, §6]. Since the beginning of the twentieth century, this third, representation theory approach has so dominated the field that it has often been difficult to perceive character theory as a separate topic. The one area in which the second approach has continued to remain viable has been the study of the characters of the symmetric and related linear groups [Ma]. Subsequently, at the latest since the publication of Delsarte's thesis [De], the second approach has become part of the theory of association schemes [Bi, §2.2, Example 2.1 (2)]. The three approaches that Frobenius adopted to the problem of extending character theory from finite abelian groups to general finite groups may thus be characterised as

$$(2.11) \qquad \left\{ \begin{array}{ll} (i) & \text{quasigroup determinants,} \\ (ii) & \text{association schemes,} \\ (iii) & \text{ordinary representation theory.} \end{array} \right.$$

Given the extremely successful generalisation from commutative groups to non–commutative groups, i.e. to associative quasigroups, it is now natural to turn one's attention to the question of further generalisation from associative quasigroups to non–associative quasigroups. Since multiplication of finite matrices is irredeemably associative, a naive attempt to apply the standard modern approach (2.11) (iii) fails. A more sophisticated attempt may be described as follows. (If the jargon is too daunting, skip to the end of the paragraph.) Observe that a complex vector space M on which a group Q acts as a group of automorphisms furnishes a split extension $M]Q$ having a projection $\pi : M]Q \to Q$. This projection $\pi : M]Q \longrightarrow Q$ is a complex vector space object in the comma category of groups over Q. Conversely, any such object $\pi : E \longrightarrow Q$ gives a Q–module $\pi^{-1}(1)$. The ordinary representation theory of a finite, non–empty quasigroup Q lying in a given variety $\mathfrak{V}$ of quasigroups may thus be construed as the study of the so–called *complex Q-modules in* $\mathfrak{V}$, the complex vector space objects in the comma category of $\mathfrak{V}$–quasigroups over Q. For appropriate varieties $\mathfrak{V}$, these objects turn out to be equivalent to complex representations of a group $U(Q; \mathfrak{V})$ known as the *universal multiplication group* of Q in $\mathfrak{V}$. However, $U(Q; \mathfrak{V})$ may turn out to be infinite. As an extreme example, if $\mathfrak{V}$ is just the variety of all quasigroups, then $U(Q; \mathfrak{V})$ is the free group on the disjoint union $Q \dot\cup Q$. The Q–modules are characterised by almost periodic functions on a subgroup of this free group, leading to what is called the *analytic character theory* of the quasigroup Q. The current, nascent state of the theory is described in [S4] [S5]. For present purposes it suffices to summarise by saying that the ordinary representation theory approach (2.11) (iii) leads to analytic character theory.

Despite its apparent intractability, the quasigroup determinant approach (2.11) (i) now begins to gain points in its favour. To start with, presence or lack of associativity in Q has little direct effect on the formulation of the basic concept or the factorisation problem (2.6). This is why Dedekind's term "group determinant" was replaced by "quasigroup determinant" above. Secondly, the availability of symbolic computation packages has facilitated the study of small examples (i.e. $|Q|$ up to the order of twenty at present). Indeed, an optimist might hope that ninety years of explosive development of mathematics would have provided more powerful analytic tools than those that Frobenius had at his disposal. (To which a pessimist might reply that there has not been a comparable development in the most vital analytic tool of all, the one between the ears.) The quasigroup determinant does have one significant feature. Two quasigroups $(Q,.)$ and $(P,*)$ are said to be *isotopic*, written $(Q,.) \sim (P,*)$, if there is an *isotopy*, an ordered triple (α, β, γ) of bijections $Q \longrightarrow P$, such that

$$(2.12) \qquad\qquad x^\alpha * y^\beta = (x.y)^\gamma$$

for all x, y in Q. The relation of isotopy is an equivalence relation. For certain purposes, such as the coordinatisation of nets [BS] [B3] [Pi], it is the isotopy classes of quasigroups, rather than individual quasigroups themselves, that are important. And, to within sign, quasigroup determinants are invariants of isotopy classes. They may thus prove to give the most appropriate version of character theory in such contexts. These factors have led K.W. Johnson to begin a new study of quasigroup determinants ([J2] and work in progress).

It is the association scheme approach (2.11) (ii) which is the main topic of the current survey. This approach leads to what is now referred to as the *combinatorial character theory* of quasigroups (to distinguish it from the analytic character theory that results from the representation theory approach (2.11) (iii)). The initial inspiration came from the examples in Delsarte's thesis [De], and from the work on S–rings done by Tamaschke (e.g [Ta]) and Wielandt (e.g. [Wi]). After preparatory papers showing how S–rings (or "Gel'fand pairs" or "(commutative) association schemes") arose from loops and quasigroups [J1] [S2], the basic theory was started in [J3] (written in 1982 at the Technische Hochschule Darmstadt). Over the following six years the theory has been developed in a series of papers [J4], [J6]–[J8], [S6]. Some important examples have been studied by Song in his Ph.D. thesis [So] at Ohio State University under Bannai's direction. A detailed introduction to the earlier parts of the theory, with full proofs virtually from first principles, is given in [S4, Ch. 5]. References [S4, Ch. 6] and [S5] discuss the few tenuous connections between the analytic and combinatorial character theories that have so far been established.

3. Quasigroups: examples and some theory. This section discusses a number of important examples of quasigroups and classes of quasigroups together with certain aspects of their general theory that impinge directly on the combinatorial character theory. Bruck's work (e.g. [B1]–[B3]) gives a good guide to quasigroup theory (particularly loop theory) up to the 1950's. Subsequent developments up to the 1980's, including an intriguing range of applications, are presented in [Ch].

By the defining property (2.1) for a quasigroup Q, it follows that for each x in Q, the *right multiplication*

$$(3.1) \qquad R(x) : Q \longmapsto Q; \; y \longmapsto yx$$

and *left multiplication*

$$(3.2) \qquad L(x) : Q \longrightarrow Q; \; y \longmapsto xy$$

are permutations of Q. The subgroup of the group $Q!$ of all permutations on Q generated by $\{R(x), L(x) | x \in Q\}$ is called the *multiplication group* of Q, denoted by $Mlt(Q, .), MltQ$, or generically by G. Much of the structure of a quasigroup Q is embodied in the transitive permutation group action of G on Q. For an element q of Q, the stabiliser of q in G will be denoted by G_q.

Example 3.3 (groups). If Q is a group, then its multiplication group G is given by the exact sequence of group homomorphisms

$$(3.4) \qquad 1 \longrightarrow Z(Q) \xrightarrow{\Delta} Q \times Q \xrightarrow{T} G \longrightarrow 1 \,,$$

where the diagonal $\Delta : Z(Q) \longrightarrow Q \times Q; z \longmapsto (z, z)$ embeds the centre of Q in its direct square, and where $T : Q \times Q \longrightarrow G; (x, y) \longmapsto L(x)^{-1}R(y)$. The stabiliser $G_1 = \{T(x, x) | x \in Q\}$ is the group $InnQ$ of inner automorphisms of Q. For general quasigroups Q, it is often helpful to think of the stabilisers G_q as generalisations of the inner automorphism group of a group. These stabilisers G_q need not consist of automorphisms of Q: this is true even for a group Q if $q \neq 1$. ☐

Example 3.5 (Latin squares). By the defining property (2.1), the (unbordered) multiplication table of a finite quasigroup Q is a Latin square. (Recall that a *Latin square of size n* has each element of a fixed set of n elements appearing (precisely once) in each row and each column of the square.) Conversely, a Latin square becomes the (bordered) multiplication table of a quasigroup $(Q,.)$ on its set Q of entries when the columns and the rows are each headed by the distinct elements of Q. For example, the quasigroup Q given thus

$$(3.6) \qquad \begin{array}{c|ccc|cccc} Q & 1 & 2 & 3 & 4 & 5 & 6 & 7 \\ \hline 1 & 1 & 3 & 2 & 5 & 6 & 7 & 4 \\ 2 & 3 & 2 & 1 & 6 & 7 & 4 & 5 \\ 3 & 2 & 1 & 3 & 7 & 4 & 5 & 6 \\ \hline 4 & 5 & 6 & 7 & 4 & 3 & 2 & 1 \\ 5 & 6 & 7 & 4 & 3 & 5 & 1 & 2 \\ 6 & 7 & 4 & 5 & 2 & 1 & 6 & 3 \\ 7 & 4 & 5 & 6 & 1 & 2 & 3 & 7 \end{array} \qquad ,$$

together with its subquasigroup $P = \{1,2,3\}$, will prove useful below in the study of induced characters. Note that the vast number of Latin squares with a given set of entries produces an even vaster number of quasigroup structures on that set, scarcely diminished by the usual algebraic tricks such as identifying members of the same isomorphism or isotopy classes [B3]. Combinatorial character theory is useful in helping to come to terms with this plethora of quasigroups. In particular, it provides generally (although not universally) valid criteria for judging which are "uninteresting", singling out many of those which are worth examining. ☐

In the guise of Latin squares, the concept of quasigroup dates back at least to 1782 and Euler's famous problem of the 36 officers. This raises the question as to why the theory of quasigroups was not developed at least in parallel with its core,

the theory of groups. Why, for example, did Dedekind not formulate the problem
of studying quasigroup determinants rather than group determinants? One answer
may be that suitable algebraic techniques did not appear until the middle of the
twentieth century, when universal algebra developed as an outgrowth of the study of
groups with operators. Even then, this (now "classical") universal algebra studies
sets with operations satisfying certain identities. Thus it does not apply directly
to quasigroups as defined by (2.1), since (2.1) is not an identity. A *quasigroup*
$(Q, ., /, \backslash)$ has to be redefined as a set Q equipped with three binary operations:
multiplication. (or juxtaposition), *right division* / and *left division* $\backslash$ satisfying the
identities

$$(3.7) \qquad \begin{cases} (x/y).y & = x \ ; \\ (x \cdot y)/y & = x \ ; \\ x \cdot (x \backslash y) & = y \ ; \\ x \backslash (x \cdot y) & = y \ . \end{cases}$$

For the equivalence of the two definitions, see [S4, 117]. Definition (3.7) enables one
to apply universal algebraic ideas such as homomorphism, subalgebra (subquasigroup), congruence, free algebra, and variety to quasigroups. A quick introduction
to these rudiments of classical universal algebra is given in [RS, Ch. 1]. Some of
the algebraic difficulties inherent in the original definition (2.1) may be appreciated
on noting that although $(\mathbf{N}, +)$ forms a subalgebra of $(\mathbf{Z}, +)$, and although $(\mathbf{Z}, +)$
is a quasigroup, it does not follow that $(\mathbf{N}, +)$ is a quasigroup.

Example 3.8 (conjugates). If $(Q, .)$, i.e. $(Q, ., /, \backslash)$, is a quasigroup, then so are
its *conjugates* $(Q, /), (Q, \backslash), (Q, .), (Q, (x, y) \longmapsto yx), (Q, (x, y) \longmapsto y/x), (Q, (x, y) \longmapsto y \backslash x)$. Taking conjugates of a known quasigroup is a useful way of generating new
ones. The most familiar not–associative quasigroup, namely the integers under
subtraction, is obtained in this way. $\quad \square$

Example 3.9 (Steiner triple systems). A element x of a quasigroup Q is said
to be *idempotent* if $x.x = x$. The quasigroup Q is itself said to be *idempotent* if
each of its elements is idempotent. (The quasigroup Q of (3.6) is idempotent.) A
quasigroup is called *totally symmetric* if it coincides with each of its conjugates.
A (finite, non–empty,) totally symmetric idempotent quasigroup Q forms a Steiner
triple system with set $\{\{x, y, xy\} | x \neq y \in Q\}$ of blocks. Conversely, a Steiner triple
system Q forms a totally symmetric idempotent quasigroup if the product xy of two
distinct elements x, y is defined to be the unique third element of the unique block
containing them. The representation theory of Steiner triple systems is discussed
in [S4, 4.3]. $\quad \square$

Both within combinatorial character theory and in many other parts of the
theory of quasigroups, the mapping

$$(3.10) \qquad \rho : Q \times Q \longrightarrow G; \ (x, y) \longmapsto \rho(x, y) = R(x \backslash x)^{-1} R(x \backslash y)$$

from the direct square of a quasigroup Q to its multiplication group G plays an
important role. For given x in Q, the set $\{\rho(x, y) | y \in Q\}$ is a transversal from G

to the stabiliser G_x. Moreover, $\rho(x,x) = 1$ and $x\rho(x,y) = y$. This means that the ternary operation

$$(3.11) \qquad\qquad P : Q^3 \longrightarrow Q; (x,y,z) \longmapsto x\rho(y,z)$$

is a *Mal'cev parallelogram operation* [Ml] [S3, 1.4]: it satisfies the identities

$$(3.12) \qquad\qquad P(x,x,y) = y = P(y,x,x) \ .$$

The existence of such an operation makes quasigroups very well behaved from the universal–algebraic point of view. They are "Mal'cev algebras", to which the centrality theory of [S1] presented in [S3] applies. A subquasigroup N of a quasigroup Q is said to be a *normal subquasigroup*, notation $N \lhd Q$, if there is a congruence α on Q such that N is an α–class. In this case the quotient Q^α is denoted by Q/N. Now a congruence α on Q is a subquasigroup of $Q \times Q$ containing the diagonal $\widehat{Q} = \{(q,q)|q \in Q\}$ as a subquasigroup. (One of the pleasant consequences following from the Mal'cev property of quasigroups is that any quasigroup α with $\widehat{Q} \le \alpha \le Q \times Q$ is a congruence on Q [S3,143][S4, 135].) The congruence α is said to be *central* if the diagonal $\widehat{Q}$ is a normal subquasigroup of α. If Q is a group, then α is central if and only if the congruence class 1^α containing 1 is contained in the centre $Z(Q)$ of Q. There is a unique maximal central congruence $\zeta(Q)$ on a quasigroup Q, known as the *centre congruence* [Ch, Th. III.3.10] [S3, 2.2–3]. Furthermore, there is a congruence $(Q^2|\zeta)$ on the (congruence considered as a) quasigroup $\zeta(Q)$ such that

$$(3.13) \qquad \forall\ (x_1,x_2) \in \zeta(Q),\ \pi_1 : (x_1,x_2)^{(Q^2|\zeta)} \longrightarrow Q; (y_1,y_2) \longmapsto y_1 \quad \text{bijects}$$

[Ch, Prop. III. 3.5] [S3, 2.1–2]. Two quasigroups $(Q,.,/,\backslash)$ and $(P,.,/,\backslash)$ are said to be *centrally isotopic*, written $(Q,.,/,\backslash) \approx (P,.,/,\backslash)$, if there is a bijection $\theta : P \longrightarrow Q$ such that for each (postfix) operation $\omega = .,/,\backslash$, there is an element $(q_\omega, \overline{q}_\omega)$ of $\zeta(Q)$ such that for all p_1, p_2 in P,

$$(3.14) \qquad\qquad (p_1^\theta p_2^\theta \omega, p_1 p_2 \omega^\theta)(Q^2|\zeta)(q_\omega, \overline{q}_\omega)$$

[Ch, Defn. III.4.1] [S3, 4.1]. Central isotopy is an equivalence relation [Ch, Th. III.4.5] [S3, 412], stronger than isotopy but weaker than isomorphism. As with isotopy, there are occasions when central isotopy classes are more important than individual quasigroups or isomorphism classes. One of the most striking illustrations is that finite quasigroups P and Q are centrally isotopic if and only if there is a finite quasigroup Z such that the direct products $Z \times P$ and $Z \times Q$ are isomorphic [S3, 4.2]. Such non–cancellation phenomena cannot be found amongst finite groups.

Example 3.15 (loops and piques). A *loop* $(Q,.,1)$ is a quasigroup $(Q,.)$ equipped with an *identity element* 1 such that

$$(3.16) \qquad\qquad 1.x = x = x.1$$

for all x in Q. In universal–algebraic terms, loops are best considered as algebras $(Q, ., /, \backslash, 1)$ having the three binary operations forming a quasigroup, and then a nullary operation $1 : Q^0 = \{1\} \longrightarrow Q; 1 \longmapsto 1$ selecting the identity element. All groups are loops, but there are also many non–associative loops. For example, given an element q of a quasigroup $(Q, .)$, there is a loop $(Q, (x, y) \longmapsto P(x, q, y), q)$ with identity q constructed using the Mal'cev parallelogram (3.12). The quasigroup and loop are isotopic via the isotopy $(R(q\backslash q), L(q), 1)$. Sometimes the full strength of the loop property (3.16) is not required, merely the existence of the special subquasigroup $\{1\}$. A *pique* is thus defined as an algebra $(Q, ., /, \backslash, e)$ such that $(Q, ., /, \backslash)$ is a quasigroup with a nullary operation selecting an idempotent e of $(Q, .)$. The abbreviated notations $(Q, ., e)$ or Q_e are often used. The name "pique" is an acronym for *Pointed Idempotent QUasigroupE*. Motivated by the discussion at the end of Example 3.3, the inner multiplication group $Inn(Q_e)$ of a pique or loop $(Q, ., e)$ is the stabiliser G_e of e in the multiplication group G. □

There is a hierarchy

$$(3.17) \qquad \text{abelian groups} \longrightarrow \text{groups} \longrightarrow \text{loops} \longrightarrow \text{piques} \longrightarrow \text{quasigroups}$$

of increasingly general classes of quasigroups. The classes of this hierarchy provide natural stages at which to test a proposition about quasigroups.

The *stability congruence* $\sigma(Q)$ on a quasigroup Q with multiplication group G is the congruence

$$(3.18) \qquad \sigma(Q) = \{(x, y) \in Q \times Q | G_x = G_y\}$$

[Ch, §III.6]. If Q is a loop, then the stability and centre congruences coincide. In general, however, the stability congruence may be a proper subcongruence of the centre congruence.

Example 3.19 (abelian quasigroups and 3–quasigroups). A quasigroup Q is said to be *abelian* if it is commutative and associative, i.e. is empty or an abelian group. In other words, $\sigma(Q) = Q \times Q$. A quasigroup Q is said to be a *3–quasigroup* if $\widehat{Q} \lhd Q \times Q$. In other words, $\zeta(Q) = Q \times Q$. This is the origin of the designation: such quasigroups are "all centre" (3entrum). If a 3–quasigroup Q is a group or a loop, then it is abelian. Every 3–quasigroup is centrally isotopic to a 3–pique, namely $(Q^2/\widehat{Q}, ., \widehat{Q})$ [Ch, Prop. III.5.5] [S3,417]. Given a 3–pique $(Q, ., e)$, the corresponding loop $(Q, (x, y) \longmapsto P(x, e, y), e)$ of Example 3.15 is an abelian group $(Q, +, e)$. The pique may be recovered from knowledge of the automorphisms $R = R(e)$ and $L = L(e)$ of $(Q, +, e)$ via

$$(3.20) \qquad x.y = xR + yL .$$

Indeed, (3.20) may be used to construct a 3–pique $(A, ., 0)$ from any pair (R, L) of automorphisms of an abelian group $(A, +, 0)$. (The 3–pique $(\mathbf{Z}, -, 0)$ mentioned in Example 3.8 is constructed in this way.) The inner multiplication group $Inn(A, ., 0)$ is the subgroup $\langle R, L \rangle$ of $Aut(A, +, 0)$ generated by $\{R, L\}$, and the full multiplication group $Mlt(A, .)$ is the split extension $(A, +, 0)] \langle R, L \rangle$. For example, $Mlt(\mathbf{Z}_n, -) \cong D_n$, the dihedral group. □

4. Quasigroup conjugacy classes and character tables. Throughout this section, Q will denote a quasigroup of positive integral order n with multiplication group G. The combinatorial character theory arises from the transitive permutation group action of G on Q, and investigates the extent to which such actions govern and reflect the algebraic structure of Q. If Q is a group, then its group conjugacy classes are subsets of Q : the orbits on Q of the inner multiplication group Inn Q, the stabiliser G_1 of the pointed idempotent 1. Working across the hierarchy (3.17), analogous decompositions make natural sense as far as piques, but not at the general quasigroup level. A similar problem arises with kernels of homomorphisms. In group theory, kernels of homomorphisms from a group Q are taken to be subsets of Q, namely normal subgroups. For general quasigroups Q, universal algebra suggests the definition of kernels of homomorphisms from Q as relations on Q (subsets of $Q \times Q$), namely congruences. One is thus led to a definition of quasigroup conjugacy classes as relations. The multiplication group G has a *diagonal action* on $Q \times Q$ given by

$$(4.1) \qquad g : Q \times Q \longrightarrow Q \times Q ; (x,y) \longmapsto (xg, yg)$$

for g in G. The *(quasigroup) conjugacy classes* of Q are then defined to be the orbits under the diagonal action of G on $Q \times Q$. They provide the *conjugacy class partition*

$$(4.2) \qquad \Gamma = \{C_1 = \widehat{Q}, C_2, \ldots, C_s\}$$

of $Q \times Q$. The incidence matrices of the conjugacy classes $C_1 = \widehat{Q}, C_2, \ldots, C_s$ are the matrices with respect to Q of complex vector space endomorphisms $a_1 = 1, a_2, \ldots, a_s$ of the complex vector space $\mathbb{C}Q$. The action of G on Q extends by linearity to make $\mathbb{C}Q$ a right module for the complex group algebra $\mathbb{C}G$. Denote the $\mathbb{C}$–algebra of $\mathbb{C}G$–module endomorphisms of $\mathbb{C}Q$ by $\mathrm{End}_{\mathbb{C}G}\,\mathbb{C}Q$. In Wielandt's language [Wi], this algebra is the *Vertauschungsring* or *centraliser ring* $V(G,Q)$ of G on Q. The fundamental theorem of the combinatorial character theory of quasigroups then has a number of essentially equivalent formulations in various terms as follows:

THEOREM 4.3. *Let G be the multiplication group of a finite non–empty quasigroup Q.*

(i) *The action of G on Q is multiplicity–free.*

(ii) *(Q, Γ) is a (commutative) association scheme.*

(iii) *For any q in Q, the pair (G, G_q) is a Gel'fand pair.*

(iv) *$\mathrm{End}_{\mathbb{C}G}\,\mathbb{C}Q = V(G,Q)$ is commutative, with vector space basis $\{a_1, \ldots, a_s\}$.* $\quad\square$

Theorem 4.3 (ii) means that

$$(4.4) \quad \begin{cases} \text{(A1)} & C_1 = \hat{Q} \ ; \\[4pt] \text{(A2)} & \text{for each } C_i \text{ in } \Gamma, \text{ the converse } C_i^{-1} \\ & \text{is an element } C_{i'} \text{ of } \Gamma \ ; \\[4pt] \text{(A3)} & \forall \ C_i \in \Gamma, \ \forall C_j \in \Gamma, \ \forall C_k \in \Gamma, \ \exists c_{ijk} \in \mathbf{N} \ . \\ & \forall (x,y) \in C_k, |\{z \in Q | (x,z) \in C_i, (z,y) \in C_j\}| = c_{ijk} \ ; \\[4pt] \text{(A4)} & \forall \ 1 \le i,j,k \le s, \quad c_{ijk} = c_{jik} \ . \end{cases}$$

The critical (A4) follows from Theorem 4.3 (iv) on noting that $a_i a_j = \sum\limits_{k=1}^{s} c_{ijk} a_k$. The algebra $\mathbf{C}\Gamma$ of complex linear combinations of the a_i, with this product, is called the *Bose–Mesner algebra* of (Q,Γ). It is isomorphic to $V(G,Q)$. Theorem 4.3(i) means that each irreducible representation of G appears at most once in the permutation representation of G on Q. It follows from (A4) via [BI, Ch. 2, Th. 1.4]. For Theorem 4.3 (iii) and the terminology of Gel'fand pairs, see [Dg, Ch. 3] [He, Defn. 4.1]. For current purposes Theorem 4.3 (iv) is the most convenient formulation. An explicit proof is given in [S4, 523]. The crucial step [S4, 522] goes back to [J1] [S2]. The proof is computational rather than conceptual, involving the mapping ρ of (3.10). A better understanding of the proof would be helpful in the continuing search for new Gel'fand pairs, and in recognising new areas in which something like the current combinatorial character theory holds. The best that can be said at present, vague though it is, is that the proof is using a sort of linearised version of the centrality theory of [S1] [S3]. To work properly this theory appears to need categories, such as the category of quasigroup homomorphisms or the category of topological groups, in which group objects are necessarily abelian.

Theorem 4.3 (iv) achieves the desired continuation of Dedekind's programme extending character theory from abelian groups beyond groups to quasigroups. In analogy with (2.2) and (2.8), the semisimple commutative algebra $\mathrm{End}_{\mathbf{C}G}\, \mathbf{C}Q$ has the direct decomposition

$$(4.5) \qquad \mathrm{End}_{\mathbf{C}G}\ \mathbf{C}Q = \bigoplus_{i=1}^{s} \mathbf{C}e_i$$

into a sum of sets $\mathbf{C}e_i$ of scalar multiples of idempotents e_i. The analogue of (2.3) and (2.9) is the expression

$$(4.6) \qquad a_i = \sum_{j=1}^{s} \xi_{ij} e_j \ .$$

Setting $\Xi = (\xi_{ij})$, one has $\Xi^{-1} = H = (\eta_{ij})$ with

$$(4.7) \qquad e_i = \sum_{j=1}^{s} \eta_{ij}\, a_j \ .$$

Corresponding to the special numbering $a_1 = 1$, the idempotent e_1 is chosen to be the projection onto the 1–dimensional submodule $\mathbf{C} \sum_{q \in Q} q$. Set $f_i = tr\, e_i$ and $|C_i| = nn_i$. Then $f_i \xi_{ji} = nn_j \bar{\eta}_{ij}$ [J3, p. 47] [S4, p. 94]. This leads to the following

Definition 4.8. The *character table* Ψ of the quasigroup Q is the $(s \times s)$–matrix $\Psi = (\psi_{ij})$ with entries

$$(4.9) \qquad \psi_{ij} = \frac{\sqrt{f_i}}{n_j}\, \xi_{ji} = \frac{n}{\sqrt{f_i}}\, \bar{\eta}_{ij} \,.$$

The character table of a quasigroup Q is completely determined by the action of the multiplication group G on Q. By [Ch, Prop. III.4.6], centrally isotopic quasigroups have similar multiplication group actions, whence the same character table. One may thus compare the approaches (2.11) (i) and (ii) to the continuation of Dedekind's programme by noting that (2.11)(i) leads to quasigroup determinants, which are isotopy invariants, whereas (2.11)(ii) leads to character tables, which are central isotopy invariants.

In the course of generalising character theory from abelian groups to non–commutative groups, Proposition 2.5 was weakened to Proposition 2.10. In the combinatorial character theory of quasigroups, one of the first concerns is to see how much of Proposition 2.10 carries over, suitably rephrased to reflect the change from subsets of Q to relations on Q Let $\mathbf{C}(Q \times Q)$ denote the set of all complex-valued functions on $Q \times Q$. This set carries a lot of algebraic structure. To begin with, it has the *pointwise* or *Hadamard* involutive $\mathbf{C}$–algebra structure induced from $\mathbf{C}$ with complex conjugation. Secondly, it has a right $\mathbf{C}G$–module structure given by

$$(4.10) \qquad g : \mathbf{C}(Q \times Q) \longrightarrow \mathbf{C}(Q \times Q); \theta \longmapsto (\theta^g : (x, y) \longmapsto \theta(xg^{-1}, yg^{-1}))$$

for g in G. Thirdly, it has a bilinear, associative *convolution* $*$ given by

$$(4.11) \qquad \theta * \varphi(x, y) = \sum_{z \in Q} \theta(x, z)\varphi(z, y)$$

for x, y in Q. The group G is a group of automorphisms of both the Hadamard and convolution algebra structures on $\mathbf{C}(Q \times Q)$. It follows that the set $\mathbf{C}Cl(Q)$ of G–invariant functions forms a Hadamard and convolution subalgebra. These G–invariant functions are (*quasigroup*) *class functions* on Q. Their restrictions to conjugacy classes are constant. The isomorphism

$$(4.12) \qquad \mathbf{C}(Q \times Q) \longrightarrow \mathrm{End}_{\mathbf{C}}\, \mathbf{C}Q; \theta \longmapsto (\tilde{\theta} : x \longmapsto \sum_{y \in Q} \theta(x, y)y)$$

preserves all the algebraic structure on $\mathbf{C}(Q \times Q)$. It may be used to give a non–degenerate, associative bilinear form

$$(4.13) \qquad \langle \theta, \varphi \rangle = |Q \times Q|^{-1}\, tr(\tilde{\theta}\tilde{\varphi})$$

making $C(Q \times Q)$ a Frobenius algebra [CR, 9.5]. Each row ψ_i of the character table Ψ gives a class function ψ_i whose restriction to C_j is ψ_{ij}. These functions $\psi_1 = 1, \psi_2 \ldots, \psi_s$ are known as the *basic (combinatorial) characters* of Q. By mild abuse of notation, the set $\{\psi_1 = 1, \psi_2, \ldots, \psi_s\}$ is also labelled Ψ. If Q is a group, then

$$(4.14) \qquad \psi_i(x,y) = \chi_i(x^{-1}y)$$

with appropriate numbering. The analogue of Proposition 2.10(i) for general quasi-groups Q is

PROPOSITION 4.15. *The set Ψ forms an orthonormal basis for $CCl(Q)$ under the inner product (4.13) [J3, Th. 3.4] [S4, 541].* $\qquad\qquad$ $\Box$

Along with the one orthogonality relation

$$(4.15) \qquad \sum_{k=1}^{s} \psi_{ik}\overline{\psi}_{jk}n_k = n\delta_{ij}$$

embodied in Proposition 4.15, the character table also satisfies the other orthogonality relation

$$(4.17) \qquad \sum_{k=1}^{s} \psi_{ki}\overline{\psi}_{kj} = n\delta_{ij}/n_i$$

[J3;(3.3), (3.4)] [S4;541(a),(b)]. The table contains enough information to specify n, s, the $n_i, f_i, \eta_{ij}, \xi_{ij}$, and c_{ijk}[J3,Cor. 3.5][S4,542–3]. It does determine the stability congruence $\sigma(Q)$ [J8, Prop. 5.1], but not the centre congruence $\zeta(Q)$, as will become apparent below. Further:

THEOREM 4.18. *The character table of Q specifies the congruence lattice of Q.* $\qquad\qquad$ $\Box$

The proof of Theorem 4.18 is easy in the group case: the normal subgroups are just the kernels of the characters. The quasigroup case [J3, Th. 3.6] [S4, 545] is less immediate. It uses the idea of [CG, Prop. 3.1].

A quasigroup Q is said to be a *rank 2 quasigroup* if it has only 2 conjugacy classes, namely $C_1 = \widehat{Q}$ and $C_2 = Q^2 - \widehat{Q}$. Using the orthogonality relations (4.16), (4.17), it follows that the character table of Q is

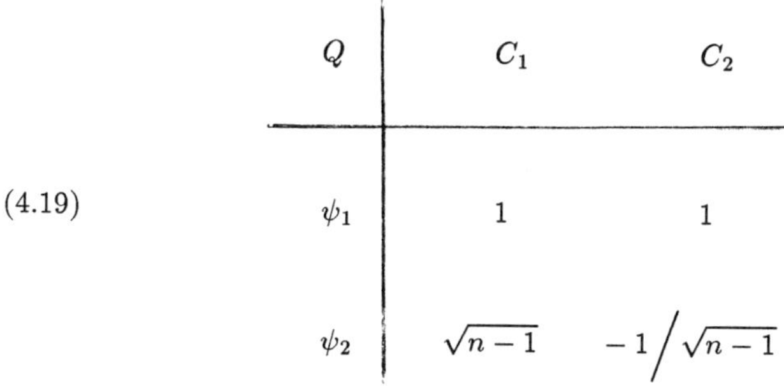

(4.19)

$$\begin{array}{c|cc} Q & C_1 & C_2 \\ \hline \psi_1 & 1 & 1 \\ \psi_2 & \sqrt{n-1} & -1\Big/\sqrt{n-1} \end{array}$$

From the standpoint of combinatorial character theory, such quasigroups are essentially "uninteresting". This is one of the criteria discussed at the end of Example 3.8. Note, however, that the 7–element Steiner triple system coming from the Fano plane $PG(2,2)$ gives a rank 2 quasigroup according to Example 3.9, and this structure hardly qualifies as "uninteresting". It is conjectured that almost all quasigroups are rank 2 quasigroups. More precisely [J4, Conj. 5.2]:

CONJECTURE 4.20. *Let $l(n)$ denote the number of Latin squares of of order n. Let $r(n)$ denote the number of Latin squares of order n that are multiplication tables of rank 2 quasigroups. Then $\lim\limits_{n\to\infty} \dfrac{r(n)}{l(n)} = 1$.* $\square$

Rank 2 quasigroups Q (with $n > 2$) do serve to show that the analogue of Proposition 2.10 (ii) breaks down for quasigroups. Indeed,

$$(4.21) \qquad \psi_2\psi_2 = \psi_1 + (n-2)(n-1)^{-1/2}\psi_2$$

from (4.19). The breakdown may be attributed to the divergence of the combinatorial character theory from the representation theory of quasigroups. Some of its implications are investigated in the final section of this survey.

Now suppose that $\theta : Q \longrightarrow P$ is a quasigroup epimorphism. If Q is a group, and $D : P \longrightarrow \mathrm{Aut}_{\mathbf{C}} V$ represents P as a group of automorphisms of a complex vector space V, then the composite $\theta D : Q \longrightarrow \mathrm{Aut}_{\mathbf{C}} V$ represents Q. Composing with the trace map $tr : \mathrm{Aut}_{\mathbf{C}} V \longrightarrow \mathbf{C}$, it is a trivial matter to lift characters from the quotient P up to Q. For general quasigroups Q, a comparable lifting result, the Quotient Theorem, holds. The proof [J6, Th.2.1] is much less direct.

THEOREM 4.22. *Let $\theta : Q \longrightarrow P$ be a quasigroup epimorphism, with corresponding diagonal $\widehat{\theta} : Q \times Q \longrightarrow P \times P; (x,y) \longmapsto (x\theta, y\theta)$. Then for each basic character $\varphi_k : P \times P \longrightarrow \mathbf{C}$ of P, the lift $\widehat{\theta}\varphi_k = Q \times Q \longrightarrow \mathbf{C}$ is a basic character of Q.* $\square$

Lifting characters from a quotient quasigroup is one way of finding characters of a given quasigroup, helping to complete its character table. Another method is to induce characters from known characters of a subquasigroup. If P is a subgroup of a group Q, then the induction map $\uparrow_P^Q \colon Cgc(P) \longrightarrow Cgc(Q); f \longmapsto f^Q$ is defined by the Frobenius formula

$$(4.23) \qquad f^Q(s) = \frac{1}{|P|} \sum_{\substack{u \in Q \\ u^{-1}su \in P}} f(u^{-1}su)$$

[Se, 7.2]. In the combinatorial character theory of quasigroups, the corresponding formula (4.24) below becomes much simpler. Let P be a non–empty subquasigroup of Q, with conjugacy class partition $\{B_{ij} | 1 \leq i \leq s, 1 \leq j \leq r_s\}$ such that each B_{ij} is a subset of the corresponding C_i. If $P \times P$ does not intersect C_i, then $r_i = 0$. Set $B_i = \cup \{B_{ij} | 1 \leq j \leq r_i\}$. Then the *induction* map $\uparrow_p^Q \colon CCl(P) \longrightarrow CCl(Q); f \longmapsto f^Q$ is given by

$$(4.24) \qquad |P \times P| \sum_{(x,y) \in C_i} f^Q(x,y) = |Q \times Q| \sum_{(x,y) \in B_i} f(x,y)$$

[J4, (2.1)] [S4, (551)]. If Q is a group, the isomorphisms $CCl(P) \cong Cgc(P)$ and $CCl(Q) \cong Cgc(Q)$ given by (4.14) commute with the induction maps $\uparrow_P^Q$, so that the simple formula (4.24) subsumes the more complicated (4.23) [J4, §3][S4, 5.5]. The definition (4.24) works for general association schemes [J5]. This illustrates one of the side benefits of the development of the combinatorial character theory of quasigroups: it may suggest new developments in the general theory of association schemes. In [S7], induced class functions of association schemes defined according to (4.24) are interpreted as conditional expectations in the sense of J. Doob [Do, Ch. 1].

Along with the induction map $\uparrow_p^Q \colon CCl(P) \longrightarrow CCl(Q)$ given by (4.24), there is also a *restriction* map $\downarrow_P^Q \colon CCl(Q) \longrightarrow CCl(P); f \longmapsto f|_{P \times P}$. Under the inner products (4.13), namely $\langle , \rangle_P$ on $CCl(P)$ and $\langle , \rangle_Q$ on $CCl(Q)$, these linear mappings are mutually adjoint:

$$(4.25) \qquad \langle f, g \uparrow_P^Q \rangle_Q = \langle f \downarrow_P^Q, g \rangle_P$$

for f in $CCl(Q)$ and g in $CCl(P)$ [J4, Th. 4.3] [S4, 557]. This relationship (4.25) is the so–called *Frobenius reciprocity*. Easily derived from (4.24), it subsumes Frobenius reciprocity for groups via (4.14).

Abelian quasigroups form a variety, so each quasigroup Q has an abelian "replica" [RS, p. 17], a maximal abelian quotient $Q^{\gamma(Q)}$. The congruence $\gamma(Q)$ is called the *abelian replica congruence* of Q. If Q is non–empty, the quotient $Q^{\gamma(Q)}$ has a unique idempotent, whose preimage is a normal subquasigroup of Q called the *derived subquasigroup* Q' of Q. The abelian replica may then be written as Q/Q'. Of course, if Q is a group, then Q' is the commutator subgroup, generated by all the commutators $(xy)/(yx)$. If Q is a loop, then Q' is the normal subloop generated by all the commutators $(xy)/(yx)$ and associators $(x.yz)/(xy.z)$. For the general quasigroup Q of positive integral order n, the order m of Q' divides n. By the Quotient Theorem 4.22, the n/m basic characters of the abelian group Q/Q' lift to n/m basic characters $\psi_1, \ldots, \psi_{n/m}$ of Q. A basic character of Q is called *linear* if it restricts to 1 on $\widehat{Q}$. Certainly the characters $\psi_1, \ldots, \psi_{n/m}$ are linear. The first part of the following theorem is the analogue of Proposition 2.10 (iii). The other two parts show that the linear characters retrieve some of the content of the failed analogue of Proposition 2.10 (ii).

THEOREM 4.26. *(i) [J8, Th. 3.1] The basic characters $\psi_1, \ldots, \psi_{n/m}$ form the complete set Λ of linear basic characters of Q. Under Hadamard multiplication, Λ forms an abelian group isomorphic to* Hom $(Q/Q', \mathbf{C}^*)$.

(ii)[J8, Prop. 4.2] For a linear basic character λ of Q, Hadamard multiplication by λ gives an isometry of $CCl(Q)$.

(iii) [J8, Th. 4.3 (i)] The abelian group Λ of linear basic characters acts by Hadamard multiplication on the full set Ψ of basic characters. $\square$

5. Induction, products, and 3–quasigroups. The previous section covered the fundamentals of the combinatorial character theory of quasigroups. Once the right definitions and notations had been set up, these fundamental parts provided direct generalisations and analogues of the character theory of finite groups. The only point of divergence was the breakdown (4.21) of the analogue of Proposition 2.10(ii). This section, by contrast, concentrates on those aspects of the theory where new phenomena begin to emerge. Their origin is usually related to the "misbehaviour" of products, and to the evolution of the abelian/non–abelian dichotomy for groups into an abelian/3/ non–3 trichotomy for quasigroups. Unless explicitly stated otherwise, the notation of the previous section is used. Thus again Q is normally a quasigroup of positive integral order n, etc.

By Proposition 2.10 (ii) and (4.14), the set of integral combinations of basic characters of a group Q forms a ring under Hadamard multiplication. For a general quasigroup Q, the *coefficient ring* $\mathbf{Z}[Q]$ is defined to be the ring $\mathbf{Z}[\langle \psi_i \psi_j, \psi_k \rangle_Q | 1 \leq i, j, k \leq s]$. The *character ring* $R[Q]$ is then defined to be the ring of $\mathbf{Z}[Q]$–linear combinations of basic characters under Hadamard multiplication. If Q is associative, this agrees with the usual group–theoretic definition [Se, 9.1]. If Q is a rank 2 quasigroup, (4.21) shows that the coefficient ring $\mathbf{Z}[Q]$ is $\mathbf{Z}[(n-1)^{-1/2}] = \mathbf{Z}[X]/\langle(n-1)X^2 - 1\rangle$. Now let P be a non–empty subquasigroup of a quasigroup Q. If Q is associative, the induction map $\uparrow_P^Q \colon CCl(P) \longrightarrow CCl(Q)$ restricts to an abelian group homomorphism $\uparrow_P^Q \colon (R[P], +) \longrightarrow (R[Q], +)$. If Q is not associative, this need no longer be true. Consider the two rank 2 quasigroups P and Q of (3.6), with character tables

P	B_1	B_2		Q	C_1	C_2
(5.1) φ_1	1	1		ψ_1	1	1
φ_2	$\sqrt{2}$	$-1/\sqrt{2}$		ψ_2	$\sqrt{6}$	$-1/\sqrt{6}$

Then $\varphi_2^Q = (7\sqrt{3}/9)\psi_2$, although $7\sqrt{3}/9$ does not lie in the coefficient ring $\mathbf{Z}[Q] = \mathbf{Z}[6^{-1/2}]$. To study rings of quasigroup characters under inducing, it appears to be necessary to admit at least the ring $\mathbf{A}$ of algebraic numbers as coefficients. Let $\mathsf{A}Cl(Q)$ denote the ring of class functions on Q taking values in A. The set Ψ of basic characters of Q forms an A–basis for $\mathsf{A}Cl(Q)$, and the induction map $\uparrow_P^Q \colon \mathsf{C}Cl(P) \longrightarrow \mathsf{C}Cl(Q)$ restricts to $\uparrow_P^Q \colon \mathsf{A}Cl(P) \longrightarrow \mathsf{A}Cl(Q)$. Moreover,

$$(5.2) \qquad\qquad f \uparrow_P^Q \cdot g = (f \cdot g \downarrow_P^Q) \uparrow_P^Q$$

for f in $\mathsf{C}Cl(P)$ and g in $\mathsf{C}Cl(Q)$, so that $\mathsf{A}Cl(P) \uparrow_P^Q$ is an ideal of $\mathsf{A}Cl(Q)$ and $\mathsf{C}Cl(P) \uparrow_P^Q$ is an ideal of $\mathsf{C}Cl(Q)$ [J4, §6] [S4, 562]

A set $\{P_j | 1 \leq j \leq N\}$ of non–empty subquasigroups of a quasigroup Q is said to be *protrusive* if $\cup\{P_j \times P_j | 1 \leq j \leq N\}$ contains a member of each conjugacy class C_i of Q (so that some $P_j \times P_j$ "protrudes" into each C_i). For example, the set of cyclic subgroups of a group is protrusive, since an element $(1, x)$ of C_i is contained in $\langle x \rangle \times \langle x \rangle$. If Q is associative, Artin's Theorem [Se, 9.2] shows that each character of Q is a rational linear combination of characters induced by characters of members of any protrusive set of subquasigroups of Q. These results do not apply verbatim to non–associative quasigroups. In the quasigroup Q of (3.6), the set $\{\langle x \rangle | x \in Q\} = \{\{x\} | x \in Q\}$ of "cyclic" or singly generated subquasigroups is not protrusive, since $\cup\{\{x\} \times \{x\} | x \in Q\} = \widehat{Q}$ does not intersect the conjugacy class C_2. As for Artin's Theorem, the singleton $\{P\}$ is protrusive, but $\psi_1 = \varphi_1^Q - (2\sqrt{2}/7)\varphi_2^Q$ and $\psi_2 = (3\sqrt{3}/7)\varphi_2^Q$, so the characters of Q are not obtained as rational linear combinations of characters induced by characters of P. The closest analogue of Artin's Theorem holding for general quasigroups Q appears to be the following

THEOREM 5.3. *Let $\{P_j | 1 \leq j \leq N\}$ be a protrusive set of subquasigroups of Q. Then the direct sum maps* $\bigoplus_{j=1}^{N} \uparrow_{P_j}^Q \colon \bigoplus_{j=1}^{N} \mathsf{A}Cl(P_j) \longrightarrow \mathsf{A}Cl(Q)$ *and* $\bigoplus_{j=1}^{N} \uparrow_{P_j}^Q \colon \bigoplus_{j=1}^{N} \mathsf{C}Cl(P_j) \longrightarrow \mathsf{C}Cl(Q)$ *surject* [J4, Th. 7.1] [S4, 565] . □

One of the long–term programmes of the combinatorial character theory of quasigroups is to investigate the dependence and influence of the coefficient ring

$\mathbf{Z}[Q]$ on the algebraic structure of Q. Quasigroups with a unique non–linear basic character form a suitable nursery for the earliest stage of the programme. The most elementary quasigroups of this type are described by the following theorem [J8, Th. 5.2]. The notation is that of Theorem 4.26, with $\Psi(P)$ denoting the character table of a quasigroup P.

THEOREM 5.4. *For $|Q| > 2$, the following are equivalent:*

(a) *Q has a unique non–linear basic character, whose square is the sum of all the linear basic characters of Q;*

(b) *The character table $\Psi(Q)$ of Q has the form*

Q	C_1	C_2	C_3	C_s
ψ_1	1	1	1	1
$\vdots$	$\vdots$		$\Psi(Q/Q')$	$\vdots$
$\psi_{n/2}$	1	1		
ψ_s	$\sqrt{n/2}$	$-\sqrt{n/2}$	0	0

$;$

(c) *the congruences $\gamma(Q)$ and $\sigma(Q)$ coincide, each having order $2n$.* $\quad\square$

Examples of quasigroups described by Theorem 5.4 are the symmetric group S_3, the dihedral group D_4, the quaternion group Q_8, and the octonion loop K_{16} [J4, §8][S4,558] which does for the octonion algebra what the quaternion group does for the quaternion algebra. Another example is Parker's Moufang loop P used in Conway's construction of the Fischer–Griess monster group [Co]. One curious feature of this loop is that all its character table entries are integral [J8, Prop. 5.3]. Each quasigroup Q described by Theorem 5.4 has the integers $\mathbf{Z}$ as its coefficient ring $\mathbf{Z}[Q]$. In fact [J8, Th. 5.4],

THEOREM 5.5. *Suppose $|Q| = n > 2$, $\quad |Q'| = m$, and that Q has a unique non–linear basic character. Then Q has integral coefficient ring if and only if one of the following two (mutually exclusive) conditions is satisfied:*

    (a) *Q satisfies the conditions of Theorem 5.4;*

    (b) *the Diophantine equation $p^2 m(m-1) = n(m-2)^2$ has a positive integral solution p.* $\square$

An immediate topic for subsequent research is to study quasigroups with a unique non–linear basic character from the standpoint of the cohomology theory for quasi-groups given in [S3, Ch. 6]. Indeed, examination of the relationship between the character ring $R[Q]$ and the cohomology of Q is one of the major tasks facing the combinatorial character theory. There are many mysteries, even in the associative case.

The Quotient Theorem 4.22 relates the character tables $\Psi(Q)$ and $\Psi(P)$ when there is a quasigroup epimorphism $Q \twoheadrightarrow P$. Such an epimorphism induces an epimorphism $MltQ \twoheadrightarrow MltP$ of the corresponding multiplication groups. A dual situation arises when there are two quasigroup structures $(Q, +)$ and $(Q, .)$ on the same underlying set Q, such that $Mlt(Q, +)$ embeds as a subgroup of $Mlt(Q, .)$ with the monomorphism $Mlt(Q, +) \rightarrowtail Mlt(Q, .)$. The construction (3.20) of **3**–piques provides many natural examples of this. Set $H = Mlt(Q, +)$. Suppose that $\{D_{ij}|1 \leq i \leq s, 1 \leq j \leq r_i\}$ is the conjugacy class partition of $(Q, +)$, with $C_i = \bigcup_{j=1}^{r_i} D_{ij}$ for $i = 1, \ldots, s$. The partition $\{\{D_{ij}|1 \leq j \leq r_i\}|1 \leq i \leq s\}$ and the corresponding partition of the columns of $\Psi(Q, +)$ are called the *G–fusion of H–classes* or the *$(Q, .)$–fusion of $(Q, +)$–classes*. Since $V(G, Q)$ is a subring of $V(H, Q)$, each idempotent e_i from (4.5) is a sum $e_i = \displaystyle\sum_{j=1}^{t_i} f_{ij}$ of idempotents

of $V(H, Q) = \displaystyle\bigoplus_{i=1}^{s} \bigoplus_{j=1}^{t_i} \mathbb{C} f_{ij}$. Set $\Psi(Q, +) = (\psi_{ij,kl}^{H})_{1 \leq i \leq s, 1 \leq j \leq t_i; 1 \leq k \leq s, 1 \leq l \leq r_k}$. The partition $\{\{f_{ij}|1 \leq j \leq t_i\}|1 \leq i \leq s\}$ and the corresponding partition of the rows of $\Psi(Q, +)$ are called the *G–fusion of H–characters* or the *$(Q, .)$–fusion of $(Q, +)$–characters*. The dual of the Quotient Theorem 4.22, the Fusion Theorem [J6, Th.3.1] may then be formulated as follows.

THEOREM 5.6. *The character table $\Psi(Q, .)$ is determined by the character table $\Psi(Q, +)$ along with the $(Q, .)$–fusion of $(Q, +)$–classes and $(Q, +)$–characters.* $\square$

The exact form of the determination is best stated geometrically. Consider the specification of the i-th basic character ψ_i^G of $(Q, .)$. In the fusion data, this character corresponds to the fusion of the t_i basic characters $\psi_{i1}^{H}, \ldots, \psi_{it_i}^{H}$ of $(Q, +)$. For each conjugacy class D_{kl} of $(Q, +)$, there is a t_i–dimensional complex vector $\underline{w}_{kl} = [\psi_{i1,kl}^{H}, \ldots, \psi_{it_k,kl}^{H}]$. These vectors may be taken to lie in $W = \mathbb{C}^{t_i}$. The subspace $W_0 = \mathbb{C}\underline{w}_{11}$ is called the *principal subspace*. An inner product $(\underline{x}|\underline{y}) = \underline{x}\,\underline{y}^*$ is given on W, where $*$ denotes the conjugate transpose. The corresponding norm

182

is $\|x\| = (\underline{x}|\underline{x})$. The character value ψ_{ik}^G is then given as the unique scalar λ minimising the expression $\|\underline{w}_{kl} - \lambda(\underline{w}_{11}/\|\underline{w}_{11}\|)\|$ for each $l = 1, \ldots, r_k$, namely [J6, Th. 4.1]

$$(5.6) \qquad \psi_{ik}^G = (\underline{w}_{kl}|\underline{w}_{11})/\|\underline{w}_{11}\| \; .$$

Thus $\lambda\underline{w}_{11}/\|\underline{w}_{11}\|$ is the unique best approximation, in the principal subspace, to the vectors $\underline{w}_{kl}$. Another condition, very useful for the completion of partial fusion data, is the *magic rectangle condition* [J6, Th. 6.1]. This says that for fixed $i, k \in \{1, \ldots, s\}$, and then for each $l \in \{1, \ldots, t_i\}$, $l' \in \{1, \ldots, r_k\}$, the relation

$$(5.7) \qquad \frac{\displaystyle\sum_{j=1}^{r_k} |D_{kj}|\psi_{il,kj}}{\displaystyle\sum_{j=1}^{r_k} |D_{kj}|\psi_{il,11}^H} = \frac{\displaystyle\sum_{j'=1}^{t_i} \psi_{ij',11}\,\psi_{ij',kl'}}{\displaystyle\sum_{j'=1}^{t_i} \psi_{ij',11}^H\,\psi_{ij',11}^H}$$

holds. As an example of its use, consider the problem of constructing the character table of the 3–pique $(\mathbf{Z}_5, -)$ from the character table of $(\mathbf{Z}_5, +)$. The $(\mathbf{Z}_5, -)$–fusion of $(\mathbf{Z}_5, +)$–classes is $\{\{0\}, \{\pm 1\}, \{\pm 2\}\}$. The condition (5.7) then fixes the $(\mathbf{Z}_5, -)$–fusion of $(\mathbf{Z}_5, +)$–characters, giving the character table of $(\mathbf{Z}_5, -)$ as

$$(5.8) \qquad \begin{bmatrix} 1 & 1 & 1 \\[2ex] \sqrt{2} & \sqrt{2}\,\cos\frac{2\pi}{5} & -\sqrt{2}\,\cos\frac{\pi}{5} \\[2ex] \sqrt{2} & -\sqrt{2}\,\cos\frac{\pi}{5} & \sqrt{2}\,\cos\frac{2\pi}{5} \end{bmatrix}$$

[J6, §7]. By [Ch,Th, III.5.9], the 3–quasigroups of prime order are the quasigroups of prime order whose multiplication groups are soluble. By Burnside's Theorem [Hu, Satz V.21.3] that a transitive permutation group of prime degree is either soluble or doubly transitive, all the prime order quasigroups that are not 3–quasigroups are rank 2 quasigroups. Since loops that are 3–quasigroups are abelian, loops of prime order are either abelian or rank 2. Thus character tables such as (5.8) with $2 < s < n$ for prime n cannot be loop character tables.

It is easy to recognise abelian quasigroups Q from their character tables, e.g. via $n = s$ or $\sigma(Q) = Q \times Q$ or $\forall\, 1 \le i \le s$, $n_i = 1$. On the other hand, the character table $\Psi(Q)$ of a quasigroup Q does not determine the centre congruence $\zeta(Q)$, or even whether Q is a 3–quasigroup or not. For example, a non–abelian loop of order 5 and the 3–pique $(\mathbf{Z}_5, ., 0)$ with $x.y = 2x + y$ share the same character table, both having rank 2. However, the character table $\Psi(Q^2)$ of the direct Q^2 of a quasigroup Q does determine whether Q is a 3–quasigroup or not [J7, Th. 3.1]. One implication is that the character table $\Psi(Q)$ of a quasigroup Q does not determine the character table $\Psi(Q^2)$. By contrast, the character table of a direct product $P \times Q$ of two loops P and Q is the tensor product $\Psi(P) \otimes \Psi(Q)$ [J7, Th. 2.1]. The problem of interpreting the tensor square $\Psi(Q) \otimes \Psi(Q)$ of a quasigroup character table $\Psi(Q)$ remains. One solution is provided by the concept of a "superscheme" [J7, §4].

An association scheme (Q, Γ) on an underlying finite non–empty set Q is a partition Γ of Q^2 satisfying (4.4). A *superscheme* (Q, Γ^*) on an underlying finite non–empty set Q is a partition $\Gamma^n = \{C_1^n, \ldots, C_{s_n}^n\}$ of Q^{n+2}, for each natural number n, such that

$$
(5.9) \quad
\begin{cases}
\text{(S1)} & C_1^0 = \hat{Q} \ ; \\[4pt]
\text{(S2)} & \forall f : \{1, \ldots, m+2\} \to \{1, \ldots, n+2\}, \ \forall \, C_j^n \in \Gamma^n \ , f^*(C_j^n) = \\[2pt]
& \{(x_1, \ldots, x_{m+2}) \mid \exists (y_1, \ldots, y_{n+2}) \in C_j^n . \ \forall \, 1 \le i \le m+2, x_i = y_{if}\} \\[4pt]
\text{(S3)} & \forall \, m \in \mathbf{N}, \ \forall \, n \in \mathbf{N}, \ \forall \, C_i^m \in \Gamma^m, \ \forall \, C_j^n \in \Gamma^n, \ \forall \, C_k^{m+n} \in \Gamma^{m+n} \ , \\[2pt]
& \exists c(i, j, k; m, n) \in \mathbf{N}. \ \forall (x_0, \ldots, x_m, y_0, \ldots, y_n) \in C_k^{m+n} \ , \\[2pt]
& |\{z \in Q \mid (x_0, \ldots, x_m, z) \in C_i^m, (z, y_0, \ldots, y_n) \in C_j^n\}| \\[2pt]
& = c(i, j, k; m, n), \text{ and} \\[4pt]
\text{(S4)} & \forall \, 1 \le i, j, k \le s_0, \quad c(i, j, k; 0, 0) = c(j, i, k; 0, 0) \ .
\end{cases}
$$

In particular, (5.9) implies that (Q, Γ^0) is an association scheme, the *associated scheme* of the superscheme. Note how (5.9)(S2) for the bijection $f : 1 \longmapsto 2$, $2 \longmapsto 1$ reduces to (4.4) (A2). The exponential generating function

$$
(5.10) \qquad f(x) = 1 + x + \sum_{n=0}^{\infty} s_n \frac{x^{n+2}}{(n+2)!}
$$

is called the *augmented Poincaré series* of (Q, Γ). If G is a multiplicity–free transitive permutation group with permutation character π acting on Q (e.g. the multiplication group of a quasigroup Q), then taking Γ^n to be the set of orbits of G in its diagonal action on Q^{n+2} makes (Q, Γ^*) a superscheme, with augmented Poincaré series given by

$$
(5.11) \qquad f(x) = \frac{1}{|G|} \sum_{g \in G} e^{x \pi(g)} \ .
$$

For each natural number n, take a complex vector space $\mathbf{C}\Gamma^n$ with basis Γ^n. Set $\mathbf{C}\Gamma = \bigoplus_{n \in \mathbf{N}} \mathbf{C}\Gamma^n$, the complex vector space direct sum of the $\mathbf{C}\Gamma^n$. Then $\mathbf{C}\Gamma$ carries an algebra structure defined by

$$
(5.12) \qquad C_i^m \, C_j^n = \sum_{k=1}^{s_{m+n}} c(i, j, k; m, n) C_k^{m+n} \ ,
$$

called the *Bose–Mesner superalgebra* of the superscheme (Q, Γ). This algebra is associative [J7, Th. 5.1] and graded: $\mathbf{C}\Gamma^m . \mathbf{C}\Gamma^n \le \mathbf{C}\Gamma^{m+n}$. The subspace $\mathbf{C}\Gamma^n$ is called the *homogeneous component of degree n*. The homogeneous component of degree 0 is the Bose–Mesner algebra of the associated scheme (Q, Γ°). Each

184

homogeneous component $C\Gamma^n$ is a bimodule for this Bose–Mesner algebra, under left multiplication

$$(5.13) \qquad L : C\Gamma^\circ \longrightarrow \mathrm{End}_{\mathbf{C}} \, C\Gamma^n; x \longmapsto (y \longmapsto xy)$$

and right multiplication

$$(5.14) \qquad R : C\Gamma^\circ \longrightarrow \mathrm{End}_{\mathbf{C}} \, C\Gamma^n; x \longmapsto (y \longmapsto yx) \ .$$

The crucial result [J7, Th. 6.2] is

THEOREM 5.15. *The algebra homomorphism* $L \otimes R : C\Gamma^\circ \otimes C\Gamma^\circ \longrightarrow \mathrm{End}_{\mathbf{C}} \, C\Gamma^1$ *embeds the tensor square* $C\Gamma^\circ \otimes C\Gamma^\circ$ *as a commutative subalgebra of the endomorphism ring* $\mathrm{End}_{\mathbf{C}} \, C\Gamma^1$. $\quad\square$

Considering the case of the multiplication group G acting on the quasigroup Q, the character table $\Psi(Q)$ is obtained via (4.9) from the relationships (4.5)–(4.7) in the commutative algebra $C\Gamma^\circ = V(G,Q)$. Theorem 5.15 enables one to obtain the tensor square $\Psi(Q) \otimes \Psi(Q)$ in a similar way from the commutative subalgebra $C\Gamma^\circ \otimes C\Gamma^\circ$ of $\mathrm{End}_{\mathbf{C}} \, C\Gamma'$. In other words [J7, Th. 7.1],

THEOREM 5.16. *The tensor square* $\Psi(Q) \otimes \Psi(Q)$ *is determined by the two–sided action of* $V(G,Q)$ *on the orbits of* G *on* Q^3. $\quad\square$

A recent approach [S6] to the problem of locating quasigroups within the abelian/3/ non–3 trichotomy has used two numerical invariants, the "entropy" and "asymptotic entropy". The *entropy* $H(Q)$ of the quasigroup Q is defined to be

$$(5.17) \qquad H(Q) = \sum_{i=1}^{s} \frac{n_i}{n} \log \frac{n}{n_i} \quad ,$$

logarithms being taken to a fixed base. This base is usually 2, in which case entropy has the units of *bits*.

PROPOSITION 5.18 [S6, PROP. 1.4]. *The entropy* $H(Q)$ *of a quasigroup* Q *of finite positive order* n *satisfies*

$$(5.19) \qquad \log n - (1 - n^{-1})\log(n-1) \leq H(Q) \leq \log n \ .$$

Equality obtains on the left if and only if Q *has rank 2. Equality obtains on the right if and only if* Q *is abelian.* $\quad\square$

The *asymptotic entropy* $h(Q)$ is defined to be

$$(5.20) \qquad h(Q) = \limsup_{m \to \infty} \frac{1}{m} H(Q^m) \ .$$

THEOREM 5.21 [S6; (1.5), TH. 3.1]. *The asymptotic entropy* $h(Q)$ *of a quasigroup* Q *of finite order* n *satisfies*

$$(5.21) \qquad 0 \leq h(Q) \leq \log n \ .$$

Equality obtains on the right if and only if Q *is a* 3*–quasigroup.* $\quad\square$

REFERENCES

[BI]   E. BANNAI AND T. ITO, *Algebraic Combinatorics I*, Benjamin/Cummings, Menlo Park 1984.

[BS]   A. BARLOTTI AND K. STRAMBACH, *The geometry of binary systems*, Adv. in Math. 49 (1983), 1–105.

[B1]   R.H. BRUCK, *Contributions to the theory of loops*, Trans. Amer. Math. Soc. 60 (1946), 245–354.

[B2]   R.H. BRUCK, *A Survey of Binary Systems*, Springer–Verlag, Berlin 1958.

[B3]   R.H. BRUCK, *What is a loop?*, in Studies in Modern Algebra (A.A. Albert ed.), M.A.A. Studies in Mathematics No. 2, Prentice Hall, Enlewood Cliffs 1963.

[CG]   P.J. CAMERON, J.M. GOETHALS, AND J.J. SEIDEL, *The Krein condition, spherical designs, Norton algebras and permutation groups*, Indag. Math. 81 (1978), 196–206.

[Ch]   O. CHEIN, H. PFLUGFELDER AND J.D.H. SMITH (EDS.), *Theory and Applications of Quasigroups and Loops*, Heldermann Verlag, Berlin 1989.

[Co]   J.H. CONWAY, *A simple construction for the Fischer–Griess monster group*, Inv. Math. 79 (1985), 513–540.

[Cr]   C.W. CURTIS AND I. REINER, *Methods of Representation Theory*, Vol. I, Wiley, New York 1981.

[De]   P. DELSARTE, *An algebraic approach to the association schemes of coding theory*, Philips Res. Repts. Supp. 10 (1973).

[Dg]   P. DIACONIS, *Group Representations in Probability and Statistics*, Institute of Mathematical Statistics Lecture notes–Monograph Series Vol. 11, Institute of Mathematical Statistics, Hayward California, (1988).

[Di]   P.G.L.–DIRICHLET (R. DEDEKIND ED.), *Vorlesungen über Zahlentheorie*, (3rd. ed.), Braunschweig 1879.

[Do]   J.L. DOOB, *Stochastic Processes*, Wiley, New York 1953.

[Fr]   F.G. FROBENIUS (J.-P. SERRE ED.), *Gesammelte Abhandlungen Bd. III*, Springer, Berlin 1968.

[Ga]   C.F. GAUSS (A.A. CLARKE TR.), *Disquisitiones Arithmeticae*, Yale University Press, New Haven 1966.

[H1]   T. HAWKINGS, *The origin of the theory of group characters*, Archive Hist. Exact Sci. 7 (1971), 142–170.

[H2]   T. HAWKINS, *New light on Frobenius' creation of the theory of group characters*, Archive Hist. Exact Sci. 12 (1974), 217–243.

[He]   H. HEYER, *Convolution semigroups of probability measures on Gelfand pairs*, Expo. Math. 1 (1983), 3–45.

[Hu]   B. HUPPERT, *Endliche Gruppen I*, Springer–Verlag, Berlin 1967.

[J1]   K.W. JOHNSON, *S–rings over loops, right mapping groups and transversals in permutation groups*, Math. Proc. Comb. Phil. Soc. 89 (1981), 433–422.

[J2]   K.W. JOHNSON, *Latin square determinants*, in proceedings of the 1986 Montréal conference on Extremal Set Theory and Relational Structures (I.G. Rosenberg ed.), Cambridge University Press, Cambridge 1988.

[J3]   K.W. JOHNSON AND J.D.H. SMITH, *Characters of finite quasigroups*, Europ. J. Combinatorics 5 (1984), 43–50.

[J4]   K.W. JOHNSON AND J.D.H. SMITH, *Characters of finite quasigroups II: induced characters*, Europ. J. Combinatorics 7 (1986), 131–137.

[J5]   K.W. JOHNSON AND J.D.H. SMITH, *A note on character induction in association schemes*, Europ. J. Combinatorics 7 (1986), 139.

[J6]   K.W. JOHNSON AND J.D.H. SMITH, *Characters of finite quasigroups III: quotients and fusion*, Europ. J. Combinatorics, 10 (1989), 47–56.

[J7]   K.W. JOHNSON AND J.D.H. SMITH, *Characters of finite quasigroups IV: products and superschemes*, Europ. J. Combinatorics, to appear.

[J8]   K.W. JOHNSON AND J.D.H. SMITH, *Characters of finite quasigroups V: linear characters*, IMA preprint series # 413 (1988).

[Ma]   I.G. MACDONALD, *Symmetric Functions and Hall Polynomials*, Clarendon Press, Oxford 1979.

[Ml]   A.I. MAL'CEV, *On the general theory of algebraic systems (Russian)*, Mat. Sb. N.S. 35 (77) (1954), 3–20.

[Mo]   T. MOLIEN, *Ueber die Invarianten der Linearen Substitutionsgruppen*, Sitzungsber. d. Akad. d. Wiss. Berlin 1897, 1152–1156.

[Pi]   G. PICKERT, *Projektive Ebene*, Springer–Verlag, Berlin 1975.

[RS]   A.B. ROMANOWSKA AND J.D.H. SMITH, *Modal Theory–An Algebraic Approach to Order Geometry, and Convexity*, Heldermann Verlag, Berlin 1985.

[Se]   J.-P. SERRE (L.L. SCOTT TR.), *Linear Representations of Finite Groups*, Springer–Verlag, New York 1977.

[S1]   J.D.H. SMITH, *Centrality*, Ph.D. Thesis (unpublished), Cambridge University, 1974.

[S2]   J.D.H. SMITH, *Centraliser rings of multiplication groups on quasigroups*, Math. Proc. Camb. Phil. Soc. 79 (1976), 427–431.

[S3]   J.D.H. SMITH, *Mal'cev Varieties*, Springer Lecture Notes in Mathematics No. 554, Springer–Verlag, Berlin 1976.

[S4]   J.D.H. SMITH, *Representation Theory of Infinite Groups and Finite Quasigroups*, Séminaire de Mathématiques Supérieures No. 101, Université de Montréal, Montréal 1986.

[S5]   J.D.H. SMITH, *Quasigroups, association schemes, and Laplace operators on almost–periodic functions*, in proceedings of the 1986 Montréal conference on Extremal Set Theory and Relational Structures (I.G. Rosenberg ed.), Cambridge University Press, Cambridge 1988.

[S6]   J.D.H. SMITH, *Entropy, character theory and centrality of finite quasigroups*, IMA preprint series #416 (1988).

[S7]   J.D.H. SMITH, *Induced class functions are conditional expectations*, preprint.

[So]   S.Y. SONG, *The Character Tables of Certain Association Schemes*, Ph.D. Thesis (unpublished), Ohio State University, 1987.

[Ta]   O. TAMASCHKE, *S–Ringe und verallgemeinerte Charaktere auf endlichen Gruppen*, Math. Zeitschr. 84 (1964), 101–119.

[W1]   H. WEBER, *Beweis des Satzes dass jede eigentlich primitive quadratische Form unendlich viele Primzahlen darzustellen fähig ist*, Math. Ann. 20 (1882), 301–329.

[W2]   H. WEBER, *Theorie der Abel'schen Zahlkïrper*, Acta Math. 8 (1886), 193–263.

[W3]   H. WEBER, *Theorie der Abel'schen Zahlkörper*, Acta Math. 9 (1887), 105–130.

[W4]   H. WEBER, *Lehrbuch der Algebra*, Bd. 2, Braunschweig 1896.

[Wi]   H. WIELANDT, *Finite Permutation Groups*, Academic Press, New York 1964.

SELF-DUAL CODES AND SELF-DUAL DESIGNS

PATRICK SOLÉ*

Abstract. We construct self-orthogonal binary codes from projective $2 - (v, k, \lambda)$ designs with a polarity, k odd, and λ even. We give arithmetic conditions on the parameters of the design to obtain self-dual or doubly even self-dual codes. Non existence results in the latter case are obtained from rationality conditions of certain strongly regular graphs.

Key words. Self-dual codes, symmetric designs, null polarities, symplectic polarities, Hadamard designs, biplanes, strongly regular graphs

AMS(MOS) subject classifications. 05, 05B05, 05B20, 05C50, 94B25

1. Introduction. A well known technique [1], [2], [3], to study designs and construct self-dual codes consists of taking the linear span of the incidence matrix over $GF(p)$. However, this approach assumes that p divides the order $n = k - \lambda$ of the design.

By replacing the incidence matrix A by $I + A$, we construct binary self-orthogonal codes when k is odd, λ even and A symmetric. Using the theory of invariant factors [3] we give conditions on n to lowerbound the binary rank of $I + A$. To achieve this construction we need the design to be self-dual. When the design admits a null polarity, or a polarity with no absolute points, we show that our construction can lead to doubly even codes. Strongly regular graphs then arise naturally.

2. Definitions and notations. A *symmetric* (v, k, λ) *design* (also called projective design) is an incidence structure consisting of v blocks and v points, each block containing k points and every pair of blocks having exactly λ points in common. The *order* of such a design is then $n = k - \lambda$. A *polarity* of an incidence structure is an order two permutation on the set of blocks and points such that points are mapped to blocks, blocks are mapped to points, and incidence is preserved. An *absolute* point is a point incident with its image by a polarity. A *null* polarity is a polarity where every point is absolute.

The *incidence matrix* of such a design is the $v \times v$ matrix A with entries in $\{0, 1\}$ with rows (columns) indexed by points (resp. blocks) such that

$$A_{ij} = \begin{cases} 1 \text{ if } i \text{ is incident to } j \\ 0 \text{ otherwise.} \end{cases}$$

We denote by A^T the transpose of A.

The *Hamming weight* of a finite dimensional binary vector is the number of nonzero coordinates it contains. An $[n, k, d]$ *code* is a k-dimensional subspace of the n-dimensional vector space over $GF(2)$ such that the minimum Hamming weight

---

*School of Computer and Information Science, 313 Link Hall, Syracuse University, Syracuse, NY 13244.
Work partially supported by a grant from INRIA, France

over all nonzero vectors it contains is d. A code is said to be *self-orthogonal* if it is included in its dual, and *self-dual* in case of equality. We shall say that a code is *even* (resp. *doubly even*) if the weight of every codeword is even (resp. a multiple of 4).

A finite simple undirected graph Γ on v vertices is said to be *strongly regular* of parameters (v, k, λ, μ) if it is regular of degree k, and if the number of common neighbors of two adjacent (resp. nonadjacent) vertices is λ (resp. μ).

3. Self-orthogonal codes:. Let A be the incidence matrix of a symmetric (v, k, λ) design D with k odd and λ even. Suppose that D admits a polarity and that $A^T = A$. Call C the binary code spanned by the rows of $I + A$.

THEOREM 1. *C is self-orthogonal: $C \subset C^\perp$.*

Proof. By definition

$$(1) \qquad AA^T = (k - \lambda)I + \lambda\, J$$

Over $GF(2)$ this reduces to

$$(2) \qquad AA^T = I.$$

Now we use the fact that $A^T = A$ to get

$$(3) \qquad A^2 = I,$$

or equivalently

$$(4) \qquad (A + I)^2 = 0 = (A + I)(A + I)^T.$$

$\square$

Assume that v is odd. Call $\bar{C}$ the code of length $v + 1$ obtained from C by appending the all-one vector to it and adding an overall parity check. Then an immediate corollary is

Corollary 1. $\bar{C}$ is self-orthogonal: $\bar{C} \subset \bar{C}^\perp$.

4. Self-dual codes. In this section we suppose furthermore that the order of D is an odd integer which is not a perfect square. In order to lowerbound the dimension of C, we need a lemma.

LEMMA 1. *The eigenvalues of A are k and $\pm\sqrt{n}$ with multiplicities 1, $\frac{v-1}{2}$, $\frac{v-1}{2}$, respectively.*

Proof. Starting from

$$(5) \qquad A^2 = nI + \lambda J$$

and

(6) $$AJ = kJ$$

we obtain, by multiplication of (5) by A,

(7) $$A^3 = nA + k\lambda J.$$

Eliminating J between (5) and (7) we get:

$$(A - kI)(A^2 - nI) = 0.$$

k is an eigenvalue associated to the all-one vector. Denote by α its multiplicity. Interpreting A as the incidence matrix of a graph we see that $\alpha = 1$ because the graph is connected. The trace of A has to be an integer. Hence $\sqrt{n}$ and $-\sqrt{n}$ have the same multiplicity, m, say. Trivially, all multiplicities sum to v: $2m + \alpha = v$.

$$\square$$

Remark. As a byproduct, we have that $tr(A)$, which counts the number of absolute points of the polarity, is k.

We write $a\|b$ to mean that a divides b, but that a^2 does not.

THEOREM 2. *If* $2\,\|\,n-1$ *and* $2\,\|\,k+1$, *then* $\dim(C) = \frac{v-1}{2}$ *and* $\bar{C}$ *is self-dual.*

Proof. First we note that v has to be odd since n is a nonsquare, and $\det A = \pm k n^{\frac{v-1}{2}}$ [2]. Since C is self-orthogonal, $\dim(C) \leq \frac{v-1}{2}$.

By the lemma, we see that

$$\det(I + A) = (k+1)(1-n)^{\frac{v-1}{2}}.$$

By an argument similar to [3], p. 383, we deduce that $\dim(C) \geq \frac{v-1}{2}$. Since the all-one vector is not in C, we see that $\dim(\bar{C}) = \frac{v+1}{2}$.

5. Doubly even codes:. Suppose C or $\bar{C}$ is doubly even. Since they contain words of weight $k+1$ or $k-1$, only two possibilities may occur:

Case 1 D has no absolute points and $k \equiv -1 (\mathrm{mod}\ 4)$

Case 2 D has a null polarity and $k \equiv 1 (\mathrm{mod}\ 4)$.

Conversely, it is easy to check that cases (1) (or (2)) is sufficient to ensure that C is doubly even.

Case (1) is equivalent to the existence of a strongly regular graph with parameters (v, k, λ, λ) [2, p. 46], the incidence matrix of which is then A.

Case (2) is equivalent to the existence of a strongly regular graph with parameters $(v, k-1, \lambda - 2, \lambda)$ [2, p. 46], the incidence matrix of which is then $I + A$ (modulo 2). The design of section 6.3 is an example of this latter situation. If v is a multiple of 4, and D satisfies the hypothesis, then $\bar{D}$, obtained by complementing the blocks of D, satisfies the hypothesis (2). The same statement with (1) and (2) interchanged also holds.

We can use rationality conditions on the multiplicities of eigenvalues of a strongly regular graph to rule out the existence of doubly even self-dual codes (see section 6.2), *obtained from our construction.*

6. Examples. We note first that there are polarities in every design with an abelian group acting regularly on it [6, p. 13]. In particular, in cyclic difference sets [3], shifting v times the first row to the left will symmetrize the incidence matrix.

6.1 Hadamard Designs:. These are designs with parameters $(4t - 1, 2t - 1, t - 1)$ and $n = t$, associated to normalized Hadamard matrices [2], [3]. When t is odd and $2||t - 1$ we can apply Theorem 3.2. This yields, e.g., for $t = 3$ and D a quadratic residue difference set a [12,6,4] even code. However, the construction works for $t = 9$ yielding a [20,10] code (computer proof), even though $t - 1 = 2^3$. Provided suitable Hadamard matrices exist, we obtain an infinite series of self-dual codes of parameters $[16m + 12, 8m + 6]$, m an integer. We can even suppress this proviso by assuming that $16m + 11$ is a prime and applying Paley's construction [3]. There is an infinity of such primes by Dirichlet's theorem.

6.2 Biplanes.

These are symmetric designs with $\lambda = 2$ [2,3], $k = n + 2$, and $v = \frac{n^2 + 3n + 4}{2}$. The following table summarizes what I know.

n	v	k	C or $\bar{C}$	Comments	Existence	Doubly Even
3	11	5	[12,6,4]	Th .2 + comp.	Hadamard design	No
7	37	9	[38,19]	Th .2	Biquadratic residues	No
9	56	11	$[56, \leq 28]$	Th 1.	See [3] and [4]	No
11	79	13	[80,60]	Th .2	B_1 (11) not self-dual	No

For $n = 3$ or 7 the code lengths are not multiples of 8: we cannot expect a doubly even code.

For $n = 9$, it is not clear if the code is self-dual, but it cannot be doubly even. If so, there should be a (56,11,2,2) strongly regular graph. And the rationality conditions are [2, p. 45]: $\frac{1}{2} [55 \pm \frac{11}{3}] \in \mathbf{Z}$. Contradiction.

For $n = 11$, we don't know if we can construct a code. (Is there a (79,13,2) projective design admitting a polarity?). If the code exists it is self-dual. It cannot be doubly even, for there would exist a (79,12,0,2) strongly regular graph. The rationality conditions [2, p. 47] are $\frac{1}{2}[78 \pm \frac{66}{\sqrt{11}}] \in \mathbf{Z}$. Contradiction.

6.3 Projective Geometries. Taking as D the design with points and blocks the points and hyperplanes of the projective geometry $PG(m, q)$, with parameters: $(\frac{q^{m+1} - 1}{q - 1}, \frac{q^m - 1}{q - 1}, \frac{q^{m-1} - 1}{q - 1})$, we see that n is odd and λ even if and only if both m and q are odd. Then v is even. To symmetrize the incidence matrix, we can use a symplectic polarity [2, p. 48]. For a complete classification of polarities of finite desarguesian geometries, see [6, p. 43]. Elementary number theory, and the fact that C is self-orthogonal, shows that

$$C \text{ is doubly even if and only if } q \equiv -1(\mathrm{mod}\ 4) \text{ or } \begin{cases} q \equiv 1(\mathrm{mod}\ 4) \\ m \equiv 1(\mathrm{mod}\ 4) \end{cases}$$

Example. Let $q = m = 3$; we obtain a $(40, 13, 4)$ projective design. Let M be the matrix

$$\begin{pmatrix} 0 & 1 & 0 & 0 \\ -1 & 0 & 0 & 0 \\ 0 & 0 & 0 & 1 \\ 0 & 0 & -1 & 0. \end{pmatrix}$$

(This is indeed a canonical form for a symplectic polarity [7].) We define a polarity π by association to the projective point of representative $X \in \mathbf{F}_3^4$ the hyperplane $\pi(X) = \{Y \in \mathbf{F}_3^4 / X^T M Y = 0\}$. We obtain in that way a $[40, 16, \leq 8]$ self-orthogonal doubly even code.

7. Open problems and conclusion. There is ample space for future research. First, an analogue to theorem 3.2 would be needed when v is even (and now n is a perfect square). Even for v, adding the restriction that n be a non-square seems unnecessary, as shown by the example in section 5.1. Clearly, the examples where v is even and C is doubly even deserve further study. More examples can be found in [2, pp. 47–48]. Strongly regular graphs emerge therefrom as interesting structures to construct self-dual codes.

Finally, we have said nothing concerning the minimum weight of all these codes. An algebraic argument like the square root bound, or a combinatorial one like what is known concerning the codes of projective planes, seems to be needed.

8. Acknowledgement. Electronic computations were performed in MAC-SYMA, on Syracuse University's ACSVAX. We thank H. F. Mattson, Jr., and Luther Rudolph for helpful comments, and Ms. Elaine Weinman for careful LATEX-processing.

REFERENCES

[1] E. F. ASSMUS, JR., H. F. MATTSON, JR., *Algebraic theory of codes II*, AFCRL-71-0013, Final Report, 15 October 1970, Part II.

[2] P. CAMERON, J. H. VAN LINT, *Graphs, codes, and designs*, Cambridge University Press, 1980.

[3] M. HALL, JR., *Combinatorial Theory*, Wiley, 1986.

[4] R. H. F. DENNISTON, *On biplanes with 56 points*, Ars. Combin., 9 (1980), pp. 167–169.

[5] V. PLESS, *A classification of self-orthogonal codes over GF(2).*, Discr. Math., 3 (1972), pp. 209–346.

[6] P. DEMBOWSKI, *Finite Geometries*, Springer, 1968.

[7] J. W. P. HIRSCHFELD, *Projective Geometries over Finite Fields*, Clarendon Press, 1979.

THE INCIDENCE ALGEBRA OF
A UNIFORM POSET

PAUL TERWILLIGER*

Abstract. Let $P, \leq$ denote a finite graded poset of rank $N \geq 2$, with fibers P_0, P_1, ..., P_N. Let the matrices L_i, R_i, E_i^* ($0 \leq i \leq N$) have rows and columns indexed by P, and entries

$$(L_i)_{xy} \;=\; 1 \quad \text{if } x \in P_{i-1},\; y \in P_i,\; x \leq y, \quad \text{and} \quad 0 \text{ otherwise} \quad (1 \leq i \leq N),$$

$$(R_i)_{xy} \;=\; 1 \quad \text{if } x \in P_{i+1},\; y \in P_i,\; y \leq x, \quad \text{and} \quad 0 \text{ otherwise} \quad (0 \leq i \leq N{-}1),$$

$$(E_i^*)_{xy} \;=\; 1 \quad \text{if } x,\, y \in P_i,\; x = y, \quad\quad\quad \text{and} \quad 0 \text{ otherwise} \quad (0 \leq i \leq N),$$

and $L_0 = R_N = 0$. The *incidence algebra* of P is the real matrix algebra generated by L_i, R_i, E_i^* ($0 \leq i \leq N$). P is *uniform* if there exists real numbers e_i^+, e_i^-, f_i ($1 \leq i \leq N$) (satisfying a certain condition) such that

$$e_i^- R_{i-2} L_{i-1} L_i \;+\; L_i R_{i-1} L_i \;+\; e_i^+ L_i L_{i+1} R_i \;=\; f_i L_i \quad (1 \leq i \leq N)$$
$$(R_{-1} = L_{N+1} = 0).$$

We show the incidence algebra T of a uniform poset takes a very simple form, and present a method for computing the irreducible T-modules. We give 11 families of examples that show many of the classical geometries are uniform. In each case we compute the irreducible T-modules. We present some open problems, and discuss a connection with P- and Q-polynomial association schemes.

Key words. Graded poset, Partial geometry, Partial geometric lattice, Association scheme.

AMS(MOS) subject classifications. Primary 05B25, 06A12, 05C50.

1. Introduction. In [2], Bose introduced a semi-linear incidence structure of points and lines called an (R, K, T)-*partial geometry*. The structure provided a uniform way of studying examples such as the *Steiner systems* (where $2 \leq T = K \leq R$), *transversal designs* or equivalently *nets* (where $2 \leq T = K - 1 \leq R$), and *generalized quadrangles* (where $T = 1 < R, K$). To include more examples, the concept has since been generalized in two main directions. To get the higher rank analogs of the nets and generalized quadrangles, namely the d-*nets* and *polar spaces*, respectively, the point-line system has been replaced with a ranked semi-lattice satisfying various axioms. This has given rise to the *partial d-space* of Laskar [17], the *partial geometric lattice* of Bose and Miskimins [5], and the *regular semi-lattice* of Delsarte [9]. We refer the reader to the papers of Liebler and Meyerowitz [20], Laskar and Dunbar [18], Laskar and Sprague [19], Meyerowitz [21], and Meyerowitz and Miskimins [22] for more information on partial geometric lattices. Another approach is to eliminate the semi-linear condition on the point-line system, in order to get more general partially balanced incomplete block designs as examples. This approach has given rise to the *partial geometric design* of Bose, Shrikhande and

---

*Department of Mathematics, University of Wisconsin, Madison, WI 53706.
Research partially supported by NSF grant DMS-8600882.

Singhi [6], (see also Bose, Bridges, and Shrikhande [3], [4]) and the equivalent $1\frac{1}{2}$-*design* of Neumaier [24], [25]. The M_n- and S_n-*designs* of Neumaier [23] combine both approaches to an extent. They are certain rank N graded posets, where the removal of the upper fiber P_N yields a semi-lattice.

In this paper we introduce the notion of a *uniform poset*. This is a certain finite graded poset with arbitrary rank $N \geq 2$, that retains the simple algebraic properties of a partial geometry, but neither it, nor any truncation or interval is assumed to be a semi-lattice. In spite of this, uniform posets are in a sense less general than the above constructions. Very roughly, the axioms for a partial geometric lattice and regular semi-lattice endow the upper fiber of the poset with a simple algebraic structure. In a uniform poset, this structure is extended to all fibers. This gives a more complete description of the structure of the poset, and also happens to simplify many of the calculations. We note that a uniform poset that is also a semi-lattice has a very restricted structure, and can probably be classified if the rank is sufficiently large. (See Conjecture 3 in Section 4). We will consider this special case in a future paper, and focus here on the algebraic properties of arbitrary uniform posets.

For the rest of this section we define our terms and give background information. In Section 2 we define a uniform poset, and give a method for finding its algebraic structure. The main result is Theorem 2.5. In Section 3, we give 11 infinite families of uniform posets, and in each case compute the algebraic structure using the method of Section 2. We acknowledge that in many cases some or all of this structure has previously been found by authors such as Delsarte [9], [10], [11], Dunkl [13], [14], and Stanton [29], [30], [31], but we wish to stress the essential similarity of the examples. In Section 4, we give some conjectures relating uniform posets and P- and Q-polynomial association schemes.

In this paper, $P, \leq$ is always assumed to be a finite, partially ordered set, or *poset*. Usually we just refer explicitly to P. If x and y are elements of P, then we write $x < y$ if $x \leq y$ and $x \neq y$. We say y *covers* x if $x < y$, but there is no $z \in P$ with $x < z < y$. A *grading* of P is a partition of P into disjoint non-empty sets $P_0, P_1, \ldots, P_N$, called *fibers*, such that for all $x, y \in P$, $x \in P_i$ and y covers x implies $i \leq N-1$ and $y \in P_{i+1}$. The *height function* $h: P \to \{0, 1, \ldots, N\}$ of the grading satisfies $h(x) = i$ if $x \in P_i$ ($x \in P$, $0 \leq i \leq N$). The integer N is the *rank* of the grading. A *graded poset* is a poset, together with a grading. Now let P be a graded poset of some rank $N \geq 2$, with fibers $P_0, P_1, \ldots, P_N$. The *dual* of P is the poset $\overline{P} = P$ with grading $\overline{P}_i = P_{N-i}$ ($0 \leq i \leq N$), where $x \leq y$ in $\overline{P}$ if and only if $y \leq x$ in P. Also, P is said to be ϕ-*regular* if the following conditions (1), (2), (3) hold.

(1) For all integers i, j, k ($0 \leq i \leq j \leq k \leq N$) and all $x, y \in P$ with $x \in P_i$, $y \in P_k$, and $x \leq y$, the number of $z \in P_j$ with $x \leq z \leq y$ is a constant denoted $\phi(i, j, k)$.

(2) For all integers i, j ($0 \leq i \leq j \leq N$) and all $x \in P_i$, the number of $z \in P_j$ with $x \leq z$ is a positive constant denoted $\phi(i, j, \infty)$.

(3) For all integers j, k $(0 \leq j \leq k \leq N)$ and all $y \in P_k$, the number of $z \in P_j$ with $z \leq y$ is a positive constant denoted $\phi(-\infty, j, k)$.

Now again let P be any graded poset of rank $N \geq 2$. Define the *lowering matrices* L_i, the *raising matrices* R_i, and the *projection matrices* E_i^* $(0 \leq i \leq N)$ of P to have rows and columns indexed by P, and entries

$$(L_i)_{xy} = \begin{cases} 1 & \text{if} \quad x \in P_{i-1}, \ y \in P_i, \ x \leq y \\ 0 & \text{otherwise} \end{cases} \qquad (1 \leq i \leq N)$$

$$(R_i)_{xy} = \begin{cases} 1 & \text{if} \quad x \in P_{i+1}, \ y \in P_i, \ y \leq x \\ 0 & \text{otherwise} \end{cases} \qquad (0 \leq i \leq N-1)$$

$$(E_i^*)_{xy} = \begin{cases} 1 & \text{if} \quad x, \ y \in P_i, \ x = y \\ 0 & \text{otherwise} \end{cases} \qquad (0 \leq i \leq N),$$

and $L_0 = R_N = 0$. The *incidence algebra* T of P is the real matrix algebra generated by the L_i, R_i, E_i^* $(0 \leq i \leq N)$. The irreducible T-modules are of interest in several contexts. For example, they can give those irreducible representations of the automorphism group of P that exist in $\mathbf{R}P$. See Dunkl [13] for the subset lattice, Dunkl [14] for the subspace lattice, Stanton [29] for the polar spaces, and Stanton [30], [31] for certain posets associated with the bilinear, alternating, hermitian, and quadratic forms (i.e. $A_q(N, M)$, $Alt_q(N)$, $Her_q(N)$ and $Quad_q(N)$ in Section 3 of this paper). We refer the reader to Stanton [32], [33] for related information on group representations. In another application, the integrality of the T-module multiplicities can give feasibility conditions governing the existence of certain posets. This was done (implicitly) for (R, K, T)-partial geometries by Bose [2] and extended (implicitly) to partial geometric lattices by Liebler and Meyerowitz [20], Meyerowitz [21], and Meyerowitz and Miskimins [22]. The irreducible T-modules can also be used to compute eigenvalues of graphs that may exist on a fiber of P. We refer the reader to Delsarte [9], [10], [11] and the above mentioned papers by Stanton and Meyerowitz for further details.

Now let P be a graded poset of rank N, with incidence algebra T. Let V be the vector space $\mathbf{R}^m$ $(m = |P|)$, with standard basis identified with P. We view V as a Euclidean space with the usual inner product $\langle \ , \ \rangle$, and call V the *standard module* of P. A subspace W of V is a *module* of T if it is invariant under T, that is, if $t(w) \in W$ for all $w \in W$ and all $t \in T$. A module W of T is *irreducible* if it is non-zero, and the only non-zero module it contains is W itself. T-modules W and Y are *isomorphic* if there exists an isomorphism of vector spaces $\sigma : W \to Y$ such that $t(\sigma(w)) = \sigma(t(w))$ for all $w \in W$ and all $t \in T$. We do not distinguish between isomorphic T-modules.

2. The structure of a uniform poset. In this section we define a uniform poset, and give a method for computing the irreducible modules of its incidence algebra.

DEFINITION 2.1. Let N be an integer at least 2. A *parameter matrix of order* N is a tri-diagonal real matrix $E := (e_{ij})_{1 \leq i, j \leq N}$ satisfying

(1) $e_{ii} = 1$ $(1 \leq i \leq N)$,

(2) $e_{i,i-1} \neq 0$ $(2 \leq i \leq N)$ or $e_{i,i+1} \neq 0$ $(1 \leq i \leq N-1)$,

(3) The principal submatrix $E(r,p) := (e_{ij})_{r+1 \leq i, j \leq p}$ is nonsingular for all integers r, p $(0 \leq r \leq p \leq N)$.

We denote $e_i^- := e_{i,i-1}$ $(2 \leq i \leq N)$, $e_i^+ := e_{i,i+1}$ $(1 \leq i \leq N-1)$, and for convenience set $e_1^- = e_N^+ = 0$. The purpose of (2) will become clear from the proof of part (2) of Theorem 2.5, and the purpose of (3) will become clear from part (1) of Definition 2.4.

DEFINITION 2.2. Let P be a finite graded poset of rank $N \geq 2$, with lowering and raising matrices L_i, R_i $(0 \leq i \leq N)$. Then P is *uniform* if there exists a parameter matrix E of order N and a vector $F := (f_i)_{1 \leq i \leq N}$ in $\mathbf{R}^N$ satisfying

$$(2.1) \quad e_i^- R_{i-2} L_{i-1} L_i + L_i R_{i-1} L_i + e_i^+ L_i L_{i+1} R_i = f_i L_i \quad (1 \leq i \leq N)$$
$$(R_{-1}, L_{N+1} = 0).$$

Here e_i^+, e_i^- are entries in E as indicated in Definition 2.1. We call E, F a *set of parameters* for P. These parameters need not be unique.

Note 1. The *partial geometric design* of Bose, Shrikhande, and Singhi [6] is equivalent to a ϕ-regular uniform poset with $N = 2$ and $|P_0| = 1$.

Note 2. The transpose of R_i is L_{i+1} $(0 \leq i \leq N - 1)$. In particular, If P is a uniform poset then the dual poset $\overline{P}$ is also uniform, with parameters $\overline{e}_i^\pm = e_{N-i+1}^\mp$, $\overline{f}_i = f_{N-i+1}$ $(1 \leq i \leq N)$.

Some infinite families of uniform posets with unbounded rank can be found in Section 3. Our purpose for the rest of this section is to show how the incidence algebra of a uniform poset has a very simple structure, and can be readily computed. We first define three sets of constants $c(r,p)$, $x_i(r,p)$, $m(r,p)$, whose meaning will become clear in our main Theorem 2.5.

DEFINITION 2.3. Let P be a uniform poset of rank $N \geq 2$. For each pair of integers r, p $(0 \leq r \leq p \leq N)$, denote by $c(r,p)$ the number of sequences $(x_r, x_{r+1}, \ldots, x_p, x_r', x_{r+1}', \ldots, x_p')$, where $x_i, x_i' \in P_i$ $(r \leq i \leq p)$, $x_r = x_r'$, $x_p = x_p'$, and $x_i < x_{i+1}$, $x_i' < x_{i+1}'$ $(r \leq i \leq p-1)$. We note x_i, x_i' may coincide for any and all i $(r \leq i \leq p)$.

Note. If P is ϕ-regular (see Introduction) then

$$c(r,p) = |P_r| \prod_{j=r}^{p-1} \phi(j, j+1, \infty) \prod_{j=r+1}^{p} \phi(r, j-1, j) \quad (0 \leq r \leq p \leq N),$$

where

$$|P_r| \;=\; |P_0| \prod_{j=0}^{r-1} \phi(j, j+1, \infty) \left(\prod_{j=1}^{r} \phi(0, j-1, j) \right)^{-1} \qquad (0 \le r \le N).$$

DEFINITION 2.4. Let P be a uniform poset of rank $N \ge 2$, with parameters E, F.

(1) For each pair of integers r, p $(0 \le r < p \le N)$, define the real numbers $x_i(r, p)$ $(r+1 \le i \le p)$ to be the solution to the linear system

$$E(r, p) \begin{pmatrix} x_{r+1}(r, p) \\ x_{r+2}(r, p) \\ \vdots \\ x_p(r, p) \end{pmatrix} = \begin{pmatrix} f_{r+1} \\ f_{r+2} \\ \vdots \\ f_p \end{pmatrix}$$

Here $E(r, p)$ is from Definition 2.1.

(2) For each pair of integers r, p $(0 \le r \le p \le N)$, let $m(r, p)$ be the unique real number satisfying

(2a) $\quad m(r, p) = 0$ if $r < p$ and $x_{r+1}(r, p) x_{r+2}(r, p) \cdots x_p(r, p) = 0$, and

(2b) $\quad c(r, p) = \displaystyle\sum_{r'=0}^{r} \sum_{p'=p}^{N} m(r', p') x_{r+1}(r', p') x_{r+2}(r', p') \cdots x_p(r', p')$ otherwise.

Here $c(r, p)$ is from Definition 2.3.

We note the $m(r, p)$ constants can be found recursively by solving (2a), (2b) in the order $(r, p) = (0, N)$, $(0, N-1)$, $(1, N)$, $(0, N-2)$, $(1, N-1)$, $(2, N)$, $\ldots$.

We are now ready to give the irreducible modules for the incidence algebra of any uniform poset.

THEOREM 2.5. *Let P be a uniform poset of rank $N \ge 2$, with lowering, raising, and projection matrices L_i, R_i, E_i^* $(0 \le i \le N)$. Let T be the incidence algebra of P acting on its standard module V. Then*

(1) V decomposes into an orthogonal direct sum of irreducible T-modules.

(2) Each irreducible T-module has a basis of the form w_r, $w_{r+1}, \cdots, w_p$ for some integers r, p $(0 \le r \le p \le N)$, where

(2a) $\quad w_i \in E_i^* V$ $(r \le i \le p)$,

(2b) $\quad L_i w_i = w_{i-1}$ $(r+1 \le i \le p)$, and $L_r w_r = 0$,

(2c) $\quad R_i w_i = x_{i+1}(r, p) w_{i+1}$ $(r \le i \le p-1)$, and $R_p w_p = 0$.

(The $x_i(r,p)$ are from Definition 2.4). In particular, the isomorphism class of an irreducible T-module is determined by the integers r, p.

We refer to the integers r, p in (2) as the endpoints of the module.

(3) *Let r, p be any integers $(0 \leq r \leq p \leq N)$. Then the irreducible T-module with endpoints r, p occurs in V with multiplicity $m(r,p)$. ($m(r,p)$ is from Definition 2.4.) If there is no such T-module then $m(r,p) = 0$.*

Proof of (1). Let $W \subseteq V$ be any T-module. Then it suffices to show $W^{\perp} := \{v \mid v \in V, \langle v, w \rangle = 0 \text{ for all } w \in W\}$ is also a T-module. Now T is closed under transposition, since each E_i^* is symmetric $(0 \leq i \leq N)$, and since $R_j^t = L_{j+1}$ $(0 \leq j \leq N-1)$. Thus for all $w \in W$, $v \in W^{\perp}$, and $A \in T$, we have $A^t \in T$ and therefore $A^t w \in W$, forcing $\langle Av, w \rangle = \langle v, A^t w \rangle = 0$ and $Av \in W^{\perp}$. Thus $W^{\perp}$ is a T-module, as desired.

Proof of (2). From (2) in Definition 2.1, we can assume either (a) $e_i^{-} \neq 0$ $(2 \leq i \leq N)$, or (b) $e_i^{+} \neq 0$ $(1 \leq i \leq N-1)$. First assume Case (a).

Let $W \subseteq V$ be an irreducible T-module, and let p be the maximal integer where $E_p^* W \neq 0$. Then $E_p^* W$ is a module for the symmetric matrix $R_{p-1} L_p = L_p^t L_p$, so there exists a nonzero vector $w_p \in E_p^* W$, and a real number λ such that $R_{p-1} L_p w_p = \lambda w_p$. Note $R_p w_p = 0$ by the maximality of p. Now define $w_i := L_{i+1} L_{i+2} \cdots L_p w_p$ $(-1 \leq i \leq p)$, and let r denote the minimal integer where $w_r \neq 0$. Then $w_i \neq 0$ $(r \leq i \leq p)$. Now (2a) and (2b) hold. If $r = p$ there is nothing further to prove, so assume $r < p$. From our above remarks, and upon applying (2.1) to w_i, we obtain

$$(2.2) \qquad\qquad R_{p-1} w_{p-1} = \lambda w_p$$

$$(2.3) \quad e_i^{-} R_{i-2} w_{i-2} + L_i R_{i-1} w_{i-1} + e_i^{+} L_i L_{i+1} R_i w_i = f_i w_{i-1} \quad (r+1 \leq i \leq p).$$

Now by induction on $i = p, \, p-1, \ldots$ in (2.3), we find $R_i w_i \in \operatorname{Span}\{w_{i+1}\}$ $(r \leq i \leq p-1)$. Now let y_i $(r+1 \leq i \leq p)$ denote the real number satisfying $R_i w_i = y_{i+1} w_{i+1}$ $(r \leq i \leq p-1)$, and set $y_r = y_{p+1} = 0$. Substituting this in (2.3), we find

$$e_i^{-} y_{i-1} + y_i + e_i^{+} y_{i+1} = f_i \qquad (r+1 \leq i \leq p).$$

But by (1) of Definition 2.4, $y_i = x_i(r,p)$ $(r+1 \leq i \leq p)$ is the unique solution to this system. This proves (2c), and we are done with Case (a).

Now assume Case (b), and again let W be an irreducible T-module. Applying Case (a) to the dual of P, we conclude W has a basis $w_r', w_{r+1}', \ldots, w_p'$ where, (in the original poset P), $w_i' \in E_i^* V$ $(r \leq i \leq p)$, $L_i w_i' = x_i(r,p) w_{i-1}'$ $(r+1 \leq i \leq p)$, $L_r w_r' = 0$, $R_i w_i' = w_{i+1}'$ $(r \leq i \leq p-1)$, and $R_p w_p' = 0$. Note $x_i(r,p) \neq 0$ $(r+1 \leq i \leq p)$, otherwise $\operatorname{Span}\{w_i', \ldots, w_p'\}$ is a T-module, contradicting the irreducibility of W. Now set $w_r = w_r'$ and

$$w_i = w_i' \left(\prod_{j=r+1}^{i} x_j(r,p)^{-1} \right) \qquad (r+1 \leq i \leq p).$$

Then w_i $(r \leq i \leq p)$ is the desired basis for W.

Proof of (3). Let $m(r, p)$ be the multiplicity of the irreducible T-module with endpoints r, p, if this module exists, and set $m(r, p) = 0$ if this module does not exist. We must show $m(r, p)$ satisfies (2a), (2b) of Definition 2.4. To prove (2a), suppose $x_i(r, p) = 0$ for some integer i $(r+1 \leq i \leq p)$. If there exists an irreducible T-module with endpoints r, p, then, using the notation of (2) in the present theorem, $\mathrm{Span}\{w_r, w_{r+1}, \ldots w_{i-1}\}$ would be a T-module, contradicting the irreducibility of W. Hence W does not exist, and $m(r, p) = 0$, as desired. To prove (2b), we consider the trace of the element $A = L_{r+1}L_{r+2} \cdots L_p R_{p-1} R_{p-2} \cdots R_{r+1} R_r$ of T. Elementary counting arguments give $\mathrm{trace}(A) = c(r, p)$. Now fix a decomposition of V into a direct sum of irreducible T-modules. Then $\mathrm{trace}(A)$ is equal to the sum of the traces of the restrictions of A to these modules, and this sum is just the right side of (2b). $\square$

As a consequence of Theorem 2.5, the incidence algebra of a uniform poset has the following simple basis.

COROLLARY 2.6. *Let P be a uniform poset of rank $N \geq 2$, with lowering, raising, and projection matrices L_i, R_i, E_i^* $(0 \leq i \leq N)$, and incidence algebra T. For each 4-tuple of integers s, r, p, t $(0 \leq s \leq r \leq p \leq t \leq N)$, define*

$$\theta^+(s, r, p, t) = L_{p+1}L_{p+2} \cdots L_{t-1}L_t R_{t-1} R_{t-2} \cdots R_{s+1} R_s L_{s+1} L_{s+2} \cdots L_{r-1} L_r$$
$$\theta^-(s, r, p, t) = R_{r-1} R_{r-2} \cdots R_{s+1} R_s L_{s+1} L_{s+2} \cdots L_{t-1} L_t R_{t-1} R_{t-2} \cdots R_{p+1} R_p$$
$$= \text{transpose of } \theta^+(s, r, p, t).$$

We interpret $\theta^{\pm}(r, r, r, r) = E_r^*$ $(0 \leq r \leq N)$.

Then T has a basis B of the form

$$(2.4) \qquad B = \{\theta^+(s, r, p, t) \mid 0 \leq s \leq r \leq p \leq t \leq N, \quad m(s, t) \neq 0\}$$

$$(2.5) \qquad \cup \{\theta^-(s, r, p, t) \mid 0 \leq s \leq r < p \leq t \leq N, \quad m(s, t) \neq 0\}.$$

Proof. The dimension of T as a real vector space is certainly at most $\Sigma(t - s + 1)^2$, where the sum is over all pairs $\{s, t \mid 0 \leq s \leq t \leq N, \ m(s, t) \neq 0\}$. Since this is the number of matrices in B, it suffices to show those matrices are independent. If not, let C be a minimal subset of B containing dependent matrices. Then C is a subset of (2.4) or (2.5), and the indices r, p of all matrices in C are identical. Without loss, we can assume C is contained in the set (2.4). Suppose

$$(2.6) \qquad \Sigma a_{st} \theta^+(s, r, p, t)$$

is a dependency among the matrices in C. Pick an element $\theta^+(s', r, p, t') \in C$ where $t' - s'$ is maximal, and consider the restriction of (2.6) to an irreducible T-module with endpoints s', t'. Then every element in C is 0 on this module except $\theta^+(s', r, p, t')$ itself. But this forces $a_{s't'} = 0$, contradicting the minimality of C. $\square$

COROLLARY 2.7. *Let P be a uniform poset of rank $N \geq 2$, with incidence algebra T. Then for each integer i $(0 \leq i \leq N)$, the subalgebra $E_i^* T E_i^* \subseteq T$ is commutative with dimension at most $(N - i + 1)(i + 1)$.*

Proof. Pick any integer i $(0 \leq i \leq N)$, and pick any matrices $a, b \in E_i^* T E_i^*$. Then a and b commute, since by Theorem 2.5, this is true of their restrictions to any irreducible T-module. The dimension bound is obtained by counting matrices in (2.4), (2.5). $\Box$

3. Examples of Uniform Posets. In this section we give 11 infinite families of uniform posets. For each example we give the irreducible modules of the incidence algebra using Theorem 2.5. We suppress the details of our calculations.

EXAMPLE 3.1. *In each of the 11 examples that follow, $P, \leq$ is a ϕ-regular graded poset with $|P_0| = 1$ and height function h. Basic combinatorial information on the examples can be found in the stated references.*

1. The truncated subset semi-lattice $S(N, M)$ $(2 \leq N \leq M)$ [9], [13].

$P = $ all subsets of $\{1, 2, \ldots, M\}$ with size at most N,

$u \leq v$ if u is a subset of v $(u, v \in P)$,

$h(u) = $ size of u $(u \in P)$,

$\phi(i, j - 1, j) = j - i, \quad \phi(i, i + 1, \infty) = M - i \quad (0 \leq i < j \leq N)$.

2. The Hamming semilattice $H(N, M)$ $(N \geq 2, \ M \geq 3)$ [9].

$P = $ all N-tuples of elements from the set $\{0, 1, 2, \ldots, M - 1\}$,

$u \leq v$ if u, v agree on all non-zero coordinates of u $(u, v \in P)$,

$h(u) = $ number of non-zero coordinates of u $(u \in P)$,

$\phi(i, j - 1, j) = j - i, \quad \phi(i, i + 1, \infty) = (M - 1)(N - i) \quad (0 \leq i < j \leq N)$.

This the poset of type II (with $q = 1$) in [9].

3. The folded Hamming poset $H^*(N, 3)$ $(N \geq 2)$ [9]

Let u, v be any elements of the poset $H(N, 3)$ in the above example, with $u = (u_1, \ldots, u_N)$ and $v = (v_1, \ldots, v_N)$ $(u_i, v_i \in \{0, 1, 2\}, 1 \leq i \leq N)$. Call u, v *antipodal opposites* if $(u_i, v_i) = (0, 0)$, $(1, 2)$, or $(2, 1)$ for all integers i $(1 \leq i \leq N)$.

$P = $ all unordered pairs (u, v) where u, v are antipodal opposites in $H(N, 3)$

$(u, v) \leq (u', v')$ if at least one of $u \leq u', \ u \leq v', \ v \leq u', \ v \leq v'$

holds in $H(N, 3)$ $((u, v), (u', v') \in P)$,

$h(u, v) = $ number of non-zero coordinates in u or v $((u, v) \in P)$,

$\phi(i, j - 1, j) = j - i \quad (0 \leq i < j \leq N)$,

$\phi(0, 1, \infty) = N$,

$\phi(i, i + 1, \infty) = 2(N - i) \quad (1 \leq i < N)$.

4. The bipartition poset $Part(2N)$ $(N \geq 3)$ **[9].** Let $X = \{1, 2, \ldots, 2N\}$.

P = all unordered pairs (u, v) where $u, v \subseteq X$, $\quad u \cap v = \phi$, $\quad u \cup v = X$.

$(u, v) \leq (u', v')$ if at least one of $u \subseteq u'$, $u \subseteq v'$, $v \subseteq u'$, $v \subseteq v'$, $((u, v), (u', v')) \in P)$,

$h(u, v) = \min\{|u|, |v|\}$ $((u, v) \in P)$,

$\phi(i, j - 1, j) = j - i$ $(0 \leq i < j \leq N)$ $(i, j) \neq (0, N)$,

$\phi(0, N - 1, N) = 2N$,

$\phi(i, i + 1, \infty) = 2N - i$ $(0 \leq i < N)$.

5. The truncated subspace semi-lattice $S_q(N, M)$ $(2 \leq N \leq M)$ **[7,Section 9.3], [9], [14].**

P = all subspaces of dimension at most N in an M-dimensional vector
      space over the finite field $GF(q)$,

$u \leq v$ if u is a subspace of v $(u, v \in P)$,

$h(u)$ = dimension of u $(u \in P)$,

$$\phi(i, j - 1, j) = \frac{q^{j-i} - 1}{q - 1}, \quad \phi(i, i + 1, \infty) = \frac{q^{M-i} - 1}{q - 1} \quad (0 \leq i < j \leq N).$$

6. The polar spaces of rank N $(N \geq 2)$ **[7, Section 9.4], [29].**

Let H be a vector space over $GF(q)$ that possesses one of the following nondegenerate forms:

name	dim(H)	form	e
$B_N(q)$	$2N + 1$	quadratic	0
$C_N(q)$	$2N$	symplectic	0
$D_N(q)$	$2N$	quadratic (Witt index N)	-1
$^2D_{N+1}(q)$	$2N + 2$	quadratic (Witt index N)	1
$^2A_{2N}(r)$	$2N + 1$	Hermitian $(q=r^2)$	$\frac{1}{2}$
$^2A_{2N-1}(r)$	$2N$	Hermitian $(q=r^2)$	$-\frac{1}{2}$

The parameter e will appear in later calculations. A subspace of H is called *isotropic* whenever the form vanishes completely on that subspace. In each of the above cases, the dimension of any maximal isotropic subspace is N.

P = all isotropic subspaces of H,

$u \leq v$ if u is a subspace of v $(u, v \in P)$,

$h(u)$ = dimension of u $(u \in P)$,

$$\phi(i, j - 1, j) = \frac{q^{j-i} - 1}{q - 1}, \quad \phi(i, i + 1, \infty) = \frac{(q^{N-i+e} + 1)(q^{N-i} - 1)}{q - 1} \quad (0 \leq i < j \leq N).$$

7. The attenuated space $A_q(N, M)$ $(2 \leq N \leq M)$ [7, Section 9.5], [9], [28], [31].

Let H be a vector space of dimension $M + N$ over $GF(q)$, and fix a subspace $w \subseteq H$ of dimension M.

$P = $ all subspaces u of H where $u \cap w = 0$,

$u \leq v$ if u is a subspace of v $(u, v \in P)$,

$h(u) = $ dimension of u $(u \in P)$,

$$\phi(i, j-1, j) = \frac{q^{j-i} - 1}{q - 1}, \quad \phi(i, i+1, \infty) = \frac{q^{M+N-i} - q^M}{q - 1} \quad (0 \leq i < j \leq N).$$

This poset is equivalent to the poset of type II (with $q \neq 1$) in [9]. If $N \geq 3$, it is also equivalent to an N-net [28].

8. The poset $Alt_q(N)$ **of alternating forms** $(N \geq 2)$ [7, Section 9.5], [30], [31].

Let H be a vector space of dimension N over $GF(q)$.

$P = $ all pairs (u, f), where u is a subspace of H and f is an alternating
     bilinear form on u,

$(u, f) \leq (u', f')$ if $u \subseteq u'$ and $f = f'|_u$ $((u, f), (u', f') \in P)$,

$h(u, f) = $ dimension of u $((u, f) \in P)$,

$$\phi(i, j-1, j) = \frac{q^{j-i} - 1}{q - 1}, \quad \phi(i, i+1, \infty) = \frac{q^N - q^i}{q - 1} \quad (0 \leq i < j \leq N).$$

9. The poset $Her_q(N)$ **of Hermitian forms** $(N \geq 2)$ [7, Section 9.5], [30], [31].

Same as 8, except H is over $GF(q^2)$ and f is a Hermitian form.

$$\phi(i, j-1, j) = \frac{q^{2j-2i} - 1}{q^2 - 1}, \quad \phi(i, i+1, \infty) = \frac{q(q^{2N} - q^{2i})}{q^2 - 1} \quad (0 \leq i < j \leq N).$$

10. The poset $Quad_q(N)$ **of quadratic forms** $(N \geq 2)$ [7, Section 9.5], [30], [31].

Same as 8, except f is a quadratic form. We allow q even or odd. See Bannai and Ito [1, p. 309] for the definition of a quadratic form if q is even.

$$\phi(i, j-1, j) = \frac{q^{j-i} - 1}{q - 1}, \quad \phi(i, i+1, \infty) = \frac{q(q^N - q^i)}{q - 1} \quad (0 \leq i < j \leq N).$$

11. Hemmeters' poset $Hem_q(N)$ $(N \geq 2)$ (q odd) [15].

Let X^+, X^- denote two copies of the graph of the dual polar space $X = C_{N-1}(q)$, $(q$ odd) (Bannai and Ito [1, p. 303]). Let Y be the bipartite graph with vertex set $X^+ \cup X^-$, where vertices $x^+ \in X^+$, $y^- \in X^-$ are adjacent in Y if and only if $x = y$ or x, y are adjacent in X. Then Y is the new distance-regular graph discovered by Hemmeter [15]. (Y has the same intersection numbers as the graph $D_N(q)$). Now let ∂ be the usual distance function in Y, and fix any vertex $u_0 \in Y$ (the choice of u_0 is irrelevant since Y is vertex transitive). Now define

$$P = Y,$$
$$u \le v \quad \text{if} \quad \partial(u_0, u) + \partial(u, v) = \partial(u_0, v) \quad (u, v \in P),$$
$$h(u) = \partial(u_0, u) \quad (u \in P),$$
$$\phi(i, j-1, j) = \frac{q^{j-i} - 1}{q - 1}, \quad \phi(i, i+1, \infty) = \frac{q^N - q^i}{q - 1} \quad (0 \le i < j \le N).$$

THEOREM 3.2. *Let P denote any of the posets in Example 3.1. Then P is uniform. Indeed*

$$(3.1) \qquad e_i^- R_{i-2} L_{i-1} L_i + L_i R_{i-1} L_i + e_i^+ L_i L_{i+1} R_i = f_i L_i \qquad (1 \le i \le N),$$

where $e_i^\mp, f_i$ are given below

Example	e_i^- $(2{\leq}i{\leq}N)$	e_i^+ $(1{\leq}i{\leq}N{-}1)$	f_i $(1{\leq}i{\leq}N)$	Case
1. $S(N,M)$	$-\frac{1}{2}$	$-\frac{1}{2}$	1	$1{\leq}i{\leq}N{-}1$
	-1		$M{-}2N{+}2$	$i{=}N$
2. $H(N,M)$	$-\frac{1}{2}$	$-\frac{1}{2}$	$M{-}1$	
3. $H^*(N,3)$		$-\frac{1}{4}$	1	$i{=}1$
	-1	$-\frac{1}{2}$	2	$i{=}2$
	$-\frac{1}{2}$	$-\frac{1}{2}$	2	$3{\leq}i$
4. $Part(2N)$	$-\frac{1}{2}$	$-\frac{1}{2}$	1	$i{\leq}N{-}2$
	-1	0	4	$i{=}N{-}1$
	-2		4	$i{=}N$
5. $S_q(N,M)$	$-q(q{+}1)^{-1}$	$-(q{+}1)^{-1}$	q^{M-i}	$1{\leq}i{\leq}N{-}1$
	-1		$\dfrac{q^{M-N+1}-q^{N-1}}{q-1}$	$i{=}N$
6. $Polar\ spaces$ $of\ rank\ N$	$-(q+1)^{-1}$	$-q(q+1)^{-1}$	$q^{e+2N+1-2i}+q^{i-1}$	
7. $A_q(N,M)$	$-q(q+1)^{-1}$	$-(q+1)^{-1}$	q^{N+M-i}	
8. $Alt_q(N)$	$-q^2(q+1)^{-1}$	$-q^{-1}(q+1)^{-1}$	q^{N-1}	
9. $Her_q(N)$	$-q^4(q^2+1)^{-1}$	$-q^{-2}(q^2+1)^{-1}$	q^{2N-1}	
10. $Quad_q(N)$	$-q^2(q+1)^{-1}$	$-q^{-1}(q+1)^{-1}$	q^N	
11. $Hem_q(N)$	$-q^2(q+1)^{-1}$	$-q^{-1}(q+1)^{-1}$	q^{N-1}	

Proof. Pick any integer i $(1 \leq i \leq N)$ and pick any $x \in P_{i-1}$, $y \in P_i$. Then $(L_i R_{i-1} L_i)_{xy}$ counts the number of ordered pairs w, $z \in P$, where $z \in P_{i-1}$, $w \in P_i$, $x \leq w$, $z \leq w$, and $z \leq y$. The x, y entries of $R_{i-2}L_{i-1}L_i$, $L_i L_{i+1} R_i$, and L_i have similar interpretations. The following table displays these counts in all cases where at least one of them is nonzero.

Example	$(R_{i-2}L_{i-1}L_i)_{xy}$	$(L_iR_{i-1}L_i)_{xy}$	$(L_iL_{i+1}R_i)_{xy}$	$(L_i)_{xy}$	Comments
$S(N,M)$	$2(i-1)$	M	$2(M-i)$	1	$i<N$
	$2(N-1)$	M	0	1	$i=N$
	2	2	2	0	$2\le i<N$
	2	2	0	0	$i=N$
$H(N,M)$	$2(i-1)$	$N(M-1)-(i-1)(M-2)$	$2(N-i)(M-1)$	1	
	2	2	2	0	$2\le i<N$
	2	1	0	0	$2\le i$
$H^*(N,3)$	0	N	$4(N-1)$	1	$i=1$
	2	$2N$	$4(N-2)$	1	$i=2$
	$2(i-1)$	$2N-i+1$	$4(N-i)$	1	$3\le i$
	4	2	0	0	$i=3$
	2	1	0	0	$3<i$
	2	4	4	0	$i=2$
	2	2	2	0	$3\le i<N$
$Part(2N)$	$2(i-1)$	$2N$	$4N-2i$	1	$i\le N-1$
	$2(N-1)$	$4N$	0	1	$i=N$
	2	2	2	0	$2\le i\le N-1$
	2	4	0	0	$i=N$
	0	0	6	0	$i=N-1,\ N\ge 4$
$S_q(N,M)$	$\frac{(q^{i-1}-1)(q+1)}{q-1}$	$\frac{q^i+q^{M-i+1}-q-1}{q-1}$	$\frac{(q^{M-i}-1)(q+1)}{q-1}$	1	$i<N$
	$\frac{(q^{N-1}-1)(q+1)}{q-1}$	$\frac{q^N+q^{M-N+1}-q-1}{q-1}$	0	1	$i=N$
	$q+1$	$q+1$	$q+1$	0	$2\le i<N$
	$q+1$	$q+1$	0	0	$i=N$
$PolarSpaces$	$\frac{(q^{i-1}-1)(q+1)}{q-1}$	$\frac{(q^{N-i+1}-1)(q^{N-i+1+e}+1)+q^i-q}{q-1}$	$\frac{(q^{N-i+e}+1)(q^{N-i}-1)(q+1)}{q-1}$	1	
	$q+1$	$q+1$	$q+1$	0	$2\le i<N$
	$q+1$	1	0	0	$2\le i$
$A_q(N,M)$	$\frac{(q^{i-1}-1)(q+1)}{q-1}$	$\frac{q^{N+M-i+1}-q^M+q^i-q}{q-1}$	$\frac{(q^{M+N-i}-q^M)(q+1)}{q-1}$	1	
	$q+1$	$q+1$	$q+1$	0	$2\le i<N$
	$q+1$	q	0	0	$2\le i$
$Alt_q(N)$	$\frac{(q^{i-1}-1)(q+1)}{q-1}$	$\frac{q^N-q^2+q^{i+1}-q^{i-1}}{q-1}$	$\frac{(q^N-q^i)(q+1)}{q-1}$	1	
	$q+1$	$q(q+1)$	$q^2(q+1)$	0	$2\le i<N$
	$(q+1)^2$	$q^2(q+1)$	0	0	$3\le i$
$Her_q(N)$	$\frac{(q^{2i-2}-1)(q^2+1)}{q^2-1}$	$\frac{q^{2N+1}-q^4+q^{2i+2}-q^{2i-1}}{q^2-1}$	$\frac{q(q^{2N}-q^{2i})(q^2+1)}{q^2-1}$	1	
	q^2+1	$q^2(q^2+1)$	$q^4(q^2+1)$	0	$2\le i<N$
	q^2+1	q^4	0	0	$2\le i$
	$(q+1)(q^2+1)$	$q^4(q+1)$	0	0	$3\le i$
$Quad_q(N)$	$\frac{(q^{i-1}-1)(q+1)}{q-1}$	$\frac{q^{N+1}-q^2+q^{i+1}-q^i}{q-1}$	$\frac{q(q^N-q^i)(q+1)}{q-1}$	1	
	$q+1$	$q(q+1)$	$q^2(q+1)$	0	$2\le i<N$
	$q+1$	q^2	0	0	$2\le i$
	$2(q+1)$	$2q^2$	0	0	$3\le i$
$Hem_q(N)$	$\frac{(q^{i-1}-1)(q+1)}{q-1}$	$\frac{q^N-q^2+q^{i+1}-q^{i-1}}{q-1}$	$\frac{(q^N-q^i)(q+1)}{q-1}$	1	
	$q+1$	$q(q+1)$	$q^2(q+1)$	0	$2\le i<N$
	$2(q+1)$	$(q+1)(2q-1)$	$q(q^2-1)$	0	$3\le i<N$
	0	$q+1$	$q(q+1)^2$	0	$3\le i<N$
	$(q+1)^2$	$q^2(q+1)$	0	0	$3\le i$

This establishes (3.1). Conditions (2) and (3) of Definition 2.1 must now be verified. But condition (2) is immediate and condition (3) holds since $\det E(r,p)$ in the following table is never 0.

$Example$	$\det E(r,\ p)\ \ (0\leq r<p\leq N)$	$Case$
$S(N,M)$	$(p-r+1)2^{r-p}$	$p<N$
	2^{r-p+1}	$p=N$
$H(N,M)$	$(p-r+1)2^{r-p}$	
$H^*(N,3)$	$(p-r+1)2^{r-p}$	
$Part(2N)$	$(p-r+1)2^{r-p}$	$p<N-1$
	2^{r-p+1}	$p=N-1$
	2^{r-p+2}	$r+1<p=N$
	1	$r+1=p=N$
$S_q(N,M)$	$\left(\dfrac{q^{p-r+1}-1}{q-1}\right)(q+1)^{r-p}$	$p<N$
	$q^{p-r-1}(q+1)^{r-p+1}$	$p=N$
$Polar\ spaces$	$\left(\dfrac{q^{p-r+1}-1}{q-1}\right)(q+1)^{r-p}$	
$A_q(N,M)$	same	
$Alt_q(N)$	same	
$Quad_q(N)$	same	
$Hem_q(N)$	same	
$Her_q(N)$	$\left(\dfrac{q^{2p-2r+2}-1}{q^2-1}\right)(q^2+1)^{r-p}$	$\square$

Recall that for any integer $r\geq 0$,

$$(a)_r = 1 \quad \text{if} \quad r=0, \quad \text{and} \quad a(a-1)\cdots(a-r+1) \quad \text{if} \quad r>0.$$

Also,

$$(a;q)_r = 1 \quad \text{if} \quad r=0, \quad \text{and} \quad (1-a)(1-aq)\cdots(1-aq^{r-1}) \quad \text{if} \quad r>0.$$

THEOREM 3.3. *Let P denote any poset in Example 3.1. Then the parameters determining the irreducible modules of the incidence algebra (by Theorem 2.5) are as follows. All $m(r,p)$ not listed are 0.*

1. $S(N,M)$.

$$x_i(r,p) \;=\; \begin{cases} (i-r)(p-i+1) & \text{if } p < N \\[2ex] (i-r)(M-r-i+1) & \text{if } p = N \end{cases} \qquad (1 \le r+1 \le i \le p \le N)$$

$$m(r,p) \;=\; \frac{(M)_r(M-2r+1)}{r!(M-r+1)} \quad \text{if } p = \min\{M-r,N\} \qquad (0 \le r \le p \le N).$$

2. $H(N,M)$.

$$x_i(r,p) \;=\; (M-1)(i-r)(p-i+1) \qquad (1 \le r+1 \le i \le p \le N)$$

$$m(r,p) \;=\; \frac{(N+1)_r(M-2)^{r+p-N}(p-r+1)}{(N-p)!(r+p-N)!(N+1)} \qquad (0 \le r \le p \le N \le r+p).$$

3. $H^*(N,3)$.

$$x_i(r,p) = \begin{cases} p & \text{if } r = 0 \text{ and } i = 1 \\[2ex] 2(i-r)(p-i+1) & \text{otherwise} \end{cases} \qquad (1 \le r+1 \le i \le p \le N)$$

$$m(r,p) = \frac{(N+1)_r(p-r+1)}{(N-p)!(r+p-N)!(N+1)} \qquad (0 \le r \le p \le N \le r+p, \ \ r+p-N \text{ even})$$

4. $Part(2N)$.

$$x_i(r,p) = \begin{cases} 2(N-r)(N-r+1) & \text{if } i = p = N \\[2ex] (i-r)(2N-r-i+1) & \text{if } 1 \le i \le N-1 \text{ and } p \ge N-1 \\[2ex] (i-r)(p-i+1) & \text{if } p < N-1 \end{cases}$$

$$(1 \le r+1 \le i \le p \le N)$$

$$m(r,p) = \frac{(2N)_r(2N-2r+1)}{r!(2N-r+1)} \quad \text{where } p = N \ (r \text{ even}) \qquad \text{or} \quad p = N-1 \ (r \text{ odd})$$

$$(0 \le r \le p \le N \le r+p).$$

5. $S_q(N, M)$.

$$x_i(r,p) = \begin{cases} \dfrac{(q^i - q^r)(q^p - q^{i-1})}{(q-1)^2 q^{i-1}} & \text{if } p < N \\[2ex] \dfrac{(q^i - q^r)(q^{M-r} - q^{i-1})}{(q-1)^2 q^{i-1}} & \text{if } p = N \end{cases} \qquad (1 \le r+1 \le i \le p \le N)$$

$$m(r,p) = \frac{(q^N; q^{-1})_r (q^N - q^{2r-1})}{(q; q)_r (q^N - q^{r-1})} \quad \text{if} \quad p = \min\{N, M-r\} \qquad (0 \le r \le p \le N).$$

6. Polar spaces of rank N.

$$x_i(r,p) = \frac{(q^{2N+e-r-p-i+1} + 1)(q^i - q^r)(q^p - q^{i-1})}{q^{i-1}(q-1)^2} \qquad (1 \le r+1 \le i \le p \le N)$$

$$m(r,p) =$$

$$\frac{(q^N; q^{-1})_r (-q^{e+N}; q^{-1})_{2r} (-q^{e-r}; q)_{N-p} (q^{-r}; q)_{N-p} (q^{r-N}; q)_{N-p} (-q^{e+N-2r+2}; q)_{N-p}}{(q; q)_r (-q^{e+N-2r+2}; q)_r (-q^{e+1-r}; q)_r (q; q)_{N-p} (-q^{e+1}; q)_{N-p} (-q^{e+N-2r+1}; q)_{N-p}}$$

$$\times \frac{(1 + q^{e-r+2N-2p})}{(q^{r-N-1}; q)_{N-p} (1 + q^{e-r})} q^{(er+2r-\binom{r+1}{2}+(N-p)(2r-N+p-1)+ep-eN)} (-1)^{p-N}$$

$$(0 \le r \le p \le N \le r+p).$$

7. $A_q(N, M)$.

$$x_i(r,p) = \frac{q^{M+N-p-r-i+1}(q^i - q^r)(q^p - q^{i-1})}{(q-1)^2} \qquad (1 \le r+1 \le i \le p \le N)$$

$$m(r,p) = \frac{(q^M; q^{-1})_{r+p-N} (q^N; q^{-1})_{r+N-p} q^{\binom{r+p-N}{2}} q^{N-p} (-1)^{r+p-N}}{(q^{N-r+1}; q^{-1})_{N-p} (q; q)_{N-p} (q; q)_{r+p-N}}$$

$$(0 \le r \le p \le N \le r+p \le M+N).$$

8. $Alt_q(N)$.

$$x_i(r,p) = \frac{q^{N-r-p}(q^i - q^r)(q^p - q^{i-1})}{(q-1)^2} \qquad (1 \le r+1 \le i \le p \le N)$$

$$m(r,p) =$$

$$\frac{(q^N; q^{-1})_{r+p-N} (q^{2N-r-p}; q^{-1})_{N-p} (q^{N-r+1} - q^{N-p}) q^{(\frac{r+p-N}{2})(\frac{r+p-N-2}{2})} (-1)^{\frac{r+p-N}{2}}}{(q^2; q^2)_{\frac{r+p-N}{2}} (q; q)_{N-p} (q^{N-r+1} - 1)}$$

$$(0 \le r \le p \le N \le r+p, \quad r+p-N \text{ even}).$$

208

9. $Her_q(N)$.

$$x_i(r,p) = \frac{q^{2N-2p-2r+1}(q^{2i} - q^{2r})(q^{2p} - q^{2i-2})}{(q^2 - 1)^2} \qquad (1 \le r+1 \le i \le p \le N)$$

$$m(r,p) =$$

$$\frac{(q^{2N};q^{-2})_{r+p-N}(q^{4N-2r-2p};q^{-2})_{N-p}(q^{2N-2r+2} - q^{2N-2p})(-q)^{\binom{r+p-N}{2}}(-1)^{r+p-N}}{(-q;-q)_{r+p-N}(q^2;q^2)_{N-p}(q^{2N-2r+2} - 1)}$$

$$(0 \le r \le p \le N \le r+p).$$

10. $Quad_q(N)$.

$$x_i(r,p) = \frac{q^{N-p-r+1}(q^i - q^r)(q^p - q^{i-1})}{(q - 1)^2} \qquad (1 \le r+1 \le i \le p \le N)$$

$$m(r,p) = \frac{(q^N;q^{-1})_{r+p-N}(q^{2N-r-p};q^{-1})_{N-p}(q^{N-r+1} - q^{N-p})(-1)^{r+p-N}}{(q^{-2};q^{-2})_{[\frac{r+p-N}{2}]}(q;q)_{N-p}(q^{N-r+1} - 1)}$$

$$(0 \le r \le p \le N \le r+p).$$

11. $Hem_q(N)$. Same as $Alt_q(N)$.

Proof. The $x_i(r,p)$ constants are found by solving the linear system in (1) of Definition 2.4. Since $E(r,p)$ is tri-diagonal, this amounts to solving a 3-term linear recurrence equation. To get the $m(r,p)$ constants, we first find the $c(r,p)$ constants using the Note after Definition 2.3, and then apply (2) of Definition 2.4 and induction. We note that much of this data has been found by other authors using different methods. See Dunkl [14] for $S_q(N,M)$ and $A_q(N,M)$, and Stanton [29], [30], [31] for the polar spaces, $Alt_q(N)$, $Her_q(N)$, and $Quad_q(N)$. $\square$

4. Remarks. In this section we give some directions for future research. Let X denote a d-class symmetric association scheme with Bose Mesner algebra M (defined in Bannai and Ito [1, p. 56]), and let P denote a uniform poset with rank N and incidence algebra T. Call X and P *compatible* if X can be identified with the upper fiber P_N of P so that M is a subalgebra of $E_N^* T E_N^*$. Note this implies $d \le N$ by Corollary 2.7. Each uniform poset in Example 3.1 is compatible with at least one P- and Q-polynomial association scheme with $d \ge 2$. Denoting by A the first associate matrix of the scheme, we have, using the notation of Bannai and Ito [1, p. 301]:

Poset	Compatible d – class scheme	Comments
1. $S(N,M)$	Johnson scheme $J(N,M)$ $d=\min\{N,M-N\}$	$A = R_{N-1}L_N - NE_N^*$
2. $H(N,M)$	Hamming scheme $H(N,M-1)$ $d=N$	$A = R_{N-1}L_N - NE_N^*$
2a. $H(N,3)$	$\frac{1}{2}H(N+1,2)$ $d=[\frac{N+1}{2}]$	$A = \frac{1}{4}R_{N-1}R_{N-2}L_{N-1}L_N -$ $(N-2)R_{N-1}L_N + \frac{N(N-3)}{2}E_N^*$
3. $H^*(N,3)$	Antip. quot. of $H(N,2)$ $d=[N/2]$	$A = R_{N-1}L_N - NE_N^*$ $(N \geq 3)$
4. $Part(2N)$	Antip. quot. of $J(N,2N)$ $d=[N/2]$	$A = \frac{1}{2}R_{N-1}L_N - NE_N^*$
5. $S_q(N,M)$	q-Johnson scheme $J_q(N,M)$ $d=\min\{N,M-N\}$	$A = R_{N-1}L_N - (\frac{q^N-1}{q-1})E_N^*$
6. $Rank\ N\ polarspaces$	schemes of dual polar spaces $d=N$	$A = R_{N-1}L_N - (\frac{q^N-1}{q-1})E_N^*$
6a. $C_N(q)$ (q odd)	Ustimenko's scheme [16] $d=[\frac{N+1}{2}]$	$A = (q+1)^{-2}R_{N-1}R_{N-2}L_{N-1}L_N -$ $\frac{q(q^{N-2}-1)}{q-1}R_{N-1}L_N +$ $(\frac{q^N-1}{q-1})(\frac{q^N-q}{q^2-1} - 1)E_N^*$
6b. $B_N(q)$	$\frac{1}{2}D_{N+1}(q)$ $d=[\frac{N+1}{2}]$	same as 6a.
7. $A_q(N,M)$	bilin. forms scheme $H_q(N,M)$ $d=\min\{N,M\}$	$A = R_{N-1}L_N - (\frac{q^N-1}{q-1})E_N^*$
8. $Alt_q(N)$	alt. forms scheme Alt $d=[N/2]$	$A = (q+1)^{-1}$ $\times (R_{N-1}L_N - (\frac{q^N-1}{q-1})E_N^*)$
9. $Her_q(N)$	Herm. forms scheme Her $d=N$	$(q+1)A^2 + 2A - q(q-1)R_{N-1}L_N$ $= (\frac{q^{2N}-1}{q+1})E_N^*$
10. $Quad_q(N)$	quad. forms scheme $Quad$ $d=[\frac{N+1}{2}]$	no simple relationship
11. $Hem_q(N)$	$Quad$ $d=[N/2]$	same as 8.

We note $A \in E_N^* T E_N^*$ for Examples 9, 10. For Example 9, this follows since T is the full commuting algebra of $\mathrm{Aut}(P)$, which contains A (see [30, Theorem 4.10]). For Example 10, this follows from the averaging technique of Stanton [31, p.304]. Call a symmetric association scheme *geometric* if it is compatible with some uniform poset. Then the above information shows that most of the known P- and Q-polynomial schemes with $d \geq 7$ are geometric. Indeed, the catalog in [7, Section 8.5] shows that apart from the ordinary cycles, the known P- and Q-polynomial schemes with $d \geq 7$ that are possibly not geometric are (i) the Doob schemes [12] (with the same parameters as the Hamming schemes $H(d,4)$), and (ii) the Hemmeter schemes [15] (with the same parameters as $D_d(q)$, q odd), and (iii) the antipodal quotient of the half cube $\frac{1}{2}H(n,2)$, (with n even).

Problem 1. Determine if the examples (i), (ii), (iii) above are geometric. If not, can the definition of "geometric" be slightly generalized so that they are?

Conjecture 2. All geometric association schemes are P- and Q-polynomial.

Conjecture 3. For sufficiently large N, the only uniform ϕ-regular semi-lattices of rank N are those in 1, 2, 5, 6, 7 of Example 3.1.

Problem 4. Find a simple axiom system for the *points* P_N and *lines* P_{N-1} (and if necessary, *planes* P_{N-2}) that characterizes the 11 examples in Section 3 (or all uniform posets). See Cameron [8] for Example 6 and Sprague [26], [27], [28] for Examples 1, 2, 5, 7 .

Acknowledgements. The author would like to thank Tatsuro Ito, Arnold Neumaier and Dennis Stanton for helpful discussions on the subject of this paper.

REFERENCES

[1]   E. BANNAI, T. *Ito, Algebraic combinatorics I: Association Schemes*, Benjamin-Cummings Lecture Note 58. New York, 1984.

[2]   R. C. BOSE, *Strongly regular graphs, partial geometries and partially balanced designs*, Pacific J. Math. 13 (1963), 389-419.

[3]   R. C. BOSE, W. G. BRIDGES, M. S. SHRIKHANDE, *A characterization of partial geometric designs*, Discrete Math. 16 (1976), 1-7.

[4]   R. C. BOSE, W. G. BRIDGES, M. S. SHRIKHANDE, *Partial geometric designs and two-class partially balanced designs*, Discrete Math. 21 (1978), 97-101.

[5]   R. C. BOSE, R. MISKIMINS, *Partial geometric spaces of m dimensions*, Algebraic methods in graph theory, Szeged (1978), 37-45.

[6]   R. C. BOSE, S. S. SHRIKHANDE, N. M. SINGHI, *Edge regular multigraphs and partial geometric designs*, Proceedings of the International Colloquium on Combinatorial Theory, Acad. Lincei, Rome (1973), 49-81.

[7]   A. BROUWER, A. COHEN, A. NEUMAIER, *Distance-regular graphs*, Springer, Berlin, 1988. preprint.

[8]   P. J. CAMERON, *Dual polar spaces*, Geom. Dedicata 12 (1982), 75-85.

[9]   P. DELSARTE, *Association schemes and t-designs in regular semilattices*, J. Combin. Theory Ser. A 20 (1976), 230-243.

[10]   P. DELSARTE, *Bilinear forms over a finite field with applications to coding theory*, J. Combin. Theory Ser. A 25 (1978), 226-241.

[11]   P. DELSARTE, J. GOETHALS, *Alternating bilinear forms over $GF(q)$*, J. Combin. Theory Ser. A 25 (1978), 26-50.

[12]   M. DOOB, *On graph products and association schemes*, Utilitas Math. 1 (1972), 291-302.

[13] C. DUNKL, *An addition theorem for Hahn polynomials: the spherical functions*, SIAM J. Math. Anal. 9 (1978), 627-637.

[14] C. DUNKL, *An addition theorem for some q-Hahn polynomials*, Monatsh. Math. 85 (1977), 5-37.

[15] J. HEMMETER, *A new family of distance-regular graphs*, preprint.

[16] A. A. IVANOV, M. E. MUZICHUK, V. A. USTIMENKO, *On a new family of (P and Q)-polynomial schemes*, preprint.

[17] R. LASKAR, Proc. 10th Southern Conference on Combinatorics, Graph Theory and Computing, Vol. 2 (Congress Numeratium XXIV) (1979), 645-650.

[18] R. LASKAR, J. DUNBAR, *Partial geometry of dimension three*, J. Combin. Theory Ser. A 24 (1978), 187-201.

[19] R. LASKAR AND A. SPRAGUE, *A characterization of partial geometric lattices of rank 4*, Enumeration and Design, (Jackson and Vanstone, eds), Academic Press, Toronto (1984), 215-224.

[20] R. LIEBLER AND A. MEYEROWITZ, *Partial geometric lattices II: Association schemes*, J. Statist. Plann. Inference 18 (1988), 161-176.

[21] A. MEYEROWITZ, *Partial geometric lattices with generalized quadrangles as planes*, Algebras Groups Geom. 2 (1985), 436-454.

[22] A. MEYEROWITZ, R. MISKIMINS, *Partial geometric lattices I. Regularity conditions*, J. Statist. Plann. Inference 17 (1987), 21-50.

[23] A. NEUMAIER, *Distance matrices and n-dimensional designs*, European J. Combin. 2 (1981), 165-172.

[24] A. NEUMAIER, *Quasi-residual 2-designs, $1\frac{1}{2}$-designs, and strongly regular multigraphs*, Geom. Dedicata 12 (1982), 351-366.

[25] A. NEUMAIER, *Regular cliques in graphs and special $1\frac{1}{2}$-designs, Finite geometries and designs*, Proc. Second Isle of Thorns Conference, London Math. Soc. Lecture Notes Ser. 49 (P. J. Cameron, J. W. Hirschfield, D. R. Hughes, eds.), Cambridge University Press, Cambridge, 1981.

[26] A. P. SPRAGUE, *A characterization of 3-nets*, J. Combin. Theory Ser. A 27 (1979), 223-253.

[27] A. P. SPRAGUE, *Pasch's axiom and projective spaces*, Discrete Math. 33 (1981), 79-87.

[28] A. P. SPRAGUE, *Incidence structures whose planes are nets*, European J. Combin. 2 (1981), 193-204.

[29] D. STANTON, *Some q-Krawtchouk polynomials on Chevalley groups*, Amer. J. Math. 102 (4) (1980), 625-662.

[30] D. STANTON, *Three addition theorems for some q-Krawtchouk polynomials*, Geom. Dedicata 10 (1981), 403-425.

[31] D. STANTON, *A partially ordered set and q-Krawtchouk polynomials*, J. Combin. Theory Ser. A 30 (1981), 276-284.

[32] D. STANTON, *Orthogonal polynomials and Chevalley groups*, Special Functions: Group theoretical aspects and applications, (Askey et. al., eds) (1984), 87-128.

[33] D. STANTON, *Harmonics on posets*, J. Combin. Theory Ser. A 40 (1985), 136-149.

[34] V. A. USTIMENKO, *On some properties of the geometry of the Chevalley groups and their generalizations*, preprint, 1988.

SOME RECENT RESULTS ON SIGNED GRAPHS
WITH LEAST EIGENVALUES ≥ -2

G.R. VIJAYAKUMAR† AND N.M. SINGHI‡

Abstract. A survey of some results concerning the class of sigraphs represented by root–systems D_n, $n \in N$ and E_8 is given and some unsolved problems are described.

1. Introduction. A sigraph S is a pair (X, ϕ) where X is a finite set (called the *set of vertices* and denoted by $V(S)$)) and $\phi : X \times X \longrightarrow \{-1, 0, 1\}$ satisfying for all x, y in X, $\phi(x, y) = \phi(y, x)$ and $\phi(x, x) = 0$(ϕ is called the *edge of function*). If for any x, y in $X, \phi(x, y) \neq 0$, we say that the set $\{x, y\}$ is an *edge* of S and x and y are *adjacent* in S.

Let $S = (X, \phi)$ be a sigraph and X_1, a subset of X. Let Φ_1 be the restriction of ϕ to $X_1 \times X_1$. Then (X_1, ϕ_1) is said to be the *induced subgraph* of S on X_1 and it is denoted by $S[X_1]$. If a sigraph R is an induced subgraph of S, sometimes we will write $R \subseteq S$.

A sigraph S is said to be *minimal forbidden* for a family of sigraphs $\mathcal{F}$, if S is not in $\mathcal{F}$ but every proper induced subgraph of S is in $\mathcal{F}$.

For various graph theoritic definitions not given and notations not explained in this paper we refer to [H1].

Let $\mathbf{R}^\infty$ be the countably infinite dimensional Euclidean space with usual inner product $\langle \cdot, \cdot \rangle$ and W, a subset of $\mathbf{R}^\infty$. We say that W *represents* a sigraph $S = (X, \phi)$ if there is a map $\Psi : X \longrightarrow W$ such that for all x, y in X,

$$\langle \Psi(x), \Psi(y) \rangle = \begin{cases} \phi(x, y), & \text{if} \quad x \neq y \\ 2 & \text{if} \quad x = y. \end{cases}$$

Ψ is called a *representation* of S in W and S is said to be *represented* by W.

Let $R(W)$ denote the family of sigraphs represented by W and $\mathcal{M}(W)$, the class of minimal forbidden sigraphs for $R(W)$. Since $R(W)$ is *hereditary* (i.e. $S \in R(W)$ and $S^1 \subset S \Rightarrow S^1 \in R(W)$), it can be completely described if all of its minimal forbidden sigraphs are known.

Let $\mathcal{B} = \{e_i | i = 1, 2, \dots \}$ be an orthonormal basis for $\mathbf{R}^\infty$.

Define $D_\infty = \{\pm e_i \pm e_j | i \neq j; i, j = 1, 2, \dots \}$; for any $n \in N$,

$$D_n = \left\{ \pm e_i \pm e_j \,\middle|\, i \neq j; i, j = 1, 2, \dots n \right\}.$$

---

†School of Mathematics, Tata Institute of Fundamental Research, Colaba, Bombay 400 005

‡School of Mathematics, Tata Institute of Fundamental Research, Colaba, Bombay 400 005. The paper was written when the author was visiting Institute for Mathematics and its Applications, U.S.A.

and

$$E_8 = \left\{ \pm\sqrt{2}\, e_i \big| i = 1, \ldots 8 \right\} \cup \left\{ \frac{1}{\sqrt{2}} \left(\pm e_i + e_j \pm e_k \pm e_\ell \right) \big| i, j, k, \ell \in S(3,4,8) \right\}$$

where $S(3,4,8)$ is the set of blocks of the unique $3-(8,4,1)$–design with $\{1,2,\ldots 8\}$ as base set.

The aim of this paper is to survey some old and recent results concerning the sigraphs in $\mathcal{R}(\mathbf{R}^\infty)$, which include the following:

    (i) Classification of the sigraphs in $\mathcal{R}(\mathbf{R}^\infty)$.

    (ii) Characterizing the graphs and sigraphs of the subclass $\mathcal{R}(D_\infty)$.

    (iii) Description of the graphs in $\mathcal{M}(\mathbf{R}^\infty)$.

Finally we will discuss some unsolved problems, concerning $\mathcal{M}(E_8)$ and $\mathcal{M}(\mathbf{R}^\infty)$.

2. Some Classical Results. We first quote an old result of Hoffman and Raychaudhuri [HR]

THEOREM 2.1. *G is regular connected graph with all eigenvalues ≥ -2 and degree ≥ 13. Then either G is a linegraph or G is cocktail party graph.*

A cocktail party graph is a graph on $2n$ vertices obtained from the complete graph on these by deleting edges in a matching.

A.J. Hoffman later proved in [H2] the following

THEOREM 2.2. *A connected graph with all eigenvalues ≥ -2 is either a generalized line graph or its number of vertices ≤ 36. (Generalized line graphs are precisely the graphs represented by D_∞; but Hoffman defined them differently by using line graphs and Cock–tail party graphs; Cameron, Goethals, Seidel and Shult observed the equivalence of these two definitions; see Theorem 4.2 of [CGSS].)*

THEOREM 2.3. *Let G be a graph and $\alpha(G)$, its least eigenvalue. Then $\alpha(G) \geq -2$ if and only if G is represented by $\mathbf{R}^\infty$.*

Cameron, Goethals, Seidel and Shult first observed this theorem. They improved the Theorem 2.2 to the following one (our terminology is different from that they used in [CGSS].):

THEOREM 2.4. *Let S be a connected sigraph and $\lambda(S)$, its least eigenvalue. Then the following are equivalent:*

(2.3.1) $\lambda(S) \geq -2$.

(2.3.2)   *S is represented by $\mathbf{R}^\infty$.*

(2.3.3)   *S is represented by D_∞ or E_8.*

The equivalence of (2.3.2) and (2.3.3) is also a particular case of Witt's Theorem (See [W].).

Using this theorem, they also improved some earlier theorems including Theorem 2.1 and gave simpler proofs. We mention a few (see also [S]):

THEOREM 2.4. *If G is a regular connected graph with least eigenvalue -2, then one of the following holds:*

(2.4.1)   *G is a line–graph.*

(2.4.2)   *G is a cock–tail party graph.*

(2.4.3)   *G is represented by E_8.*

THEOREM 2.5. *If G is a connected strongly regular graph with least eigenvalue -2, then either*

(2.5.1)   *$G = L(K_n)$, $L(K_{n,n})$ or $CP(n)$; or*

(2.5.2)   *G is represented by E_8*

3. Some New Results. Using Theorem 2.3, attempts were made to characterize some hereditary subclasses of $\mathbf{R}(\mathbf{R}^\infty)$, in terms of minimal forbidden sigraphs. A.J. Hoffman asked the following question in [H3]: What are the minimal forbidden graphs of the family of graphs represented by D_∞?

In [RSV] these graphs were found by using Hoffman's definition of generalized line graphs. In [CDS], by the second definition and partly by the computer search, this class was found. These graphs are 31 in number and order of any such graph is either 5 or 6.

Van Rooij and Wilf gave the following characterization for line graphs which has become a classical result by now.

THEOREM 3.1. *A graph G is a line graph if and only if it satisfies the following conditions:*

(3.1.1)   *$K(1,3)$ is not an induced sigraph of G.*

(3.1.2)   *If an induced subgraph H of G is $K(1,1,2)$ then one of the triangles of H is even in G (See [H1] for proof.)*

Motivated by this an analogous characterization has been given for $R(D_\infty)$ in [CV]. We need some definitions for giving that characterization here.

Two sigraphs $S_i = (X_i, \phi_i), i = 1, 2$ are said to be *switching equivalent* if there are functions $f : X_1 \longrightarrow X_2$ and $\eta : X_1 \longrightarrow \{-1, 1\}$ such that f is a bijection and for all s, y in X_1.

$$\eta(x)\phi_1(x, y)\eta(y) = \phi_2(f(x), f(y)).$$

A sigraph is said to be *positive* if it is switching equivalent to a graph; otherwise it is said to be *negative.*

Let S be a sigraph and T, a *triangle* in S, i.e., its underlying graph is K_3. T is said to be *odd* in S if there is a vertex a in $V(S)$ which is adjacent to odd number of vertices in $V(T)$; otherwise it is said to be *even* in S.

215

Definition 3.2. Let $S = (X, \phi)$ be a sigraph. A function $* : X \longrightarrow X$--for any $x \in X$, we will denote its image by x^*- is said to be a *symmetry* of S if it has the following properties:

(3.2.1)   For all $x \in X$, $N(x) = N(x^*)$ and $x^{**} = x$.

(3.2.2)   If an induced subgraph R is switching equivalent to $K(1,3)$ then there exist distinct vertices $a, b \in V(R)$ such that $a^* = b$.

(3.2.3) If there are vertices a, b, c in X such that $S[a, a^*, b, c]$ is switching equivalent to $K(2,2)$, then $b^* = c$.

(3.2.4)   If there are vertices a, b, x, y in X such that $S[a, b, x, y]$ is switching equivalent to $K(1,1,2)$ where $\phi(x, y) = 0$, then one of the following holds:

    (a) $x^* = y$

    (b) $S[a, b, x^*]$ is even; it is positive only when $x^* = x$.

    (c) $S[a, b, y^*]$ is even; it is positive only when $y^* = y$.

Note that $*$ is an automorphism of the underlying graph.

Now we can state the theorem which gives the characterization of $R(D_\infty)$ (see[CS])

THEOREM 3.3. *A sigraph $S = (X, \phi)$ has a representation in D_∞ if and only if it satisfies the following:*

(3.3.1)   *S admits a symmetry $*$ in it.*

(3.3.2)   *Any negative triangle T in S is even and whenever two vertices of T are adjacent to a vertex of $V(S) - V(T)$, then these three form a positive triangle..*

4. Root System E_8. The following property of E_8 system can be easily seen (see [VRS])

PROPOSITION 4.1. *Let $A_1, A_2 \subset E_8$ be two sets of eight mutually orthogonal vectors, each. Then there exists an automorphism f of E_8 such that $f(A_1) = A_2$.*

Using this Proposition 4.1, the Theorem 2.3 and by analyzing the properties of the graphs in $\mathcal{M}(D_\infty)$, a description of the graphs in $\mathcal{M}(\mathbf{R}^\infty)$, has been given in [VRS].

As it involves a lot of technical definitions, we are not giving it here; Any graph in $\mathcal{M}(\mathbf{R}^\infty)$ has at most 10 vertices. One such graph is given below

Figure 1.

In [V] it has been proved that 10 is also the upper bound for $|V(S)|$, where S is any sigraph in $\mathcal{M}(\mathbf{R}^\infty)$. Using this, the following application to quadratic forms is given there.

THEOREM 4.2. *Let*

$$Q(\tilde{x}) = \sum_{i=1}^{n} x_i^2 + \sum_{1 \le i < j \le n} \epsilon_{ij} x_i \, x_j, \quad \epsilon_{ij} \in \mathbf{Z},$$

$\tilde{x} = (x_1, x_2, \ldots x_n) \in \mathbf{R}^n$, *be a quadratic form which is not positive semidefinite. Then there exists $\tilde{x}_0 \in \mathbf{R}^n$ with atmost 10 non zero coordinates such that $Q(\tilde{x}_0) < 0$.*

5. Further Problems. (1) So far, except for Proposition 4.1, little have been found out about E_8 system. Though it is finite it seems to be difficult to get a characterization of $R(E_8)$. In this regard we mention the following Conjecture:

Any minimal forbidden sigraph for E_8 system has atmost 9 vertices.

(2) The graphs in $\mathcal{M}(\mathbf{R}^\infty)$ have been described in [VRS]. Is there an analogue for the whole family $\mathcal{M}(\mathbf{R}^\infty)$ itself?

Finally, one can consider analogous more general question related to the multigraphs with eigenvalues $-k$, k an integer ≥ 2, which will have many useful implications for the theory of designs etc.

In a multigraph the function ϕ can take any nonnegative integral value, instead of $0, 1$. Such a multigraph (x, ϕ) is said to be k–represented by a set $W \subseteq \mathbf{R}^\infty$ iff there is a map $\Psi : X \longrightarrow W$ such that for all x, y in X, $\Psi(x, y) = \phi(x, y)$ if $x \ne y$ and $\psi(x, y) = k$ if $x = y$. In this paper we have discussed only the case $k = 2$.

Conjecture. For any k, if n is sufficiently large compared to k then any connected multigraph with n vertices and with a eigenvalues $\ge -k$ is represented by the set $D_n^k = \{x_1 e_1 + \cdots + x_n e_n \,|\, x_i$'s integers, $x_1^2 + x_2^2 + \cdots + x_n^2 = k\}$

REFERENCES

[CDS] D. CVETKOVIC, M. DOOB AND S. SIMIC, *Generalized line graphs*, Journal of Graph Theory, 5 (1981), pp. 385–399.

[CV] P.D. CHAWATHE AND G.R. VIJAYAKUMAR, *Signed graphs represented by D_∞*, submitted.

[CGSS] P.J. CAMERON, J.M. GOETHALS, J.J. SEIDEL AND E.E. SHULT, *Line graphs, root systems and elliptic geometry*, J. Alg., 43 (1976), pp. 305–327.

[H1] F. HARARY, *"Graph Theory"*, Addison–Wesley, Reading Mass, 1972.

[H2]   A.J. HOFFMAN, $-1 - \sqrt{2}$? in "Combinatorial Structures and their Applications", R. Guy. Ed. Gordon and Breech, New York (1970) 173–176.

[H3]   A.J. HOFFMAN, On graphs whose least eigenvalue exceeds $-1 - \sqrt{2}$, J. Linear Algebra and its Applications, 16 (1977).

[HR]   A.J. HOFFMAN AND D.K. RAY CHAUDHURI, On a spectral characterization of regular line graphs, unpublished, manuscript (1965).

[RSV]   S.B. RAO, N.M. SINGHI AND K.S. VIJAYAN, the minimal forbidden graphs for generalized line graphs, "Proceedings of International Symposium in Combinatorics, Calcutta 1980, Ed. S.B. Rao, Springer Verlag lecture notes No. 885, 459–472.

[RW]   A. VAN ROOIJ AND H. WILF, The interchange graph of a finite graph, Acta. Math. Acad. Scie. Hungar., 16 (1965), pp. 263–269.

[S]   J.J. SEIDEL, Strongly regular graphs with $(-1, 1, 0)$-adjacency matrix having eigenvalue 3, Linear Algebra Appl. 1 (1968), pp. 281–298.

[VI]   G.R. VIJAYAKUMAR, Signed graphs represented by D_∞, Europ. J. Comb, 8 (1987), pp. 103–112.

[VRS]   VIJAYAKUMAR, S.B. RAO AND N.M. SINGHI, Graphs with eigenvalues at least -2, Linear Algebra and its Applications, 46 (1982), pp. 27–42.

[W]   E. WITT, Spiegelungsgruppan and Auf zahlung halbein facher Leicher Ringe, Abh. Math. Sem. Hamburg, 14 (1941), pp. 289–337.

SELF-ORTHOGONAL CODES
AND THE TOPOLOGY OF SPINOR GROUPS

JAY A. WOOD*

Abstract. Maximal doubly-even self-orthogonal binary linear codes correspond to the maximal elementary abelian 2-groups of the spinor group $\mathrm{Spin}(n)$. We will describe the correspondence and discuss various techniques from the algebraic topology of $\mathrm{Spin}(n)$ which may be useful in studying self-orthogonal codes. In particular, Quillen's results in equivariant cohomology theory coupled with some Morse theory may allow one to address certain questions on the minimum weight of doubly-even self-orthogonal codes.

Key words. self-orthogonal codes, spinor groups, flat connections, equivariant cohomology, Morse theory

AMS(MOS) subject classifications. Primary 94B05, 57R70; Secondary 11T71, 22E40, 53C05, 22E70, 55R40, 57T10

1. Introduction. The purpose of this paper is to offer a new way to view the self-orthogonal binary linear codes—as certain abelian 2-subgroups of the spinor groups $\mathrm{Spin}(n)$—and then to propose some ideas on how the topology of $\mathrm{Spin}(n)$ may be able to answer questions on the minimum weights of self-orthogonal codes.

The reader should be warned of the speculative nature of trying to apply algebraic topology to coding theory. One may only be translating one intractable problem into another intractable problem. Nevertheless, viewing the self-orthogonal codes as subgroups of $\mathrm{Spin}(n)$ offers a fresh perspective on the codes, and the new ideas are interesting and worth a try. The other direction may also be useful: using codes to say something about the topology of $\mathrm{Spin}(n)$.

An outline of the contents of the paper follows. My original interest was in understanding the gauge equivalence classes of flat connections on principal G-bundles over a compact manifold X, where G is a compact Lie group. Such objects arise in the study of the ends of Yang-Mills moduli spaces. Gauge equivalence classes of flat connections are parameterized by homomorphisms from the fundamental group $\pi_1(X)$ of the base manifold X into the structure group G of the bundle, up to conjugation in G, i.e., by the space

$$\mathcal{F} = \mathrm{Hom}(\pi_1(X), G)/\mathrm{Ad}(G),$$

where $\mathrm{Ad}(G)$ indicates G acting via the adjoint representation (conjugation). In the special case where $\pi_1(X)$ is abelian, considering only the image subgroups appearing in $\mathcal{F}$ leads one to the set of conjugacy classes of maximal abelian subgroups of G,

*Department of Mathematics, Bowdoin College, Brunswick, ME, 04011. This research was supported in part by grants from the Faculty Research Committee of Bowdoin College, by NSA Grant Number MDA904-88-H-2026, and by the Institute for Mathematics and its Applications with funds provided by the National Science Foundation. The United States Government is authorized to reproduce and distribute reprints notwithstanding any copyright notation hereon. E-mail: jwood@bowdoin.bitnet.

where G is a compact Lie group. In Section 2 we discuss these issues in more detail and outline what happens when $G = \mathrm{SU}(n)$, $\mathrm{Sp}(n)$, or $\mathrm{SO}(n)$.

In Section 3 we discuss $G = \mathrm{Spin}(n)$, the universal double covering group of $\mathrm{SO}(n)$. $\mathrm{Spin}(n)$ is described concretely in terms of the Clifford algebra. The maximal abelian subgroups of $\mathrm{Spin}(n)$ have a continuous piece and a discrete piece, and the discrete piece corresponds to a self-orthogonal code. The basic idea is this: View the diagonal matrices in $\mathrm{SO}(n)$ as a binary vector space V. *Question*: When does a subspace W (i.e., a matrix subgroup) of V lift to an abelian subgroup of $\mathrm{Spin}(n)$? *Answer*: Precisely when W is a self-orthogonal code. Moreover, the doubly-even self-orthogonal codes lift to the elementary abelian 2-subgroups of $\mathrm{Spin}(n)$.

The elementary abelian 2-subgroups of $\mathrm{Spin}(n)$ (call them 2-*tori*) are especially important in understanding the $\mathbf{Z}/2$-topology of $\mathrm{Spin}(n)$. After reviewing some topological background in Section 4, we summarize in Section 5 some results of Borel on how the 2-tori in $\mathrm{Spin}(n)$ reflect 2-torsion in the cohomology of $\mathrm{Spin}(n)$ and its classifying space. For example, the existence of inequivalent maximal doubly-even self-orthogonal codes implies the presence of 2-torsion in the cohomology of $\mathrm{Spin}(n)$.

The interaction between 2-tori and cohomology was greatly extended by Quillen in his study of equivariant cohomology theory. In this case, $\mathrm{Spin}(n)$ acts on some space X. Among the results of Quillen which are summarized in Section 6 is the one-to-one correspondence between the minimal prime ideals of the equivariant cohomology ring $H^*_{\mathrm{Spin}(n)}(X; \mathbf{Z}/2)$ and the conjugacy classes of maximal 2-tori in $\mathrm{Spin}(n)$ which have fixed points when acting on X. Already when X is a point (so every 2-torus has a fixed point), the conjugacy classes of maximal 2-tori, i.e., the equivalence classes of maximal doubly-even self-orthogonal codes, are in one-to-one correspondence with the minimal prime ideals of $H^*_{\mathrm{Spin}(n)}(\mathrm{point}; \mathbf{Z}/2) \cong H^*(B\mathrm{Spin}(n); \mathbf{Z}/2)$.

In order to address weight-theoretic questions of codes, one studies the function

$$f = -\mathrm{trace} \circ \pi : \mathrm{Spin}(n) \to \mathbf{R},$$

where π is the double covering map $\pi : \mathrm{Spin}(n) \to \mathrm{SO}(n)$. In Section 7 we view f as a Morse function on $\mathrm{Spin}(n)$ and examine the structure of its critical points.

Finally, in Section 8 we couple Quillen's equivariant cohomology theory for $\mathrm{Spin}(n)$ acting on some space X with the Morse theory of the function f, by letting $X = X_{\alpha,\beta} = \{x \in \mathrm{Spin}(n) \mid \alpha < f(x) < \beta\}$. By varying the values of α and β, the 2-tori which have fixed points on $X_{\alpha,\beta}$ (and hence contribute prime ideals to $H^*_{\mathrm{Spin}(n)}(X_{\alpha,\beta})$) will change. Thus it might be possible to detect the existence of doubly-even self-orthogonal codes of high minimum weight via the prime ideal structure of the equivariant cohomology rings $H^*_{\mathrm{Spin}(n)}(X_{\alpha,\beta})$.

Acknowledgements. We thank Haynes Miller for hed interest in this work and for suggesting the use of Morse filtrations to study weight problems. Thanks go to the Institute for Mathematics and its Applications for its hospitality during the Workshops on Coding Theory and Design Theory, June 1988. Lastly, we thank the referee for some helpful suggestions.

2. Maximal abelian subgroups of compact connected Lie groups. The correspondence between self-orthogonal codes and abelian subgroups of $\mathrm{Spin}(n)$ originated in studying the conjugacy classes of maximal abelian subgroups of compact Lie groups. This in turn stemmed from studying the gauge equivalence classes of flat connections on principal bundles in Yang-Mills theory. This section describes briefly this chain of ideas.

Let G be a compact, simple Lie group. A Lie group is *simple* if it has no proper connected normal subgroups of positive dimension. A compact, simple Lie group G need not be simple as an abstract group; however, $G/\mathrm{center}(G)$ is simple in both senses.

In Simon Donaldson's applications of Yang-Mills theory to the study of the topology of smooth 4-manifolds (see [11] and [13]), the ends of the moduli spaces of self-dual connections on a principal bundle play an important role. If the principal bundle is $P \to X$ with structure group G, then the ends of the moduli space turn out to be parameterized by the space of flat connections on P, modulo gauge equivalence.

By making use of the holonomy subgroups associated to the flat connections (see [15, Chapter II]), one can show that the space of flat connections on P, modulo gauge equivalence, is equal to

$$\mathcal{F} = \mathrm{Hom}(\pi_1(X), G)/\mathrm{Ad}(G),$$

the space of group homomorphisms from the fundamental group $\pi_1(X)$ of X to the structure group G of the bundle, modulo the adjoint action $\mathrm{Ad}(G)$ of G (G acting by conjugation). For more details, see [28, §2].

To simplify matters somewhat, we assume that $\pi_1(X)$ is abelian, and we consider only the image subgroups of the homomorphisms appearing in $\mathcal{F}$. This leads one to study the space of conjugacy classes of abelian subgroups of G, where G is a compact, simple Lie group. The most important are the conjugacy classes of maximal abelian subgroups of G.

The compact, simple Lie groups up to local isomorphism were classified by Élie Cartan. There are four infinite families of examples:

(A_n) $\mathrm{SU}(n+1)$: the $(n+1) \times (n+1)$ complex unitary matrices of determinant 1, $n \geq 1$,

(B_n) $\mathrm{SO}(2n+1)$: the $(2n+1) \times (2n+1)$ real orthogonal matrices of determinant 1, $n \geq 2$,

(C_n) $\mathrm{Sp}(n)$: the $n \times n$ quaternionic unitary matrices, $n \geq 3$,

(D_n) $\mathrm{SO}(2n)$: the $2n \times 2n$ real orthogonal matrices of determinant 1, $n \geq 4$,

and five exceptional groups: G_2, F_4, E_6, E_7, and E_8. See, for example, [14, p. 516]. We discuss the conjugacy classes of maximal abelian subgroups in G, for G equaling $\mathrm{SU}(n)$, $\mathrm{Sp}(n)$ or $\mathrm{SO}(n)$. We will not discuss the exceptional groups.

When G equals $\mathrm{SU}(n)$ or $\mathrm{Sp}(n)$, theorems in linear algebra on simultaneous diagonalization of commuting unitary operators imply that every abelian subgroup of G is conjugate to a subgroup of diagonal matrices. Thus there is only one maximal abelian subgroup of G up to conjugation: the subgroup of all diagonal matrices in G. This subgroup is a maximal torus in G. (An l-dimensional *torus* is a group isomorphic to a product of l circle groups. A *maximal torus* is a torus which is not properly contained in another torus.)

When $G = \mathrm{SO}(n)$, there are theorems in linear algebra on commuting orthogonal operators which say that abelian subgroups of G can be conjugated into a certain normal form consisting of some 2×2 rotation blocks down the main diagonal, supplemented by diagonal elements thereafter. Up to conjugation, the maximal abelian subgroups of $\mathrm{SO}(n)$ are thus of the form

$$T^l \times V(n - 2l),$$

where T^l is an l-dimensional torus in $\mathrm{SO}(2l)$, thought of as l 2×2 rotation blocks down the diagonal, and

$$V(k) = \{\text{diagonal matrices in } \mathrm{SO}(k)\}.$$

The possible values of l are $l = 0, 1, 2, \ldots, [n/2]$, except $l \neq n/2 - 1$, when n is even. ($V(2)$ is not maximal abelian in $\mathrm{SO}(2)$.) $[a]$ denotes the greatest integer $\leq a$.

Example. In $\mathrm{SO}(3)$, the two maximal abelian subgroups, up to conjugation, are:

$$T^1 = \left\{ \begin{pmatrix} \cos t & -\sin t & 0 \\ \sin t & \cos t & 0 \\ 0 & 0 & 1 \end{pmatrix} \right\}$$

and

$$V(3) = \left\{ \begin{pmatrix} 1 & 0 & 0 \\ 0 & 1 & 0 \\ 0 & 0 & 1 \end{pmatrix}, \begin{pmatrix} -1 & 0 & 0 \\ 0 & -1 & 0 \\ 0 & 0 & 1 \end{pmatrix}, \begin{pmatrix} -1 & 0 & 0 \\ 0 & 1 & 0 \\ 0 & 0 & -1 \end{pmatrix}, \begin{pmatrix} 1 & 0 & 0 \\ 0 & -1 & 0 \\ 0 & 0 & -1 \end{pmatrix} \right\}$$
$$\cong \mathbb{Z}/2 \oplus \mathbb{Z}/2.$$

Cartan's classification of the simple, compact Lie groups was only up to local isomorphism. The groups $\mathrm{SU}(n)$ and $\mathrm{Sp}(n)$ are simply-connected, but the special orthogonal groups $\mathrm{SO}(n)$ are not simply-connected. Since $\pi_1(\mathrm{SO}(n)) = \mathbb{Z}/2$, for $n \geq 3$, $\mathrm{SO}(n)$ has a universal covering group which double covers $\mathrm{SO}(n)$. This is the spinor group $\mathrm{Spin}(n)$. We define $\mathrm{Spin}(n)$ more concretely and examine its maximal abelian subgroups in the next section.

3. Abelian subgroups of $\mathrm{Spin}(n)$ and self-orthogonal codes. In order to study the conjugacy classes of maximal abelian subgroups of $\mathrm{Spin}(n)$, and how they relate to self-orthogonal codes, we define $\mathrm{Spin}(n)$ by means of the Clifford algebra C_n. The reader may refer to [2] or [26, Appendix A] for more details.

On $\mathbf{R}^n$, choose an orthonormal basis $e_1, e_2, \ldots, e_n$. The *Clifford algebra* C_n is the associative algebra with 1 over $\mathbf{R}$ generated by $e_1, e_2, \ldots, e_n$, subject to the relations

$$e_i e_j + e_j e_i = -2\delta_{ij}.$$

$\mathbf{R}^n$ injects linearly into C_n as the linear combinations of $e_1, e_2, \ldots, e_n$. Every non-zero $x \in \mathbf{R}^n$ is a unit in C_n with inverse $x^{-1} = -x/\|x\|^2$. The unit sphere $S^{n-1} \subset \mathbf{R}^n$ also sits inside C_n, and any $x \in S^{n-1}$ is a unit with $x^{-1} = -x$.

DEFINITION. $\text{Spin}(n)$ is defined to be the (multiplicative) subgroup of the group of units of C_n generated by products of an even number of factors from S^{n-1}.

The double covering homomorphism $\pi : \text{Spin}(n) \to SO(n)$ is defined by using Clifford multiplication: for $x \in \text{Spin}(n)$, $y \in \mathbf{R}^n \subset C_n$, Clifford conjugation

$$\pi_x : y \mapsto xyx^{-1}$$

maps $\mathbf{R}^n \to \mathbf{R}^n$, is orthogonal (since the factors in x are of unit length), and has determinant 1 (x has an even number of factors). Thus $\pi : x \mapsto \pi_x$ maps $\text{Spin}(n) \to SO(n)$. π is surjective, as follows from the next lemma, and $\ker \pi = \{\pm 1\}$.

For an index set $I = \{i_1 < i_2 < \cdots < i_r\} \subset \{1, 2, \dots, n\}$, set

$$e_I = e_{i_1} e_{i_2} \cdots e_{i_r},$$

with $e_\emptyset = 1$, by convention. Similarly, let v_I be the diagonal matrix with -1's in diagonal positions $i_1, i_2, \dots, i_r$, and 1's elsewhere on the diagonal. The next lemma is an easy exercise for the reader.

LEMMA 3.1.

(1) $|I \cup J| = |I| + |J| - |I \cap J|$.

(2) $e_I^2 = \begin{cases} +1, & \text{if } |I| \equiv 0, 3 \bmod 4 \\ -1, & \text{if } |I| \equiv 1, 2 \bmod 4. \end{cases}$

(3) $e_I e_J = \begin{cases} +e_J e_I, & \text{if } |I||J| + |I \cap J| \text{ is even} \\ -e_J e_I, & \text{if } |I||J| + |I \cap J| \text{ is odd.} \end{cases}$

(4) $e_I e_j e_I^{-1} = \begin{cases} +(-1)^{|I|} e_j, & \text{if } j \notin I \\ -(-1)^{|I|} e_j, & \text{if } j \in I. \end{cases}$

Recall from Section 2 that $V(n) = \{\text{diagonal matrices in } SO(n)\}$. Let

$$\tilde{V}(n) = \{\pm e_I \mid |I| \text{ is even }\} \subset \text{Spin}(n).$$

Lemma 3.1 implies that $\tilde{V}(n)$ is a non-abelian subgroup of $\text{Spin}(n)$ and that $\tilde{V}(n) = \pi^{-1}(V(n))$. Clearly, $\pi(e_I) = v_I$. Moreover, $V = V(n)$ and $\tilde{V} = \tilde{V}(n)$ fit into the following exact sequence of groups:

$$(3.2) \qquad\qquad 1 \to \mathbf{Z}/2 \overset{i}{\to} \tilde{V} \overset{\pi}{\to} V \to 1,$$

where $\mathbf{Z}/2 \cong \{\pm 1\} = \ker \pi \subset \tilde{V}$, i is the inclusion, and π is the projection from $\text{Spin}(n)$ to $SO(n)$, restricted to $\tilde{V}$.

Recall also from Section 2 that, up to conjugation, the maximal abelian subgroups of $SO(n)$ are of the form

$$B_l = T^l \times V(n - 2l),$$

where T^l is an l-dimensional torus in $SO(2l)$. We now wish to discuss the maximal abelian subgroups of $\text{Spin}(n)$. Let A be a maximal abelian subgroup of $\text{Spin}(n)$, so

223

that $\pi(A)$ is an abelian subgroup of SO(n). Some conjugate of $\pi(A)$ is contained in a B_l, so that a conjugate of A is contained in $\pi^{-1}(B_l)$. Now

$$\pi^{-1}(B_l) = \tilde{T}^l \cdot \tilde{V}(n - 2l),$$

where $\tilde{T}^l$ is an l-dimensional torus in Spin($2l$) which double covers T^l. Because $\tilde{V}$ is non-abelian, $\pi^{-1}(B_l)$ itself cannot be a maximal abelian subgroup of Spin(n). However, the discussion above leads to the next theorem, a more detailed proof of which is contained in [27, Theorem 5.6].

THEOREM 3.3. *Any maximal abelian subgroup of* Spin(n) *is conjugate to*

$$\tilde{T}^l \cdot M,$$

for some $l = 0, 1, 2, \ldots, [n/2]$, ($l \neq n/2 - 1$, *when* n *is even*), *where* $\tilde{T}^l$ *is an l-dimensional torus in* Spin($2l$), *and M is a maximal abelian subgroup of* Spin($n - 2l$) *which is contained in* $\tilde{V}(n - 2l)$.

Remark. Two maximal abelian subgroups of Spin(n) of the form $\tilde{T}^l \cdot M_1$, $\tilde{T}^l \cdot M_2$ are conjugate if and only if M_1 and M_2 are conjugate in Spin($n - 2l$) by an element of the normalizer $\tilde{N}$ of $\tilde{V}(n - 2l)$ in Spin($n - 2l$). See [27, Theorem 5.8].

Thus we see that the study of the conjugacy classes of maximal abelian subgroups of Spin(n) reduces to the study of the maximal abelian subgroups of $\tilde{V}(k)$, up to the action of the normalizer $\tilde{N}$ of $\tilde{V}(k)$ in Spin(k).

Because $\tilde{V}$ and V fit into the exact sequence (3.2), the basic question before us is: Which subgroups of V lift to give abelian subgroups of $\tilde{V}$? To answer this question, we follow Quillen [24, §4] in using (3.2) to define two $\mathbf{F}_2$-valued forms. Note that V is an elementary abelian 2-group of rank $n - 1$, i.e., an $(n - 1)$-dimensional vector space over $\mathbf{F}_2$.

DEFINITION. $\mathbf{F}_2$ is the two element field which we identify with $\mathbf{Z}/2 = \{\pm 1\}$ in the usual way. Define $B : V \times V \to \mathbf{F}_2$ by

$$iB(x,y) = \bar{x}\bar{y}\bar{x}^{-1}\bar{y}^{-1}, \quad \pi\bar{x} = x, \pi\bar{y} = y,$$

and define $Q : V \to \mathbf{F}_2$ by

$$iQ(x) = \bar{x}^2, \quad \pi\bar{x} = x.$$

Note that B and Q are well-defined: the two pre-images of x under π are of the form $\pm\bar{x}$, and -1 is central in $\tilde{V}$.

By using Lemma 3.1, one can prove the following proposition.

PROPOSITION 3.4.

(1) $B : V \times V \to \mathbf{F}_2$ *is a symmetric, bilinear form, and* $B(v_I, v_J) \equiv |I \cap J| \bmod 2$.

(2) $Q : V \to \mathbf{F}_2$ *is a quadratic form, with* $Q(x + y) + Q(x) + Q(y) = B(x, y)$ *and* $Q(v_I) \equiv \frac{1}{2}|I| \bmod 2$.

224

The matrix subgroups W of V are just the $\mathbf{F}_2$-linear subspaces of $\tilde{V}$. A subspace W of V is *B-isotropic* (resp. *Q-isotropic*) if B (resp. Q) vanishes identically when restricted to W. Then the definitions of B and Q and the correspondence $W \mapsto \pi^{-1}(W)$ yield the next theorem.

THEOREM 3.5. *Let W be a subgroup of V. Then $\pi^{-1}(W)$ is an abelian subgroup (resp. elementary abelian 2-subgroup) of $\tilde{V}$ if and only if W is B-isotropic (resp. Q-isotropic).*

Finally, we wish to show the relationship between abelian subgroups of $\tilde{V}$ and self-orthogonal codes. Let us recall some definitions from coding theory [17]. Let V' be an n-dimensional vector space over $\mathbf{F}_2$, with a fixed basis. The choice of basis allows one to define a *dot product* "$\cdot$", with values in $\mathbf{F}_2$: just take the inner product with respect to which the basis is orthonormal. A *binary, linenary, linear code* is an $\mathbf{F}_2$-subspace W of V'. W is *self-orthogonal* if $W \subset W^\perp$, where

$$W^\perp = \{y \in V' \mid w \cdot y = 0, \text{ for all } w \in W\}.$$

W is *self-dual* if $W = W^\perp$. The *weight* $\mathrm{wt}(x)$ of $x \in V'$ is the number of non-zero coefficients in the expression of x in terms of the fixed basis. Since $\mathrm{wt}(x) \equiv x \cdot x \bmod 2$, every element of a self-orthogonal code has even weight. A self-orthogonal code W is *doubly-even* if every element of W has weight divisible by 4.

Of particular interest in coding theory is the *minimum weight*

$$d(W) = \min\{\mathrm{wt}(x) \mid 0 \neq x \in W\}$$

of a code W. The minimum weight determines the error-correcting capability of the code, as W can correct $< [d(W)/2]$ errors. Finding codes with high minimum weight is an important problem in coding theory, one we return to in Section 8.

Let $V' = V'(n) = \{\text{diagonal matrices in } \mathrm{O}(n)\}$, with basis $v_1, v_2, \ldots, v_n$, where v_i is the diagonal matrix with a -1 at diagonal position i and 1's elsewhere on the diagonal. It is easy to check that the dot product on V', when restricted to the subspace $V \subset V'$, is exactly the bilinear form B of Proposition 3.4. Thus the B-isotropic subspaces are precisely the self-orthogonal codes. Similarly, an element x has weight divisible by 4 if and only if $Q(x) = 0$. In summary, we have:

THEOREM 3.6.

(1) *Abelian subgroups of $\tilde{V}$ which contain -1 are in one-to-one correspondence with B-isotropic subspaces of V, which in turn are in one-to-one correspondence with self-orthogonal codes.*

(2) *Elementary abelian 2-subgroups of $\tilde{V}$ which contain -1 are in one-to-one correspondence with Q-isotropic subspaces of V, which in turn are in one-to-one correspondence with doubly-even self-orthogonal codes.*

Remark. The equivalence relations behave nicely as well. Two abelian subgroups of $\tilde{V}$ are conjugate via an element of the normalizer $\tilde{N}$ of $\tilde{V}$ in $\mathrm{Spin}(n)$ if and only if their corresponding self-orthogonal codes in V are permutation equivalent. For details, see [28, Theorem 4.6].

4. Topological background. Several concepts from algebraic topology are reviewed in this section. The treatment is not exhaustive—only those features needed in later sections are covered. The reader may consult the references for further information.

If X is a topological space and R is a commutative ring, then the *singular cohomology groups* $H^n(X; R)$, $n \geq 0$, fit together to form a graded ring, the *singular cohomology ring*

$$H^*(X; R) = \bigoplus_{n=0}^{\infty} H^n(X; R).$$

The multiplication is given by the cup product

$$\smile : H^m(X; R) \otimes H^n(X; R) \to H^{m+n}(X; R).$$

The multiplication is commutative in the sense of graded rings: if $a \in H^m(X; R)$, $b \in H^n(X; R)$, then $b \smile a = (-1)^{mn} a \smile b$. Any continuous map $f : X \to Y$ induces a ring homomorphism $f^* : H^*(Y; R) \to H^*(X; R)$.

When $R = \mathbf{Z}/p$, p prime, the cohomology ring $H^*(X; \mathbf{Z}/p)$ admits certain cohomology operations, especially the Steenrod reduced power operations $\mathcal{P}^i$. The cases $p = 2$ and p odd behave slightly differently. Since we shall only need the case $p = 2$ in later sections, this is the only case that will be covered.

When $p = 2$, the relevant Steenrod operations are called the *Steenrod squares*, denoted Sq^i. The Steenrod squares have the following four properties [20, pp. 90–91].

(1) For any space X and any two non-negative integers n, i, Sq^i is an additive homomorphism

$$Sq^i : H^n(X; \mathbf{Z}/2) \to H^{n+i}(X; \mathbf{Z}/2).$$

(2) If $f : X \to Y$, then $Sq^i \circ f^* = f^* \circ Sq^i$.

(3) If $a \in H^n(X; \mathbf{Z}/2)$, then $Sq^0(a) = a$, $Sq^n(a) = a \smile a$, and $Sq^i(a) = 0$, for all $i > n$.

(4) (*Cartan formula*) Whenever $a \smile b$ is defined,

$$Sq^k(a \smile b) = \sum_{i+j=k} Sq^i(a) \smile Sq^j(b).$$

The Steenrod squares will play an important role in Quillen's work on equivariant cohomology theory.

In order to explain equivariant cohomology, one needs the concept of the classifying space of a group. Let G be a compact Lie group (not necessarily connected—any finite group works!). Associated to G is a topological space BG, called the *classifying space* of G. BG is the base space of a principal G-bundle $EG \to BG$, where EG is contractible. It is well-known that BG exists, for every G, and is unique up to homotopy [25, §19]. In general, BG is infinite dimensional.

Example 4.1. The exponential map $\mathbf{R} \to S^1$, $x \mapsto e^{2\pi i x}$, is a principal $\mathbf{Z}$-bundle over S^1. Since $\mathbf{R}$ is contractible, $B\mathbf{Z} = S^1$.

Example 4.2. The standard projection $S^n \to \mathbf{R}P^n$ is a principal $\mathbf{Z}/2$-bundle over the real projective space $\mathbf{R}P^n$. Alas, S^n is not contractible. Taking the limit as $n \to \infty$ leads to the principal $\mathbf{Z}/2$-bundle $S^\infty \to \mathbf{R}P^\infty$, and S^∞ is contractible. Thus $B\mathbf{Z}/2 = \mathbf{R}P^\infty$.

Example 4.3. Similar arguments for the projections $S^{2n+1} \to \mathbf{C}P^n$ and $S^{4n+3} \to \mathbf{H}P^n$ give that

$$BU(1) = BSO(2) = BS^1 = \mathbf{C}P^\infty$$

and

$$BSp(1) = BSU(2) = BS^3 = \mathbf{H}P^\infty.$$

Example 4.4. Using the projection from Stiefel manifolds to Grassmann manifolds, plus taking limits, implies that

(1) $BO(n) = Gr(n, \mathbf{R}^\infty)$, the Grassmannian of unoriented n-planes in $\mathbf{R}^\infty$.

(2) $BSO(n) = \widetilde{Gr}(n, \mathbf{R}^\infty)$, the Grassmannian d n-planes in $\mathbf{R}^\infty$.

(3) $BU(n) = Gr(n, \mathbf{C}^\infty)$, the Grassmannian of complex n-planes in $\mathbf{C}^\infty$.

(4) $BSp(n) = Gr(n, \mathbf{H}^\infty)$, the Grassmannian of quaternionic n-planes in $\mathbf{H}^\infty$.

For details, see [20, pp. 145, 163].

The importance of the classifying spaces is that they classify principal G-bundles. Denote by ξ_G the principal G-bundle $EG \to BG$ in the definition of BG. To every map $f : X \to BG$, one can define the *pull-back* of ξ_G, denoted $f^*(\xi_G)$, which is a principal G-bundle over X. The basic fact is that all principal G-bundles on X occur in this way [25, §19].

THEOREM 4.5. *The homotopy classes $[X, BG]$ of maps $f : X \to BG$ are in one-to-one correspondence with isomorphism classes of principal G-bundles on X, via $f \mapsto f^*(\xi_G)$.*

One use of this theorem is to assign cohomology classes to principal G-bundles on X. If ξ is a principal G-bundle on X, then $\xi = f^*(\xi_G)$, for some $f : X \to BG$. Then $f^*(H^*(BG; R)) \subset H^*(X; R)$ is the *characteristic subring* associated to ξ, which is very important in the study of bundles ξ. This is the theory of characteristic classes of bundles; see [20].

Now suppose that a compact Lie group G acts on a space X on the left. The constructions that follow are due originally to Borel (see, for example, [3, Chapter 4]). In the principal G-bundle $EG \to BG$, G acts on the total space EG on the right. The space $EG \times_G X$ is the space of equivalence classes of pairs of points $(e, x) \in EG \times X$, where $(e, x) \sim (e', x')$ if there exists $g \in G$ such that $e' = eg$ and $x' = g^{-1}x$. The bundle $EG \times_G X \to BG$ is the *associated bundle* (to $EG \to BG$) with typical fiber X. The *equivariant cohomology ring* of X with respect to its G-action is defined by

$$H_G^*(X) = H^*(EG \times_G X).$$

If X is a point, then $EG \times_G \mathrm{pt} = BG$, so that $H_G^*(\mathrm{pt}) = H^*(BG)$. Equivariant cohomology will play a prominent role in later sections.

Remark. When G is a finite group, the equivariant cohomology $H_G^*(\mathrm{pt}) = H^*(BG)$ is equal to the group cohomology of G [16, Theorem IV.11.5].

5. Results of Borel on p-torsion. We review some early results of Borel which relate the behavior of the elementary abelian p-subgroups of a compact, connected Lie group G to various properties of the cohomology of G and its classifying space.

DEFINITIONS. For convenience of notation, an elementary abelian p-group will be called a *p-torus*. A p-torus A is isomorphic to a product of r copies of $\mathbf{Z}/p$, where r is the *rank* of A. If G is a compact, connected Lie group, the *p-rank* of G, denoted $r_p(G)$, is the maximum of the ranks of p-tori which are subgroups of G. The *rank* $l(G)$ of G is the dimension of a maximal torus of G. That the rank is well-defined follows from the next theorem. See [9, p. 159].

THEOREM 5.1 (MAXIMAL TORUS THEOREM). *Let G be a compact, connected Lie group. Then every element of G is contained in a maximal torus, and any two maximal tori in G are conjugate.*

If T is a maximal torus of G, a compact, connected Lie group, then the subgroup $_pT$ of T consisting of points of order p is a p-torus. This shows that $r_p(G) \geq l(G)$, for all primes p. One should not expect equality to hold, as the next example illustrates.

Example 5.2. Let $G = \mathrm{SO}(n)$. The rank $l(\mathrm{SO}(n)) = [n/2]$. $V(n)$, the subgroup of all diagonal matrices in $\mathrm{SO}(n)$, is a 2-torus of maximal rank $r_2(\mathrm{SO}(n)) = n - 1$.

There are some general results relating $r_p(G)$ and $l(G)$:

PROPOSITION 5.3.

(1) (BOREL AND SERRE, [6, PROPOSITION 6])

$$l(G) \leq r_p(G) \leq \begin{cases} 2\,l(G), & \text{if } p = 2, \\ (3/2)\,l(G), & \text{if } p \text{ is an odd prime,} \end{cases}$$

and $l(G) = r_p(G)$, *if p does not divide the order of the Weyl group of G.*

(2) (BOREL, [5]) $l(G) = r_p(G)$, *for p an odd prime.*

There are two more results of Borel related to p-tori which we wish to discuss. The first result relates torsion in the cohomology groups to p-tori which are not contained in maximal tori.

THEOREM 5.4 (BOREL, [4, THEOREM 4.5]). *Let G be a compact, connected Lie group, and let p be a prime. BG is the classifying space of G. The following conditions are equivalent.*

(1) $H^*(G; \mathbf{Z})$ *has no p-torsion.*

(2) $H^*(BG; \mathbb{Z})$ has no p-torsion.

(3) Every p-torus is contained in a maximal torus.

(4) Every p-torus of rank ≤ 3 is contained in a maximal torus.

The second result lists the p-torsion that occurs amongst the simple compact Lie groups (see the list in Section 2).

THEOREM 5.5 (BOREL, [4, THEOREM 2.5]). *Suppose that G is a compact, connected, simply-connected, simple Lie group, and that p is prime. Then $H^*(G; \mathbb{Z})$ has p-torsion in exactly the following cases:*

$$p = 2 : G = \mathrm{Spin}(n), n \geq 7; G_2, F_4, E_6, E_7, E_8;$$
$$p = 3 : G = F_4, E_6, E_7, E_8;$$
$$p = 5 : G = E_8.$$

Discussion. Theorem 5.4 says that $H^*(G; \mathbb{Z})$ has p-torsion if and only if there exists a p-torus which is not contained in a maximal torus. There are two basic ways in which this can occur. First, one might have $r_p(G) > l(G)$: rank reasons alone would preclude a p-torus of maximal rank from being contained in a maximal torus. By Borel's result in Proposition 5.3, this case will only occur when $p = 2$. Example 5.2 shows that $r_2(G) > l(G)$, for $G = \mathrm{SO}(n)$, $n \geq 3$.

For $G = \mathrm{Spin}(n)$, one can show that the 2-rank of $\mathrm{Spin}(n)$ behaves as follows. See [24, Table 6.2 $(r_2 = n - h)$] or [27, Theorem 3.18].

PROPOSITION 5.6.

$$r_2(\mathrm{Spin}(n)) = \begin{cases} [n/2] + 1, & \text{if } n \equiv 0, 1, 7 \bmod 8, \\ [n/2], & \text{if } n \equiv 2, 3, 4, 5, 6 \bmod 8. \end{cases}$$

Since $l(\mathrm{Spin}(n)) = [n/2]$, we see that $r_2 > l$, when $n \equiv 0, 1, 7 \bmod 8$. This accounts for 2-torsion in $H^*(\mathrm{Spin}(n); \mathbb{Z})$, $n = 7, 8, 9$, for example.

The second way for a p-torus not to be contained in a maximal torus (when $r_p = l$) is for there to exist at least two distinct conjugacy classes of maximal p-tori. One conjugacy class which always exists is the conjugacy class of the p-torus $_pT$ of order p points on a maximal torus. Thus there exists a p-torus not contained in a maximal torus if and only if its conjugacy class is distinct from that of $_pT$. Whenever G has p-torsion, p odd, it follows that G has non-conjugate maximal p-tori.

When $G = \mathrm{Spin}(n)$, $n \geq 7$ and $n \equiv 2, 3, 4, 5, 6 \bmod 8$, the presence of 2-torsion in $H^*(\mathrm{Spin}(n); \mathbb{Z})$ implies the existence of non-conjugate maximal 2-tori, i.e., inequivalent maximal doubly-even self-orthogonal codes. This explains why inequivalent maximal doubly-even codes begin to appear at $n = 10$.

In the next section p-tori are related to the prime ideal structure of equivariant cohomology rings.

6. Results of Quillen on equivariant cohomology. We now outline some results of Quillen [23] which relate the collection of p-tori in a compact Lie group G to the prime ideal structure of $H^*(BG; \mathbf{Z}/p)$. If G acts on some space X, it is the p-tori together with information about their fixed point sets on X which is related to prime ideals in the equivariant cohomology ring $H^*_G(X; \mathbf{Z}/p)$. We borrow shamelessly from [23] and the reader should see Quillen's paper for the full story.

Throughout this section G will be a compact Lie group (not necessarily connected), and X will be a compact topological space on which G acts. Let p be a fixed prime. A will denote a p-torus in G, and all cohomology will be with $\mathbf{Z}/p$-coefficients. We assume in addition that $H^*(X)$ is finite dimensional. This implies that the fixed point set

$$X^A = \{x \in X \mid ax = x, \text{ for all } a \in A\}$$

has only finitely many connected components [23, Corollary 4.3].

From the p-tori in G and their fixed point sets, we build a category $\mathcal{A}(G, X)$. The objects of $\mathcal{A}(G, X)$ are all pairs (A, c), where A is a p-torus in G and c is a connected component of X^A. A morphism

$$\theta : (A, c) \to (A', c')$$

in $\mathcal{A}(G, X)$ is a triple $((A, c), (A', c'), \bar{\theta})$, where $\bar{\theta}$ is a homomorphism $\bar{\theta} : A \to A'$ of the form $\bar{\theta}(a) = gag^{-1}$, for some $g \in G$ which has the properties that $gAg^{-1} \subset A'$ and $gc \supset c'$. Composition of morphisms is just composition of the corresponding homomorphisms of p-tori.

For any $(A, c) \in \mathcal{A}(G, X)$, every map from $(A, \mathrm{pt}) \to (G, X)$ consisting of the inclusion homomorphism $A \subset G$ and any map taking the one-point space to the component c, induces a homomorphism

$$(6.1) \qquad\qquad (A, c)^* : H^*_G(X) \to H^*_A$$

on equivariant cohomology. (We denote $H^*_A(\mathrm{pt})$ simply by H^*_A.) If $\theta : (A, c) \to (A', c')$ is any morphism in $\mathcal{A}(G, X)$, then $\theta^*(A', c')^* = (A, c)^*$. The family (6.1) of homomorphisms then defines a homomorphism

$$H^*_G(X) \longrightarrow \mathop{\mathrm{proj\,lim}}_{(A,c)\in\mathcal{A}(G,X)} H^*_A$$

to the projective limit. The main theorem of Quillen is

THEOREM 6.2 (QUILLEN, [23, THEOREM 6.2, (8.5)]). *The homomorphism*

$$h : H^*_G(X) \longrightarrow \mathop{\mathrm{proj\,lim}}_{(A,c)\in\mathcal{A}(G,X)} H^*_A$$

is an F-isomorphism. That is, every element in $\ker h$ *is nilpotent, and, for any* $y \in \mathrm{proj\,lim}\, H^*_A$, $y^{p^n} \in \mathrm{image}(h)$, *for some* n.

Remark. Speaking loosely, h being an F-isomorphism means that h is an isomorphism "modulo nilpotents." The condition on the image of h is that $\mathrm{coker}\, h$ consists of nilpotent elements which are killed by a pth power.

Theorem 6.2 has several consequences which will be of use in later sections. Since our main interest is the case of 2-tori in $\mathrm{Spin}(n)$, it will simplify the exposition to assume $p = 2$ from here on. The reader may consult [23] for the changes necessary for the p odd case.

Remember from Section 4 that any cohomology ring $H^*(X; R)$ is commutative in the graded sense: $b \smile a = (-1)^{mn} a \smile b$, for $a \in H^m(X; R)$, $b \in H^n(X; R)$. When $R = \mathbb{Z}/2$, $-1 = 1$, so that $H^*(X; \mathbb{Z}/2)$ is also commutative in the usual sense. The machinery of commutative algebra, e.g., prime ideals, can be applied to $H^*(X; \mathbb{Z}/2)$.

A 2-torus A of rank r can be viewed as an r-dimensional vector space over $\mathbb{Z}/2$. As such, it has a dual vector space denoted $A^\sharp$. There is a canonical isomorphism $H_A^1 \cong A^\sharp$ from which one can prove that $H_A^* \cong S(A^\sharp)$, where $S(A^\sharp)$ is the symmetric algebra on $A^\sharp$.

Because $S(A^\sharp)$ is a polynomial ring, the kernel $\wp_{A,c}$ of the homomorphism $(A, c)^* : H_G^*(X) \to H_A^*$ of (6.1) is a prime ideal in $H_G^*(X)$. One can characterize the prime ideals of $H_G^*(X)$ which are of the form $\wp_{A,c}$. Remember that the Steenrod squaring operations were defined in Section 4.

THEOREM 6.3 (QUILLEN, [23, THEOREM 12.1]). *A prime ideal of $H_G^*(X)$ is of the form $\wp_{A,c}$ for some pair (A, c) if and only if it is homogeneous and stable under the Steenrod squaring operations Sq^i, $i \geq 0$.*

Further relations among the $\wp$'s are summarized in the next theorem of Quillen.

THEOREM 6.4 (QUILLEN, [23, PROPOSITION 11.2]).

(1) *One has $\wp_{A,c} \supset \wp_{A',c'}$ if and only if there is a morphism $(A, c) \to (A', c')$; in particular $\wp_{A,c} = \wp_{A',c'}$ if and only if (A, c) and (A', c') are isomorphic.*

(2) *There is a one-to-one correspondence between conjugacy classes of maximal pairs (A, c) and minimal prime ideals of $H_G^*(X)$ given by associating to (A, c) the prime ideal $\wp_{A,c}$.*

Remark. Theorems 6.3 and 6.4 show that there is an order-reversing correspondence between the category $\mathcal{A}(G, X)$ and the category of homogeneous, Sq^i-stable, prime ideals of $H_G^*(X)$. When $X = \mathrm{pt}$, $\mathcal{A}(G, X)$ is just the category of 2-tori in G, while $H_G^*(\mathrm{pt}) = H^*(BG)$ is the cohomology of the classifying space of G. When $G = \mathrm{Spin}(n)$, more details on this correspondence, plus examples, can be found in [27, §5].

One final consequence of Quillen's main theorem relates the Krull dimension of H_G^* to the 2-rank of G.

THEOREM 6.5 (QUILLEN, [23, THEOREM 7.7, COROLLARY 7.8]). *The Krull dimension of $H_G^*(X)$ equals the maximum rank of a 2-torus A of G such that $X^A \neq \emptyset$. In particular, when $X = pt$, the Krull dimension of H_G^* equals $r_2(G)$, the maximum rank of a 2-torus of G.*

Looking ahead, the basic strategy in Section 8 will be to find actions of $G = \mathrm{Spin}(n)$ on various X such that the minimum weight $d(A)$ of a 2-torus A affects whether or not X^A is empty. It is only when $X^A \neq \emptyset$ that (A, c) can contribute a prime ideal to $H_G^*(X)$.

By examining the Morse theory of the trace functional on $\mathrm{Spin}(n)$, various candidates arise for $\mathrm{Spin}(n)$-actions with weight-theoretic importance. This is the topic we start in the next section.

7. Morse theory on $\mathrm{Spin}(n)$. In its broadest sense, Morse theory relates the topology of a manifold to the behavior of the critical points of a function on the manifold. Morse's original formulation of the theory, where the critical points are isolated, is expounded in [19]. Bott's generalization of the theory to non-isolated critical points appears in [7] and [8]. The main features of Morse theory are summarized in this section, drawing heavily on the cogent account of Atiyah and Bott [1, §1]. Then the Morse theory of the trace functional on $\mathrm{Spin}(n)$ is examined.

Throughout this section, let X be a smooth, compact manifold, and let $f : X \to \mathbf{R}$ be a smooth function on X. A point $x \in X$ is a *critical point* of f if the differential df of f vanishes at x. (In local coordinates on X, all the partial derivatives of f vanish at x.) At a critical point x, the *Hessian $H_x f$* is a well-defined symmetric bilinear form on the tangent space $T_x X$ of X at x. (In local coordinates, $H_x f$ is represented by the matrix of second-order partial derivatives of f at x.) The critical point x is *non-degenerate* if $H_x f$ is non-degenerate, and the *index $\lambda_x(f)$* of f at a non-degenerate critical point x is the number of negative eigenvalues in a diagonalization of $H_x f$.

If $f : X \to \mathbf{R}$ has only non-degenerate critical points, define the *Morse counting series $M_t(f)$* by
$$M_t(f) = \sum_{x \text{ critical}} t^{\lambda_x(f)},$$
where the sum is over the (finite number of) critical points of f.

Information about the topology of X, in particular its cohomology, can be summarized in the Poincaré series of X. If K is any field, the *Poincaré series* of X relative to K is defined as
$$P_t(X; K) = \sum_i t^i \dim H^i(X; K).$$

One of the fundamental results in Morse theory is the relationship between the Morse counting series and the Poincaré series. The relationship is called the Morse inequalities.

THEOREM 7.1 (MORSE INEQUALITIES). *There exists a polynomial $R(t)$ with non-negative coefficients such that*
$$M_t(f) - P_t(X; K) = (1 + t)R(t).$$

In particular, the coefficients of $M_t(f)$ dominate those of $P_t(X; K)$, and $M_{-1}(f) = P_{-1}(X) = \chi(X)$, the Euler number of X.

Remark. The Morse inequalities follow from the main structure theorem of Morse theory, which tells how the sub-level sets $X_a = \{x \in X \mid f(x) \leq a\}$ relate.

232

More precisely, X_a is homotopy equivalent to X_b if there are no critical values of f between a and b. Also, X_b is obtained from X_a by attaching a λ-cell, if there is one critical point x of index λ in $X_b - X_a$. Thus the information on non-degenerate critical points and indices describes the handlebody structure of X.

In many examples of functions $f : X \to \mathbf{R}$ (in particular, the trace functional on a Lie group), the critical points of f are not isolated, hence degenerate. Although the Morse theory above does not apply in this situation, Bott has a generalization of Morse theory which often does apply.

Let $Y \subset X$ be a connected submanifold of X. We say that Y is a *non-degenerate critical manifold* for f if $df \equiv 0$ on Y and $H_Y f$ is non-degenerate on the normal bundle $\nu(Y)$ of Y. A function $f : X \to \mathbf{R}$ is called *non-degenerate* if its set of critical points is a union of non-degenerate critical manifolds. To emphasize, at every point $y \in Y$, the Hessian $H_y f$ at y vanishes when restricted to the tangent space $T_y Y$ to Y at y (because $df \equiv 0$ on Y). The non-degeneracy condition is that $H_y f$ is non-degenerate when restricted to a normal space $\nu_y(Y)$ to Y at y.

By putting a Riemannian metric on the normal bundle $\nu(Y)$, $H_Y f$ can be thought of as a non-degenerate self-adjoint operator $\nu(Y) \to \nu(Y)$. It then defines an orthogonal splitting $\nu(Y) = \nu^+(Y) \oplus \nu^-(Y)$ into spaces spanned by the positive and negative eigenvectors, respectively. The *index* λ_Y of Y as a critical manifold of f is defined to be the fiber dimension of $\nu^-(Y)$ (a constant, since Y is connected). To avoid technical difficulties, we assume the negative normal bundle $\nu^-(Y)$ is orientable.

The generalization of the Morse counting series for non-degenerate f is defined as

$$M_t(f) = \sum_{Y \text{ critical}} t^{\lambda_Y} P_t(Y),$$

where the summation is over all the non-degenerate critical manifolds Y of f, and where a coefficient field K has been fixed. Once again, the Morse inequalities are true.

THEOREM 7.2 (MORSE-BOTT INEQUALITIES). *If f is a non-degenerate function on X, then*

$$M_t(f) - P_t(X) = (1+t)R(t),$$

where $R(t)$ is a polynomial with non-negative coefficients.

We next wish to examine the Morse theory of the trace functional on $X = \mathrm{Spin}(n)$. More specifically, let $f : \mathrm{Spin}(n) \to \mathbf{R}$ be $f = -\mathrm{tr} \circ \pi$, where $\pi : \mathrm{Spin}(n) \to \mathrm{SO}(n)$ is the standard projection of Section 3, and tr is the trace. If $x \in \mathrm{Spin}(n)$ actually belongs to $\tilde{V}(n)$, so that $\pi(x)$ is a diagonal matrix, then $f(x)$ equals the number of -1's minus the number of $+1$'s on the diagonal in $\pi(x)$. Viewing x as a binary code word, we see that $f(x) = 2\,\mathrm{wt}(x) - n$, where $\mathrm{wt}(x)$ is the weight of x (Section 3). Since questions concerning the weights of code words are of crucial importance in coding theory, f is a natural function to investigate.

The Morse theory of the trace functional on the classical matrix groups has been studied by Frankel [12]. (We learned of this work from Haynes Miller and his paper [18], which generalizes Frankel's results.) Much of Frankel's work on $SO(n)$ carries over directly to the case of $Spin(n)$. In succeeding paragraphs, we follow closely Frankel's line of argument.

We fix a bi-invariant Riemannian metric on $Spin(n)$, and use the metric to identify the differential df of f with the gradient vector field $grad\, f$. The argument will proceed by restricting f to a maximal torus of $Spin(n)$.

We fix a choice of maximal torus $\tilde{T}$ in $Spin(n)$ as follows. Let $k = [n/2]$, so that $n = 2k$ or $n = 2k + 1$, if n is even or odd, respectively. In terms of Clifford algebra multiplication from Section 3,

$$(7.3) \qquad \tilde{T} = \left\{ \prod_{j=1}^{k} (\cos 2\pi t_j - e_{2j-1} e_{2j} \sin 2\pi t_j) \mid t_j \in \mathbf{R}/\mathbf{Z} \right\}$$

is a maximal torus of $Spin(n)$ which double covers the standard maximal torus T of $SO(n)$. Explicitly, T is of the form

$$T = \left\{ \begin{pmatrix} R(\theta_1) & & & \\ & \ddots & & \\ & & R(\theta_k) & \\ & & & (1) \end{pmatrix} \right\},$$

where

$$R(\theta) = \begin{pmatrix} \cos 2\pi\theta & -\sin 2\pi\theta \\ \sin 2\pi\theta & \cos 2\pi\theta \end{pmatrix}, \qquad \theta \in \mathbf{R}/\mathbf{Z},$$

and the 1 appears only if $n = 2k+1$ is odd. Denote the element $R(\theta_1) \times \cdots \times R(\theta_k) \in T$ by $(\theta_1, \ldots, \theta_k)$. The double covering map $\tilde{T} \to T$ sends

$$\prod_{j=1}^{k} (\cos 2\pi t_j - e_{2j-1} e_{2j} \sin 2\pi t_j) \mapsto (2t_1, \ldots, 2t_k).$$

(The reader should be aware of the conventions used for factors of 2π—the mapping doubles the angles.)

For any point $x \in Spin(n)$, let $M_x = \{gxg^{-1} \mid g \in Spin(n)\}$ be the space of conjugates of x. It is well-known that M_x is an embedding of the homogeneous space $Spin(n)/C(x)$, where $C(x) = \{g \in Spin(n) \mid gxg^{-1} = x\}$ is the *centralizer* of x in $Spin(n)$. Because the trace is a class function, we have $f(gxg^{-1}) = f(x)$, for all $g, x \in Spin(n)$. It will be useful to know the center of $Spin(n)$. See [27, Remark 1.4].

PROPOSITION 7.4. *The center of* $Spin(2k+1)$ *is* $\{\pm 1\}$. *The center of* $Spin(2k)$ *is* $\{\pm 1, \pm e_1 e_2 \cdots e_{2k}\}$, *which is isomorphic to* $\mathbf{Z}/2 \oplus \mathbf{Z}/2$ *when k is even and isomorphic to* $\mathbf{Z}/4$ *when k is odd.*

To examine the critical points of f, note that if $grad\, f = 0$ at x, then $grad\, f = 0$ at gxg^{-1}, for any $g \in Spin(n)$. This holds because f is a class function. Consequently, if x is a critical point, the conjugacy class M_x of x is a critical manifold.

By Theorem 5.1, x is contained in some maximal torus, so x is conjugate to some element h in the fixed maximal torus $\tilde{T}$. Thus the critical set of f on $\mathrm{Spin}(n)$ consists of the conjugates of the critical points of f which lie on $\tilde{T}$. Frankel [12, Lemma 1] has shown that $\mathrm{grad}\, f$ is tangent to $\tilde{T}$ at each point $h \in \tilde{T}$, so that the critical points of f (as a function on $\mathrm{Spin}(n)$) which lie on $\tilde{T}$ are the same as the critical points of f restricted to $\tilde{T}$ (as a function on $\tilde{T}$). This reduces the problem of finding the critical points of f on $\mathrm{Spin}(n)$ to finding the critical points of f on $\tilde{T}$.

To determine the critical points of f on $\tilde{T}$, we use a slightly different parameterization of $\tilde{T}$. The problem with (7.3) is that the mapping $\mathbf{R}^k/\mathbf{Z}^k \to \tilde{T}$ sending

$$(t_1, \ldots, t_k) \mapsto \prod_{j=1}^{k} (\cos 2\pi t_j - e_{2j-1} e_{2j} \sin 2\pi t_j)$$

is not injective. (Let one $t = 1/2$, the rest 0; the result is always $-1 \in \tilde{T}$.) To remedy this, we follow Bröcker and tom Dieck [9, p. 174]. There is an isomorphism $\beta : \mathbf{R}^k/\mathbf{Z}^k \to \tilde{T}$ sending $(\zeta_1, \ldots, \zeta_k) \mapsto \beta_1 \beta_2 \cdots \beta_k$, $\zeta_\nu \in \mathbf{R}/\mathbf{Z}$, where

$$\beta_1 = \cos 2\pi\zeta_1 - e_1 e_2 \sin 2\pi\zeta_1,$$

and

$$\beta_j = (\cos \pi\zeta_j + e_1 e_2 \sin \pi\zeta_j)(\cos \pi\zeta_j - e_{2j-1} e_{2j} \sin \pi\zeta_j), \quad j > 1.$$

Simplifying the product $\beta_1 \beta_2 \cdots \beta_k$, we have

(7.5)
$$\beta_1 \beta_2 \cdots \beta_k = (\cos \pi(2\zeta_1 - \zeta_2 - \cdots - \zeta_k) - e_1 e_2 \sin \pi(2\zeta_1 - \zeta_2 - \cdots - \zeta_k))$$
$$\times \prod_{j=2}^{k} (\cos \pi\zeta_j - e_{2j-1} e_{2j} \sin \pi\zeta_j).$$

Thus we see that $\pi(\beta_1 \beta_2 \cdots \beta_k) = (2\zeta_1 - \zeta_2 - \cdots - \zeta_k, \zeta_2, \ldots, \zeta_k) \in T$. (Beware the 2π-conventions!) Computing the trace we have

$$f(\zeta_1, \ldots, \zeta_k) \equiv -2 \cos 2\pi(2\zeta_1 - \zeta_2 - \cdots - \zeta_k) - 2 \sum_{j=2}^{k} \cos 2\pi\zeta_j \bmod 1.$$

At critical points we see that $\sin 2\pi(2\zeta_1 - \zeta_2 - \cdots - \zeta_k) = \sin 2\pi\zeta_j = 0$, $j > 1$ ($\zeta_\nu \in \mathbf{R}/\mathbf{Z}$). Then $\zeta_j \equiv 0, 1/2 \bmod 1$ ($j > 1$), and $2\zeta_1 - \zeta_2 - \cdots - \zeta_k \equiv 0, 1/2 \bmod 1$, also. In (7.5), this implies that $\beta_1 \beta_2 \cdots \beta_k$ is $\pm$ a product of pairs of the form $e_{2j-1} e_{2j}$, for various j. More precisely, write

$$\beta_1 \beta_2 \cdots \beta_k = \pm \prod_{j \in J} e_{2j-1} e_{2j},$$

where $J \subset \{1, 2, \ldots, k\}$.

In general, any two elements σ of the form $\pm \prod_{j \in J} e_{2j-1} e_{2j}$ will be conjugate if their index sets J have the same number of elements. (For example, $-\sigma$ is conjugate

235

to σ, in general.) There are some exceptions. When $J = \emptyset$, $\sigma = 1$ and $-\sigma = -1$ are not conjugate, since they are central in $\mathrm{Spin}(n)$. Also, when $n = 2k$ is even, and $J = \{1, 2, \ldots, k\}$, then $\sigma = e_1 e_2 \cdots e_n$ and $-\sigma = -e_1 e_2 \cdots e_n$ are not conjugate, because they too are central. Since M_σ is connected, each M_σ passes through all the conjugates of σ. Thus to discuss the critical manifolds of f, we need only take one σ from each conjugacy class. Hence we may assume that σ has the form $\pm \sigma_0 = \pm 1$ ($J = \emptyset$) or, for $j = 1, 2, \ldots, k$,

$$\sigma_j = \prod_{q=1}^{j} e_{2q-1} e_{2q}.$$

When $n = 2k$ is even, we need both $\pm e_1 e_2 \cdots e_n$.

The critical submanifolds $M_j = M_{\sigma_j}$ are homogeneous spaces of the form $\mathrm{Spin}(n)/C(\sigma_j)$, where C denotes the centralizer. Both ± 1 are in the center of $\mathrm{Spin}(n)$, so $C(\pm 1) = \mathrm{Spin}(n)$ and both $+M_0 = \{+1\}$ and $-M_0 = \{-1\}$ are one point critical manifolds. When $n = 2k$ is even, $\pm e_1 e_2 \cdots e_n$ are both central, so $M_k = \{e_1 e_2 \cdots e_n\}$ and $-M_k = \{-e_1 e_2 \cdots e_n\}$ are also single points. In the general case, $C(\sigma_j) = \mathrm{Spin}(2j) \times \mathrm{Spin}(n - 2j)$, so that $M_j = \mathrm{Spin}(n)/(\mathrm{Spin}(2j) \times \mathrm{Spin}(n - 2j))$ is isomorphic to $\mathrm{SO}(n)/(\mathrm{SO}(2j) \times \mathrm{SO}(n - 2j)) \cong \widetilde{Gr}(2j, \mathbf{R}^n)$, the Grassmannian of oriented $2j$-planes in $\mathbf{R}^n$. Summarizing, we have

THEOREM 7.6. *The function $f = -\,\mathrm{tr} \circ \pi$ on $\mathrm{Spin}(n)$ has critical manifolds as follows.*

$$n = 2k + 1 : \{+1\}, \{-1\} \text{ and } \widetilde{Gr}(2j, \mathbf{R}^{2k+1}),\ j = 1, 2, \ldots, k.$$
$$n = 2k : \{+1\}, \{-1\}, \{e_1 e_2 \cdots e_{2k}\}, \{-e_1 e_2 \cdots e_{2k}\}, \text{ and } \widetilde{Gr}(2j, \mathbf{R}^{2k}),\ j = 1, 2, \ldots, k - 1.$$

Remark. The critical values of $f = -\,\mathrm{tr} \circ \pi$, i.e., the values of f at its critical manifolds, are: $f(\pm 1) = -n$, $f(\widetilde{Gr}(2j, \mathbf{R}^n)) = 4j - n$. When $n = 2k$ is even, $f(\pm e_1 e_2 \cdots e_n) = n$. The critical points ± 1 are global minima; the critical points $\pm e_1 e_2 \cdots e_n$ ($n = 2k$) are global maxima. When $n = 2k + 1$, $\widetilde{Gr}(2k, \mathbf{R}^{2k+1})$ consists of global maxima.

The arguments dealing with the non-degeneracy of the critical manifolds and their indices are technical, and we choose not to include them here. Basically they follow Frankel's method of attack and yield the following result.

THEOREM 7.7. *The critical manifolds of $f = -\,\mathrm{tr} \circ \pi$ on $\mathrm{Spin}(n)$ are all non-degenerate. Their indices are:*

$$\lambda(\{+1\}) = \lambda(\{-1\}) = 0,$$
$$\lambda(\widetilde{Gr}(2j, \mathbf{R}^n)) = j(2j - 1),$$
$$\lambda(\{e_1 e_2 \cdots e_n\}) = \lambda(\{-e_1 e_2 \cdots e_n\}) = k(2k-1) = \dim \mathrm{Spin}(n), \quad \text{when } n = 2k.$$

In addition, all the negative normal bundles $\nu^-(M_\sigma)$ are orientable.

In summary, the function $f = -\,\mathrm{tr} \circ \pi$ on $\mathrm{Spin}(n)$ is related to the weight properties of codes. It also is a non-degenerate Morse function on $\mathrm{Spin}(n)$, whose critical manifolds are well-known spaces. In the next section we describe a program for detecting doubly-even codes of high minimum weight by using both the Morse theory and equivariant cohomology.

8. Detection of maximal 2-tori with high minimum weight. Armed with several topological tools from preceding sections, we wish to address a coding theory question: How can one detect the existence of maximal doubly-even self-orthogonal codes with high minimum weight? We offer one approach to a solution in this section.

The basic tool is Theorem 6.4, which, given an action of $\mathrm{Spin}(n)$ on X, establishes a one-to-one correspondence of conjugacy classes of maximal pairs (A, c) of 2-tori A and components of their fixed point sets with minimal prime ideals of $H^*_{\mathrm{Spin}(n)}(X)$. Already when $X = \mathrm{point}$, maximal 2-tori in $\mathrm{Spin}(n)$, i.e., maximal doubly-even self-orthogonal codes, are in one-to-one correspondence with minimal prime ideals in $H^*_{\mathrm{Spin}(n)} \cong H^*(B\mathrm{Spin}(n))$. Quillen [24, Theorem 6.5] has determined the ring structure of $H^*(B\mathrm{Spin}(n))$, but to determine the minimal prime ideals seems too general and too hard a problem to carry out at this time. (It is equivalent to classifying the maximal doubly-even self-orthogonal codes. This has been done for $n \leq 32$ by Conway, Pless, and Sloane [21], [22], and [10]. It is well-near impossible for $n = 40$ [10, pp. 52–53].) See [27, §5] for other details.

Part of the problem with taking $X = \mathrm{point}$ is that $H^*(B\mathrm{Spin}(n))$ might provide too much information: we are getting information about all the doubly-even codes with no special emphasis being placed on those of high minimum weight. It is for this reason that we bring the trace functional $f = -\mathrm{tr} \circ \pi$ on $\mathrm{Spin}(n)$ into play, since $f(x) = 2\,\mathrm{wt}(x) - n$. We use f to define special spaces X on which $\mathrm{Spin}(n)$ can act.

Remember that $\mathrm{Spin}(n)$ acts on itself by conjugation and that f is a class function: $f(gxg^{-1}) = f(x)$, for all $g, x \in \mathrm{Spin}(n)$. Thus any subspace of $\mathrm{Spin}(n)$ of the form

$$X_{\alpha,\beta} = \{x \in \mathrm{Spin}(n) \mid \alpha < f(x) < \beta\} \quad (\alpha < \beta)$$

inherits a $\mathrm{Spin}(n)$ action. One can understand the topology of $X_{\alpha,\beta}$ by using Morse theory—as in Section 7. Only those critical manifolds with critical values between α and β will contribute to the Morse-Bott inequalities for $X_{\alpha,\beta}$.

If one uses $X_{\alpha,\beta}$ as the space on which $\mathrm{Spin}(n)$ acts, minimal prime ideals of $H^*_{\mathrm{Spin}(n)}(X_{\alpha,\beta})$ correspond to maximal 2-tori A such that $X_{\alpha,\beta}{}^A \neq \emptyset$, i.e., only those maximal 2-tori A which have fixed points on $X_{\alpha,\beta}$. What are the fixed points of A on $X_{\alpha,\beta}$? The fixed points of A on $\mathrm{Spin}(n)$ itself are just the centralizer

$$C(A) = \{x \in \mathrm{Spin}(n) \mid axa^{-1} = x, \text{ for all } a \in A\}$$

of A in $\mathrm{Spin}(n)$. Thus $X_{\alpha,\beta}{}^A = C(A) \cap X_{\alpha,\beta}$, i.e., those elements of the centralizer of A whose "weights" are restricted by the inequalities $\alpha < f(x) < \beta$.

For the rest of the section, let us assume that $n \equiv 0, 1, 7 \bmod 8$. In these cases, maximal 2-tori are also maximal abelian subgroups of $\mathrm{Spin}(n)$ ([27, Theorem 3.20]), i.e., $C(A) = A$. Then $X_{\alpha,\beta}{}^A = A \cap X_{\alpha,\beta}$. Remember that $f(\pm 1) = -n$ and that

± 1 are always in the center of $\mathrm{Spin}(n)$, hence in any $C(A)$. If α is chosen so that $\alpha \geq -n$, then $\pm 1 \notin X_{\alpha,\beta}$. Now fix an integer $d > 0$ and suppose that β is chosen so that $\beta \leq 2d - n$. If A is any maximal 2-torus whose minimum weight

$$d(A) = \min\{\mathrm{wt}(x) \mid \pm 1 \neq x \in A\}$$

satisfies $d \leq d(A)$, then $X_{\alpha,\beta}{}^A = \emptyset$. Such a maximal 2-torus makes no contribution to the prime ideals in $H^*_{\mathrm{Spin}(n)}(X_{\alpha,\beta})$. We summarize.

THEOREM 8.1. *Assume $n \equiv 0, 1, 7 \bmod 8$, and $d > 0$. A maximal 2-torus A of $\mathrm{Spin}(n)$ has fixed points on $X_{-n,2d-n}$ if and only if the minimum weight $d(A) < d$. In particular, only those maximal 2-tori A with minimum weight $d(A) < d$ contribute prime ideals to $H^*_{\mathrm{Spin}(n)}(X_{-n,2d-n})$.*

Once the principle behind Theorem 8.1 is understood, there are several directions to explore. One can now vary the values of α and β, for example. If $\alpha < -n$, then $\pm 1 \in X_{\alpha,\beta}$, so that every maximal 2-torus A has $X_{\alpha,\beta}{}^A \neq \emptyset$. Thus all maximal 2-tori contribute prime ideals to $H^*_{\mathrm{Spin}(n)}(X_{-n-\epsilon,2d-n})$, while only those with $d(A) < d$ contribute to $H^*_{\mathrm{Spin}(n)}(X_{-n,2d-n})$.

Similar reasoning applies when one varies β. Maximal 2-tori A with $d(A) = d$ do not contribute prime ideals to $H^*_{\mathrm{Spin}(n)}(X_{-n,2d-n})$, but they do contribute prime ideals to $H^*_{\mathrm{Spin}(n)}(X_{-n,2d-n+\epsilon})$. By step-wise increasing β, one gets contributions from maximal 2-tori of increasingly higher minimum weight. The problem then is to understand precisely how the prime ideals of $H^*_{\mathrm{Spin}(n)}(X_{-n,\beta})$ change as β varies from $2d - n$ to $2d - n + \epsilon$. This should allow one to detect maximal 2-tori A with $d(A) = d$.

The stategy of changing β and seeing how cohomology changes is precisely the idea behind the fundamental structure theorem of Morse theory (see Remark following Theorem 7.1), only now it is being applied in the context of equivariant cohomology theory. The author is continuing to pursue these methods, and ideas of Atiyah and Bott [1, §1] may be of use.

Concluding Remarks. My goal in this paper has been to outline in some depth the interrelationships between coding theory and the topology of $\mathrm{Spin}(n)$. I hope I have succeeded in showing that equivariant Morse theory may be of use in detecting the existence of maximal doubly-even codes of high minimum weight. There is more work to be done, and I hope the reader agrees that it is worth the effort.

REFERENCES

[1] Michael F. Atiyah and Raoul Bott, *The Yang-Mills equations over Riemann surfaces*, Philosophical Transactions of the Royal Society of London, A 308 (1982), pp. 523–615.

[2] Michael F. Atiyah, Raoul Bott and Arnold Shapiro, *Clifford Modules*, Topology, 3(Supp 1) (1964), pp. 3–38.

[3] Armand Borel, *Seminar on Transformation Groups*, Annals of Mathematics Studies 46, Princeton University Press, Princeton, N. J., 1960.

[4] ——————, *Sous-groupes commutatifs et torsion des groupes de Lie compacts connexes*, Tôhoku Mathematical Journal, 13 (1961), pp. 216–240.

[5] ——————, *On the p-rank of compact connected Lie groups*, preprint 1987.

[6] Armand Borel and Jean-Pierre Serre, *Sur certains sous-groupes des groupes de Lie compacts*, Commentarii Mathematici Helvetici, 27 (1953), pp. 128–139.

[7] Raoul Bott, *Nondegenerate critical manifolds*, Annals of Mathematics, 60 (1954), pp. 248–261.

[8] ——————, *The stable homotopy of the classical groups*, Annals of Mathematics, 70 (1959), pp. 313–337.

[9] Theodor Bröcker and Tammo tom Dieck, *Representations of Compact Lie Groups*, Graduate Texts in Mathematics 98, Springer-Verlag, New York, Berlin, Heidelberg, Tokyo, 1985.

[10] John H. Conway and Vera Pless, *On the enumeration of self-dual codes*, Journal of Combinatorial Theory, Series A, 28 (1980), pp. 26–53.

[11] Simon K. Donaldson, *An application of gauge theory to the topology of 4-manifolds*, Journal of Differential Geometry, 18 (1983), pp. 279–315.

[12] Theodore Frankel, *Critical submanifolds of the classical groups and Stiefel manifolds*, in *Differential and Combinatorial Topology: A Symposium in Honor of Marston Morse*, Stewart S. Cairns, editor, Princeton University Press, Princeton, N. J., 1965, pp. 37–53.

[13] Daniel S. Freed and Karen K. Uhlenbeck, *Instantons and Four-Manifolds*, Mathematical Sciences Research Institute Publications 1, Springer-Verlag, New York, Heidelberg, Berlin, 1984.

[14] Sigurdur Helgason, *Differential Geometry, Lie Groups, and Symmetric Spaces*, Pure and Applied Mathematics 80, Academic Press, New York, San Francisco, London, 1978.

[15] Shoshichi Kobayashi and Katsumi Nomizu, *Foundations of Differential Geometry*, Interscience Tracts in Pure and Applied Mathematics 15, Interscience Publishers, New York, London, Sydney, 1963/1969.

[16] Saunders MacLane, *Homology*, Grundlehren der mathematischen Wissenschaften 114, Springer-Verlag, Berlin, Göttingen, Heidelberg, 1963.

[17] F. J. MacWilliams and N. J. A. Sloane, *The Theory of Error-Correcting Codes*, North-Holland Mathematical Library 16, North-Holland, Amsterdam, New York, Oxford, 1978.

[18] Haynes Miller, *Stable splittings of Stiefel manifolds*, Topology, 24 (1985), pp. 411–419.

[19] John W. Milnor, *Morse Theory*, Annals of Mathematics Studies 51, Princeton University Press, Princeton, N. J., 1969.

[20] John W. Milnor and James D. Stasheff, *Characteristic Classes*, Annals of Mathematics Studies 76, Princeton University Press, Princeton, N. J., 1974.

[21] Vera Pless, *A classification of self-orthogonal codes over $GF(2)$*, Discrete Mathematics, 3 (1972), pp. 209–246.

[22] Vera Pless and N. J. A. Sloane, *On the classification and enumeration of self-dual codes*, Journal of Combinatorial Theory, Series A, 18 (1975), pp. 313–335.

[23] Daniel Quillen, *The spectrum of an equivariant cohomology ring I,II*, Annals of Mathematics, 94 (1971), pp. 549–602.

[24] ——————, *The mod 2 cohomology rings of extra-special 2-groups and the spinor groups*, Mathematische Annalen, 194 (1971), pp. 197–212.

[25] Norman Steenrod, *The Topology of Fibre Bundles*, Princeton University Press, Princeton, N. J., 1951.

[26] George W. Whitehead, *Elements of Homotopy Theory*, Graduate Texts in Mathematics 61, Springer-Verlag, New York, Heidelberg, Berlin, 1978.

[27] Jay A. Wood, *Spinor groups and algebraic coding theory*, Journal of Combinatorial Theory, Series A (to appear).

[28] ——————, *Flat connections, spinor groups and error-correcting codes*, submitted to the Proceedings of the 1988 Northwestern International Conference on Algebraic Topology.